QUALITY MANAGEMENT
IN THE IMAGING SCIENCES

QUALITY MANAGEMENT
IN THE IMAGING SCIENCES

JEFFREY PAPP, PhD

Associate Professor of Physics and Radiologic Science
College of DuPage
Glen Ellyn, Illinois

with 233 illustrations

 Mosby

St. Louis Baltimore Boston Carlsbad Chicago Minneapolis New York Philadelphia Portland
London Milan Sydney Tokyo Toronto

Publisher: Don Ladig
Senior Editor: Jeanne Rowland
Senior Developmental Editor: Carolyn Kruse
Project Manager: Mark Spann
Production Editor: Beth Hayes
Interior Design: Liz Young
Manufacturing Supervisor: Debbie LaRocca
Book Design Manager: Judi Lang
Cover Design: Teresa Breckwoldt

Every effort has been made to ensure the accuracy of the information presented, including website addresses. However, Mosby, Inc., its editors, authors, and contributors cannot be responsible for errors, omissions, or changes in addresses.

Printed in the United States of America
Composition by Top Graphics
Printing/binding by Von Hoffmann Press, Inc.

Mosby, Inc.
11830 Westline Industrial Drive
St. Louis, Missouri 63146

Library of Congress Cataloging-in–Publication Data

Papp, Jeffrey.
      Quality management in the imaging sciences / Jeffrey Papp.—
   1st ed.
         p.   cm.
      Includes bibliographical references and index.

      ISBN 0-8151-2968-8

      1. Diagnostic imaging—Quality control.   2. Radiography, Medical—
   Image quality.
      [DNLM: 1. Diagnostic Imaging—standards.   2. Diagnostic Equipment—
   standards.   3. Quality Control.   WN 180 P218q 1998]
   RC78.7.D53P35   1998
   616.07′54′0685—dc21
   DNLM/DLC
   for Library of Congress   97-46903
                                                                           CIP

98 99 00 01 02 / 9 8 7 6 5 4 3 2 1

Contributors

Luann Culbreth, MEd, RT (R) (MR)
Manager, MRI Department
Baylor University Medical Center
Dallas, Texas

Lorrie Kelley, MS, RT (R) (MR) (CT)
Associate Professor
Director, CT/MRI Program
Boise State University
Boise, Idaho

Joanne M. Metler, MS, CNMT
Assistant Professor
Coordinator, Nuclear Medicine Technology Program
College of DuPage
Glen Ellyn, Illinois

James A. Zagzebski, PhD
Professor
Department of Medical Physics, Human Oncology, and
    Radiology
University of Wisconsin
Madison, Wisconsin

Reviewers

Joseph R. Bittengle, MEd, RT(R), ARRT
Chairman and Assistant Professor
Department of Radiologic Technology
College of Health Related Professions
University of Arkansas for Medical Sciences
Little Rock, Arkansas

Neil Bosch, BS, RT(R)(CT)
CT Imaging Services
Merit Care Hospital
Fargo, North Dakota

Neal M. Boucher, BS, CNMT, RSO, CSM, CSS
Radiation Safety Officer
President Glass Med, Inc.,
Technical Director, Joint Imaging Program
Kensington, New Hampshire
Technical Director, Nuclear Medicine
Anna Jaques Hospital
Newburyport, Massachusetts

Debbie Caldwell, MBA, RT(R)(M)
Assistant Professor
Medical Imaging Technology
Oregon Institute of Technology
Klamath Falls, Oregon

Cheri A. Dyke, BS, RT(R)
Radiography Program Director
All Saints Healthcare System, Inc.
School of Radiologic Technology
Racine, Wisconsin

Michael Fugate, MEd, RT(R)
Lead Didactic Faculty
Radiography Program
Santa Fe Community College
Gainesville, Florida

Julie Gill, MEd, RT(R)
Program Director
Radiologic Technology Program
Muskingum Area Technical College
Zanesville, Ohio

Michael Grey, RT(R)(CT)(MR)
Department of Health Care Professions
CASA
Southern Illinois University, Carbondale
Carbondale, Illinois

Ginger S. Griffin, RT(R) FASRT
Education Coordinator
School of Radiologic Technology
Baptist Medical Center
Jacksonville, Florida

Josephine M. Latini, MS, RT(R)(M)
Assistant Manager of Radiology
Lack Haven Hospital
Lack Haven, Pennsylvania

Starla L. Mason, MS, RT(R)
Program Coordinator, Radiography
Laramie County Community College
Cheyenne, Wyoming

Kathy McGarry, PhD, RT(R)(QM)
Program Director
Burdette Tomlin Memorial Hospital
School of Radiologic Technology
Cape May Court House, New Jersey

Christine Mehlbaum, BS, RT(R)
Program Director
Radiographer Program
Pennsylvania State University
Schuylkill, Pennsylvania

Lori M. Oberholzer, MS, RT(R)
Clinical Coordinator
Muskingum Area Technical College
Radiography Program
Zanesville, Ohio

Gary P. Randle, MS, RT(R), ARRT

Professor
Program Director
Radiography Program
Manatee Community College
Brudenton, Florida

Sandra L. Saletta, MBA, RT(R)(M)

Program Director
Northwest Community Hospital
School of Radiologic Technology
Arlington Heights, Illinois

Stephen Schultz, MSEd, RT(R)(CT)

Assistant Professor
Department of Medical Imaging Technology
Oregon Institute of Technology
Klamath Falls, Oregon

Linda A. Shields, MEd, RT(R)(M)

Instructor
Radiologic Technology Program
Department of Health Occupations
El Paso Community College
El Paso, Texas

Debra M. Snider, RT(R), CDT

Instructor
Diagnostic Imaging
Oregon Institute of Technology
Director, Osteoporosis Center
Nuclear Medicine
Merle West Medical Center
Klamath Falls, Oregon

Marsha M. Sortor, MHE, RT(R)(N)(M)(QC)

Associate Professor
Department of Radiologic Science
Midwestern State University
Wichita Falls, Texas

Keith Steeves, RT(R)(CT)

Chief CT Technologist
CT Scan Department
William W. Backus Hospital
Norwich, Connecticut

*To my wife, Anna,
my daughter, Ashley Marie,
and all of my students
past, present, and future.*

Preface

Quality management and its associated topics, quality assurance and quality control, are vitally important in modern diagnostic imaging departments. Government and accreditation agencies now mandate procedures to ensure that equipment is functioning within accepted standards and that it is operated properly. Such procedures must also be appropriately documented. Because these responsibilities have been delegated to technologists, they now need additional knowledge. The American Registry of Radiologic Technologists (ARRT) has recognized this need by offering an advanced level examination in Quality Management as of March, 1997.

I have been teaching a course in Quality Assurance/Quality Management since 1983 and have never required a textbook because I could not find one single book that contained all of the necessary material. Instead, I have had to reserve different books and government publications in our library for students to consult as reference sources or suggest that they consult individual chapters, research papers, and literature from various equipment manufacturers and suppliers. During discussions with other radiologic science educators, I discovered that most of them had the same problem in teaching this topic. I have also recently been besieged with requests from practicing technologists for study material for the Quality Management Advanced Level Examination. I can only respond by supplying a listing of several reference books.

Out of these many years of frustration came the impetus to write *Quality Management in the Imaging Sciences*. This comprehensive resource will fill several needs. Radiography educators will find it to be a tailor-made text for instruction in quality management. It will also serve as a practical reference for day-to-day consultation by practitioners responsible for implementing quality management programs in diagnostic imaging departments. This comprehensive resource also allows those practicing technologists studying for the Quality Management Advanced Level Examination to use a single reference book. It should be noted that the material contained in Chapters 12, 13, 14, and 15 pertains to specialized areas of imaging (CT, MRI, ultrasonography, and nuclear medicine) and is *not* covered on the advanced level examination offered by the ARRT. Those readers preparing for the examination will find Chapter 16 particularly useful, because it contains a sample test based on the content outline developed by the ARRT for the quality management examination.

Quality Management in the Imaging Sciences includes the most up-to-date information available on the quality management aspects of darkrooms, processing, equipment and accessories, fluoroscopic and advanced imaging equipment, artifacts, repeat analysis, and silver recovery. Quality assurance organizations and their websites are listed in an appendix, and full-page documentation forms are included throughout, with additional forms in an appendix.

The following special features are included

- Federal regulations are set in bold-face type in the text, and this symbol ☻ appears beside them.
- Procedures are highlighted as separate elements with step-by-step guidelines.
- Experiments and analysis of them are presented in relevant chapters.
- Key terms are identified at the beginnings of chapters, set in bold-face type, and explained within chapters.
- Learning objectives, chapter outlines, and chapter review questions (with answers) are provided as study tools.
- Key term definitions are collected in a glossary.
- A 140-question mock examination encourages self-testing and is particularly convenient for those readers preparing for the advanced level examination.
- The accompanying instructors' manual is filled with additional teaching tools, including more review questions, additional laboratory experiments, and troubleshooting/critical thinking exercises.

Quality Management in the Imaging Sciences provides the wealth of information now needed for instructors to guide students through quality management issues, for students and practitioners to prepare for the ARRT examination, and for technologists to succeed in delivery of high-quality services.

ACKNOWLEDGEMENTS

As with almost any technical book, this text reflects the help of many persons who contributed in diverse ways to its production. I am grateful to my associates at the College of DuPage, namely Paul Laudicina (especially for the use of his camera lens), Gina Rigoni, and Pam Jankovsky for their patience and support during the writing of this book. I also wish to thank Charles Gauthier of ComDisco Corporation for his help in the research of much of the technical data. Special thanks also goes to Vito Raimondi of Konica Corporation for material on processors and image receptors.

I am deeply indebted to my contributing authors Joanne Metler, Coordinator for Nuclear Medicine at the College of DuPage; James Zagzebski, Professor of Medical Physics at the University of Wisconsin, Madison; Lorrie Kelley, Program Director for MRI/CT at Boise State University; and Luann Culbreth, Manager of MRI Department at Baylor University Medical Center.

I would also like to thank Jeanne Rowland, Carole Glauser, Carolyn Kruse, Tamara Myers, Beth Hayes, and everyone at Mosby for their help and support in the publication of this book.

Finally, I must thank my wife, Anna, for her support and patience while I was writing this book (especially because she gave birth to our daughter, Ashley, during this time).

Jeffrey Papp, PhD

Contents

6 Quality Control of Radiographic Equipment   67

7 Radiographic Ancillary Equipment   93

8 Quality Control of Fluoroscopic Equipment   115

9 Advanced Imaging Equipment   135

10 Additional Quality Management Procedures   150

11 Mammographic Quality Standards   171

12 Quality Control in Computed Tomography   189

13 Quality Control for Magnetic Resonance Imaging Equipment   200

14 Ultrasound Equipment Quality Assurance   208

QUALITY MANAGEMENT
IN THE IMAGING SCIENCES

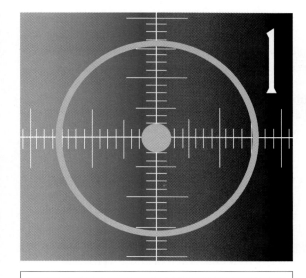

1

Introduction to Quality Management

Objectives

At the completion of this chapter the reader will be able to:

- Identify the need for quality management in diagnostic imaging
- Discuss the impact of government regulation and JCAHO accreditation on quality management
- Explain the differences between quality assurance, quality control, and quality management
- Identify the five steps of a process
- List the various tools of group dynamics
- Discuss the seven types of graphs and charts used to organize and present data in total quality management
- Explain the JCAHO 10-step monitoring and evaluation process and cycle for improving performance

Key Terms

action
aggregate data indicator
appropriateness of care
benchmarking
brainstorming
cause and effect diagram
concurrent data
continuity of care
control chart
critical path
customer
effectiveness of care
efficacy of care
efficiency of care
flowchart
focus group
FOCUS-PDCA
histogram
indicators
input
Mammography Quality Standards Act
Pareto chart
process
quality assurance
quality control
Safe Medical Devices Act
scatter plot
sentinental event indicator
supplier
threshold
trend chart

Diagnostic imaging is a multistep **process** by which information concerning patient anatomy and physiology is gathered and displayed using modern technology. Unfortunately, there are numerous sources of variability, in both human factors and equipment factors, that can produce subquality images if not properly controlled. This can result in repeat exposures increasing patient dose and department cost and decreasing the accuracy of image interpretation. The purpose of a quality management program is to control or minimize these variables as much as possible. In a diagnostic imaging department, these variables include equipment, image receptor, processing, viewing conditions, and competency of the technologist, support staff, and the observer or interpreter.

Since the early 1980s, healthcare delivery in the United States has undergone dramatic changes, which have affected diagnostic imaging departments. These changes include the following:

- *Advances in technology, equipment, and procedures.* Expensive technologies such as magnetic resonance imaging, spiral CT, PET scanning, digital radiography and fluoroscopy, SPECT, and so on, have increased the cost of equipment acquisition, installation, and maintenance.
- *Legislation and government regulations.* The **Mammography Quality Standards Act** (MQSA) and the **Safe Medical Devices Act** (SMDA) of 1990 have increased the responsibility of diagnostic imaging department managers and staff to document proper equipment operation and procedures. This is in addition to requirements from the Occupational Safety and Health Administration (OSHA), the Environmental Protection Agency (EPA), and the Food and Drug Administration (FDA) that affect matters ranging from blood-borne pathogens to disposal of processing chemicals.
- *Joint Commission on the Accreditation of Healthcare Organizations Accreditation Procedures.* The Joint Commission on the Accreditation of Healthcare Organizations Accreditation Procedures (JCAHO) has gone from a philosophy of quality assurance to one of total quality management (explained in more detail later in this chapter).
- *Corporate buyouts and mergers.* Since 1980, over 750 hospitals have closed in the United States. Many others have been purchased by "for profit" healthcare organizations or have merged to condense costs and/or reduce competition.
- *Methods of reimbursement for services rendered.* The previous method of "fee for service" reimbursement of healthcare expenses is rapidly being replaced by managed care plans, such as HMO's. The lower rate of reimbursement from these plans has reduced the operating budgets of many diagnostic imaging departments.

These changes have made a quality management program essential to the operation and survival of a diagnostic imaging department. The cost of such a program in the form of personnel time and test equipment is more than offset by the savings from lower repeat rates, less equipment downtime, film and chemical savings, greater department efficiency, and increased **customer** satisfaction because waiting time can be reduced.

HISTORY OF QUALITY MANAGEMENT IN RADIOLOGY

Many diagnostic imaging departments have been systematically monitoring their equipment and procedures dating back to the 1930s, independent of any government regulation or accreditation agency. The main motivations were to save money and increase efficiency and quality of care.

Governmental Action

The federal government's first step toward quality management came in 1968 with the Radiation Control for Health and Safety Act. This required the U.S. Department of Health, Education and Welfare (now called Health and Human Services) to develop and administer standards that would reduce human exposure to radiation from electronic products. The Bureau of Radiological Health (BRH) (now called the National Center for Devices and Radiological Health) was given the responsibility for implementing this act. The BRH set forth regulatory action, beginning in 1974 with several amendments to control the manufacture and installation of medical and dental diagnostic equipment to reduce the production of useless radiation. In 1978 they published the "Recommendations for Quality Assurance Programs in Diagnostic Radiology Facilities." JCAHO and most state public health agencies adopted these recommendations.

In 1981, the Consumer-Patient Radiation Health and Safety Act addressed issues such as unnecessary repeat examinations, quality assurance techniques, referral criteria, radiation exposure, and unnecessary mass screening programs. It also established minimum standards for accreditation of educational programs in the radiologic sciences and for the certification of radiographic equipment operators.

In the mid-1980s OSHA, in response to the outbreak of human immunodeficiency virus (HIV) and hepatitis B virus (HBV), mandated a policy on blood-borne pathogens. This policy states that an exposure control plan must be in place for all industries in which workers may come in contact with blood and other infectious materials. Included in this policy are standard precaution procedures, education programs for employees, personal protective equipment supplied by the employer (including gloves, gowns, laboratory coats, face shields, eye protection, pocket masks, and ventilation devices), and disposal procedures. The complete OSHA policy on blood-borne pathogens can be found in the Federal Register under 29 CFR 1910.

The SMDA of 1991 requires a medical facility to report to the FDA any medical devices that have caused a serious injury or death of a patient (malfunctioning bed, nonworking defibrillator, nonworking pacemaker, malfunctioning radiation therapy unit, etc.) or employee. It also authorizes civil penalties to healthcare workers or facilities that do not report defects and failures in medical devices.

In 1992 the MQSA mandated quality assurance programs for all facilities performing mammographic procedures, to obtain FDA approval. It also includes specific requirements for dedicated equipment, physicians interpreting the images, medical physicists, and technologists. Most of these standards were formulated by or in conjunction with the American College of Radiology and were in use by many facilities before enactment of MQSA. This law became effective on October 1, 1994. More specific information on MQSA can be found in Chapter 12.

Joint Commission on the Accreditation of Healthcare Organizations

In the 1970s JCAHO began requiring specific quality management procedures for facilities to obtain accreditation. This accreditation is voluntary, but hospitals and medical centers that do not have it may not possess Medicaid certification, hold certain licenses, have a residency program for training physicians, obtain reimbursements from insurance companies, or receive malpractice insurance. JCAHO not only accredits hospitals but also facilities for long-term care, ambulatory care, mental health, and chemical dependency.

Before 1991 JCAHO used the concepts of quality assurance and quality control as quality management methods requiring systematic monitoring and evaluation, with the responsibility left to the medical director or department head.

Quality Assurance

Quality assurance is an all-encompassing management program used to ensure excellence in healthcare through the systematic collection and evaluation of data. The primary objective of a quality assurance program is the enhancement of patient care; this includes patient selection parameters and scheduling, management techniques, departmental policies and procedures, technical effectiveness and efficiency, inservice education, and image interpretation with timeliness of reports. The main emphasis of the program is on the human factors that can lead to variations in quality care.

Quality Control

Quality control is the part of the quality assurance program that deals with techniques used in monitoring and maintenance of the technical elements of the systems that affect the quality of the image. Therefore quality control is the part of the quality assurance program that deals with instrumentation and equipment. A quality control program includes the following three levels of testing.

Level I: Noninvasive and Simple. Noninvasive and simple evaluations can be performed by any technologists and include tests such as the wire mesh test for screen contact and the spinning top test for timer accuracy.

Level II: Noninvasive and Complex. Noninvasive and complex evaluations should be performed by a technologist trained in quality control procedures, because more sophisticated equipment, such as special test tools, meters, or the NERO (Noninvasive Evaluation of Radiation Output) computerized multiple function unit, is used. Many educational programs now include this level of competency for graduation, so the number of technologists with these skills is increasing. The American Society of Radiologic Technologists includes quality control and quality assurance duties in their scopes of practice for radiographers, sonographers, nuclear medicine technologists, CT technologists, and MRI technologists.

Level III: Invasive and Complex. Invasive and complex evaluations involve some disassembly of the equipment and are normally performed by engineers or physicists. This textbook focuses on Levels I and II quality control testing. The following are the three types of quality control tests on various levels:

- Acceptance testing is performed on new equipment to demonstrate that it is performing within the manufacturers specifications and criteria.
- Routine performance evaluations are specific tests performed on the equipment in use after a certain amount of time has elapsed.
- Error correction tests evaluate equipment that is malfunctioning or not performing at specification.

Continuous Quality Improvement

The older quality assurance/quality control program ensured that a certain level of quality was met; it required monitoring only periodically for maintenance. It was segmented in approach, because each department in a facility monitored and evaluated their own structural outcomes, creating a tendency to view individual performances rather than the process or system in which that individual was functioning. In turn, the program was externally motivated, because its emphasis was on demonstrating compliance with externally developed standards. As long as the standards were met, no further work was required to improve the system.

In 1991 JCAHO developed the concept of continuous quality improvement (CQI), also referred to as *total quality management (TQM), total quality control (TQC), total quality leadership (TQL), total quality improvement (TQI), and statistical quality control (SQC)*. This concept is based on the "14 Points for Management" developed by W. Edwards Deming (Box 1-1) and on the Japanese management style.

The CQI concept does not replace the concept of quality assurance but incorporates it in a higher conceptual level. Instead of just ensuring and maintaining quality, it continually improves quality by focusing on improving the system or process in which individual workers function rather than on the individuals themselves. To improve these processes, it is essential to focus on the organization as a whole, rather than on individual departments. Every employee should be actively involved in CQI (rather than just management or the quality control technologist), for the program to be successful. In this way, CQI can be internally motivated, by making employees believe they are tied to the success of the hospital, and therefore create an atmosphere in which employees are motivated to do better because they are participating actively. Management must take the responsibility to promote this atmosphere, effectively allocate resources needed for improvement, treat employees as assets and not expenses, and work together toward shared goals.

PROCESS IMPROVEMENT THROUGH CQI

As mentioned earlier, CQI focuses on the process or system in which employees operate rather than on the individual employees themselves. The rationale is that problems and variability with the process are the main cause of poor quality. The premise of process improvement is based on the following ratios:

- *85/15*—The process is the problem 85% of the time, and the people are the problem 15% of the time.
- *80/20*—Eighty percent of the problems are the result of 20% of the causes.

A process is an ordered series of steps that help achieve a desired outcome. The parts of a process include the following:

- *Supplier:* One who provides goods or services such as film, chemistry, equipment; referring physicians; and so on.
- *Input:* **Input** is information or knowledge necessary to achieve the desired outcome. Examples include patient information, examination requested, knowledge of procedures, workload, and so on.

Box 1-1 14 Points for Management

1. Create constancy of purpose toward improvement of product and service, with the aim to become competitive and stay in business and provide jobs.
2. Adopt a new philosophy.
3. Cease dependence on mass inspection to achieve quality. Build quality into the product in the first place.
4. End the practice of awarding business on the basis of price alone. Instead, minimize total cost. Move toward a single **supplier** for any one item, based on a long-term relationship built on loyalty and trust.
5. Improve constantly and forever the system of production and service, in order to improve quality and productivity and thus constantly reduce costs.
6. Institute training on the job.
7. Institute leadership to help people do the job better.
8. Drive out fear so that everyone can work effectively for the good of the organization.
9. Break down barriers between departments.
10. Eliminate slogans, exhortations, and targets for the work force.
11. Eliminate work quotas. Substitute leadership.
12. Eliminate merit rating systems.
13. Institute a vigorous program of education and self-improvement.
14. Involve everyone in the organization in the transformation of total quality improvement.

From Deming WE: *Out of the crisis,* Cambridge, Mass, 1986, Center for Advanced Educational Services.

- *Action:* **Action** is the activity to achieve the desired outcome. Examples include computer entry and form completion, assignment of patient to appropriate room, and so on.

These first three steps are variable factors that influence the output.

- *Output:* The desired outcome or the characteristics that satisfy the customer. Examples include completed paperwork, completed diagnostic examination, and so on.
- *Customer:* A person, department, or organization that needs or wants the desired outcome. This can be broken down into the following groups:

  Internal customers: Referring physicians, hospital employees, departments, and department employees
  External customers: Patients and their families, third party payers, and the community

The satisfaction of the customer, both internal and external, is the driving force behind CQI because it focuses on the needs and expectations of customers and the continuous improvement of the product or service. By continually meeting or exceeding customer satisfaction, the process is considered to be successful.

Problem Identification and Analysis

Group Dynamics

To continually improve the processes involved in customer satisfaction, several tools must be used to identify problems and analyze the data obtained. To help with problem identification in CQI, groups of individuals that are familiar with or are using the processes receive the most valid input. Group dynamic tools include brainstorming, focus groups, and quality improvement teams.

Brainstorming. Brainstorming is a group process used to develop a large collection of ideas without regard to their merit or validity. For example, a department meeting of all staff could be used to solicit ideas or suggestions for a particular topic. The leader of this session should encourage participation by everyone, not criticize any contribution made, and record all ideas for future assessment.

Focus Groups. A focus group is a smaller group that focuses on a particular problem and derive a solution. Generally, the applicable ideas on a particular problem obtained from brainstorming are considered in this smaller group, which can come to a consensus. A focus group must have a skilled facilitator to be successful.

Quality Improvement Team. A quality improvement team is a group of individuals who implement the solutions derived by the focus group. This may or may not include members of the focus group.

Information Analysis

For these groups to facilitate a solution to a problem, data obtained through various collection methods must be organized and presented in a format that will be easy to analyze. To accomplish this, several different charts or graphs may be used.

Flowchart. A flowchart is a pictorial representation of the individual steps required in a process. It shows the relationship among various steps and can help identify sites of possible system failure. It also helps document current processes, redesign current processes, and design new processes. For an explanation of the symbols used in a flowchart, see Box 1-2.

An example of a flowchart is shown in Figure 1-1.

Cause and Effect Diagram. A cause and effect diagram is a causal analysis tool (also called a *fishbone chart* or

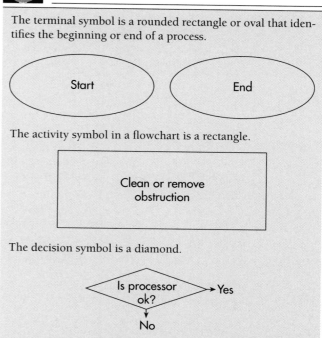

Box 1-2 The Flowchart

The terminal symbol is a rounded rectangle or oval that identifies the beginning or end of a process.

Start   End

The activity symbol in a flowchart is a rectangle.

Clean or remove obstruction

The decision symbol is a diamond.

Is processor ok? → Yes / No

Ishikawa diagram, in honor of the person who developed it) (Figure 1-2). It is used to demonstrate graphically the causes and effects of different variables or conditions on a key quality characteristic and thereby identify potential areas for improvement.

Histogram. A histogram is a data display tool in the form of a bar graph that plots the most frequent occurrence of a quantity in the center (Figure 1-3). The distribution of continuous data often is best accomplished with a histogram. It also helps to demonstrate the amount of variation within a process.

Pareto Chart. A Pareto chart is a causal analysis tool named after Wilfredo Pareto, an Italian political economist. This is a variation of the histogram, which prioritizes the most frequent problems at the Y axis and the other problems in decreasing order to the right (Figure 1-4). The horizontal, or X, axis contains the factors or problems; the vertical, or Y, axis contains the frequency. Most Pareto charts include a horizontal reference, or norm. The Pareto chart is useful in identifying the main causes of problems.

Scatter Plot. A scatter plot (also called a *scatter diagram*) is a traditional two-axis graph (X and Y), with several points plotted throughout (Figure 1-5). If the points seem

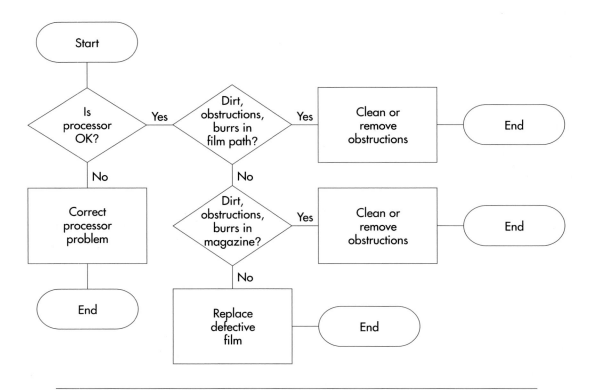

FIGURE 1-1

Flowchart. Flowchart diagrams the process of eliminating scratches on images caused by film processors.

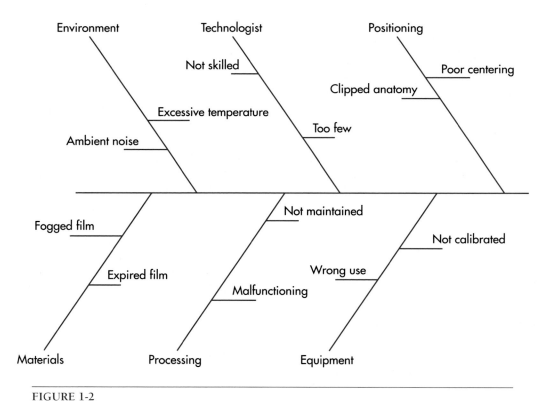

FIGURE 1-2

Fishbone chart. Chart shows the effect of various parameters on key quality characteristic or outcome of proper image quality.

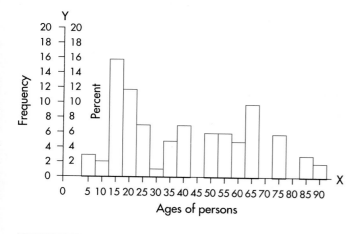

FIGURE 1-3

Histogram. Frequency of occurrence is demonstrated on the Y axis, and category or class interval is demonstrated on the X axis. This example plots percentage of patients undergoing diagnostic procedures versus ages of patients.

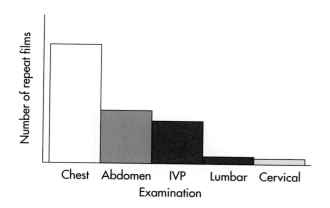

FIGURE 1-4

Pareto chart. Chart indicates specific areas that cause unsatisfactory outcomes, so that improvement actions can be appropriately directed.

to be scattered in a particular pattern, a correlation can be obtained.

Trend Chart. A **trend chart** (also called a *run chart*) pictorially demonstrates whether key **indicators** are moving up or down over a given period (Figure 1-6).

Control Chart. A **control chart** is a modification of the trend chart, in which statistically determined upper and lower control limits are placed with a central line that indicates an accepted norm (Figure 1-7). The control chart is often used for demonstrating film processor operation and variation.

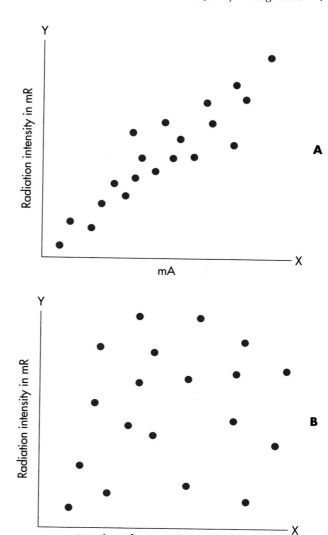

FIGURE 1-5

Scatter plot. Graph shows relationship between a key outcome or characteristic (Y axis) and a key process variable (X axis). Graph **A** indicates a positive correlation between two values, and graph **B** indicates that no correlation exists.

Specific Quality Management Processes

JCAHO 10-Step Process

In 1985 JCAHO introduced the 10-step monitoring and evaluation process as the mechanism for satisfaction of accreditation. Although it is still in use today, the emphasis of some of its steps have changed from quality assurance (QA) to continuous quality improvement (CQI).

Step 1: Assign Responsibility. In QA, the medical director is ultimately responsible, but the task usually is del-

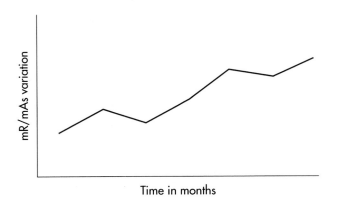

FIGURE 1-6

Trend chart. Graph displays amount of variation of indicator (radiation emitted from an x-ray generator) as a function of time.

egated to a supervisor or QA technologist. With CQI, both intradepartment and interdepartment committees work together with participation of hospital management.

Step 2: Delineate the Scope Of Care and Service. With the QA model, the major services of a particular department are listed (imaging modalities offered, types of patients served, credentials of staff, etc.), whereas under CQI, the scope of care or service for the hospital as a whole is defined.

Step 3: Identify Important Aspects Of Care and Service. Under QA, specific departmental tasks or functions are identified, with emphasis on high volume (chest radiography), high risk (mammography interpretations and angiography) and high risk/problem prone (IVP and examinations requiring intravenous [IV] contrast media). With CQI, the entire hospital determines the key functions to be monitored. This should include important functions relating to patients, care of patients, leadership, use of medications, use of blood and blood components, and determination of the appropriateness of admissions and continued hospitalization.

Step 4: Identify Indicators. JCAHO defines an indicator as a valid and reliable quantitative process or outcome measure related to one or more dimensions of performance. There are two important types of indicators.

SENTINENTAL EVENT INDICATOR. A **sentinental event indicator** identifies an individual event or phenomenon that is significant enough to trigger further review each time it occurs. Most of these events are undesirable and occur infrequently, such as death during a diagnostic examination as a result of contrast media reaction.

AGGREGATE DATA INDICATOR. An **aggregate data indicator** quantifies a process or outcome related to many cases. It may occur frequently and may be desirable or undesirable. Examples include the number of cesarean sections and the number of reported medication errors.

Using QA, each department identifies indicators, whereas under CQI, an interdisciplinary team identifies indicators that will focus more on the process of care. The main dimensions of performance indicators include the following:

- *Appropriateness of care.* **Appropriateness of care** is whether the type of care is necessary.
- *Continuity of care.* **Continuity of care** is the degree to which the care is coordinated among practitioners and/or organizations.
- *Effectiveness of care.* **Effectiveness of care** is the level of benefit when services are rendered under ordinary circumstances by average practitioners for typical patients, as defined by K.N. Lohr.*
- *Efficacy of care.* **Efficacy of care** is the level of benefit expected when health care services are applied under ideal conditions and the best possible circumstances. Most healthcare systems deliver care that places somewhere between effectiveness and efficacy. QA attempts to bring effectiveness to efficacy, whereas CQI goes a step further in allowing for continued improvement once effectiveness has been reached.
- *Efficiency of care.* **Efficiency of care** is the highest quality of care delivered in the shortest amount of time with the least amount of expense and with a positive outcome for the patient condition.
- *Respect and caring.* Respect and caring refer to how well patients are treated during delivery of healthcare service, the level of patient satisfaction, and how well complaints are handled by staff and management.
- *Safety in the care environment.* Safety in the care environment includes equipment, universal precautions, and competency of staff.
- *Timeliness of care.* Timeliness of care refers to delivery of healthcare within a reasonable amount of time, with minimal waiting time.
- *Cost of care.* Cost of care refers to healthcare reasonable for the current marketplace.
- *Availability of care.* Availability of care refers to availability at the clinical facility of the type of care or procedure required by the patient.

Step 5: Establish a Means To Trigger Evaluation. Under QA, a **threshold** is be identified for each indicator. JCAHO

---

*Lohr, KN: Outcomes measurement: concepts and questions, *Inquiry* 25:37-50, 1988.

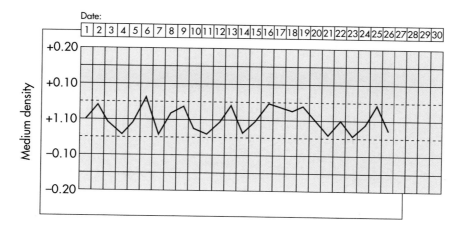

FIGURE 1-7

Control chart. Graph displays amount of variation of indicator (speed or medium density value from a sensitometry film) as a function of time, with upper and lower control limits indicated.

identifies a threshold as a preestablished level of performance applied to a specific indicator. Thresholds may be determined internally (based on past performance of the facility) or externally (based on federal and state regulations or professional guidelines, such as those of JCAHO). As long as the indicator is below the threshold in a negative event or condition, no further action or evaluation is required. For a highly desirable condition or event, the threshold is set at 100%. Under CQI, interdisciplinary teams use statistical methods to determine levels or patterns that trigger evaluation.

Step 6: Collect and Organize Data. Under QA, the department determines the protocol for data collection. First, the method of collection is determined. Options for collection include the following:

- *Patient surveys and questionnaires.* These should be sent to patients 3 to 7 days after discharge or on service date for outpatients.
- *Patient records.*
- *Staff reports.* These include patient care logs, diaries, drug reaction reports, medication variance reports, and so on.
- *Focus groups.* These include quality improvement teams.
- *Computer data base.*

Next, the size of the sample is determined (how many patients, cases, etc.). Then the frequency of collection is determined (concurrently, daily, weekly, monthly, etc.) **Concurrent data** is any data collected during the time of care. Data that should be collected and processed on a continuous basis include patient deaths (dependent upon the patient mix and regional factors) and serious complications to treatment. The frequency at which data are collected for

a specific indicator is reviewed annually to indicate whether the data are adequately capturing the desired information. The final task is to determine how the data will be manipulated for comparison with the threshold. Under CQI, an interdisciplinary team determines the protocol for data collection from various areas of the hospital.

Step 7: Initiate Evaluation. With QA the staff evaluate the level of performance for an indicator by comparing it with the threshold level. With CQI, the leaders identify areas for evaluation based on the data collected.

Step 8: Take Actions To Improve Care and Service. With QA, individuals are evaluated as to whether or not threshold levels were achieved and corrective action taken accordingly. The CQI method looks at the process used in providing the care or service rather than at the individual.

Step 9: Assess Effectiveness Of Actions and Maintain Improvements. The QA method examines whether the actions taken in Step 8 are effective in ensuring quality, whereas the CQI method shows that improvement is continually being sustained. Documentation of these methods is very important.

Step 10: Communicate Results To Affected Individuals and Groups. With the QA method, all results are given to a QA committee and then shared with the department staff and hospital QA committee, whereas with CQI, all results are reported to the leaders and other affected individuals. A common method of presenting such results is with a storyboard (Figure 1-8). A storyboard can summarize a whole report or process using photographs and graphs with a minimum of text.

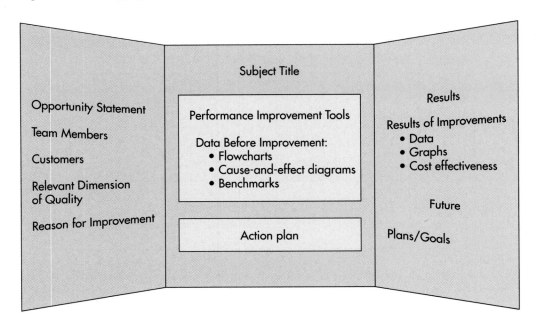

FIGURE 1-8

Model for a storyboard. (From Managing hospital quality, risk, and cost: storyboards showcase performance improvement, *QRC Advisor* 12(9), 1996.)

JCAHO Cycle for Improving Performance

The JCAHO 10-step monitoring and evaluation process is still valid and is the basis of JCAHO's "Cycle for Improving Performance," which identifies the steps *design, measure, assess,* and *improve.*

Design. Systematic planning and implementation are key to the design of any function or process. When designing and planning for new functions and processes, the following factors should be considered:

- The organization's overriding purpose (mission), how it sees itself in the future (vision), and strategies for carrying out its mission and fulfilling its vision (strategic plan)
- Needs and expectations of patients, staff, accreditors, and payers (customers and suppliers)
- Current knowledge about organizational and clinical activities both from inside and outside the organization
- Current and relevant data
- Availability of resources such as funds, staff time, and equipment

Measure. Measure is defined by JACHO as collection of valid and reliable data to demonstrate effectiveness and efficiency of care and performance improvement.

Assess. Accessment is defined by JCAHO as translating data collected during measurement into information that can be used to change processes and improve performance. Proper assessment usually requires comparing data with a reference point or standard. These include the following:

Internal:

- *Historical patterns of performance in the organization* (also called *baseline performance*). This is a comparison of current performance levels with those occurring previously, such as comparing a current department repeat rate with those of the previous year.
- *Desired performance limits.* The patient population and referring physicians expect a certain level or performance. This should be compared with the level achieved, as indicated by the current data. The healthcare organization may also establish its own control limits, targets, and specifications that could be compared with the data obtained.

External:

- *Practice guidelines and parameters.* Procedures developed by professional societies, expert panels, or in-house practitioners, which represent a consensus about the best practices for a given diagnosis, treatment, or procedure. These are usually described in the form of a

Cycle for Improving Performance

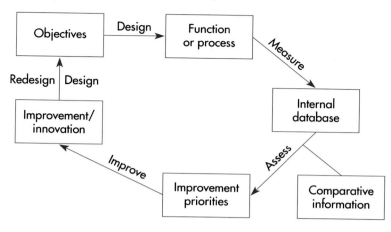

FIGURE 1-9

Cycle for improving performance, showing the important steps, including inputs and outputs, of a systematic approach to improvement. (From *Forms, charts, & other tools for performance improvement*, Oakbrook Terrace, Ill, 1994, JCAHO.)

critical path that documents the basic treatment or action sequence in an effort to eliminate unnecessary variation.
- *Aggregate external reference database.* These allow an organization to compare its performance with that of other organizations, using information such as patient outcomes, costs, lengths of stay for certain treatments, mortality and morbidity rates, and so on. Examples are the JCAHO Indicator Measurement System (IMS), and databases maintained by federal and state governments and third party payers.
- *Benchmarking.* **Benchmarking** involves comparing one organization's performance with that of another; however, it focuses on the other organization's key processes that achieve performance rather than the numbers and statistical data obtained in an aggregate external reference database.

Improve. Once knowledge is gained through measurement and analysis, action can be taken to improve processes by refining or redesigning a process to improve its level of performance. This cycle of *design, measure, assess,* and *improve* should be continually repeating in a CQI program (Figure 1-9).

Other Quality Management Methods

The following are other specific quality management methods that are currently acceptable:

- The **FOCUS-PDCA** approach developed by the Hospital Corporation of America combined with the *plan, do, check,* and *act* cycle used by Deming in Japanese industry.

F Find a problem and define it.
O Organize a team and work on improvement.
C Clarify the problem and current knowledge of the process.
U Understand the problem and the causes of process variation.
S Select the method to improve the process.
P Plan to implement a new method.
D Do the implementation and measure the change.
C Check the results of the change.
A Act to hold the improvements and continue further improvements.

- Evangelical Health Systems CQI Monitoring system.
- FADE, created by Organizational Dynamics (a private consulting firm).
- The Five Stage Plan developed by Joiner and Associates (a quality consulting group).

SUMMARY

In modern diagnostic imaging departments, the radiologists, department administrators and supervisors, technologists, and support staff should work together to ensure that adequate processes are in place in order to properly care for the patient, achieve the highest quality image possible, and obtain the correct diagnosis from that image. These processes should be continuously reviewed by all parties and modified as the need arises.

Review Questions

1. Which levels of quality control testing can usually be performed by a quality assurance technologist?
    1. Level I
    2. Level II
    3. Level III
    a. 1 and 2
    b. 1 and 3
    c. 2 and 3
    d. 1, 2, and 3
2. Which government agency mandates a policy on exposure to blood-borne pathogens?
    a. FDA
    b. EPA
    c. OSHA
    d. CDRH
3. Information or knowledge necessary to achieve a desired outcome is termed:
    a. supplier
    b. input
    c. action
    d. output
4. The desired outcome or the characteristics that satisfy the customer is termed:
    a. supplier
    b. input
    c. action
    d. output
5. An activity to achieve a desired outcome is termed:
    a. supplier
    b. input
    c. action
    d. output

6. A person, department, or organization who needs or wants a desired outcome is termed:
    a. supplier
    b. input
    c. action
    d. output
7. A cause and effect diagram is also known as a:
    a. histogram
    b. Pareto chart
    c. scatter plot
    d. fishbone chart
8. A chart that pictorially demonstrates whether key indicators are moving up or down over a given period is termed:
    a. histogram
    b. Pareto chart
    c. trend chart
    d. scatter plot
9. A valid and reliable quantitative process or outcome measure related to one or more dimensions of performance is termed:
    a. external customer
    b. indicator
    c. threshold
    d. sentinental event
10. The highest quality of care delivered in the shortest amount of time with the least amount to expense and a positive outcome is termed _____ of care.
    a. appropriateness
    b. continuity
    c. effectiveness
    d. efficiency

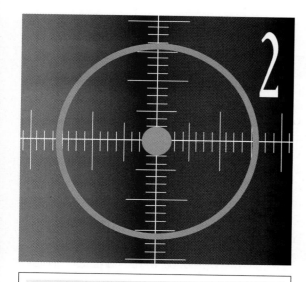

2 Film Darkrooms

Objectives

At the completion of this chapter the reader will be able to do the following:

- State the function and characteristics of a darkroom used for diagnostic imaging
- Explain the importance of proper safelight type and function
- Perform a safelight evaluation test
- Perform an evaluation of white light leakage and processing area condition
- Explain the conditions for proper film and chemical storage
- Discuss the importance of proper viewbox illuminator function on image quality
- Perform a viewbox quality control test
- Explain the evaluation process of image duplicators

Outline

DARKROOM FUNCTION

The function of a radiographic **darkroom** is to protect the film from white light and ionizing radiation during handling and processing. After a film has been exposed to light or ionizing radiation (such as in a cassette during a radiographic examination) it can be as much as two to eight times more sensitive to subsequent exposure as an unexposed film (depending upon the type of emulsion). This means that any accidental exposure from an unwanted source (such as a darkroom light leak) can destroy a diagnostic image. Film can also be affected by excess heat, humidity, static electricity, pressure, and chemical fumes. All of these variables must be carefully controlled to obtain a diagnostic quality image. The most common result if they are not controlled is the presence of fog on the manifest image. *Fog* is defined as noninformational density that occurs because silver grains are formed that do not represent any of the anatomic structures within the patient.

DARKROOM ENVIRONMENT

A darkroom is considered a scientific laboratory by common practice standards and the Occupational Safety and Health Administration (OSHA) and should meet all of the requirements and possess all of the equipment of a laboratory. It should also be clean, well ventilated, well organized, and safe. Eating, drinking, and smoking must be prohibited in the darkroom, because bits of food or ashes from cigarettes can get into image receptors as they are being loaded and unloaded. This can cause artifacts on the image that could mimic pathologies (especially in mammography cassettes) or otherwise degrade the diagnostic quality of the image.

Darkroom Characteristics

Countertops or other work surfaces and rubber floor mats should be grounded, to reduce the risk of **static electricity**. Static electricity creates sparks that emit white light (all colors of the visible spectrum). Because all imaging films are sensitive to some portion of the visible light spectrum, this light creates artifacts that appear on the processed image. The types of static artifacts are tree, crown, and smudge (see Chapter 10). In addition to grounding the work surfaces, static can be minimized by:

1. Proper film handling (placing a film into and out of a cassette or onto a film tray rather than sliding it), because friction is a primary cause of static electricity.
2. Wearing natural-fiber clothing (cotton) versus synthetic-fiber clothing (nylon, polyester, etc.)

3. Maintaining a proper **humidity** range (40% to 60% relative humidity). Moisture in the air absorbs the buildup of static charges. This is why static is less of a problem in the summer, when the relative humidity is greater. In some darkrooms, installation of a humidifier or ion generator may be necessary to maintain the recommended level of humidity. A **psychrometer** to measure humidity should be available or installed in the darkroom. Excessive humidity could cause films to stick together or condensation problems.
4. Cleaning screens regularly with an antistatic nonabrasive cleaner.

Appropriate screen cleaners are available from the manufacturers from whom the screen is purchased (it is important to match these products to the particular brand of screen).

The darkroom must be well ventilated to prevent buildup of heat and humidity, which will degrade the film. **Temperature** should be maintained in a range of 65° to 75° F (18° to 24° C). The fumes from the processing chemicals are considered toxic, corrosive, and potentially carcinogenic by OSHA, the Environmental Protection Agency (EPA), and the Department of Transportation. OSHA maintains a listing of Permissable Exposure Limits (PELs), which are the chemical levels to which employees can be exposed in the workplace without risk or harm. An environmental engineer can be consulted to monitor the level of a darkroom area. The following are some of the PELs for processing of chemicals:

Acetic acid: 10 parts/million (ppm)
Ammonium sulfamate: 5 mg/m^3
Hydroquinone: 2 mg/m^3 (0.44 ppm)
Phenol: 5 parts/million
Sulfur dioxide: 5 parts/million
Glutaraldehyde: 0.7 mg/m^3 (0.2 ppm)
Silver: 0.01 mg/m^3

The above values were established in 1968, and discussion is taking place to revise these figures. In recent years, many technologists and darkroom technicians have complained of hypersensitivity to darkroom chemicals, a condition sometimes called *darkroom disease* that manifests in a variety of symptoms ranging from hives to severe fatigue and impairment of the immune system. The Society of Toxicology and the American Society of Radiologic Technologists are currently collecting data on this phenomenon. Proper **ventilation** in a darkroom should keep the levels of chemical vapors well below PELs and should include a source of fresh air, slight positive air pressure (so that chemical fumes are not sucked out of the processor), and ventilation to the outside atmosphere. *This should yield about eight to ten room changes of air per hour.* A ventilator duct should be placed near the floor, either in the lower portion of the entrance door or the wall.

Many darkrooms have interior walls that are mistakenly painted black, which can make the room too dark. Instead, darkroom walls should be painted in pastels and light colors to increase the reflectance of the light emitted from the safelight. Enamels or epoxy paints are best, because they are easy to clean and more durable. However, a matte finish must be used, because a high-gloss finish could reflect and amplify light leaks. Should any darkroom wall lie adjacent to a radiation area (x-ray room, nuclear medicine area, etc.), proper lead shielding appropriate to the type and energy of radiation used must be present to protect darkroom personnel and prevent fogging of the film.

The processing of most diagnostic images requires a large quantity of clean water. The majority of automatic film processors in use today use only cold water, because they have built-in heating coils to regulate solution temperatures (see Chapter 3). Older processors and many cine film processors require a hot water supply in addition to the cold water and have a mixing valve to regulate the temperature. Adequate drainage must be in place to remove the dirty water and used chemicals after processing is completed. Adequate drainage is generally defined as the capacity to handle 2.5 times the maximum outflow of the processor when all drains are open. For most automatic film processors this is about 10 gal/min (38 L/min). A floor drain is generally desired for maximum efficiency, using 3-inch diameter cast iron or plastic (polyvinylchloride [PVC]) pipe. Local building codes should be referenced before choosing PVC pipe, because some municipalities have restrictions on its use. Copper or brass pipes and fittings should be avoided because of the corrosive effect of the processing chemicals. These drains should be dedicated only to film processors and should not share a common line with sinks and toilets, to reduce the chance of blockage. They must also be cleaned on a regular basis with a commercial drain cleaner, because buildup will form over time. This is especially important when metallic replacement silver recovery units (see Chapter 5) are used. Flooring around the drain must be easy to clean, moisture-resistant, and of a light color to allow identification of objects that may have been dropped in the dark.

Darkrooms should have adequate storage space for film and chemicals. Film must be stored upright to avoid pressure marks. Open boxes of film should be kept in a metal film bin (usually mounted under the work counter) to minimize the chance of being exposed to white light (Figure 2-1). Passboxes, also called *film transfer systems,* should also be present to prohibit white light from entering. The darkroom door should be double interlocked or revolving or a lightproof maze can be installed if floor space permits.

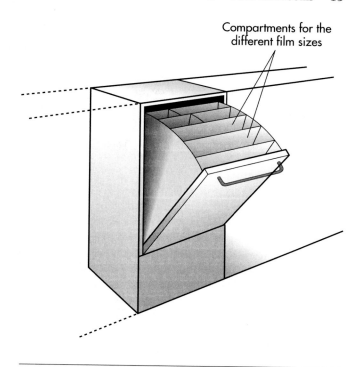

FIGURE 2-1
Standard darkroom film bin.

Darkroom Lighting

A darkroom should have two types of lighting, overhead lights and safelights.

Overhead Lighting

Overhead lighting is the standard white light that normally illuminates the interior rooms of hospitals and clinics. This standard lighting is necessary for cleaning, maintenance, and possible emergencies (e.g., darkroom personnel becoming ill). Proper overhead lighting normally requires a standard fluorescent fixture (one 2-inch × 4-inch × four fluorescent tubes) per 8 square feet (0.74 m² of floor space. The overhead light should be interlocked with the film bin(s), so that if the bin is open, the light cannot be energized. If this is not practical, a cover should be placed over the switch to prevent accidental activation. Film bin alerts are also available (at a minimal cost) that sound a continuous alarm while the film bin is open, to prevent accidental exposure to white light.

Safelight

A **safelight** is a light source that emits wavelengths to which particular types of film are not sensitive. A typical radiographic film should be able to remain in safelighting for at least 40 seconds without becoming fogged. Safelights should be mounted at least 3 to 4 feet from feed trays or loading counters.

| Red | Orange | Yellow | Green | Blue | Indigo | Violet |

FIGURE 2-2
Visible light spectrum.

The visible light spectrum consists of the primary colors shown in Figure 2-2.

Wavelengths range from about 4000Å for violet light to 8000Å for red light. The type of film to be processed in the darkroom determines the type of safelight to be used.

Blue-Violet-Sensitive Film. Blue-violet sensitive film is the most common type of film used in screen cassettes and, as its name implies, is primarily sensitive to the colors blue, indigo, and violet. An amber safelight (a mixture of red, orange, and some yellow) is normally used, with two options available. For the average-size darkroom, a fixture type of safelight containing either a 7.5- or 15-watt lightbulb is sufficient (Figure 2-3). The lightbulb is covered by an amber piece of plastic or glass, called a *filter*. The most common types of filters are the Kodak Wratten 6B or the Kodak Mor-Lite (which is slightly brighter). The other option, called a *sodium vapor lamp* (Figure 2-4) is used in a large darkroom or when bright safelight conditions are desired. This works on the same principle as mercury streetlights; however, sodium yields a bright amber color when energized. These lights are large, expensive, and require a long warm-up time to reach maximum brightness. They must be mounted on the darkroom ceiling because of their brightness level and to provide indirect lighting. To regulate the level of brightness, shutter or door openings on top are adjusted with a pull-chain.

Orthochromatic Film. Orthochromatic film is mainly sensitive to the green portion of the visible spectrum, in addition to blue-violet. A red or magenta dye is added to the film emulsion to increase the absorption of green light by the silver halide crystals. Amber is a mixture of red, orange, and yellow; therefore the safelights discussed previously are not compatible with this type of film, because orange and yellow are too close to green in the spectrum. It is necessary, therefore, to use a safelight with the same fixture and lightbulb combination mentioned previously that has a safelight filter that is pure red. The most common of this type is the Kodak GBX Series all-purpose filters. Another option is an LED safelight, which uses a light-emitting diode that consumes very low power and can last up to 15 years. These safelights are perfectly compatible for use with blue-violet-sensitive film but are not as bright as lights with amber filters.

FIGURE 2-3
Fixture type of darkroom safelight.

FIGURE 2-4
Sodium vapor lamp darkroom safelight.

New Modality Film. New modality film is designed to obtain images from either a cathode-ray tube (multiformat camera) or a laser camera (often used in CT, sonography, nuclear medicine, MRI, and digital radiography [hence the name]). The light source for these cameras usually emits red or amber color, so the film emulsion is designed accordingly. A fixture and lightbulb combination safelight with a dark green filter may be used with these emulsions. This filter is very dark, and some time is necessary for the eyes of technologists or darkroom personnel to adapt. Some types of new modality film are **panchromatic** (sensitive to all colors of the visible spectrum) and therefore cannot be exposed to any safelighting. It is best to consult the literature accompanying the box of film or the manufacturer's technical representative before using dark green safelighting.

Other Film Types. Most other types of film (duplicating, subtraction, spot, industrial, etc.) can be processed in darkrooms using any of the safelights discussed above. Cine film used in cardiac catheterization studies is black and white motion picture film (panchromatic) and cannot be exposed to safelights. It normally requires its own dedicated processor (see Chapter 8).

Light and Leakage Testing

Safelight Testing

Safelights may become unsafe over time as a result of cracks or pinholes in the filter (resulting from expansion and contraction with heat), the wrong wattage of bulb installed, or the doors on a sodium vapor lamp being open too far. Therefore a safelight test should be performed at least semiannually. Testing requires a sensitized film (preexposed), because this makes it more sensitive to safelight fog. A form for this test can be found in Appendix B.

Procedure

1. Use a ruler to verify the proper distance from the safelight to the work counters or feed trays. Also check the wattage of lightbulbs and inspect the filter for cracks or pinholes. Make sure that the filter type matches the film type.

2. Load an 8- × 10-inch (20 × 25 cm) cassette and expose it to radiation at about 60 kVp and 1 mAs at 40 inches SID tabletop. This should produce an optical density of between 0.3 and 0.5 when processed (it may be necessary to modify the above exposure factors to achieve the desired optical density, depending on the image receptor system speed).

3. Bring the cassette back into the darkroom, lay the exposed film on the counter, and cover all of it except for 1 inch with a piece of cardboard (Figure 2-5).

4. After 10 seconds, move the cardboard sheet back and expose another 1-inch strip of film. Repeat every 10 seconds until the last 1-inch strip is reached. Process the film before this strip is exposed.

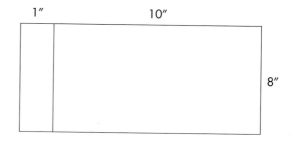

FIGURE 2-5
Placement of cardboard on film for safelight.

5. Place the film on a viewbox and label according to the total time of exposure. Use a **densitometer** to measure the optical density of each strip. The strip that shows an increase in optical density above the base-plus-fog is the maximum amount of time that the film can be placed under that safelight (should be 40 seconds or greater). If the safelight is truly safe, the strips should not vary in optical density by a value of more than 0.2.

For mammographic films (which are generally slower-speed emulsions) the darkroom fog test is performed with a slightly different procedure. A film is exposed with a **sensitometer** and placed on the counter in the darkroom. An opaque card is then placed over one half of the exposed wedge pattern on the film. After the film has been exposed for 2 minutes of safelighting, it is processed, and the step having an optical density closest to 1.4 on the unexposed portion is examined with a densitometer. The difference in the area of this step that was covered with the opaque card and the uncovered (exposed to the safelight) area of this step should be 0.02 or less.

Leakage Testing and Processing Area Condition

While testing safelights, a check for light leaks, other extraneous light sources (indicator lights on processors, duplicators, etc.), and processing area conditions also usually can be performed. A form for this test can be found in Appendix B.

Procedure

1. Turn on all white lights in the area surrounding the darkroom. Enter the darkroom and shut off all safelights and overhead lights.

2. After eyes adapt to the dark (about 5 minutes), check for white light leaks, especially near the processor, darkroom doors, water pipes, ventilation ducts, and suspended ceiling tiles.

3. Turn on the overhead lighting and inspect the counter tops and processor feed tray for foreign objects, dampness, cleanliness and sharp edges.

4. Locate the reserve fixer and developer tanks and check to ensure that they are properly ventilated and that the temperature of the area is within accepted limits.

5. Locate the film storage area and verify that the boxes of film are being stored vertically and under the proper temperature conditions. Also check the age of the film and the visibility of the expiration date.

Film and Chemical Storage

Film should be stored at a temperature range between 55° and 75° F (14° to less than 24° C), whether in the darkroom, storage closet, or warehouse. Excessive heat can cause age fog, and too low of a temperature can lead to moisture condensation on the film, causing artifacts. Humidity also must be controlled, as mentioned previously, (40% to 60% RH), because static artifacts can appear if the air is too dry. While aging, condensation and films sticking together could be a problem in high humidity. Film can be stored in a refrigerator or freezer to prolong the shelf life, provided the inner seal is unopened. If kept in a freezer at 0° F or below, the deterioration or aging process will stop and the expiration date can be extended for any time that the film was in the freezer. After removal, a 24-hour warm-up period is required before the inner seal can be opened and the film used. This is to prevent condensation and the associated artifacts from appearing on the film.

Chemicals shold be stored in a well-ventilated area under the same temperature conditions as film. The area should be darkened or have minimal lighting, because the developer solution can degrade if exposed to bright light. It is best not to store film and chemicals in close proximity to each other, because film chemistry contains quantities of potassium, a percentage of which is in the form of K^{40}, a naturally occurring radioactive isotope that can fog film over time. The majority of film manufacturers recommend that background radiation not exceed 7 µR/hr. Levels near large quantities of processing chemicals can reach 12 µR/hr. Most manufacturers of film and processing chemicals give a 12-month expiration date based on an ambient temperature of 68° F (20° C).

VIEWBOX QUALITY CONTROL

Viewbox Illuminators

Most diagnostic images are transparencies and therefore require an illuminator to view the final image. Proper functioning of the **viewbox illuminator** is essential in maintaining

image quality because it has a direct effect on the contrast. Over time, heat from the fluorescent bulb inside can discolor the plastic front of the viewbox. Dirt and dust can form on both the inside and outside of the plastic viewing surface, as well as the outside surface of the fluorescent bulb. This can reduce light output by as much as 10% per year, which will decrease image contrast. For this reason, the bulbs should be changed every 2 years (especially viewboxes used in mammography), even though the typical fluorescent bulb has a rated life of 7500 to 9000 hours. With multiple viewboxes, replace all lamps at the same time and replace them with bulbs of the same manufacturer, production lot, and color temperature to maintain consistency. All viewboxes should be cleaned weekly with an antistatic, nonabrasive cleaner, and the intensity of all viewboxes within the department should be checked for consistency. A viewbox quality control test should be performed upon acceptance and then at least once a year (weekly for those used in mammography).

Viewbox Quality Control Test

The viewbox quality control test requires a screwdriver and either a photographic light meter or a 35-mm camera with a built-in light meter.

Procedure

1. Inspect the plexiglass front of the viewbox for discoloration, dust, and other artifacts. Clean or replace the plexiglass if necessary.

2. Unplug the viewbox and remove the plexiglass front with the screwdriver. Inspect the fluorescent lightbulb for proper wattage, cleanliness, and discoloration; clean or replace if necessary. When finished, replace the plexiglass front and screws.

3. Determine the brightness level. This procedure requires a basic understanding of the concepts of photometry, which is the study and measurement of light (Box 2-1). To measure the brightness level of viewbox illuminators, a photographic light meter (photometer) is required (Figure 2-6), which ideally can measure both luminance and illuminance. The American College of Radiology (ACR) recommends measuring the luminance in nit. The aperature of the photometer should be 9 inches away from the viewbox front when measuring brightness. Make the first reading in the center viewbox. Conventional viewbox luminance should be at least 1500 nit, with 1700 nit being standard. Viewboxes used for viewing mammograms should have a luminance of about 3500 nit. The greater the brightness level of the viewbox, the greater the contrast observed

Box 2-1 Photometery

The radiant energy that strikes or crosses a surface per unit of time or radiant energy emitted by a source per unit time is called *radiant flux* and is measured in watts. Radiant flux, evaluated with respect to its capacity to evoke the sensation of brightness, is called *luminous flux*. The unit of luminous flux is the lumen and is affected by the radiant flux and the wavelength of the light. The luminous intensity of a light source is the amount of luminous flux per solid angle and is represented by the equation:

$$I = \frac{dF}{d\omega}$$

where:

I = Luminous intensity
dF = Luminous flux in lumens
dω = Solid angle in steradians

ω is equal to the area on the surface of a sphere divided by the square of the radius of that sphere. This value of lumens per steradian is also called the *candle*, or *candela*.

The actual brightness of a particular area or source can be evaluated by one of two values, illuminance and luminance.

ILLUMINANCE

Illuminance is the amount of luminous flux incident per unit area, or the amount of light that falls upon a given surface. This can be measured in units of lux (lumens/m²) or foot-candles (lumens/ft²). Conversion of foot-candles (ft-cd) to lux can be accomplished by the following equation:

$$\text{Lux} = \text{Foot-candles} \times 10.8$$

The illuminance of the interior of a typical home or office building from artificial light is approximately 100 lux or 10 ft-cd. Standard viewboxes are about 5000 lux, or 500 ft-cd. To measure illuminance, a photodetector that is covered with both a photometric filter and a cosine diffuser is required (see Figure 2-4).

LUMINANCE

Luminance is the luminous intensity per unit of projected area of source or the amount of light that is emitted or scattered from a particular surface. Units that can measure luminance include candles or candela/m² (also known as *nit*), candles/cm², or candles/ft². The range of human vision is from 6×10^{-6} nit to 10×10^{6} nit. The optimum range is from about 1000 to 10,000 nit. Another set of units can also be used for measurement of luminance and are ⅛ as great as those mentioned above. These units are the lambert, foot-lambert, and meter-lambert.

$$1 \text{ lambert} = 1/\pi \text{ candle/cm}^2$$
$$1 \text{ foot-lambert} = 1/\pi \text{ candle/ft}^2$$
$$1 \text{ meter-lambert} = 1/\pi \text{ candle/m}^2$$

For conversion of nit to foot-lamberts, the following equation can be used:

$$1 \text{ cd/m}^2 \text{ (nit)} = \text{Foot-lambert} \times 3.43$$

To equate the units of luminance and illuminance (because both can be used to measure viewbox brightness), 1 lux of illuminance may be thought of as the reflectance of a perfectly diffusing surface to 1 candle/m² (nit) of luminance (or 1 lux = 1 nit).

FIGURE 2-6

Photographic light meter (photometer) for viewbox evaluation. (Courtesy Nuclear Associates, Carle Place, N.Y.)

in the viewed diagnostic image. The luminance of each of the viewboxes in the department should be compared and should not deviate from each other by more than ±15%. The uniformity of a single viewbox should also be evaluated by dividing the viewing panel into four quadrants. Take readings from the center of each quadrant at a 9-inch distance and compare. The readings from each of the four quadrants should not deviate by more than ±15%.

If a photometer is not available, a 35-mm camera with a built-in light meter can be substituted (this will not be accepted during Mammography Quality Standards Act [MQSA] inspections). If the camera uses an exposure value (EV) scale to measure light intensity, set the film speed indicator to ASA 100. Place the camera lens in contact with the center of the viewbox front, look into the viewfinder, and record the reading. Repeat this procedure for each quadrant to verify viewbox uniformity. An EV of 13 will indicate 500 ft-cd of illumination (the minimum acceptable value for a standard viewbox). An EV of 14 indicates twice as much light (or 1000 ft-cd), and an EV of 12 is one half as much (250 ft-cd). If the light intensity is doubled, the maximum optical density that can be viewed is also doubled. For example, if 500 ft-cd can illuminate a maximum optical density of 2.5 on the image, then 1000 ft-cd can illuminate a maximum optical density of 2.8. Some cameras have a light meter that does not use an EV scale but instead indicates the shutter speed to use when taking the photograph when you look into the viewfinder. In this case, set the film speed indicator to ASA 64 and the shutter to f8. The denominator of the shutter speed indicated is the light intensity in ft-cd. For example, if the indicated shutter speed is 1/400 seconds, the light intensity is 400 ft-cd.

4. Measure the color temperature. The quality or spectrum of light emitted from a light source is defined by its color temperature. This is the temperature at which a black body radiator would emit light of a comparable color. A surface that absorbs all of the radiant energy incident upon it would appear black and is called a *black body*. The color temperature is measured in degrees kelvin (°K) and measured with a color temperature meter. Standard viewboxes should have color temperatures ranging from 5400 °K to 10,000 °K. The majority of viewbox manufacturers prefer a rating of 6250 °K.

5. Measure the ambient light conditions. The ambient light is the light level of the viewing room and the radiologist viewing area separate from the viewbox. This light must be less than that of the viewbox, or a decrease in contrast level will be observed in the image. To survey this level, turn the illuminators off and place the meter or camera 1 foot away from the viewbox to record the read-

ing. The maximum ambient room light should be 30 ft-cd (320 lux) or 8 EV. Mammographic viewing areas should be 50 lux or less (equivalent to a moonlit night).

IMAGE DUPLICATING UNITS

Film duplicating units, or copiers, are standard pieces of equipment in diagnostic imaging darkrooms (Figure 2-7). Because legal considerations make hospitals reluctant to release original images, copies are made so that patients can consult with specialty physicians without having to repeat the examinations. Most units emit **ultraviolet** (UV) light using special BLB bulbs. UV light is more penetrating than visible light; thus it can penetrate the darker areas of a processed image so that the image can be duplicated. The copy film is a single-emulsion film sensitive to UV light, so a standard safelight can be used. The emulsion side of the film should be placed against the original image during the duplication process. The emulsion is more unstable with this type of film because it has been preexposed to the point of **solarization**, or image reversal. For this reason, large quantities should not be stockpiled.

Most units have an exposure level switch to regulate the quality of the copy image. Film duplicators should faithfully copy optical densities of up to 2.5 from the original image. To verify this, make a copy of a sensitometer film, use a densitometer to measure each step and compare with the original image. They should be the same or within an optical density of 0.02 and should be evaluated on a weekly basis. To check the contact between the copy film and the original during duplication, use a radiograph of a wire mesh screen (used to evaluate film/screen contact) and

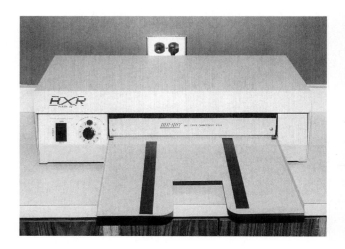

FIGURE 2-7
Duplicating unit for copying diagnostic images.

make a copy. The copy should demonstrate the same sharpness level of the mesh pattern throughout the image. This should be performed monthly.

Images obtained with a multiformat camera or laser camera can be particularly difficult to duplicate because of their single emulsion. An image from a Society of Motion Picture and Television Engineers (SMPTE) test pattern (see Chapter 8) should be produced from the camera and then duplicated with the copier. Optical density readings from the same areas of the copy and the original should be taken with a densitometer and compared. Again, they should be the same or within a value of 0.02.

SUMMARY

Maintaining proper darkroom conditions and procedures is essential to achieving the desired film image. These images must also be displayed using proper viewing conditions for optimum diagnostic capability.

Review Questions

1. The main reason to prohibit food and drink in a film darkroom is to:
   a. avoid contamination of processor solutions
   b. prevent artifacts
   c. prevent pressure marks on the film
   d. prevent static artifacts

2. The amount of light that is emitted or scattered by a surface may be referred to as:
   a. photometry
   b. luminance
   c. illuminance
   d. optical density

3. A device that can be used to measure darkroom humidity levels is known as a(an):
   a. sensitometer
   b. densitometer
   c. hydrometer
   d. psychrometer

4. Proper darkroom ventilation should include _____ _____ room changes of air per hour.
   a. 3 to 5
   b. 6 to 8
   c. 8 to 10
   d. 10 to 12

5. Most types of new modality film may be processed under a(an) _____ colored safelight.
   a. amber
   b. dark green
   c. red
   d. white

6. A darkroom safelight test should be performed at least:
   a. daily
   b. weekly
   c. monthly
   d. semiannually

7. Why should boxes of film and containers of developer solution not be stored in close proximity to each other?
   a. developer contains naturally occurring radioactive material
   b. pressure marks can occur on the film
   c. static electricity is more common
   d. none of the above

8. Photometric readings from each quadrant of a viewbox should not vary by more than plus or minus _____ _____ %.
   a. 2
   b. 5
   c. 10
   d. 25

9. The unit most commonly employed to measure luminance is the:
   a. lux
   b. nit
   c. foot-candle
   d. lumen

10. A film duplicating unit should be able to faithfully copy optical densities of up to:
    a. 0.5
    b. 1.5
    c. 2.5
    d. 3.5

Student Experiment 2.1   Darkroom Fog Check and Viewbox Illuminations

Part 1 Darkroom Fog Check

PURPOSE

To ensure that the safelights and other potential sources of "unsafe light" will not fog the film being handled in the darkroom.

EQUIPMENT NEEDED

1. X-ray film
2. Clock or stopwatch
3. Densitometer
4. Darkroom

PROCEDURE

1. Turn off all of the safelights and overhead lights in the darkroom.
2. After eyes are adjusted to the darkness (about 5 minutes), look for any sources of light that you can find. Pay particular attention to the seals around processors, passboxes, darkroom doors, and so on. Suspended ceilings can leak light from the surrounding rooms. Make note of any light leaks and indicate them in the analysis portion of this experiment. Turn the safelights back on.
3. Remove an 8- × 10-inch cassette from the passbox, take it into one of the radiographic rooms and expose it to 50 kVp, 1 mAs and 40-inch SID tabletop.
4. Return the cassette to the darkroom and remove the exposed film from the cassette. Lay it on the counter and cover the entire film except for 1 inch with a sheet of cardboard.
5. After 10 seconds, move the cardboard and expose a second 1-inch strip. Repeat this procedure until all except the last 1-inch strip is exposed.
6. Process the film before the last 1-inch strip is exposed to the safelight.
7. Label each strip and take density readings. Record each value on the data page.

Part 2 Viewbox Illuminations

PURPOSE

To verify that the illumination levels of department viewboxes are within the recommended guidelines and that the ambient light conditions within the viewing area are conducive to proper viewing.

EQUIPMENT REQUIRED

1. Photometer
2. Various department viewboxes

PROCEDURE

1. Set the photometer to measure illumination in candles/m^2 (nit). Place the aperature opening 9 inches from the center of the viewbox illuminator and record the reading on the data page.
2. Mentally divide the viewbox into quadrants and take a light measurement from the center of each quadrant. Record the readings on the data page. Compare each of these values to each other and that of the center obtained in step 1. These values should be within ± 10% of each other.
3. Measure the ambient light levels by turning off the viewbox but leave on all of the overhead room lights that are normally in use. Place the light meter 9 inches away from the viewbox front and record the reading (even though the viewbox is off). The maximum ambient light should be about 300 nit.

Student Experiment 2.1   Darkroom Fog Check and Viewbox Illuminations—cont'd

Analysis

PART 1 DARKROOM FOG CHECK

1. Were there any light leaks visible from inside the darkroom when all of the lights were out. If so, how would you correct the problem?
2. Examine the density readings taken from each strip and comment on any differences that were observed. Were they within acceptable limits? (All strips should not vary in optical density by more than a value of 0.2.)
3. How would you correct your darkroom conditions if your films are varying by more than the allowable limits.
4. What effect on radiographic quality (optical density, contrast, visibility of detail, etc.) could occur as a result of improper safelight conditions? Be specific.

PART 2 VIEWBOX ILLUMINATORS

1. How did your viewbox illuminator's light output in the center compare with accepted guidelines?
2. How did the uniformity of light output between each quadrant compare with accepted limits? How could this affect image quality if it did not meet accepted variances?
3. Did the ambient light conditions in the viewing room meet accepted guidelines? How would image quality be affected if ambient light is too great?
4. List some of the steps that could be taken to correct improper viewbox illumination and ambient light conditions.

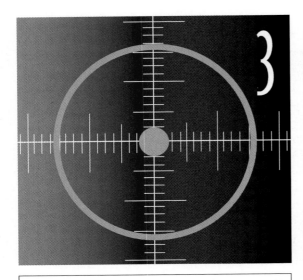

3 Film Processing

Objectives

At the completion of this chapter the reader will be able to do the following:

- Describe the main differences between manual and automatic film processing
- List the main components of the developer and fixer solutions and state the function of each component
- Explain the proper mixing procedure for developer and fixer concentrate solutions
- State the chemical safety procedures for the safe handling of processing chemicals as described by OSHA.
- Describe the basic tests for determining the archival quality of processed images
- List the six main systems of automatic film processors and state the function of each system
- Describe the methods of installing film processors in a darkroom

Outline

Outline–cont'd

After a film has been exposed to radiation, the image that it contains is still invisible to the human eye and is called a **latent image**. To convert it into a visible image, or **manifest image**, the silver contained in the film must be changed from an ionized state (Ag^+) into a neutral, or reduced, state (Ag°), in which the silver turns black. This requires the film to be processed by various solutions that convert the latent image into a visible one and also preserve the image for permanent storage. The two basic methods of film processing are manual and automatic.

MANUAL AND AUTOMATIC FILM PROCESSING

Manual Processing

In the manual processing method film is moved from one solution to the next manually, or by hand, until processing is complete. This method requires more labor and more time and is more prone to variations than automatic processing. For this reason, manual processing is seldom employed in diagnostic imaging today. To process a film manually, several steps are required after the films are hung on special hangers.

Procedure

1. *Wetting agent.* The wetting agent is a chemical that loosens the emulsion so that subsequent solutions can reach all parts of the emulsion uniformly, which reduces development time. This step is optional, because developer ingredients also soften the emulsion. If a wetting agent is used, the film should remain in the solution for about 15 seconds.

2. *Developer.* The **developer** solution converts the latent image into the visible image; therefore this is the most important processing chemical. The film remains in the developer for 3 to 5 minutes depending on the temperature of the solution.

3. *Stop bath or water rinse.* The stop bath or water rinse step stops the development process and removes excess developer from the film. A stop bath is a 1% solution of acetic acid that chemically neutralizes the developer (because it is an alkaline solution) and requires only 5 to 10 seconds of film immersion time. A water rinse relies on water to remove the excess developer and requires about 30 seconds of film immersion.

4. *Fixer.* The **fixer** solution removes the unexposed and undeveloped silver halide crystals from the film emulsion and also hardens the emulsion so that the film can be permanently stored. The time of fixation varies with solution temperature, but the general rule for manual fixation is use the following equation:

Fixing time = Clearing time + Hardening time

The clearing time is the time necessary for the fixer to clear away the unexposed and undeveloped silver halide crystals, which should be accomplished within 5 minutes. The hardening time is the time it takes the emulsion to properly harden and is usually equal to the clearing time. Therefore a film that requires 5 minutes to clear requires another 5 minutes to harden, leaving a total fixing time of 10 minutes.

5. *Washing.* Excess fixer must be removed from film before it is allowed to dry, or the fixer components will crystallize onto the film surface, a process known as **hyporetention**. This white, powdery residue can impair the diagnostic quality of the final image and must therefore be avoided. An example of an image with hyporetention can be found in Chapter 10. This step can take up to 20 minutes.

6. *Drying.* **Drying** prepares the film for viewing and storage and can be accomplished by either an electric dryer, which works in less than a minute, or by exposure to room air while the film is mounted on a special hanger, which can require an hour or more.

Automatic Processing

Automatic processing requires an electromechanical device called an *automatic film processor,* which transports the film from one solution to the next without any manual labor except for placing the film into the device. This shortens the overall processing time, increases the number of films that can be processed in a given period, and ensures less variability of overall film quality than manually processed films, because the processing time, solution temperature, and chemical replenishment are automatically controlled. The disadvantages of automatic processing include higher capital and maintenance costs, increased chemical fog because of higher processing temperatures and transport problems that can damage or destroy images during processing. In a modern diagnostic imaging department, the advantages far outweigh the disadvantages, making automatic film processing virtually exclusive.

PROCESSING CHEMICALS

Developer

As previously mentioned, the developer is the most important processing solution; it converts the latent image into a manifest image. This is accomplished by the developer solution carrying out an *oxidation/reduction reaction,* or *redox.* When a chemical is oxidized (broken down), it releases electrons. These electrons are then available to convert another compound into a more simplified, or reduced, state (hence the term *oxidation/reduction reaction*). During film processing, the developer solution ingredients are oxidized and the silver halide crystal is reduced to black metallic silver. This chemical reaction can be summarized by the following equations: *During exposure to radiation:*

$$Ag^+Br^- + radiation \ \varnothing \ Ag° \ + Br^- + Ag° \ (5 \ atoms \ latent \ image)$$

During immersion in developer:

$$Ag^+ \ + developer + Ag° \ (5 \ atoms \ latent \ image) \ \varnothing \ Ag°$$
$$(10^8 \ atoms \ visible \ image) + oxidized \ developer$$

Developer Components

Developer is composed of developing or reducing agents, preservatives, accelerators or activators, restrainers, regulators, antifoggants or starters, hardeners, solvents, and sequestering agents, all of which act on the film.

Developing or Reducing Agents. Developing or reducing agents carry out the **oxidation/reduction reaction** that converts the latent image into a manifest image. There are two different reducing agents used in standard developer solutions: phenidone and hydroquinone.

PHENIDONE (ELON OR METOL IN MANUAL DEVELOPER). Phenidone is fast-acting and produces the optical densities up to about 1.2, making it responsible for the D_{min} and speed indicators used in sensitometric testing (described in Chapter 4).

HYDROQUINONE. Hydroquinone acts more slowly than phenidone, completing the development process so that the optical densities greater than 1.2 are visualized. Hydroquinone is responsible for the D_{max} and contrast indicators used in sensitometric testing. These indicators are the first variables to show an indication of developer failure, because hydroquinone is the processing chemical most sensitive to changes in temperature, concentration, and pH and to exposure to light and to heavy metals. Hydroquinone levels should be maintained in the range of 20 to 25 g/L.

The overall optical density is created by the synergistic action of the two reducing agents. *Synergism* means that the action of the two agents working together is greater than the sum of each agent working independently. **Synergism** is also known as *superadditivity* (Figure 3-1).

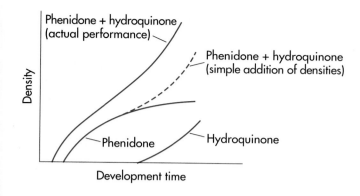

FIGURE 3-1
Graph demonstrating superadditivity effect of phenidone and hydroquinone.

Box 3-1 pH Scale

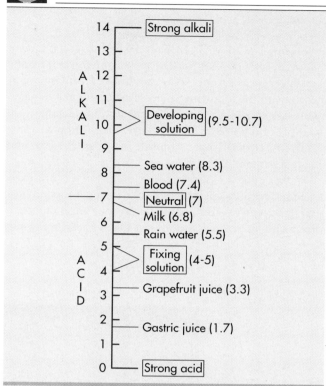

Preservative. The preservative protects the hydroquinone from both aerial oxidation (chemical reaction with air) and internal oxidation (chemical reaction with other developer ingredients). If the hydroquinone is oxidized, there is a decrease in the D_{max} and contrast indicators during a sensitometric test, along with a loss of the shoulder on the H and D curve. Oxidized developer causes the developer solution to turn from a clear, brown liquid into one that is dark and muddy. If strongly oxidized, the solution also will have the odor of ammonia, because this is a by-product of the oxidation chemical reaction. Most developer replenishment tanks have a floating lid inside of the tank, in addition to the main lid on the outside to minimize contact with the outside air. The chemicals sodium sulfite and cycon can be used as developer solution preservatives.

Accelerator or Activator. The accelerator, or activator, has two functions: to soften and swell the emulsion so that reducing agents can work on all of the emulsion and to provide an alkaline medium for the reducing agents. The developing agents must exist in an alkaline medium to have the free electrons available to reduce the silver to Ag°.

An indicator known as *pH* is used to measure the alkalinity of a solution. pH refers to the exponential (*p*) value of hydrogen or hydroxyl ions (*H*) available for a reaction. Those chemicals having a high hydrogen potential (H+) are called *acids,* and those having a high alkaline or hydroxide potential (OH−) are called bases. The pH scale ranges from 0 to 7 (acids) and 7 to 14 (bases) (Box 3-1). Pure water is neutral and has a pH of 7. Fixer is an acid solution; therefore care must be taken not to introduce it into developer solutions, because only 0.1% contamination deteriorates the developer activity enough to compromise image quality. Chemicals that can be used as accelerators include sodium carbonate, sodium hydroxide, potassium carbonate, and potassium hydroxide.

Restrainer, Regulator, Antifoggant, or Starter. The restrainer (regulator, antifoggant, or starter) holds back, or restrains, the action of the developing agents so that they reduce only the silver halide crystals that have been exposed to radiation. The chemical used in most brands of developer is potassium bromide in the form of K+Br−, which is chemically similar to Ag+Br−. If the reducing agents become too active, they attack the potassium bromide instead of the silver halide. Overdilution of water or underreplenishment can reduce the levels of restrainer, which increases the speed indicator during a sensitometric test.

Hardener. When a film enters the warm developer solution, the gelatin emulsion begins to soften and swell, which could cause the film to stick to the rollers of an automatic film processor. Therefore developer manufacturers add a weak hardener (a stronger one is present in fixer solutions) to control emulsion swelling and stickiness. If the amount of hardener is depleted because of underreplenishment, wet films, transport problems, and uncleared films can result. The chemical agent used as a hardener is glutaraldehyde.

Solvent. The above ingredients are mixed with a solvent to form developer solution. The most common and readily available solvent is water. This should be of drinking water quality, with the following characteristics: filtered to particles under 40 microns (μm), dissolved solids less than 250 ppm, pH of 6.5 to 8.5, hardness of 40 to 150 ppm, heavy metals less than 0.1 ppm, chloride less than 25 ppm, and sulfate less than 200 ppm.

Sequestering Agent. Much of the developer used in hospital darkrooms is shipped in concentrate form and then mixed with tap water at the clinical site. Because impurities can be found in tap water, many manufacturers add a sequestering agent called *EDTA* to prevent impurities from interfering with the developer chemicals. EDTA is an oily substance that causes calcium and other mineral contaminants to stick together and dissipate to the bottom of processing tanks.

Developer Activity

How well a developer functions is called the *developer activity* and is governed by the following five factors: solution temperature, immersion time, solution concentration, type of chemicals used, and solvent pH.

Solution Temperature (Figure 3-2). The greater the solution temperature, the more active the developing agents, especially hydroquinone, which increases the optical density of the film. If the temperature drops below 60° F (15.5° C),

85° F   90° F

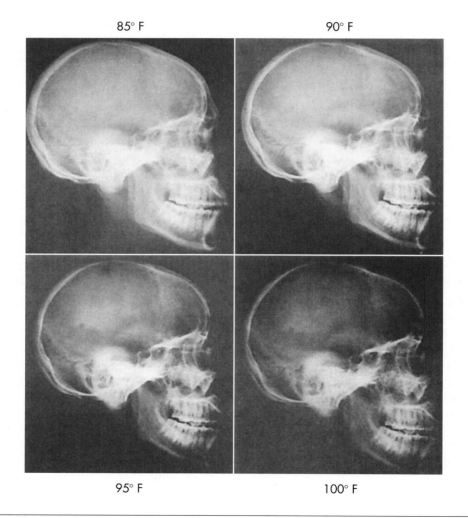

95° F   100° F

FIGURE 3-2
Radiographs showing effect of solution temperature on optical density and contrast.

the hydroquinone stops working, which causes the resulting images to decrease in optical density and contrast. At temperatures above 75° F (24° C), the developing agents become increasingly active, which increases the optical density of subsequent films.

Immersion Time (Figure 3-3). The greater the length of time in the solution, the greater the optical densities recorded on the processed image.

Solution Concentration. Solution concentration refers to the percentage of water versus other chemicals in the solution and can be measured by specific gravity (the density of a liquid compared with water). An instrument called a *hydrometer* measures specific gravity, which ranges from 1.07 to 1.1 in typical developer solutions. The specific gravity should not vary by ±0.004 from the manufacturer's specifications.

Type of Chemicals Used. Developer solutions that contain elon or metol behave differently than those that contain phenidone. The DuPont Cronex HSD system uses an acid developer solution to process the film and therefore behaves quite differently than conventional developer solutions.

Solution pH. The developer solution should maintain a pH of between 10 and 11.5 and should not vary by more than ±0.1 from the manufacturer's specifications. Excessive pH increases the optical density of a processed image, and too low of a pH value has the opposite effect.

Over time, the developer becomes exhausted and requires replenishment. Reasons for this replenishment include the following:

• Significant quantities of developer are consumed during the development process.

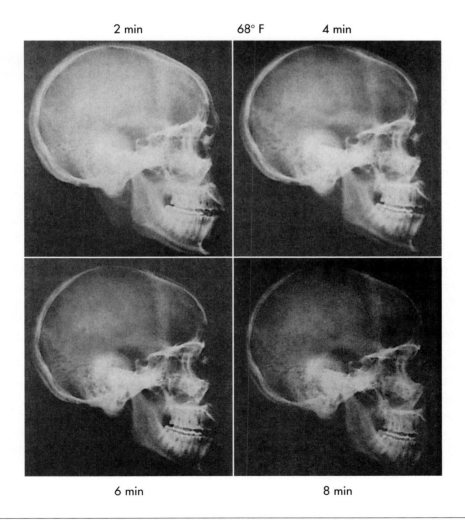

FIGURE 3-3
Radiographs showing effect of developer time on optical density and contrast.

- Bromide and hydrogen bromide acid are liberated into the developer during development, which can lower the pH and cause a decrease in activity. These bromide levels should be maintained in a range of 4 to 8 g/L.
- Aerial and internal oxidation begins as soon as the solution is mixed, which consumes developing agents.
- A certain volume of developer solution is removed by the film's emulsion each time a film is fed into the processor. The squeegee action of the crossover rack helps minimize this effect.

Developer Mixing Procedure

Developer solution is generally available in two options, as a premix or a concentrate.

Premix or Ready-Mix. As the name implies, this solution has all of the ingredients combined with the solvent, so that no mixing is required at the clinical site. They are usually delivered in 5- or 10-gal containers and should be directly into the replenishment tanks. The disadvantages of this method include a relatively short shelf life (from 2 weeks to 3 months) and higher cost (about 40% more than concentrate). Therefore large quantities should not be stockpiled, and frequent deliveries must be made.

Concentrate. The main ingredients are shipped to the clinical site in a concentrate form and must be mixed with water at the clinical site. This is less convenient but greatly reduces the cost of the solutions. The concentrate kit usually comes in three parts. Part 1 contains the hydroquinone, preservative, and accelerator and has a pH between 11 and 12. Part 2 contains the phenidone and restrainer and has a pH of 3. Part 3 contains the hardener and has a pH of 3.

The proper amount of water should be present in the tank, and then each solution added in the proper order. Large quantities of chemicals should be mixed electrically with a commercially available system. These systems use a propeller type of variable-speed mixer. The speed must be regulated, because excessive speed introduces unwanted air into the chemicals, which can oxidize the developer. These systems are not useful in facilities that use only a small volume of developer each week. Fresh chemistry should last 2 weeks and should then be discarded. Concentrate will last 1 year when stored at room temperature and away from direct sunlight. Avoid excessive **agitation** in mixing and storage.

Fixer

Fixer solutions remove all of the unexposed and undeveloped silver halide crystals from the film, halting the development process and hardening the emulsion for permanent storage.

Fixer Ingredients

Fixers are composed of the following five components: fixing agent, preservative, hardener or tanning agent, acidifier, and solvent.

Fixing Agent, Clearing Agent, or Hypo. The fixing agent (clearing agent or hypo) removes the unexposed and undeveloped silver halide crystals from the film. The chemical ammonium thiosulfate is used in most modern fixing solutions (sodium thiosulfate has been used in manual solutions). It picks up unexposed silver atoms out of the silver halide crystal to form ammonium thio-silver-sulfate. The action of this agent is controlled by dilution, replenishment, and the use of a recirculating electrolytic silver recovery unit (discussed in Chapter 11).

The effectiveness of the fixing agent can be evaluated by a clearing time test.

Procedure

1. Take a strip of undeveloped green film and dip it into the fixer solution. Use a stopwatch to measure the clearing time.
2. Film should clear in 10 seconds at room temperature and in less than 7 seconds at 90° F (32° C).

Preservative. The chemical sodium sulfite dissolves the silver out of the ammonium thio-silver-sulfate, returning or recycling it back to ammonium thiosulfate. In this way, sulfite is available to clear more of the undeveloped silver from the film. It can be depleted by excess developer carry-in, underreplenishment, and the use of recirculating electrolytic silver recovery units, which deplete sodium sulfite. The concentration of this chemical should be maintained in the range of 15 to 50 g/L.

Hardener or Tanning Agent. For the film to be stored permanently, the emulsion must be hardened to keep the image from fading or being scratched during handling. This is called *tanning*. Potassium alum, chrome alum, and aluminum chloride are the more common chemicals used as fixer hardeners.

Acidifier or Activator. The acidifier, or activator, has two functions: neutralizing any developer remaining in the emulsion and providing an acid medium for the fixing agent.

Just as the developing agents need an alkaline medium in which to function, the fixing agent can dissolve undeveloped silver only in an acid solution. Fixer pH should be maintained at a level between 4 and 4.5 and not vary more than ±0.1 from the manufacturer's specifications. Both acetic acid and sulfuric acid can be used as the acidifier.

Solvent. Water is used as the solvent in which to suspend the other chemicals. The same standards listed for the developer solvent water also apply for the fixer. The concentration of fixer can be measured by specific gravity and can range from 1.077 to 1.11. It should not vary by more than ±0.004 from the manufacturer's specifications.

Fixer Mixing Procedure

The fixer solution can be purchased in either ready-mix or concentrate form. The ready-mix can cost as much as 20% more but has the same convenience as ready-mix developer. The concentrate must be mixed with water and usually comes in two parts. Part 1 contains the ammonium thiosulfate, preservative, and acidifier. Part 2 contains the hardener in a strong acid solution.

As with developer, start with water in the tank and mix large quantities with a commercial mixing unit. It is recommended that the fixer be mixed before the developer, because inadvertent splashing of fixer could contaminate the developer.

Washing

Washing is important for the **archival quality** of the film, because it removes the fixer from the film emulsion before drying. If hyporetention is allowed to take place, the thiosulfate can react with the silver in the emulsion, producing Ag_2S, or silver sulfide, which can stain the image from pale yellow to dark brown. By law, films must be kept 5 years; groups such as the military require 40 years after death, separation, or retirement. Commercial test kits are available to measure the amount of hyporetention (Figure 3-4). These normally involve a test strip that is placed in contact with a processed film after a drop of solution is applied to its surface. The color of the strip indicates the amount of hyporetention. The American National Standards Institute (ANSI) suggests that the amount of hyporetention not exceed 2 µg/cm². These ANSI tests should be performed at least every 6 months and preferably every 3 months.

The water used in washing should have the following characteristics: hardness of 40 to 150 ppm, pH of 6.5 to 8.5, dissolved solids less than 250 ppm, and a specific gravity of 1. Washing time should be at least 50% to 100% of the developer time, and the temperature should be 5° F (3° C) below the developer temperature to help trigger the heater

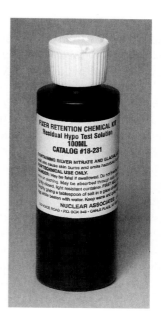

FIGURE 3-4

Hyporetention kit for evaluating residual fixer in processed films. (Courtesy Nuclear Associates, Carle Place, N.Y.)

thermostat in the automatic processor. The water flow rate should be at a rate of 1 to 3 gal/min for proper agitation and prevention of algae and bioslime. If this is a problem, a few milliliters of laundry bleach (5% sodium hypochlorite) can be added to the wash tank at shutdown.

Chemical Safety

Because OSHA considers the darkroom a scientific laboratory, it has several safety requirements in place, including the following:

- Material Safety Data Sheets (MSDS) must be displayed for all chemicals used by employees. These should contain the potentially toxic chemical agents to which a worker can be exposed. They should also contain basic warnings concerning the product and the name and address of the manufacturer. A Material Safety Data Sheet should be included with each shipment of chemistry. If not, one may be obtained by contacting the manufacturer.
- Safety equipment, such as eye protection (preferably full-face or nonvented goggles), must be available to personnel who handle, mix, transport, or use processing chemicals. An eyewash station should be prominently located in the area where the chemicals are in use. Should any amount of processing solution come in contact with the eye, wash copiously and contact a physician immedi-

ately. Shower facilities should be available, as should rubber gloves and aprons. Training programs for personnel must be established. Only trained personnel should perform mixing, cleaning, or maintenance work.

The Environmental Protection Agency (EPA) also has regulations concerning processing chemicals. The EPA-SARA Title III requires all users of developer solution to report the quantity used. The Resource Conservation and Recovery Act of 1987 limits liquid waste to a toxic level of no more than 5 mg/L, or 5 ppm. This can limit the amount of processing chemicals and wash water tank water than can be placed into public sewers and private septic systems before a special permit is required. Material with a pH of between 5.5 and 10 can safely be disposed of down the drain, which disqualifies all three parts of the concentrated developer and both parts of concentrated fixer. Shipment of scrap film, silver-laden fixer, and silver recovery cartridges from the clinical site to a refiner or treatment plant also requires a special permit from the EPA and/or the Department of Transportation.

The developer solution is considered the most dangerous processing chemical, because of its high alkalinity. This makes it especially dangerous to the eyes (hence the Occupational Safely and Health Administration [OSHA] requirement of eye protection) and skin. A main component of film emulsion is gelatin (a form of collagen), which is an organic form of protein that is broken down by chemicals with a high pH. Because human soft tissue contains collagen, the skin and eyes are at risk if contact is made with developer. Hydroquinone can be absorbed through the skin and is corrosive to the eyes and nose. Glutaraldehyde is a tanning agent and therefore a skin irritant. Wearing eye protection, rubber gloves, and an apron should always be standard operating procedure when pouring or mixing developer. Fixer is a strong acid that can burn the eyes and irritate the skin. As with developer, proper safety apparel should be worn when pouring and mixing fixer. Wash immediately any skin that has been in contact with processing solutions.

AUTOMATIC PROCESSOR MAIN SYSTEMS

All automatic film processors have six main systems: transport, temperature, circulation, replenishment, drying, and electrical.

Transport System

The transport system is responsible for transporting the film through the various steps in processing and for controlling the development and total processing times. It also plays a minor role in solution agitation and concentration. This is the largest and most complex system in an automatic processor. Because it has many moving parts, it is also the system most likely to break down. The transport system is made up of three smaller subsystems.

Roller Subsystem

The rollers are responsible for "grabbing" the film and transporting it through the various stages of processing. They also provide a squeegee action that helps prevent too much solution carryover. There are three main types of rollers:

- *Entrance rollers* are serrated rollers made of rubberized plastic to grip the film as it enters the processor (Figure 3-5).
- *Transport,* or *planetary, rollers* are responsible for the transportation of film and most often have a diameter of 1 inch. They are usually mounted in pairs, either staggered or directly opposite each other (Figure 3-6).
- *Master,* or *solar, rollers* are larger rollers with a 3-inch diameter. These rollers are found at the bottom of each solution tank, where the film must bend and turn back upward.

FIGURE 3-5
Entrance rollers for automatic film processor.

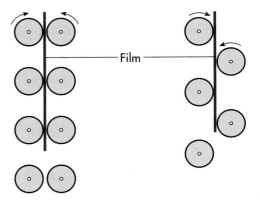

FIGURE 3-6
Transport rollers for automatic film processor.

Rollers can be made of Plexiglas, stainless steel, polyester plastic, rubberized plastic, and phenolic resin. The phenolic rollers are orange-brown and wooden in appearance. Care must be taken in cleaning phenolic rollers (no abrasive pads), because this is a relatively soft material that could be scratched, allowing liquid to be absorbed into the roller and causing subsequent warping. For this reason, rollers made of phenolic resin are normally found in the dryer section.

Transport Rack Subsystem

The transport rack subsystem is the rack or frame containing the rollers, guide shoes, and associated hardware. There are four types of transport racks.

- *Entrance rack.* The entrance rack contains the entrance rollers, guide shoe(s), and a microswitch to activate the replenishment system (in volume replenishment systems) (see Figure 3-5).
- *Vertical* or *deep racks.* Vertical or deep racks contain the transport rollers that transport the film into or up out of the tank (Figure 3-7). Side plates and tie bars hold the rollers in place. The side plates and tie bars can expand and contract over time and cause misalignment.
- *Turnaround rack.* The turnaround rack is found at the bottom of the tank and contains a master roller, transport rollers, and two guide shoes (Figure 3-8).
- *Crossover rack.* Crossover racks move from developer to fixer, fixer to wash tank, and wash tank to dryer transition. Normally, these contain a master roller, transport rollers, and two guide shoes but can vary from manufacturer to manufacturer. These racks are out of solution and therefore must be cleaned before use, because chemical residue can crystallize on the rollers during downtime. If the processor is on standby longer than 2 hours, crossover racks should be cleaned before use.

Drive Subsystem

The drive subsystem is the portion of the transport system that supplies the mechanical energy to move the film (Figure 3-9). This subsystem includes the following.

- *Drive motor.* The drive motor is a 1/20- to 1/8-HP electric motor that runs at 1725 to 1750 rpm.
- *Main drive chain.* The main drive chain is a no. 25 chain that attaches the drive motor to the gear system (similar to a bicycle chain). It is located on the side of the deep racks.
- *Gear reduction mechanism.* The gear reduction mechanism is a series of gears of different sizes that reduce the speed to between 10 and 20 rpm.
- *Gears.* Gears transfer the mechanical energy from the motor to the rollers. The two types of gears are drive gears,

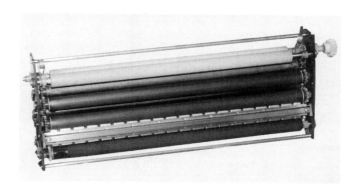

FIGURE 3-7
Vertical rack assembly.

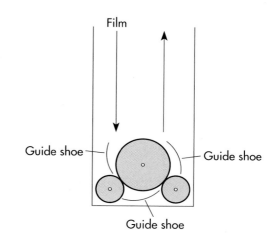

FIGURE 3-8
Turnaround rack assembly.

FIGURE 3-9
Drive system.

which are normally attached to the ends of the rollers, and worm gears, which are located on the main drive shaft and used to power the drive gears (Figure 3-10). The gears can be made of plastic or metal.

- *Main drive shaft.* The main drive shaft connects the gear reduction mechanism to the drive gears using a system of worm gears.

Gears out of solution can be coated lightly with grease. Sprockets and chains out of solution require a light coating of oil but care must be taken to avoid getting petroleum-based products in chemical solutions or on rollers. In the dryer section, lubricants must be avoided. Therefore the gears must be kept clean to minimize friction.

The average transport system speed for a 90-second processor is about 60 inches of film per minute.

Temperature Control System

The temperature control system is also called the *tempering system* and regulates the temperature of each solution. The two basic types of this system currently in use are water-controlled systems and thermostatically controlled systems.

Water-Controlled System

This is often called a *warm-water processor* and uses the wash water temperature to regulate the solution tempera-

FIGURE 3-10
Worm and drive gears.

ture by circulating the water around the outside of the stainless steel processing tanks. This method requires a large supply of hot water and a mixing valve to regulate water temperature (Figure 3-11).

Thermostatically Controlled System

Processors with this type of system are often called *cold-water processors* because they require only cold wash water to enter the unit. Heating coils are located at the bottom of each tank (Figure 3-12), and a thermostat regulates the temperature. This system is much more practical than the others, because it does not require the large hot water heater and associated utility cost to maintain the supply necessary for the water-controlled system. For this reason, most newer processors are of this type.

Regardless of the type of temperature control system used, the system must maintain the developer temperature to within ±0.5° F (0.3° C) of the manufacturer's specifications.

Circulation System

The circulation system also can be referred to as the *re-circulation and filtration system*. It uses a series of pumps to constantly circulate the solution in each tank and serves the following functions:

- *Ensures complete chemistry mixing.* During processor downtime, chemicals inside of the tanks can begin to separate, with the water rising to the top and the chemicals dissipating to the bottom (a condition known as *stratification*). Swirling of the solutions ensures uniform concentration.
- *Provides uniform temperature.* Because the heating coils are on the bottom of the tank, uneven regions of temperature could develop unless the solutions are continuously in motion.
- *Provides the equivalent of agitation performed in manual processing.*

In manual film processing the halide ions that have been separated from the silver leave the emulsion in the form of bromine gas. This gas can cause a layer of bubbles to form on the outside surface of the film. This can block developing agents from reaching the inner portion of the emulsion, which can cause areas of uneven development called *streaking*. Agitation in manual processing involves "jiggling" the film every 30 seconds to shake this layer of bubbles on the film. By having the developer swirling over the surface of the film in an automatic processor, the layer of bubbles is removed in much the same way as agitation in manual processing.

A 25-µm filter is often located in the developer loop of this system to remove gelatin and other impurities that become dissolved in the developer during processing (Figure 3-13). This filter must be replaced periodically as part of a processor maintenance program. The circulation rate of this system is roughly 3 to 5 gal/min.

Replenishment System

The replenishement system is also called the *regeneration system* and is responsible for replenishing processor solutions. It consists of a series of pumps, plastic tubing, and

plastic storage tanks. The two different types of replenishment systems available in film processors are volume replenishment and flood replenishment.

Volume Replenishment

With the **volume replenishment** system, a volume of chemicals is replaced for each film that is fed into the processor. This is the most common type of replenishment system. A

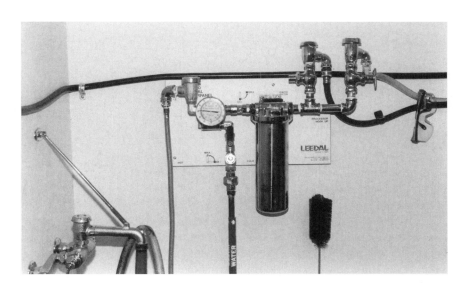

FIGURE 3-11
Mixing valve for warm water automatic processors.

FIGURE 3-12
Heater coil located in bottom of water tank in thermostatically controlled temperature system.

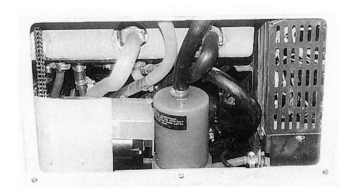

FIGURE 3-13
Developer circulation system filter.

microswitch placed at either end of the entrance rack senses the film and activates this system so that the size of the film controls the amount of replenishment that takes place.

The average replenishment rates for this system are as follows:

- *Developer:* 4 to 5 mL/in of film, or roughly 60 to 70 mL per sheet of 14- × 17-inch film (35 × 43 cm).
- *Fixer:* 6 to 8 mL/in, or roughly 100 to 110 mL per sheet of 14- × 17-inch film.

The volume replenishment system is used for relatively busy processors that process at least 25 to 50 sheets of 14- × 17-inch film per 8-hour work day.

Flood Replenishment

Flood replenishment is also called *timed* or *stand-by replenishment* and is used for processors that are not in constant use or that process less than 25 to 50 sheets of 14- × 17-inch film per day. Replenishment is controlled by a timer, which periodically replenishes the solutions, regardless of the number of films processed. The replenishment pump should operate for approximately 20 seconds out of every 5 minutes, delivering about 65 mL of each chemical. This maintains a total replenishment rate of 780 mL/hr. All developer in the processing tank should be replaced every 16 working hours.

Most processors have a replenishment rate indicator on them, so monitoring is easy. In the case of other types of processors, special test paper is available for testing certain concentrations in the developer and fixer.

For developer, the paper estimates the levels of bromide ions that are dissolved in the solution. Stable developer should have a bromide level of about 6 g/L. Levels above 8 g/L indicate underreplenishment, whereas levels below 4 g/L indicate overreplenishment.

Fixer replenishment can be estimated using silver estimating paper, which estimates the dissolved silver content in the solution. Normal fixer contains about 4 to 6 g/L (0.4 to 0.6 troy oz/gal). Levels above 8 g/L indicate underreplenishment and associated film quality problems, whereas levels below 4 g/L indicate overreplenishment, which does not adversely affect film quality but wastes fixer (and therefore money).

Dryer System

The dryer system consists of two or three heating units of between 1500 and 2500 watts that are used to dry the film. This can draw at least 10A of electric current, causing this system to consume 60% to 80% of the electrical power going into the processor. A hot-air blower moves the air at a rate of 200 ft³/min over the film. A series of air fins and air

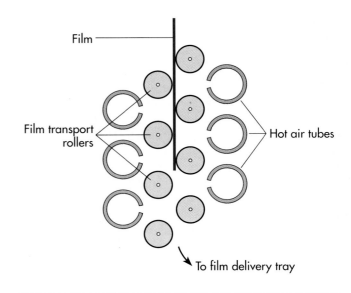

FIGURE 3-14
Dryer air tubes.

tubes are used to direct the air onto the film (Figure 3-14). These fins and tubes and the exhaust tube must be kept clean for maximum efficiency.

Electrical System

The electrical system consists of a solid-state circuit board or microprocessor that distributes electrical power to the other systems. In some newer processors, the microprocessor can be accessed to disclose quality control information such as solution temperature, replenishment rate, and so on. It normally handles 4 to 5 kW/hr and between 15 and 25 A of current. This system requires periodic replacement because of the heat, humidity, and corrosive environment inside of the processor.

TYPES OF AUTOMATIC PROCESSORS

There are several types of automatic processors, and they are usually named according to the time it takes to fully process the film, often called the *dry-to-drop time.*

- *7-minute:* the original Kodak automatic processor from the 1950s; processes about 100 films/hr.
- *3-minute:* also called a *double-capacity processor* because it processes 200 films/hr.
- *90-second:* also called a *fast-access processor,* because the film is available in 90 seconds and the processor has a capacity of 300 films/hr. This was developed by Kodak

in the mid-1960s and is still the most commonly used film processor.

- *60-second:* a newer type of processor that can process up to 350 films/hr.
- *45-second:* the newest type of processor; it requires special film and chemistry to function properly

Many newer processors come with a variable speed option, so that processing time can be varied according to the type of film used. An example of this is the "extended processing" used in mammography, which increases normal processing time to increase the film contrast. This is covered more completely in Chapter 12.

Some processors also have a stand-by option that is useful for low-volume facilities. The drive system and dryer blower are shut off and the water flow rate is reduced, but the chemical and dryer temperature are maintained. This occurs when 2 minutes pass without a film entering the unit.

Processor Size

Automatic film processors come in three basic sizes according to the number of films processed in a given period.

Floor-Size Processor

The floor-size processor is the largest processor and, as its name implies, sits on the floor of the darkroom or lightroom. It has heavy-duty rollers, gears, and drive motor so that it can handle a high volume of operation. This size of processor is normally found in the main radiology department of hospitals.

Intermediate-Size Processor

The intermediate-size processor is a smaller version of the floor-size processor and usually sits on four support legs. It is about the size of a single laundry sink. This processor is lower in cost than the floor-size model and is often found in physician offices and clinics and in specialized areas of hospitals, such as surgery.

Tabletop-Size Processor

The tabletop-size processor is the smallest and least expensive processor. It is designed for low-volume operation, such as in a mobile facility, and is small enough to fit on the countertop of a darkroom.

Processor Location

A processor can be installed in the darkroom in one of four methods: totally inside, bulk inside, bulk outside, or daylight processing.

Totally Inside

With totally inside installation, the processor is completely inside of the darkroom, which generates noise, heat, and humidity. For this reason, this is the least desirable method of installation. An advantage of this method, however, is easy retrieval of film that has jammed in the processor, because it can be removed in safelighting.

Bulk Inside

With bulk inside installation, most of the processor is inside the darkroom and only the drop tray is on the outside. This method minimizes the heat and noise in the darkroom but still allows easy retrieval of jammed film.

Bulk Outside

Bulk outside installation places the feed tray inside the darkroom but all other components outside. This method eliminates the heat, noise, and humidity inside the darkroom but makes retrieval of films more difficult, because they must be removed in white light.

The minimum space on all sides of the processor must be 24 inches, to allow for servicing.

Daylight Processing Systems and Processors

Daylight processing systems and processors are designed to eliminate the need for a darkroom. They are discussed in detail in Chapter 4.

SUMMARY

A basic understanding of film processing and automatic processing systems is essential for the performance of the quality control activities discussed in Chapter 4.

Review Questions

1. When mixing developer solution from concentrate, which part should be placed into the tank first?
   a. part A
   b. part B
   c. part C
   d. water

2. What would cause an ammonia-like odor in a darkroom?
   a. contamination of the fixer by the developer
   b. oxidation of the developer
   c. improper mixing of the developer
   d. overreplenishment of the developer

3. In an automatic processor, which of the following is not considered a part of the three principle subsystems of the film transport system?
   a. microswitch
   b. rollers
   c. transport racks
   d. drive motor

4. According to ANSI standards, the maximum amount of hyporetention allowed is _____ $\mu m/cm^2$.
   a. 2
   b. 5
   c. 8
   d. 10

5. If the developer temperature is set at 96° F, then the wash water temperature should be set at _____ ° F.
   a. 86
   b. 91
   c. 96
   d. 101

6. Which processing chemical is responsible for creating the optical densities above 1 on a diagnostic image?
   a. phenidone
   b. hydroquinone
   c. elon
   d. metol

7. Which system of the automatic processor consumes the greatest amount of electrical power?
   a. transport
   b. replenishment
   c. circulation
   d. dryer

8. Which of the following is located at the bottom of each processing tank?
   a. entrance rack
   b. vertical rack
   c. turnaround rack
   d. crossover rack

9. Which of the following materials are used in the construction of an entrance roller?
   a. Plexiglas
   b. stainless steel
   c. polyester
   d. rubberized plastic

10. Hydrogen ions (H^+) that constitute $1/10,000$ of a liquid would have a pH of:
    a. 2
    b. 4
    c. 6
    d. 8

 **Student Experiment 3.1**   Hyporetention Test

PURPOSE

To determine if the film is adequately washed following immersion into fixer solutions.

EQUIPMENT NEEDED:

1. Automatic processor
2. Fixer retention chemical kit
3. 8- × 10-inch sheet of unexposed film

PROCEDURE

1. Remove a sheet of 8- × 10-inch film from film bin and process.
2. Take the processed sheet of film into the darkroom. Place one drop of fixer retention chemical solution in the center of the film. If single emulsion film is tested, be sure to place the drop on the emulsion side.
3. Under safelight conditions, allow the solution to stand for 2 minutes. Then blot off the excess and compare the resulting stain with the density patches on the hypoestimator comparison strip as soon as possible.

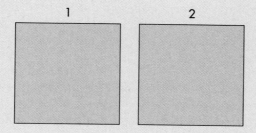

ANALYSIS

1. Was the amount of hyporetention within acceptable limits (less than 0.05 g/m²)?
2. What effect would excessive hyporetention have on image quality?
3. What effect would excessive hyporetention have on archival quality?

 **Student Experiment 3.2**   Automatic Processor Inspection

PURPOSE

To inspect an automatic processor for mechanical problems and to prepare it for proper operation.

EQUIPMENT NEEDED

1. Automatic processor
2. Thermometer
3. Paper towels

PROCEDURES

1. Turn the processor on and remove the top. Check the gears from the racks that engage the worm gear to ensure that they are functioning properly. Record the results in the appropriate area on the data page.

continued

Student Experiment 3.2   Automatic Processor Inspection—cont'd

2. Turn the processor off. Inspect the feed tray for cleanliness and record the results.
3. Remove the entrance rack and crossover racks from each section and inspect the status of the rollers, guide shoes, chains, and gears of each rack. Record the results on the data page.
4. Slowly remove the developer deep rack (be careful to avoid chemical cross-contamination) and place over a sink. Inspect the status of the rollers, chains, guide shoes, and gears of the rack and record the results.
5. Repeat the above step for the fixer deep rack (be especially careful not to contaminate the other solutions). Replace the fixer rack and repeat this step for the wash deep rack. Record the results on the data page.
6. Check the status of the dryer rollers and record the results.
7. Turn on the circulation system and look inside the developer and fixer tanks to ensure that the solutions are circulating. Record the results on the data page.
8. Check the tubing that connects the replenishment tanks to the processor for kinks, cracks, or debris.
9. Inspect the condition of the filter for the circulation system and record the results on the data page.
10. Return all racks, splash guards, and panels to their respective places and leave the top cover off of the processor.
11. Turn on the processor and feed 14- $\times$ 17-inch film into the feed tray. While the film is passing through the entrance rack, check the following: whether the detector switch started the replenishment, the rate of replenishment (this may be done by checking the gauges on the processor), and whether the bell sounded after the film entered the processor. Record the results in the appropriate area on the data page.
12. With the processor on and warmed up, check the dryer section to ensure that the blower is functioning properly. Place a thermometer in the dryer section to assess the status of the heater and thermostat. Record the results on the data page.

ANALYSIS

1. Summarize findings from the data sheet, commenting on areas that failed and possible consequences of those failures. Enclose the data sheet with the analysis.
2. What are the functions of the replenishment and recirculation systems? How are they similar? Different?
3. How often should parts of an automatic processor be inspected?
4. List three items on a transport/rack assembly that should be inspected.
5. Explain how to identify the diameter of a scratched roller from the processed radiograph.
6. How can it be determined whether scratches on a radiograph are caused by the guide shoes or by a roller?
7. Why should the plastic tubing of the replenishment system be inspected for kinks, cracks, or debris?

Automatic Film Processor Checklist

Transport System

	Rollers	Guide Shoes	Gears	Chains
Entrance rack				
Developer rack				
D-F crossover				
Fixer rack				
F-W crossover				
Wash rack				
Squeegee rack				
Dryer rollers				
Main drive motor				
Worm gear				
Feed tray cleanliness				

Circulation System

Pump	
Tubing	
Filter	
Circulation rate	

Replenishment System

Microswitch function	
Audible signal	
Replenishment rate	

continued

Automatic Film Processor Checklist–cont'd

Dryer System

Drive belt	
Heater	
Thermostat	
Air tubes	

Place a P in the column if the component passes the visual inspection and an F if it fails. Mark NA for items that are nonapplicable.

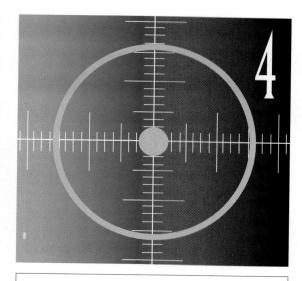

4 Processor Quality Control

Objectives

At the completion of this chapter the reader will be able to do the following:

- Understand the importance of a processor quality control program
- List the main components of a processor quality control program
- Describe the factors that affect chemical activity
- Indicate the proper processor cleaning procedures
- Describe the basic types of processor maintenance and appropriate maintenance procedures
- Perform sensitometric tests to monitor processor function and chemical activity performance
- Describe the importance of quality control in daylight systems

Key Terms

base + fog
bromide drag
chemical activity
contrast indicator
daylight system
densitometer
flow meter
hydrometer
incident light
locational effect
sensitometer
sensitometry
speed indicator
time of day variability
transmitted light

The most important part of a diagnostic imaging department quality management program is the quality control of the film processor. This is because of the large degree of variability that can occur with processing systems. Daily monitoring of processor operation and function is required to keep these variables from degrading the image quality. There are four components to a processor quality control program: chemical activity, cleaning procedures, maintenance, and monitoring.

CHEMICAL ACTIVITY

As mentioned in Chapter 3, **chemical activity** refers to how well the processing chemicals are functioning. Many variables affect chemical activity, including the solution temperature, processing time, replenishment rate, solution pH, specific gravity, and proper mixing.

Solution Temperature

Variations in developer temperature can significantly affect image contrast, optical density, and the visibility of recorded detail. Therefore developer temperature should not vary by more than ±0.5° F (0.3° C) from the manufacturer's recommendations. It should be monitored at the beginning of the work day and then periodically throughout the day. Many film processors have either an analog thermometer or an LED indicator of solution temperature built into the front panel. If this is not available, a digital thermometer with a remote probe (Figure 4-1) is the best instrument to monitor solution temperature, because it is the most accurate and will work quickly. A glass, alcohol-filled thermometer is an adequate alternative. A mercury thermometer should never be used, because mercury is a toxic substance and poses a difficult and potentially hazardous clean-up problem in the event of breakage. The accuracy of any built-in thermometer should be checked monthly with a digital thermometer and should be within ±0.5° F (0.3° C).

Fixer activity is not as temperature-sensitive as developer activity but the temperature should be maintained within ±5° F (3° C) of the developer temperature, to avoid reticulation marks (see Chapter 10) and for proper clearing of the film. Wash water temperature should be the same as that of the fixer, in order for washing to be complete.

To check the solution temperatures, place the probe in each tank, starting with the developer. Be sure the probe is clean, to avoid contamination. Next, check the wash water and then the fixer. Afterward, rinse the probe with water so that it is ready for the next inspection.

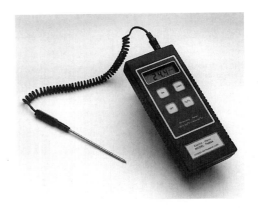

FIGURE 4-1
Digital thermometer for monitoring solution temperatures. (Courtesy Gammex/RMI, Middleton, Wis.)

Processing Time

Variations in developer time can have the same effect on image quality as solution temperature. Therefore developer time should be maintained to within ±2% to 3% of the manufacturer's specifications. As mentioned in Chapter 3, the transport system is responsible for maintaining processing time. Most of this system is made up of moving parts (and experiences the most wear-and-tear of any system), so it is subject to the most variability and breakdown. Processing time should be checked daily at the beginning of each work day (or more often if a malfunction is suspected). This can be checked using a stopwatch or digital timer. For the developer time, feed a film into the processor with the top open. When the leading edge of the film enters the solution, start the timer, and when the leading edge first emerges from the solution, stop it. For a 90-second processor, the time should be between 18 and 22 seconds, with a margin of error of roughly 0.5 seconds. To evaluate the total processing time, use the stopwatch to measure the time when the leading edge of the film enters the processor to when it begins to appear in the drop section and compare it with the manufacturer's specification.

Replenishment Rate

As film is processed during the course of the workday, the processing solutions are being depleted. If they are not adequately replenished, a decrease in image contrast and optical density will occur. Excessive replenishment will have the opposite effect. Most film processors have replenishment rate **flow meters** that indicate the replenishment rate for each solution. The values indicated should be within

±5% of the manufacturer's specification for the type of replenishment system in use (volume versus flood replenishment). These values for most processors are described in Chapter 3. The amount of replenishment should also be within 5% of these values. To verify replenishment rate and flow meter accuracy, a stop watch and a graduated cylinder can be used. With the top of the processor open, feed an 8- × 10-inch (20 × 25 cm) film lengthwise. Place the graduated cylinder under the opening of the replenisher line, so that the fresh solution pumps directly into the cylinder. When the film has passed through the entrance rack, the replenisher pump shuts off, stopping the flow of solution. When this happens, divide the volume of solution in milliliters (mL) by 10 to get the mL/in value (or divide by 25 to obtain mL/cm) and compare with manufacturer's values.

Solution pH

Most developer solutions must function in a pH range between 10 and 11.5 to convert the latent image into a visible image. A developer pH that is too low (caused by underreplenishment or contamination) decreases image contrast and optical density, whereas excessive pH has the opposite effect. Fixer solutions should maintain a pH between 4 and 4.5 for proper clearing. Although not as critical as the other factors affecting chemical activity, pH should be checked daily to avoid potential problems. A digital pH meter is recommended for evaluating pH, because of its accuracy. If one is not available, litmus paper or similar commercially available test strips are an inexpensive alternative. These are dipped into the solution and changes color to indicate the pH value. Care should be taken (wear rubber gloves) not to get processing chemicals on skin with this method.

Specific Gravity and Proper Mixing

Processing chemicals must be mixed to manufacturer's specifications of concentration to function within operating parameters. The easiest method of evaluation of solution concentration is the measurement of specific gravity.

$$\text{Specific gravity} = \frac{\text{Density of } x \text{ liquid}}{\text{Density of water in equal amount}}$$

A **hydrometer** is the instrument used to measure specific gravity. It resembles a large glass thermometer (Figure 4-2). When placed into a liquid, it sinks to a certain depth in the solution, and the level of the liquid indicates the specific gravity on the stem of the hydrometer. The developer should be measured first, the hydrometer rinsed with water, and then the fixer measured. Developer specific gravity should be in the range of 1.07 and 1.1 and should not vary more than ±0.004 from the manufacturer's specifications.

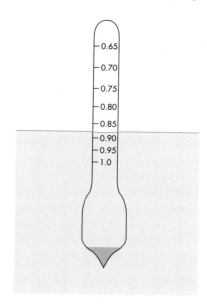

FIGURE 4-2
Floating hydrometer for measurement of specific gravity (indicating value of 0.87 g/cm^3).

Fixer solutions should be in the range of 1.077 to 1.11 and should not vary by more than ±0.004 from the manufacturer's specification.

PROCESSOR CLEANING PROCEDURES

Processors that are dirty cannot function according to established parameters and are the most common cause of processor breakdown. Therefore proper cleaning procedures should be performed daily, monthly, quarterly, and annually.

Daily

These procedures should be performed daily at start-up.

Procedure

1. With the top open, remove the splash guards and crossover racks and rinse with water. Be sure the rollers and guide shoes are free of dirt, debris, gelatin, or crystallized processing chemicals. A soft sponge or plastic cleaning pad may be used for cleaning, but steel wool pads or other metallic scrubbers should be avoided. The rollers should be turned by hand so that all surfaces can be reached.

2. Remove the deep transport racks from each solution and rinse with water. Care must be taken not to drip one solution into the next (especially fixer into developer) when lifting the racks out of the solution tanks. Stubborn dirt or residue can be removed with a soft sponge or plastic scrubber. Inspect the rollers and gears for any obvious defects. Carefully replace the racks back into the solutions to avoid contamination.

3. Activate the transport system and observe the rollers and gears for asymmetry, rotation, hesitation during operation. Replace the crossover racks and again observe the rollers and gears during operation. Replace any defective parts (especially gears and roller tension springs) and be sure that all mounting screws are tightened.

4. Observe the level of processing solutions to be sure that they are within 1 mm of specified level. Activate the replenisher pump or pour fresh solution from the storage tank if low.

5. At shut down, remove the crossover racks and store adjacent to the processor (if practical) to minimize the formation of chemical residue. The top of the processor should be raised so that a 2- to 4-inch gap exists to allow chemical fumes to escape.

The above procedure normally requires 15 to 20 minutes daily but can add several years to the life expectancy of the processor in addition to eliminating most processor artifacts.

Monthly

1. Drain all processing tanks and wash with water. A soft sponge or plastic scrubber can be used to remove stubborn dirt or residue.

2. Rinse all tanks with water and refill with the proper amount of chemical solution. The developer solution must be "seasoned" before any films can be processed, because typical replenisher solution will be too concentrated. This involves the addition of a starter solution, which is stabilized potassium bromide. This raises the bromide level to between 4 and 8 g/L, which is the normal level of a developer solution as it is processing films. Fresh developer replenisher that is used to refill the tank has levels far below this, which can increase the fog level of the film. The amount of starter solution required is about 100 mL/gal of solution.

Quarterly

1. Drain, wash, and rinse all replenishment tanks with water. Be especially careful to remove the oxidized developer from the sides of the developer replenisher tank.

2. Refill tanks with fresh solution and check the specific gravity with a hydrometer.

Yearly

Replenisher and circulation system pumps and tubing can experience a build-up of dirt and chemical residue, which can reduce the efficiency of these systems. Therefore some manufacturers suggest the use of a systems cleaner to reduce these deposits. The developer systems cleaner has an acid pH level to counteract the alkaline developer; whereas the fixer systems cleaner has an alkaline pH to counteract the acid fixer. The transport racks should be removed before using a systems cleaner, because phenolic and soft rubber rollers will absorb the cleaner and slowly contaminate future processing solutions. Most systems cleaners are either chlorine-based (which can break down hydroquinone) or sulfamic-based (which also breaks down hydroquinone and dissolves metallic silver). Great care should also be taken to flush the systems with water to remove residual cleaner. Some manufacturers do not recommend the use of a systems cleaner in their processors because of the risk of contamination, so it is best to check with your technical representative.

PROCESSOR MAINTENANCE

Poorly maintained processors (in addition to dirty ones) cannot function according to established parameters and can degrade image quality. Therefore a proper maintenance schedule must be maintained by the diagnostic imaging department to ensure continued satisfactory operation of the film processor. A log of any maintenance procedures should be kept for documentation. There are three types of processor maintenance: scheduled, preventative, and nonscheduled.

Scheduled Maintenance

Scheduled maintenance includes procedures that are performed daily, weekly, and monthly. It includes proper lubrication of moving parts, observation of all moving parts, replacement of filters in the water and developer circulation system, adjustment and/or replacement of tension springs, pulleys, and gears, and correction of any mechanical problems.

Preventive Maintenance

Preventive maintenance is a planned program whereby certain specific parts of the processor are replaced on a regular basis. It includes gear and roller replacement after a certain number of hours of operation.

Nonscheduled Maintenance

Nonscheduled maintenance is required when a system failure occurs. It can be minimized by proper cleaning, scheduled maintenance procedures, and preventive maintenance procedures.

A processor maintenance schedule should include maintenance procedures daily at start-up, daily during operation, daily at shutdown, weekly, monthly, quarterly, and yearly.

Daily at Start-Up

1. Follow daily cleaning procedures covered earlier in this chapter.

2. Make sure the processor feed tray and darkroom countertops are clean.

3. Feed four 14- × 17-inch (35 × 43 cm) green, unprocessed films into the processor. This cleans the rollers of any residual matter and also allows assessment of transport system operation. Do not use preprocessed radiographs, because they may contain residual fixer and have a hardened emulsion, which causes extra stress on the transport system.

Daily During Operation

1. Assess any changes in the normal operation of the processor, including noise level, vibration, odors, indicator buzzer, and film feeding characteristics.

2. Shut down the unit after 2 hours if no films have been processed (unless it is equipped with a stand-by option). If the unit has been shut down for 30 minutes or longer, run another 14- × 17-inch piece of green film to clean the rollers.

Daily at Shutdown

1. Follow cleaning procedure for shutdown mentioned earlier in this chapter.

2. Note any obvious problems or changes observed in the unit (abnormal odors or residues).

Weekly

1. Using a thermometer, evaluate the solution temperature and dryer thermostats for accuracy. Compare the stated value on the thermostat with the indicated value on the thermometer. Solution temperatures must be maintained at the previously mentioned parameters. The dryer thermostat should be accurate to within ±5° F (3° C).

2. Evaluate replenishment rates for accuracy, using previously mentioned procedure.

3. Lubricate main driveshaft bearings, motor, and drive chain with motor oil.

4. Inspect replenishment system microswitches on the entrance rack for proper operation on units equipped with volume replenishment.

5. For units equipped with flood replenishment, drain the developer tank, rinse with water, and fill with fresh solution.

6. Inspect and service silver reclamation unit (discussed in Chapter 5).

Monthly

1. Follow monthly cleaning procedures mentioned previously in this chapter.

2. Using a large bottle brush, remove, clean, and inspect all dryer air tubes.

3. Replace the filter in the developer circulation. This filter removes dissolved gelatin and other impurities from the developer, down to 75 μm. Before installation, it is best to soak the filter in fresh developer solution to remove any air from the system.

4. Replace water filters if the flow rate decreases by more than 10% of the accepted amount.

5. Flush the floor drain with a commercial drain cleaner.

6. Perform a safelight test (see Chapter 2).

Quarterly

Procedure

1. Follow the quarterly cleaning procedure mentioned previously.

2. Inspect all transport racks, rollers, gears, and guide shoes for wear or malfunction.

3. Check the integrity of all electrical connections and remove any dirt or corrosion.

4. Perform a hyporetention test on processed films using an ANSI test kit (see Chapter 3), to evaluate the archival quality of images.

Yearly

Procedure

1. Disassemble each transport rack and replace worn rollers, gears, or mounting springs.

2. Disassemble the drive motor and gearbox, lubricate internal components, and replace worn parts.

3. Disassemble all replenishment and circulation system pump heads and replace worn parts, including rubber diaphragms and seals.

4. Replace the tubing in the circulation and replenishment system with ⅛-inch-wall, clear PVC tubing. New clamps should also be installed because of the corrosive environment inside of the processor.

PROCESSOR MONITORING

Processor monitoring is accomplished by performing daily sensitometric tests to evaluate the performance of the processor systems and processing chemicals. **Sensitometry** measures the relationship between the intensity of radiation absorbed by the film to the optical density that is produced. Two British amateur photographers, F. Hurter

and U. Driffield, developed the current system of comparing these quantities (hence the Hurter and Driffield curve, which demonstrates film contrast). To perform sensitometric tests, the following equipment is required: sensitometer, densitometer, and control chart.

Sensitometer

The **sensitometer** is an instrument designed to expose a reproducible, uniform optical step-wedge pattern onto a film (Figure 4-3). It contains a controlled-intensity light source with a standardized optical step-wedge image (also called a *step tablet*). These patterns are available in 11- and 21-step versions (Figure 4-4). The 11-step pattern increases the optical density by a factor of 2 times (100%) between each step. The 21-step pattern increases optical density by a factor of 1.41 (41%) between each step and is more useful in sensitometric tests. A radiograph taken with an aluminum step-wedge or penetrometer should not be used in processor sensitometric tests because x-ray generators are subject to too much variation from day to day, and the origin of any differences in radiographic images could not be determined (i.e., the problem could be with the processor or with the x-ray generator). The controlled light source of the sensitometer eliminates these variations.

Densitometer

The **densitometer**, also known as a *transmission densitometer*, measures the optical density of a portion of an image

FIGURE 4-3

Sensitometer. (Courtesy Nuclear Associates, Carle Place, N.Y.)

using a 0 to 4 scale (Figure 4-5). It is a photographic light meter that measures the amount of light transmitted through a portion of film and compares it with the original amount of light incident on the film (Figure 4-6). The 0 to 4 value is then calculated using the following equation:

$$\text{Optical density} = \frac{\log_{10} \text{ Incident light}}{\text{Transmitted light}} \text{ or } \log_{10} \frac{I_i}{I_t}$$

If the **transmitted light** is 10% of the incident light, the optical density would be 1, because the equation would be:

$$\text{Optical density} = \log_{10} \frac{100}{10}$$

Because the **incident light** is the full amount of light striking the film, it has a relative value of 100%. The $\log^{10}$ symbol in the equation asks the question, "10 to what power equals the number in the equation?" Because 100 divided by 10 equals 10, the $\log_{10}$ of the number 10 is 1 ($10^1 = 10$). Therefore, if only 1% of the incident light is transmitted through the film, that portion of the image has an optical density of 2, because $^{100}\!/_1 = 100$ and $10^2 = 100$. A difference in the optical density scale of 0.3 is equivalent to a differ-

ence of 2 times in the amount of light transmission through the film, because $10^{0.3} = 2$. This means that an optical density of 1.3 would be twice as dark as an optical density of 1, and so on. The anatomic structures displayed on a diagnostic image normally have optical density values ranging from 0.5 to 2.5 when measured with a densitometer; this is known as the *diagnostic range*. Optical densities outside of this range will not contain diagnostic information when viewed on a standard viewbox illuminator.

Control Chart

A control chart is a graph that has predetermined upper and lower thresholds indicated (see Chapter 1) and is used

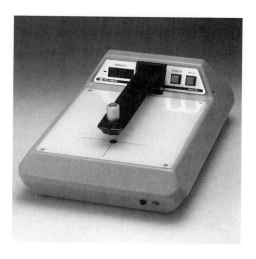

FIGURE 4-5

Densitometer for measurement of optical density. (Courtesy Gammex/RMI, Middleton, Wis.)

DATE *mAY 15, 1993*

TIME *12:00 Am*

1
2
3
4
5
6
7
8
9
10
11
12
13
14
15
16
17
18
19
20
21
COMMENTS:

FIGURE 4-4

Twenty-one step sensitometry film image.

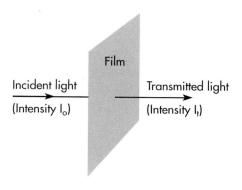

FIGURE 4-6

Diagram of incident and transmitted light.

to plot the data obtained in the sensitometric test (see Figure 4-7).

Before sensitometric tests are performed, be sure that the processor is clean and functioning properly; that fresh, properly mixed chemicals are available; and that a safelight test has been performed with satisfactory results. The processor should also be in operation for at least 20 minutes, so that the temperatures are at optimum levels.

Procedure

1. Place an 8- × 10-inch (20 × 25 cm) unexposed film in the sensitometer and expose according to the manufacturer's instructions.

2. Feed the exposed film into the processor as soon as possible. Avoid variability by keeping the time between the exposure of the sensitometer film and the processing consistent. Be sure to feed the film into the processor correctly (see below). This helps to avoid the following variables:
   - *Bromide drag.* **Bromide drag**, also called *bromide flow or directional effect,* is caused by halide ions being released by the emulsion during development and then coating the trailing areas of the film, which decreases the optical density of these areas. To minimize this effect, feed the least dense end of the sensitometric strip first, with the long axis of the wedge pattern parallel to the entrance rollers. This reduces the number of halide ions that are "dragged" over the remainder of the film.
   - *Locational effect.* **Locational effect** results from a difference in the location of the test film insertion into the processor. To minimize this effect, try to always insert the film on the same side of the feed tray each time a sensitometric test is performed.
   - *Time of day variability.* **Time of day variability** is important because chemical activity and processing system parameters can vary considerably during the course of the work day. Therefore sensitometric test films should always be processed at the same time each day, preferably early in the morning after the processor has reached optimum operating levels.

3. After the film is processed, optical density readings of each of the 21 steps and the clear portion of the film should be measured with a densitometer and recorded. After the first day, when the operating parameters of the processor are established, it should not be necessary to measure all 21 steps in succeeding days' test films.

4. From these optical density readings, the following indicators are established:
   - *Base + fog.* Often abbreviated B + F, **base + fog** is the optical density of the clear portion of the film and is the result of the blue tint added to the base of the film and any black metallic silver grains that were created by aging of the film or background radiation exposure. The B + F value for most film ranges from 0.1 to 0.2 and should never exceed 0.25. Once the value is established on the first day, it should never vary by more than an optical density value of ± 0.05 during subsequent days sensitometric test films. An above normal developer temperature, above normal developing time, overreplenishment, contaminated solution, and fogged film can increase the B + F value above accepted limits.
   - *Speed indicator or mid-density point.* This is a measure of the amount of exposure energy necessary to produce an optical density of 1 above the B + F. Once the B + F is determined, find the step with an optical density closest to 1 above this value. The value of this step is always measured and recorded as the **speed indicator**, regardless of the value obtained. For example, if the B + F is 0.2 on the first day and step 8 of the sensitometry film yields an optical density of 1.2 on the same day, then the optical density of step 8 is always used to determine the speed indicator for all future days' tests. This value should not vary by an optical density of ±0.1 from the value established on the first day. An increased developer temperature, increased developer time, overreplenishment, excessive concentration of developer or replenisher, or a contaminated solution can increase this value above the established limits. The reverse of the above decreases the speed indicator below accepted limits.
   - D_{min} *or L (low density).* D_{min}, or L (low density), is the optical density of the step closest to 0.25 above the B + F, which approximates the low end of the diagnostic range of optical densities. Again, once established on the first day, the same step is used in future days' tests, regardless of the optical density reading. The optical density of this step should not vary by more than ±5 from the first day's reading during any future test. This is primarily created by the action of phenidone, which is less sensitive to variability than hydroquinone. Essentially, the same factors affecting the B + F indicator also affect the D_{min}.
   - D_{max} *or H (high density).* D_{max}, or H (high density), is the optical density of the step closest to 2 above the B + F, which is close to the upper value of the diagnostic density range. This value should stay within ±0.1 from that determined on the first day. This optical

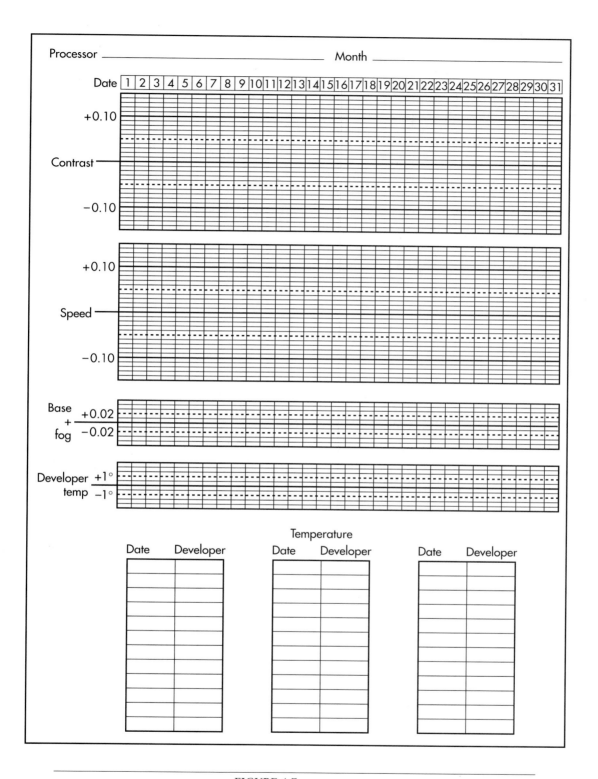

FIGURE 4-7
Processor control chart.

density value is created primarily by hydroquinone, which is more sensitive to variability than phenidone. An increase in developer time, temperature, pH, over-replenishment, or overconcentration of developer solution can increase this value above the upper limit and vice versa.

- Contrast indicator or relative density difference. Because contrast is defined as the difference between optical densities on the processed image, a **contrast indicator** can be obtained by calculating the difference between the D_{max} and D_{min} values during each day's sensitometry test. Once this value is determined on the first day, it should not vary by more than ± 0.1 during any subsequent tests. An increased developer temperature, developer time, overreplenishment, or overconcentration of developer solution can increase the contrast indicator above the upper limit. A decrease below the lower limit occurs if the above factors are decreased.

Once all of the above values are determined, they should be plotted on a control chart (see Figure 4-7). This helps monitor chemical activity and processor performance and document the quality control activities for accreditation or government agencies. A processor quality control documentation form and daily sensitometric test form are included in Appendix B.

PROCESSOR TROUBLESHOOTING

As mentioned earlier in this chapter, an automatic film processor is subject to considerable variability during the course of operation, resulting in visible changes in film quality. The troubleshooting guide in Table 4-1 is designed to identify specific processor problems and/or conditions and details the necessary corrective.

Table 4-1   Processor Control Chart Troubleshooting Guide

Processor problem	Trend in graph	Image appearance	Corrective action
Unsafe darkroom	Sharp rise in B + F with a sudden decrease in the contrast indicator but no change in developer temperature	Increased fog level	Check safelight filter; check for light leaks; check film type and safelight type; check film storage conditions
Developer temperature too high	Sharp rise in speed and contrast indicators, with a smaller increase in B + F	Excessive optical density	Check incoming water temperature or developer thermostat setting
Developer temperature too low	Slight decrease in B + F, with sharp drops in speed and contrast indicators	Optical density too low	Check incoming water temperature or developer thermostat setting
Developer concentration or pH to high	Same as developer temperature too high	Excessive optical density	Check replenishment rates and/or mix fresh solutions
Developer concentration or pH too low	Same as developer temperature too low	Optical density too low	Check replenishment rates and/or mix fresh solutions
Underreplenishment	Gradual decline in contrast and speed indicators, with normal values for B + F and developer temperature	Increased fog level and overall decrease in optical density	Check replenishment rates
Overreplenishment	Increase in B + F level and speed indicator, with a decrease in contrast indicator	Increased fog level and decrease in image contrast	Check replenishment rates
Oxidized developer	Slight increase in B+F with decrease in speed and contrast indicators	Loss of image contrast	Drain developer tank and mix fresh solution. Add correct amount of starter solution.

DAYLIGHT SYSTEMS

Many diagnostic imaging departments have eliminated traditional darkrooms in favor of **daylight systems**, which automatically load cassettes with fresh sheets of film and unload exposed cassettes directly into a processor (Figure 4-8). Because the film is loaded and unloaded from the cassette mechanically, a regular maintenance program is essential for continued proper operation. This includes cleaning and lubrication of moving parts and replacement of parts as necessary. Separate areas for loaded and unloaded cassettes should exist and be clearly marked. The processing section should be cleaned, maintained, and monitored the same way as conventional film processors.

Temperature and humidity in the area where the daylight system is used must be maintained to manufacturer's specifications, because high humidity will result in films sticking together and jamming inside of the unit. Humidity that is too low could result in static artifacts on images.

SUMMARY

A properly instituted processor quality control program should reduce variability to a minimum, which should reduce the number of repeat images and maintain the acceptable level of image quality established by the facility.

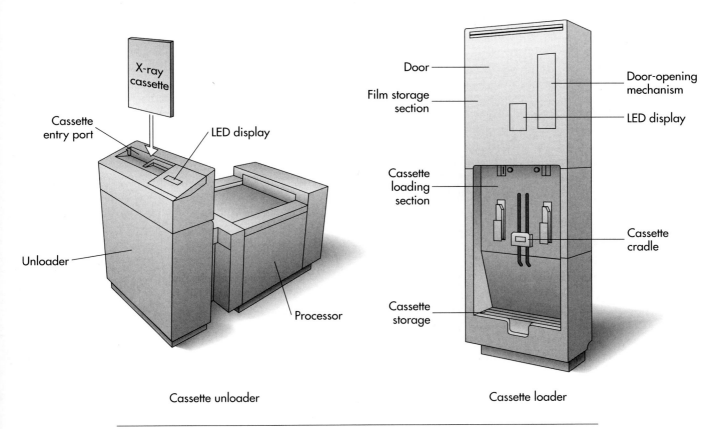

FIGURE 4-8
Daylight systems.

Review Questions

1. What is the margin of error for the specific gravity of processing solutions?
   a. 0.002
   b. 0.004
   c. 0.006
   d. 0.1

2. Which of the following cannot be determined by an H and D curve or a processor control chart?
   a. film sensitivity
   b. film contrast
   c. recorded detail
   d. base + fog

3. The presence of bromide drag produces films that are:
   a. overdeveloped
   b. underdeveloped
   c. underfixed
   d. overfixed

4. The best time to process sensitometric films is in the:
   a. morning, after the processor is warmed up
   b. late morning or midday, after peak-demand period
   c. late afternoon, during low-demand period
   d. evening, during the lowest-demand period

5. A device designed to give precise, reproducible, and graded light exposures to a film is called a:
   a. densitometer
   b. photometer
   c. sensitometer
   d. penetrometer

6. The maximum variation allowed for the contrast indicator in daily sensitometric films is plus or minus:
   a. 0.01
   b. 0.05
   c. 0.1
   d. 0.2

7. Daily quality control activities are normally required for film processing systems because of their:
   a. high degree of complexity
   b. high degree of variability
   c. high degree of consistency
   d. none of the above

8. The principle purpose of the washing process is the:
   a. stoppage of the fixation process
   b. stoppage of the development process
   c. maintenance of the solution activity
   d. removal of fixer solution

9. Temperature variations in older models of automatic processors are often related to changes in the:
   a. temperature of the dryer section
   b. incoming water supply
   c. replenisher rate
   d. film transportation rate

10. The relationship between the intensity of radiation absorbed by the film to the optical density produced defines:
    a. densitometry
    b. dosimetry
    c. sensitometry
    d. sensitivity

Student Experiment 4.1   Quality Control of Mechanized Processors

PURPOSE

The purpose of this experiment is to ensure that the automatic film processor is properly prepared for operation and that the operating levels are within the accepted values.

EQUIPMENT NEEDED

1. Sensitometer
2. Densitometer
3. Thermometer
4. Hydrometer
5. Litmus paper
6. X-ray film

PROCEDURE

1. With the processor turned off, open the top and make sure that all of the racks are in place and that they are clean.
2. Turn on the processor and the water supply.
3. After 20 minutes of operation, record the following:
   Developer temperature:
   Developer specific gravity:
   Fixer temperature:
   Fixer specific gravity:
   Water temperature:
4. Using the appropriate litmus paper, record the pH levels of both the developer and fixer.
5. Expose a sheet of film with the sensitometer and process. Take optical density readings of all 21 steps and record.
6. Determine the contrast indicator, speed indicator, and B + F for this processor using the following steps: D_{min} — step 4; speed indicator—step 11; and D_{max}—step 16.

ANALYSIS

1. Are the contrast indicator, speed indicator, and B + F within the acceptable limits? What are possible explanations for these values not being within accepted limits (even though values may have been within accepted limits)?
2. Are the solution temperatures within the proper limits? What effect(s) appear on the film if these temperatures were not within the proper limits? (Answer this question even if values were within the normal limits.)
3. Is the pH within the proper range for both the developer and fixer? What effect(s) appear on the film if these values are not within the proper range? (Answer this question even if values were within normal limits.)
4. Is the specific gravity within the proper range for both the developer and fixer? What effect(s) appear on the film if these values are not within the proper range? (Answer this question even if values were within normal limits.)

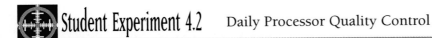

Student Experiment 4.2   Daily Processor Quality Control

PURPOSE

The purpose of this experiment is to ensure that the film processor is operating at the proper levels and producing consistent, high-quality radiographs on a day-to-day basis.

EQUIPMENT NEEDED

1. Sensitometer
2. Densitometer
3. Thermometer
4. X-ray film

PROCEDURE

1. Select an automatic film processor.
2. Using a thermometer, measure the developer temperature for 10 consecutive days if possible (some units may have a temperature readout on the front of the processor). Record these readings on the control chart.
3. Expose a sheet of film with the sensitometer and process. Take optical density readings of all steps. Repeat for 10 days.
4. Determine the B + F, speed indicator, and contrast indicator on the first day, and use the same densitometer steps to determine these values for the other 9 days. Record these values on the control chart.

ANALYSIS

1. Are the contrast indicator, speed indicator, and B + F within acceptable limits for all 10 days? If not, what are possible explanations for the variation(s)?
2. Are the solution temperatures within the proper limits for all 10 days? If not, what are possible explanations for the variation(s)?
3. What recommendations can be given to improve any processor deficiencies? Enclose control chart.

Processor Quality Control Form

DAILY SENSITOMETRIC TEST
Chemical Activity

Developer temperature	_____	Fixer temperature	_____
Developer specific gravity	_____	Fixer specific gravity	_____
Developer pH	_____	Fixer pH	_____
		Water temperature	_____

Sensitometric Test

Step number	Optical density
1	_____
2	_____
4	_____
5	_____
6	_____
7	_____
8	_____
9	_____
10	_____
11	_____
12	_____
13	_____
14	_____
15	_____
16	_____
17	_____
18	_____
19	_____
20	_____
21	_____

Base + Fog   _____

Speed indicator   _____

D_{max} _____

D_{min} _____

Contrast indicator   _____

Plot the B + F, speed indicator, and contrast indicator values daily on the control chart.

Control Chart

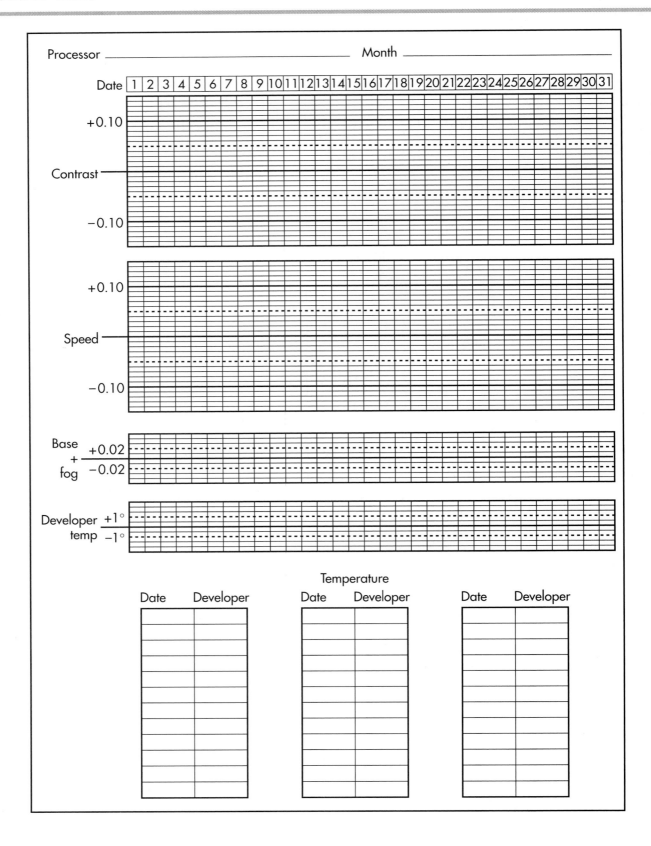

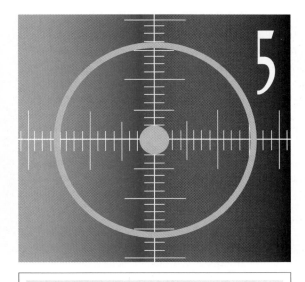

5 Silver Recovery

Objectives

At the completion of this chapter the reader will be able to do the following:

- Describe the role of silver recovery in diagnostic imaging
- List the reasons for silver recovery in diagnostic imaging
- Describe the methods of recovering silver from processing solutions
- List the factors that affect the efficiency of silver reclamation devices
- Describe the methods of recovering silver from film

Key Terms

agitation
archival film
avoirdupois ounce
channeling
dwell time
electrolysis
green film
metallic replacement
precipitation
recirculating electrolytic
scrap exposed film
sulfurization
terminal electrolytic
troy ounce

The recovery of silver has been standard practice in most hospitals and medical centers for at least 30 years. In 1967 the federal government lifted previous regulations governing the sale of silver, which escalated the price and therefore increased the demand on worldwide markets. The photographic industry is the largest single user of silver worldwide, consuming approximately 30% of the total used. This includes all film used in diagnostic imaging, which is estimated to be roughly one half of all photographic film. Medical radiographic film is the single largest consumer of silver in the medical field. Approximately 85 million troy ounces of silver are used in the photographic film consumed in the United States each year. A **troy ounce** is a unit for measuring precious metals such as silver. There are 14.58 troy ounces in 16 **avoirdupois ounces**, or standard ounces.

The next largest industrial consumer of silver is the electronics industry, using approximately 20% of all silver. Silver conducts electricity better than most substances and also resists oxidation and rusting. For this reason, most electronic devices, from the smallest electronic watch to the space shuttle, contain some quantity of silver.

The sterlingware industry consumes approximately 15% of all silver. Pure silver is relatively soft (much like lead) and is mixed with copper to create sterling silver. Generally, 925 parts pure silver are mixed with 75 parts copper to make sterling silver.

Some medical uses of silver (other than film) include the construction of metal prostheses used in repairing broken bones or joint replacement and the 1% solution of silver nitrate that physicians sometimes put into the eyes of newborns to prevent infection.

Other uses of silver include water treatment filters, in which silver is used as a bacteriocide and in the catalytic converters of some automobiles. The federal government stopped minting silver coins for general circulation in 1964.

JUSTIFICATION FOR SILVER RECOVERY

The three basic reasons for a diagnostic imaging department to institute a silver recovery program are the dwindling worldwide supply of silver, monetary return back to the diagnostic imaging department, and compliance with federal and state pollution regulations.

Worldwide Supply of Silver

The present worldwide shortage of silver is the result of very little silver being mined because of low price and high refining charges. Political instability in countries where silver is abundant also contributes to this shortage. Presently 120 million more troy ounces of silver are consumed than are produced annually in the United States. At this rate, current silver supplies may not last through the next century. The photographic industry is able to recover approximately one half of what is required annually, but eventually a serious shortfall will exist. Because diagnostic imaging is a large portion of the photographic use of silver, efforts to recover as much silver as possible are the responsibility of all department managers. It is estimated that 10% to 20% of all hospitals and 30% to 40% of doctors offices and clinics do not have silver recovery protocols in place.

Monetary Return to Department

Money obtained from silver recovery procedures can be returned to the diagnostic imaging department to help offset the cost of processing supplies, materials, and equipment. Many studies have demonstrated that about 10% of the purchase price of film can be recovered through proper silver reclamation procedures. Therefore, if a department spends $50,000 annually on film, then about $5000 can be returned to department budgets to help offset costs.

When selling silver reclaimed from processing chemistry or films, bids should be solicited from several dealers so that the best price can be negotiated. Familiarity with the current market prices based on *The Wall Street Journal* or similar business publications also is helpful. It is also better to sell only once a year so that a higher volume price can be obtained and shipping and handling costs can be reduced.

Federal and State Pollution Laws

Film processors continually replenish the chemical solutions, which means that used solutions must be disposed of in some manner. The used fixer and wash water contain silver in some form, which is a toxic heavy metal and therefore subject to strict pollution guidelines by the Environmental Protection Agency (EPA) and many state regulations. California has particularly strict pollution guidelines. Some of the important federal pollution laws are described in Box 5-1.

A silver recovery system is required for most hospitals to remove silver from used processing chemicals in order to meet the requirements of these laws. Some states and municipalities require that used wash water also be collected and disposed through approved disposal companies.

Silver recovery in a diagnostic imaging department can occur through recovery from processing solutions and recovery from film.

Box 5-1 Important Federal Pollution Laws

Water Control Act of 1972

The Water Control Act of 1972 bans the placing of toxic substances in public waterways and sewer systems.

Resources Conservation/Hazardous Waste Act of 1976

The Resources Conservation/Hazardous Waste Act of 1976 requires that available devices must be used to remove toxic substances from waste water.

Clean Water Act of 1984

The Clean Water Act of 1984 amends the previous law, in that it requires the best available methods be used to remove toxic substances from waste water.

Resource Conservation and Recovery Act of 1987 (RCRA)

The Resource Conservation and Recovery Act of 1987 (RCRA) contains many guidelines affecting film processing and silver recovery methods including the following:
1. Limits liquid waste to a toxic level of no more than 5 mg/L or 5 ppm.
2. Special permits are required to dump more than 27 gal of waste per month into public sewers. For private septic systems, a permit from the National Pollutant Discharge Elimination System (NPDES) and/or the EPA is required.
3. Shipping manifests are required to ship material such as silver recovery cartridges, scrap film, silver flake, or silver-laden fixer. The manifest forms required are EPA Forms 8700-12 and 8700-22.

SILVER RECOVERY FROM PROCESSING CHEMICALS

One of the functions of the fixer solution is to remove the unexposed and undeveloped silver halide crystals from the film. These crystals are suspended in the solution and eliminated with the used fixer by the replenishment system. This dissolved silver averages about 50% of the silver that was originally on the film and can be recovered by a variety of methods.

Metallic Replacement

This method is sometimes called the *displacement method* and is the simplest and least expensive method for a diagnostic imaging department. This makes it the most widely used method of silver recovery from processing chemicals. The metallic replacement system incorporates a plastic bucket or canister (Figure 5-1) that comes in a variety of sizes, including 3.5 gal, 5 gal (most popular in diagnostic imaging), 7.5 gal, and 10 gal, depending on the amount of films processed per month. Inside of the canister is iron in some form, which reacts chemically with the acid and silver ions in the fixer through ion exchange. When the acid in the fixer oxidizes the iron, electrons are released that are used by the silver ions to form metallic silver. The more active iron ions replace the less active silver ions, which remain in the canister as the ions are picked up and washed out in the used fixer, hence the name **metallic replace-**

FIGURE 5-1
Metallic replacement silver recovery unit.

ment. The two types of iron cartridges that can be used inside of the canister are the steel wool cartridge and the iron-impregnated foam cartridge.

Steel Wool Cartridge

Because the primary component of steel is iron, the inside of the cartridge can be packed with steel wool, yielding a large surface area in which metallic replacement can occur. One pound of steel wool can collect 3 to 4 lbs of silver. This is the more common type of cartridge insert because

Box 5-2 Advantages of Metallic Replacement Method

- No operating cost because no electric current is used.
- Low initial expense. These units can be purchased in bulk and stockpiled, which can reduce the cost per unit even further. The average service life of a metallic replacement cartridge is 6 months. After this time, it must be replaced, because most of the iron will be gone.
- There are no moving parts or electrical connections, so the unit requires very little maintenance.
- The units have a relatively high efficiency rating, because up to 95% of the recoverable silver is usually removed.

Box 5-3 Disadvantages of Metallic Replacement Method

- The units are not as efficient as the other methods discussed in this chapter. The cartridges operate at 100% efficiency for only the first quarter of life and then at about 25% efficiency for the remaining three quarters. A second unit can be connected to the primary unit to increase the efficiency. This is known as *piggy-backing* (Figure 5-2).
- The silver recovered is in the form of silver sludge. After the elapsed time of use has occurred, the unit is disconnected and the contents of the canister sold to a silver dealer. These contents are in the form of silver sludge, which is about 30% to 50% silver and 50% to 70% iron oxide. Silver refiners charge a handling fee to process the silver from this sludge, which reduces the amount of money returned to the department.
- The unit must be replaced with a new one each time it is expended in the recovery cycle.
- Payment for the silver recovered is delayed until after processing of the sludge, because the amount of actual silver content in the sludge is not known until this time.

of its lower cost, but it is subject to three potential problems: channeling, rust, and drain stoppage.

Channeling. **Channeling** occurs when an intermittent or low volume of fixer is used or by a fixer that is too acidic. In these situations, the fixer concentrates in almost a straight path, or channel, into and out of the cartridge rather than moving uniformly throughout the steep wool. Because the solution comes in contact with very little steel wool, not much silver is reclaimed. This can be avoided by filling the cartridge with fixer or water at the time of installation, allowing the fixer to dissipate throughout the cartridge as it enters.

Rusting. Iron that is exposed to moisture and air undergoes a chemical reaction that forms iron oxide, or rust. This rust forms a barrier between the silver ions and the iron ions, which prevents the metallic process from occurring or, at the very least, reduces the efficiency of the unit. This occurs with units that are used infrequently.

Drain Stoppage. As the steel wool is dissolved by the acid in the fixer, the iron ions may become deposited on the inside of the drainage pipes, which can cause obstruction. To prevent this build-up, a commercial drain cleaner composed of sodium bisulfate should be used monthly, as mentioned in Chapter 4.

Iron-Impregnated Foam Cartridge

An iron-impregnated foam cartridge uses a fine iron powder that is impregnated in a tightly wound piece of plastic foam, similar to a plastic sponge. This design helps minimize channeling and rusting, because the foam helps distribute the fixer more evenly. The suspended iron powder also provides 50% more surface area, which increases the efficiency of the unit. The advantages and disadvantages of the metallic replacement method are discussed in Boxes 5-2 and 5-3.

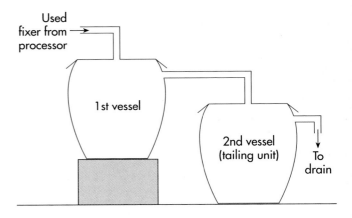

FIGURE 5-2
"Piggybacking" of metallic replacement units.

Electrolytic Silver Recovery

The electrolytic silver recovery method is based on **electrolysis**, or electroplating, and uses an electric current to reclaim the silver (Figure 5-3). Because unexposed, undeveloped silver halide is removed from the film by the fixer, the suspended silver is in the form of a positive ion (Ag^+). This means that it is attracted to a metal electrode that has a negative charge imparted on it (cathode). As these Ag^+ ions come in contact with the metal cathode, the silver collects in a layer that can be removed at a later time. The cathodes in the electrolytic recovery units are usually made of stainless steel and are either drum-shaped (Figure 5-4) or

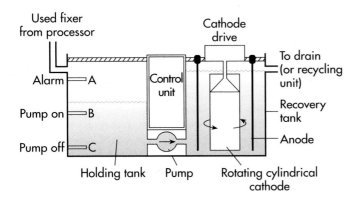

FIGURE 5-3

Diagram of electrolytic silver recovery unit.

FIGURE 5-4

Cathodes from electrolytic silver recovery unit. Top cathode is clean and unused. Left cathode contains more than 20 lb of silver flake after correct amperage has been used. Right cathode contains silver that has been "burned" by too high of an amperage setting.

disk-shaped. The solution requires **agitation** for best results to distribute the silver ions evenly over the cathode surface. This can be accomplished by rotating the cathode with a stationary anode or a stationary cathode and rotating anodes. Another design that is available keeps the cathode and anode stationary and uses a self-contained pump to swirl the solution. Systems are available that recover 3 troy ounces of silver or more per hour at 98% efficiency. The purity level of the silver ranges from 92% to 98%. The cathodes are removed periodically, and the silver is stripped off. The silver-laden cathode is replaced by a clean cathode, so that minimal interruption in film processing takes place. Once cleaned, the cathode can be reused at a later date.

The silver that is removed from the cathode is in the form of silver flake (Figure 5-5). This silver flake should be cream- or light-colored for maximum purity. The darker the flake, the less pure the silver. To control flake color and purity, an amperage control switch located on the unit regulates the amount of charge on the cathode. The amount of this current is usually around 8 A for most systems. If the flake is too dark, too much amperage is being used and is "burning" the silver. This also causes the fixing agent to be converted into sulfide, which results in a foul-smelling (like rotten eggs), yellow-brown deposit of sulfur on the cathode. This is known as *sulfating* or **sulfurization**. If the silver flake coating is very light or silver, the amperage is too low. A computerized timer and current selector available on some models of electrolytic silver reclaimers adjusts the current according to the time of day or usage.

The two types of electrolytic silver recovery units are terminal electrolytic systems and recirculating electrolytic systems.

Terminal Electrolytic System

The **terminal electrolytic** unit is connected to the fixer overflow line from the processor replenishment system.

FIGURE 5-5

Silver flake that has been removed from a cathode after correct amperage has been used.

Box 5-4 Advantages of Electrolytic Silver Recovery

- Electrolytic silver recovery is more efficient than metallic replacement, without the problems of channeling, rusting, or drain stoppage.
- The silver recovered is in the form of silver flake, which is 92% to 98% pure rather than sludge.
- Payment for the silver can be received upon delivery of the flake to the refiner, because the content is immediately apparent.
- Shipping costs of materials to the refiner are minimal.
- The system produces no new pollutants (as opposed to the sludge produced by metallic replacement).
- The system is reusable, because the cathodes can be cleaned and reused.

Box 5-5 Disadvantages of Electrolytic Silver Recovery

- Higher capital cost for the equipment as opposed to metallic replacement. These units begin at about $250.00 and can increase to several thousand dollars for larger-size units. Metallic replacement canisters can vary considerably in price but usually average about $25.00.
- There is an operating cost for these units because of the electricity consumed during operation.
- Special electrical or plumbing connections may be required in the processing area.
- Periodic monitoring and servicing of the equipment is required. Most units call for at least monthly monitoring and service to ensure maximum efficiency. This includes checking the current level and flake color of the silver deposited on the cathode. The efficiency of silver recovery is estimated with special silver paper that changes color to indicate the silver content of the fixer that has passed through the unit. These test papers are usually accurate to within ± 10% of the actual silver content. The amount of silver measured in the fixer should not exceed the values specified by the manufacturer. Otherwise, the current value must be changed or the cathode cleaned.

Once this unit recovers the silver, the used fixer is flushed down the drain. Most processor manufacturers recommend this type of electrolytic unit.

Recirculating Electrolytic System

The **recirculating electrolytic** unit is designed to recover silver from used fixer and then recirculate the fixer back into the processor. This normally does not conserve much fixer because electrolysis destroys the preservative in the fixer. Fixer replenishment is decreased by no more than 20%. The main advantage of this method is that the overall concentration of silver in the fixer tank is decreased. Therefore the amount of silver transported into the wash water through the fixer is decreased. This may allow the wash water to have a low enough silver content to avoid the thresholds of certain pollution standards. Most film manufacturers do not recommend this method because of decreased archival quality of the processed films. The advantages and disadvantages of the electrolytic silver recovery method are discussed in Boxes 5-4 and 5-5.

Direct Sale of Used Fixer

There are roughly 0.5 to 0.8 troy ounces of silver per gallon of used fixer. In small-volume facilities (less than 10 gal/wk), metallic replacement or electrolytic units may not be practical. In this case, used fixer can be collected in 55 gal drums and sold to a refiner, who will reclaim the silver from the solution. The advantages of this method are that no capital outlay for equipment is required by the facility and no pollutants other than the used developer and wash water are discharged into a sewer system. The disadvantages are that considerable handling or storage may be required, which reduces the profit margin from the sale of the silver.

Chemical Precipitation

Chemical **precipitation** is the oldest form of silver recovery. In this method compounds such as sodium sulfite and zinc chloride are mixed with used fixer, causing a chemical reaction. This results in the silver precipitating, or sinking, to the bottom of the tank or drum, where it can be removed. This is a fairly efficient method but has many disadvantages including the following:

- The chemicals used are hazardous and require special precautions.
- Toxic fumes, such as chlorine gas and hydrogen, are created by the chemical reaction.
- A large drum or vat with adequate space is required.
- The process is labor-intensive, which reduces the profit margin.

Because of these disadvantages, this method should not be attempted by diagnostic facilities and should be carried out only by licensed silver refiners. The silver in fixer sold directly to a silver refiner usually is reclaimed in this fashion.

Resin Systems

Resin systems use resin particles treated with an acid to give them a negative ionic charge. The silver is attracted to the resin, where it remains. This method requires a large

Box 5-6   Factors Affecting the Efficiency of Silver Recovery From Processing Solutions

Dwell Time

Dwell time is the time that the fixer remains within the recovery device. The longer the dwell time, the greater the efficiency.

Agitation

Agitation helps distribute the silver ions throughout the device.

Surface Area

An increase in the surface area of the recovery device increases the efficiency of silver recovery.

Solution Temperature

If the solution temperature exceeds 95° F (35° C), the efficiency of the system decreases, because it becomes more active.

Fixer pH

Silver recovery must take place in an acid solution to release the silver ions. Therefore the fixer pH must be kept below 5.

Amperage

Amperage applies only to electrolytic units. As mentioned previously, the amperage must be kept in an optimum range for maximum efficiency.

Maintenance

Poorly maintained units always lose efficiency. Severely neglected units can clog, which can cause the fixer tank in the processor to overflow, contaminating the developer or damaging internal components. On electrolytic units, excessive corrosion can cause electrical hazards and must be removed. When obtaining silver from the cathode, be sure to clean out the bottom of the unit tank and scrub the anodes. Never allow more than 1 inch of silver to accumulate on the cathode. This can cause an electrical short circuit or jam the rotating mechanism used for agitation. The excessive weight of the silver on the cathode also puts stress on the drive motor of this rotating mechanism, shortening its life span.

amount of space and is labor-intensive; therefore it is performed only by silver refiners.

Box 5-6 lists factors affecting silver recovery from processing solutions.

SILVER RECOVERY FROM FILM

As previously mentioned, 50% of the silver is dissolved in the fixer. This means that the other 50% remains on the film. For images that are not of diagnostic quality (and therefore not kept for the patient's files), the sheets of film can be stored in a bin and then sold to a silver refiner. A price per pound is negotiated for the film and the money

paid to the facility. The three basic categories of film that hospitals and medical centers can release for sale are green film, scrap exposed film, and archival film.

Green Film

Green film is film that has not been processed, such as expired film or film that was accidentally exposed to white light (open film bin). This is the most valuable, because all of the silver is in place (usually about 0.4 troy ounces per sheet of 14- × 17-inch (35 × 43 cm) film. Because of this higher value, this film should be separated from other categories of film to be sold and a higher price negotiated.

Scrap Exposed Film

Scrap exposed film is film that has been exposed and processed, such as rejects or old sensitometry films. This film contains about 0.11 troy ounces of silver per 14- × 17-inch sheet.

Archival Film

Archival film is film that has been exposed and processed and has outlived its use as a patient record. Most hospitals and associated medical facilities retain images for a minimum of 5 years (except for mammograms). It then generally is released for sale, except for film containing certain pathologic conditions or those required for litigation or pending litigation. Any film dated before 1974 contains 20% more silver (0.13 to 0.18 troy ounces per 14- × 17-inch sheet) than film manufactured since that time. This is because the price of silver escalated in 1974, and manufacturers responded by developing emulsions that could maintain image quality with less silver. Any film in this category should be separated from newer archival film and scrap exposed film so that a higher price per pound can be negotiated.

Once a refiner obtains films from a diagnostic imaging department, the silver is reclaimed by either incineration (which burns the film and removes the silver from the ash) or chemical treatments (which use chemicals to remove, or leach, the silver from the film).

SUMMARY

In many diagnostic radiology departments, the quality control technologist is given the responsibility of determining the type of silver reclamation to be used, as well as maintaining and servicing the unit during operation. A basic understanding of these systems is essential to fulfilling this responsibility.

Review Questions

1. The unit used for measurement of precious metals such as silver is the:
   a. standard ounce
   b. avoirduprois ounce
   c. troy ounce
   d. none of the above

2. The largest worldwide consumer of silver is the:
   a. photographic industry
   b. electronics industry
   c. sterlingware industry
   d. space program

3. The Resource Conservation and Recovery Act of 1987 limits liquid waste to a toxic level of no more than _____ ppm.
   a. 2
   b. 5
   c. 10
   d. 100

4. Most silver recovery systems reclaim the silver from the:
   a. developer solution
   b. fixer solution
   c. wash water
   d. dryer section

5. The simplest and least expensive method of silver reclamation is the:
   a. metallic replacement method
   b. electrolytic method
   c. chemical precipitation
   d. resin method

6. Problems with steel wool metallic replacement cartridges include:
   1. channeling
   2. rusting
   3. drain stoppage
   a. 1 and 2 only
   b. 2 and 3 only
   c. 1 and 3 only
   d. 1, 2, and 3

7. When electrolytic silver recovery units are used, the silver is deposited on the:
   a. anode
   b. cathode
   c. both cathode and anode
   d. neither cathode nor anode

8. The oldest form of silver recovery is the _____ _____ method.
   a. metallic replacement
   b. electrolytic
   c. chemical precipitation
   d. resin

9. Which of the following are factors that affect the efficiency of silver reclamation systems?
   1. dwell time
   2. agitation
   3. surface area
   a. 1 and 2 only
   b. 2 and 3 only
   c. 1 and 3 only
   d. 1, 2, and 3

10. What percentage of the silver is normally dissolved in the fixer solution during film processing?
   a. 10%
   b. 25%
   c. 50%
   d. 90%

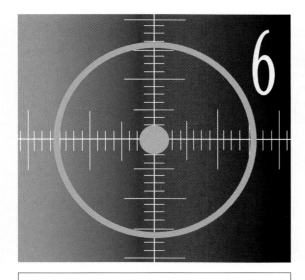

6 Quality Control of Radiographic Equipment

Objectives

At the completion of this chapter the reader will be able to do the following:

- Explain the difference between single-phase, three-phase, and high-frequency x-ray generators
- Recognize the voltage waveform characteristics of the three types of x-ray generators
- List the voltage ripple values for the three types of x-ray generators
- Calculate the power output rating for the three types of x-ray generators
- List the three main parts of a quality control program for radiographic equipment
- List and describe the performance tests for radiographic equipment

Key Terms

actual focal spot
coulomb/kilogram
effective focal spot
focal spot blooming
half-value layer
high-frequency
kilowatt rating
line focus principle
linearity
reciprocity
reproducibility
roentgen
single-phase
three-phase
voltage ripple

Outline cont'd _____

Chapter 4 discussed quality control of the film processor as the most important quality control component for a quality management program in diagnostic imaging. However, many other components of diagnostic imaging departments are subject to variability and must have separate quality control protocols to ensure safe operation and function. One such component is the equipment used as the x-ray source in conventional radiography. This includes the x-ray generator, control or operating console, x-ray tube, and accessory devices, such as the x-ray table and support mechanism.

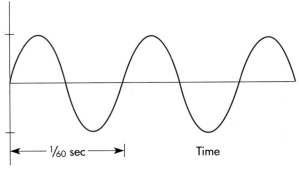

(FIGURE 6-1)

X-RAY GENERATORS

The x-ray generator is the largest component of the radiographic unit. It contains the high-voltage transformers, rectifiers, timing circuitry, and mA and kVp selectors. X-ray generators are available in three basic types: single-phase, three-phase, and high-frequency.

Single-Phase Generator

A single source of alternating current is used to power the generator in a **single-phase** unit. A graphic representation of single-phase alternating current is demonstrated in Figure 6-1.

The graph in Figure 6-1 plots the voltage on the Y axis versus time on the X axis. The peaks in the graph represent the flow of electricity changing direction throughout the circuit. Voltage values range from zero volts to a peak value (hence the term *kilovolts peak*) and back to zero volts. The two types of single-phase generators used in diagnostic radiography are half-wave rectified and full-wave rectified.

Half-Wave Rectified

In a half-wave rectified generator, one half of the normal alternating current wave is used to power the x-ray tube and the other half is shut off by the addition of one or two rectifiers. This causes the normal single-phase alternating current waveform graph to appear as shown in Figure 6-2.

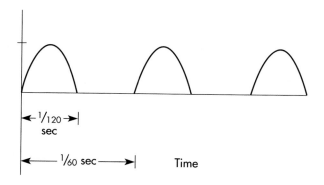

(FIGURE 6-2)

Because the standard frequency of alternating current in the United States is 60 Hertz, or 60 cycles/sec (a cycle represents the current flowing in each direction one time), only 60 pulses of electricity per second can be used to create x-rays. This means that the x-rays are emitted in pulses, or spurts, and therefore a longer amount of time is required to obtain a specific quantity of x-rays. For this reason, half-wave rectified units are generally used in dental x-ray units and some small portable x-ray units.

Full-Wave Rectified

Full-wave rectified generators use a combination of four rectifiers to channel all of the pulses through the x-ray tube to create x-rays. The resultant waveform graph for this type of unit appears as shown in Figure 6-3.

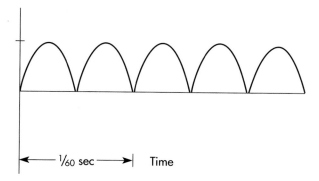

(FIGURE 6-3)

Because 120 pulses of electricity per second can be used to create x-rays, twice as many x-rays can be created in a given period compared with the half-wave unit. This allows full-wave rectified units to be used in larger x-ray generators, such as those found in the radiology department of hospitals and clinics. However, the x-rays are still emitted in pulses (as demonstrated by the number of times the pulses reach zero on the waveform graph) and therefore still require some time to achieve a specific quantity of x-rays. The shortest exposure time available for single-phase x-ray generators is $\frac{1}{120}$ second. For this reason, full-wave

rectified units are seldom found in larger hospitals but are frequently found in doctors' offices and small clinics.

Three-Phase Generator

Three-phase x-ray generators are powered by three separate sources of alternating current that have been staggered so that they are "out of phase" with each other by 120 degrees or $\frac{1}{3}$ of a cycle. The voltage waveform graph for three-phase alternating current appears as shown in Figure 6-4.

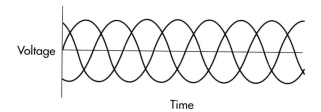

(FIGURE 6-4)

By the time one pulse of current begins to drop toward zero voltage, another pulse is heading back up to the maximum value, so the voltage never reaches zero and x-rays are continuously produced (eliminating the pulsed effect of single-phase units). This allows exposure time values as low as $\frac{1}{1000}$ second (1 ms). The x-rays created with three-phase units also have a higher average energy than those of single-phase units, because the voltage is near the peak value for a higher percentage of the time during x-ray production (which can lower patient dose compared with single-phase units). The main disadvantages of three-phase equipment are higher capital cost (at least twice as expensive as single-phase) and the size of the unit (because of the additional electronic components required). The advantages have generally outweighed the disadvantages, because the three-phase x-ray generator has been the most common type of unit in major hospitals and medical centers since the 1970s. The two types of three-phase generators are six-pulse and twelve-pulse generators.

Three-Phase, Six-Pulse

The six-pulse type of three-phase unit uses six rectifiers and one half of the three-phase alternating current pulses, with the rest of the pulses eliminated by the rectifiers. The resulting voltage waveform appears as shown in Figure 6-5.

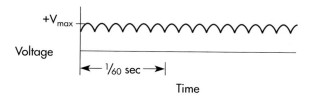

(FIGURE 6-5)

As mentioned previously, one cycle of single-phase alternating current referred to one pulse of electricity traveling each direction one time, so that two pulses are found in one cycle. Because 60 cycles occur each second, one cycle requires a time of $\frac{1}{60}$ second. In a three-phase, six-pulse x-ray generator, six pulses of electricity exist during the same cycle or $\frac{1}{60}$ second time interval (instead of two pulses per $\frac{1}{60}$ second in single-phase), hence the name three-phase, six-pulse. This means that 360 voltage pulses are now available per second.

Three-Phase, 12-Pulse

The three-phase, 12-pulse type of x-ray generator uses 12 rectifiers, which direct all of the three-phase alternating current pulses through the x-ray tube during x-ray production. This yields 12 pulses of electricity per one-cycle ($\frac{1}{60}$ second) time interval, for a total of 720 voltage pulses available per second. This unit is more efficient than the three-phase, six-pulse unit, but is more expensive in capital cost. The voltage waveform for a three-phase, 12-pulse x-ray generator appears as shown in Figure 6-6.

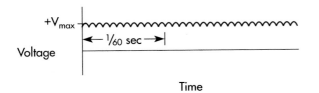

(FIGURE 6-6)

High-Frequency Generator

High-frequency x-ray generators are the newest type of generator equipment, developed in the late 1970s. They are sometimes referred to as *medium-frequency generators,* depending on the design and manufacturer. Most of these units use a single source of alternating current that is first fed into a microprocessor circuit before entering the high-voltage section. This microprocessor changes the frequency of the alternating current from the standard 60 Hz to as much as 20,000 Hz in some units. It is then rectified and smoothed with capacitors before application across the x-ray tube. This causes the pulses to merge together and results in a voltage waveform that appears as shown in Figure 6-7.

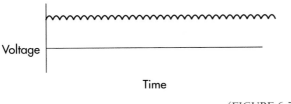

(FIGURE 6-7)

High-frequency generators and three-phase generators produce similar voltage waveforms. However, the capital cost and power requirements for high-frequency units are far less than for three-phase units. The transformers in high-frequency units can be smaller because they are much more efficient at higher frequencies (according to Faraday's Law of Electromagnetism). This accounts for the lower capital cost and also lowers the space requirement for installation. Because these units yield most of the advantages of a three-phase unit but at a fraction of the cost, they are becoming more common in hospitals, medical centers, clinics, and doctor's offices.

Voltage Ripple

A term often used to distinguish the voltage waveforms of each type of x-ray generator is **voltage ripple**. This is the amount of variation from the peak voltage that occurs during x-ray production. For single-phase units, the voltage ripple is considered to be 100%, because the voltage drops from its peak all the way to zero before rising again, so 100% of all possible voltages are obtained. For three-phase equipment, the voltage does not fall all the way to zero. One pulse is rising as soon as the previous one is falling, which yields a voltage ripple of 13% for a three-phase, six-pulse generator and 3.5% for a three-phase, 12-pulse unit. High-frequency generators can create voltage ripple values between 1% and 15%, which are comparable to three-phase.

Power Ratings

The power output of an x-ray generator is used to measure the capacity of x-ray production from the individual unit. This value is measured in kilowatts (kW) and is called the **kilowatt rating**. It is usually calculated by the maximum combination of kVp and mA that can be achieved at an exposure time of 100 ms. These values are then placed into the following equations:

$$\text{Three-phase and high-frequency} \quad kW = \frac{kVp \times mA}{1000}$$

$$\text{Single-phase } kW = \frac{kVp \times mA \times 0.707}{1000}$$

The rippling effect of the single-phase alternating current requires the 0.707 multiplier be added to the equation.

QUALITY CONTROL PROGRAM FOR RADIOGRAPHIC UNITS

The three parts of a quality control program for radiographic equipment are visual inspection, environmental inspection, and performance testing.

Visual Inspection

Visual inspection includes checking the main components of the equipment for proper function, mechanical condition, and safety. This inspection should be performed at least annually using a checklist for documentation. An example of this checklist is provided in Appendix B. The inspection should include the control panel, overhead tube crane, radiographic table, protective lead apparel, and miscellaneous equipment.

Control Panel

The control panel contains all of the selectors for controlling x-ray production (mA, kVp, and exposure time) and the various meters that monitor the operation of the generator. Control panel inspection should include function of x-ray tube heat sensors; overload protection indicator; and panel lights, meters, and switches. The inspection should ensure proper view of the exposure room through the window (should be unobstructed), correct exposure switch placement, and the presence of an up-to-date technique chart.

Overhead Tube Crane

The overhead tube crane is the mounting bracket that holds the x-ray tube over the x-ray table. Items to evaluate in this section include the condition of the high-voltage cables and other wires; condition of the cable brackets, clamps, or tie-downs; stability of the system; proper movement; SID and angulation indicator function; detent operation; lock function; Bucky center light; collimator light brightness; and interlock function.

Radiographic Table

A patient usually will be in contact with the x-ray table throughout the diagnostic procedure, so it must be kept clean and safe. Items to inspect include surface condition and cleanliness of tabletop; power top and angulation switches; Bucky tray and cassette locks; stability; table angulation indicator; and the condition of any footboard or shoulder braces.

Protective Lead Apparel

Lead aprons and gloves should be present in the radiographic room and have a minimum of 0.5 mm Pb equivalent thickness. They should be radiographed or viewed fluoroscopically (using remote fluoroscopy if possible) upon acceptance and then every 6 months following to determine if any cracks are present. When not in use, they should be properly hung to prevent cracks. Lead vinyl sheets and gonadal shields should also be evaluated in the same manner.

Miscellaneous Equipment

A measuring caliper should be present in radiographic rooms where manual technique is used. This and a technique chart aid in establishing the correct exposure factors. Positioning sponges and other patient position aids should be clean and free of contrast media. A check of the manual integrity of any step stools or intravenous fluid stands should also be included.

Environmental Inspection

Environmental inspection should be performed annually and involves checking for mechanical and electrical safety. Often, it can be performed along with the visual inspection. One item included in the environmental inspection is evaluation of the condition of the x-ray tube high-tension cables. This is accomplished by checking the covering on the outside of the cables (or any other wires that are visible on the outside of the unit). Any discoloration of the outside insulation, especially where the wire or cable bends, could be an indicator of internal heat and a potential short circuit. A service engineer should be consulted if this is present.

The mechanical condition of the x-ray tube counterweights and tracks (especially in overhead tube stands) should also be included in the environmental inspection. Proper lubrication of moving parts should be provided at this time.

Electrical safety is critical for the safety of both the patient and the equipment operator. All radiographic equipment should be grounded, and all obvious electrical connections should be intact.

Should the possibility of a short circuit exist, never touch an electrical device with one hand while the other hand is touching any type of conductor. This will help prevent the direct flow of electricity through the heart. If someone is experiencing an electric shock, do not grasp the victim directly. Instead, either open the main switch (turn the power off) or use some type of insulator (dry wooden board) to separate the person from the source of the electricity. A good rule of thumb to remember when dealing with electric current is that the combination of high voltage and low amperage tends to throw a victim, whereas a combination of low voltage and high amperage tends to hold a victim and is potentially more dangerous. For older equipment or equipment that has a history of problems with electrical safety, a service engineer should be consulted for environmental inspections. Many states require that an electrical inspection record be posted on the equipment.

Performance Testing

Performance testing evaluates the performance of the x-ray generator and x-ray tube using specialized test instrumentation, which can range from simple phantoms and test tools to sophisticated computerized systems such as the Noninvasive Evaluation of Radiation Output (NERO) system (Figure 6-8) or similar devices available from various manufacturers. These computerized systems make the gathering of data for performance evaluations very quick and easy, but they can cost several thousand dollars. It is more common for facilities to use several smaller devices to gather the necessary data. The results of these tests should be documented for governmental and accreditation agencies. Sample forms for many of these tests are provided in Appendix B.

Radiation Measurement

Much of the data obtained during performance testing includes radiation measurement. Therefore some type of radiation detector is a standard piece of equipment for many of these tests. The more common type of detector used in performance testing is the gas-filled chamber. As radiation enters this chamber, it ionizes the gas along its path (Figure 6-9). This produces a trail of ions that allows the flow of current for a split second and can be detected by a meter. A quenching material may be added to the chamber to speed the return of ions to a stable state. There are three types of gas-filled chamber detectors, which vary according to the chamber voltage (see Figure 6-10).

Ion Chamber. A voltage of 100 to 300 volts is placed on the ion chamber, making it the least sensitive of the three chambers. This makes the ion chamber useful for measuring x-rays, because a high sensitivity is not required for their detection, and ion chambers are often used in performance testing. They are usually available as pocket ionization chambers (also called *pocket dosimeters*) and analog or digital dosimeters (Figure 6-11). They can also be used as the sensor in Automatic Exposure Control systems and as the detectors in CT scanners.

Proportional Counter. A voltage of 300 to 900 volts is placed on the chamber, which increases the sensitivity. Proportional counters are often used in stationary laboratory counters to measure small quantities of radioactive material.

Geiger-Müeller Counter. A voltage of 900 to 1200 volts is placed on the chamber, which yields the greatest sensitivity. Geiger-Müeller counters are often used for contamination control in nuclear medicine departments.

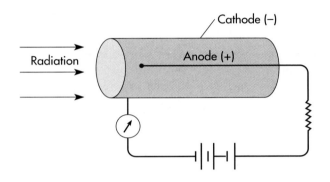

FIGURE 6-9
Schematic diagram of an ion chamber.

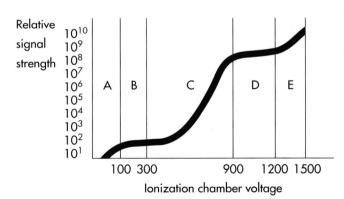

FIGURE 6-10
Graph showing how the intensity of the signal from a gas-filled detector increases as the voltage across the chamber increases. **A,** Region of recombination. **B,** Ionization region. **C,** Proportional region. **D,** Geiger-Müeller region. **E,** Region of continuous discharge.

FIGURE 6-8
NERO is a microprocessor that can be programmed to acquire and analyze exposure data, providing quality control test results for numerous parameters. (From Ballinger PW: *Merrill's atlas of radiographic positions and radiologic procedures,* ed 8, St Louis, 1995, Mosby.)

Some of the newer types of radiation-monitoring devices use a solid-state or semiconducting detector instead of an ionization chamber. This incorporates a crystal of either silicon or germanium with selected impurities added to detect the incident radiation. When the crystal is attached to an electric current, little or no current can flow through the crystal because no free electrons are available. If the crystal is exposed to radiation, electrons are dislodged within its matrix and electric current can flow through it. This increase in current is proportional to the amount of radiation incident upon the crystal and is registered by an analog or digital meter. This type of detector is relatively small and accurate but can be higher in cost than ionization chambers.

The value obtained from the radiation detector is the radiation intensity, which can be measured in a special unit called the **roentgen** (R) or in an SI unit called the **coulomb/kilogram** (C kg^{-1}).

$$1 \text{ R} = 2.58 \times 10^{-4} \text{ C/kg}^{-1}$$
$$1 \text{ C kg}^{-1} = 3.88 \times 10^{3} \text{ R}$$

Because both units measure a relatively large amount of radiation, smaller increments of milliroentgen (mR) or microcoulomb/kilogram (µC kg^{-1}) are most often obtained during performance testing. Some detectors are designed so that the exposure rate (intensity of radiation/unit of time) can be displayed in addition to the radiation intensity; these are known as *rate meters*.

Reproducibility of Exposure

An x-ray generator should always produce the same intensity of radiation each time the same set of technical factors are used to make an exposure. For example, if a technique of 80 kVp, 500 mA, and 0.02 second yields 100 mR of radiation when measured by a dosimeter, then at any future time that the same technical factors are entered into the same x-ray generator, the yield when tested should be 100 mR. This concept is known as **reproducibility.** ● *The maximum variability allowed in reproducibility is ±5%.* Evaluation of reproducibility variance requires a dosimeter (unless a computerized noninvasive system is used).

Procedure

1. Place the dosimeter on the x-ray tabletop on a lead apron, using a source-to-dosimeter distance of 40 inches.

2. Make a series of three to five separate exposures of the dosimeter using factors of 80 kVp, 100 mA, and 100 ms. The dosimeter must be cleared after each exposure. Record each reading on a documentation form.

3. Use the readings obtained to determine the reproducibility variance using the following equation:

$$\frac{\text{Reproducibility}}{\text{variance}} = \frac{(\text{mR}_{max} - \text{mR}_{min})}{(\text{mR}_{max} + \text{mR}_{min})}$$

The calculated variance should be less than 0.05 (5%) for a properly functioning x-ray generator. This test should be performed upon acceptance of new equipment and then annually or when service is performed on the x-ray generator or x-ray tube. Variations in x-ray generator performance (kVp selector, mA selector, rectifier failure, etc.) or x-ray tube operation (filament evaporation, arcing, etc.) can cause the reproducibility variance to exceed accepted limits. This can cause radiographs of inconsistent quality and necessitate repeat exposures.

Radiation Output

X-ray generators should emit a specific amount of radiation (mR or µC kg^{-1}) per unit of x-ray tube current and time (mAs). In addition, similar types of x-ray generators and tubes within a department should emit the same mR/mAs (µC kg^{-1}/mAs) values, so that technique charts can be valid in all rooms, which should reduce the number of repeat examinations. The original mR/mAs (µC kg^{-1}/mAs) value is determined upon acceptance of the unit or at the start of the quality control program.

FIGURE 6-11
Digital dosimeter. (Courtesy Gammex/RMI, Middleton, Wis.)

Procedure

1. Place a dosimeter on the x-ray tabletop on a lead apron, using a source-to-detector distance of 40 inches.

2. Make an exposure at 80 kVp, 100 mA, and 100 ms (10 mAs). Some physicists recommend that the dosimeter be placed under a homogenous phantom of aluminum or acrylic plates or in the Bucky for this measurement. Either method is satisfactory, but the test must always be performed the same way each time so that the values can be compared for variation.

3. Divide the radiation measurement recorded from the dosimeter by 10 mAs to obtain the mR/mAs, or μC kg^{-1}/mAs, value. This value should be recorded and the test repeated at least annually. ●*The original acceptance value and future values should be within ±10% of each other in a properly functioning x-ray generator.* Values obtained in different x-ray rooms with similar x-ray generators and tubes should also be compared and should fall within ± 10% of each other to establish room-to-room consistency.

Many states and the Joint Commission on the Accreditation of Healthcare Organizations (JCAHO) require the posting of this value to guarantee that the x-ray generator does not emit excessive amounts of radiation exposure for a given kVp/mAs combination.

Filtration Check

Proper filtration is necessary to remove low-energy photons from the x-ray beam, which can increase the patient skin dose by as much as 90% if not removed. This test should be performed upon acceptance and then annually or whenever service is performed on the x-ray tube or collimator. The best method to determine if adequate filtration exists is to measure the **half-value layer** (HVL) (the amount of filtration that will reduce the exposure rate to one half of its initial value), because normally it is not possible to measure inherent filtration. This is due to the fact that filament evaporation is continually taking place, which adds a layer of tungsten onto the inside of the x-ray tube window. The HVL should not vary from its original value (which is established at acceptance) or its value at the beginning of the quality control program. It is dependent upon the kVp used, the total beam filtration, and the type of x-ray generator.

1. Place a dosimeter on the x-ray tabletop on top of a lead apron or lead vinyl (to prevent backscatter).

2. Adjust the tube-to-dosimeter distance to between 60 and 80 cm and collimate to slightly larger than the dosimeter.

3. Make an exposure at 80 kVp and 50 mAs and record the amount of radiation from the dosimeter.

4. Clear the dosimeter and add a 1-mm thick aluminum plate between the bottom of the collimator and the dosimeter and expose. Record the reading and clear the dosimeter. Repeat this procedure, adding aluminum plates in 1-mm increments until a total of 6 to 8 mm are in place.

5. Use semi-log graph paper and plot a graph of x-ray intensity (dosimeter readings) on the Y axis versus absorber thickness on the X axis (Figure 6-12). Draw in a curve by connecting the dots in the graph. The HVL is determined by taking one half of the maximum dosimeter reading and then drawing a line from this point on the Y axis to the curve and then another line from this point on the curve, down to the X axis. This value on the X

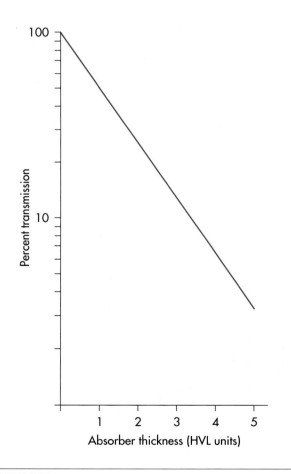

FIGURE 6-12

Semi-log plot of radiation intensity versus attenuator thickness for determination of half-value layer.

axis represents the HVL. This should be greater than or equal to 2.3 mm, because this is the minimum HVL at 80 kVp according to the Food and Drug Administration (FDA). The HVL amounts at various kVp values are given in Table 6-1.

A quick test to determine if adequate filtration is present can be performed in cases in which HVL value measurement cannot be made. However, this indicates only whether adequate filtration is present and not the actual amount of filtration. Therefore it should not take the place of HVL measurement during formal quality control testing. This method uses a dosimeter and a 2.3-mm thick aluminum plate.

Procedure

1. Place the dosimeter on the x-ray table on top of a lead apron.

2. Make an exposure at a source-to-detector distance of 40 inches at 80 kVp and 50 mAs and record the reading.

3. Clear the dosimeter and make a second exposure at the same technical factors but with the aluminum plate between the detector and the x-ray source.

4. Place the readings obtained into the following equation:

$$\frac{\text{Exposure with aluminum plate}}{\text{Exposure without aluminum plate}}$$

If adequate filtration is present, the number obtained from the equation should range between 0.5 and 0.75. If less than 0.5, the beam filtration is not adequate. If it is greater

than 0.75, excessive filtration exists, which is legally acceptable but can be an indicator of pending x-ray tube failure because of excessive tungsten deposits on the x-ray tube window as a result of filament evaporation.

kVp Accuracy

The x-ray tube voltage (kVp) has a significant effect on the image contrast and optical density, as well as the patient dose. Therefore the kVp stated on the control panel should produce an x-ray beam with a comparable and consistent amount of energy. ● *Variations between the stated kVp and the x-ray beam quality must be within ±5%.* This means that if 80 kVp is selected on the control panel, the x-ray beam energy should fall within ±4 kVp of this value. The kVp accuracy can be determined by using either a specialized test cassette, such as the Wisconsin Test Cassette (Figure 6-13), Ardan and Crook's cassette, or a digital kVp meter (Figure 6-14), according to the respective manufacturer's instructions. The digital meters are usually more accurate and easier to use (because when they are exposed the measured kVp appears automatically with an LED readout) but are more expensive than the test cassettes. The test cassettes require that a film be placed inside and exposed to a specific set of technical factors. The resulting film is then analyzed visually or with a densitometer to obtain the measured kVp. This test should be performed upon acceptance and then annually or when service is performed on the x-ray generator or tube.

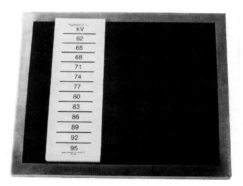

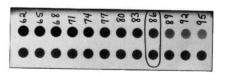

FIGURE 6-13

Wisconsin Test Cassette. (Courtesy Gammex/RMI, Middleton, Wis.)

Table 6-1 Half-Value Layer	
X-ray tube voltage	Minimum HVL in mm of aluminum
30	0.3
40	0.4
50	1.2
60	1.3
70	1.5
80	2.3
90	2.5
100	2.7
120	3.2

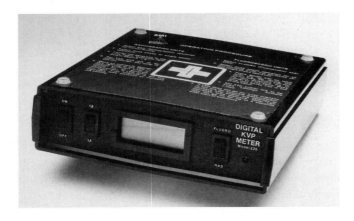

FIGURE 6-14
Digital kVp meter. (Courtesy Gammex/RMI, Middleton, Wis.)

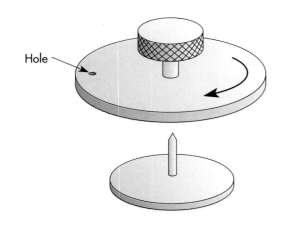

FIGURE 6-15
Manual spinning top.

Timer Accuracy

Exposure time directly affects the total quantity of radiation emitted from an x-ray tube; therefore an accurate exposure timer is critical for properly exposed radiographs and reasonable patient radiation exposure. ● *The variability allowed for timer accuracy is ±5% for exposure times greater than 10 ms and ±20% for exposures less than 10 ms.* Timer accuracy should be determined upon acceptance and then annually or when service is performed on the x-ray generator or if technique problems arise suddenly. The easiest method to validate timer accuracy is the use of a digital x-ray timer available from various manufacturers. These usually incorporate a solid-state detector that measures the total time of x-ray production and then display the time using a digital LED readout. Because these devices cost several hundred dollars, other lower-cost methods can be em-

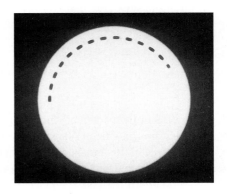

FIGURE 6-16
Image from manual spinning top on a single-phase x-ray generator.

ployed. One of the oldest methods is the spinning top test. This uses a spinning top consisting of a metal disk with a hole or slit cut into the outside edge. If evaluating a single-phase x-ray unit, a manual spinning top can be used (Figure 6-15). Single-phase generators emit x-rays in pulses, therefore each pulse creates a dot on the radiograph made of the spinning top (Figure 6-16). The number of dots appearing on this radiograph is then compared with the number that should appear, using the particular time station on the control panel that is determined by the following equations:
Half-wave rectified:

$$\text{Correct number of dots} = \text{Exposure time (seconds)} \times 60$$

Full-wave rectified:

$$\text{Correct number of dots} = \text{Exposure time (seconds)} \times 120$$

Exposures should be made at 1/10, 1/20, 1/30, and 1/40 of a second for single-phase equipment.

For three-phase and high-frequency generators, x-ray production is constant, so a solid line or arc will appear instead of a series of dots. For this reason, a manual spinning top cannot be used, and a synchronous or motor-driven spinning top is used instead (Figure 6-17). The motor rotates at a constant speed of one revolution per second, so that at the end of 1 second, a 360-degree circle is made. When placed on a cassette and exposed, this device creates an arc on the processed film that will be some fraction of 360 degrees at exposure times less than 1 second. The arc size on the image is measured using a protractor (Figure 6-18) and then compared with the ideal arc size calculated with the following equation:

$$\text{Correct arc size} = \text{Exposure time (seconds)} \times 360$$

At least four different time stations should be tested for three-phase equipment.

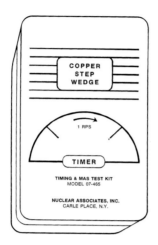

FIGURE 6-17

Synchronous spinning top. (Courtesy Nuclear Associates, Inc., Carle Place, N.Y.)

A

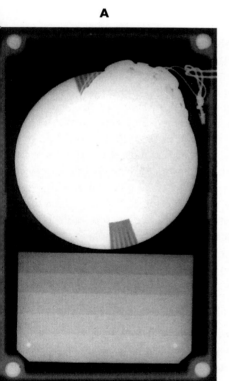

B

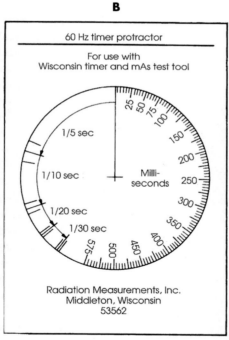

C

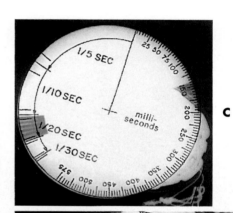

D

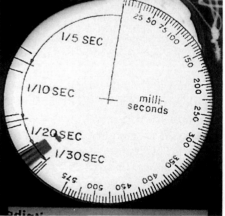

FIGURE 6-18

A, Radiograph produced at 200 mA and 1/20-second exposure. B, RMI protractor template. C, Radiograph A with template showing acceptable results for a 1/20-second exposure. D, Radiograph produced at 300 mA and 1/30-second showing unacceptable results. (From Ballinger PW: *Merrill's atlas of radiographic positions and radiologic procedures,* ed 8, St Louis, 1995, Mosby.)

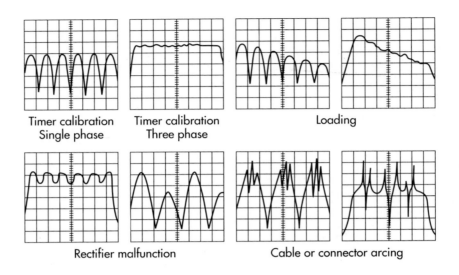

Timer calibration   Timer calibration   Loading
Single phase   Three phase

Rectifier malfunction   Cable or connector arcing

FIGURE 6-19
Voltage waveforms indicating various conditions within the x-ray generator.

FIGURE 6-20
Output detector for obtaining voltage waveforms. (Courtesy Nuclear Associates, Carle Place, N.Y.)

Many of the newer high-frequency units come equipped with mAs timers instead of separate mA and time stations. Because the exposure time is regulated by the internal microprocessor circuitry, the actual time will not be known. This means that the digital timer or spinning top test will not be of use. Instead, a digital mAs meter must be used. These devices have electrical probes that must be attached to the circuitry of the unit to obtain a reading. Only a person with adequate training on the use of these devices should attempt to access the circuitry.

Another option to determine timer accuracy is the use of an oscilloscope to display the voltage waveform, which is discussed in the next section.

Voltage Waveform

As discussed previously, each type of x-ray generator creates a distinctive voltage waveform. If the waveform could

be displayed on an oscilloscope screen during x-ray production, considerable information could be obtained concerning timer accuracy, rectifier malfunctions, loading characteristics, contactor or switching problems, and high-voltage cable or connector arcing (Figure 6-19), because these variables affect the size or shape of the waveform. The oscilloscope can be hooked up electronically to specific areas of the x-ray generator (which should be performed only by personnel with extensive electronics background, such as physicists, biomedical engineers, or service engineers) or it can be attached to a commercially available x-ray output detector (Figure 6-20). This detector is placed in the x-ray beam, and the output cable is connected to the oscilloscope input. The display is then analyzed for potential problems. This test should be performed upon acceptance and then annually or after x-ray generator service.

mA and Exposure Time Linearity and Reciprocity

The mA selector in an x-ray generator is used to regulate the x-ray tube filament temperature, which, along with the exposure time, ultimately determines the quantity of x-rays in the x-ray beam. Therefore the accuracy of the mA selected is equally important to the accuracy of the exposure timer. One method of testing mA accuracy is to make a 1-second exposure while watching the mAs meter on the control panel. A better method is to determine the reciprocity and linearity.

Reciprocity refers to the same mAs being selected but with different combinations of mA and exposure time. The radiation output should be the same as long as the kVp is kept constant. For example, an exposure of 70 kVp, 50 mA at 1 second should produce the same amount of radiation as an exposure of 70 kVp, 100 mA at ½ second, because both yield 50 mAs. ● *Any variation in reciprocity must be ± 10%.*

Procedure

1. Place a dosimeter on the x-ray tabletop on top of a lead apron placed at a distance of 40 inches from the focal spot.

2. Make three to five exposures at 80 kVp and 20 mAs. Each exposure should be at a different mA and time combination.

3. Record the dosimeter readings from each exposure and then divide each by 20 mAs to yield the mR/mAs, or μC kg^{-1}/mAs, value.

4. The minimum, maximum, and average of these three to five values are then used to determine the reciprocity variance with the following equation:

$$\text{Reciprocity variance} = \left(\frac{[\text{mR/mAs}_{max} - \text{mR/mAs}_{min}]}{\text{mR/mAs}_{average}}\right) \div 2$$

Adequate reciprocity exists when the variance is less than 0.1 (10%).

If a dosimeter is not available, exposures of an aluminum step-wedge or homogenous phantom made of aluminum or acrylic can be taken using the same factors given above. Optical density readings are then taken of the same area from each of the three to five images with a densitometer and compared. These readings should be within ± 10%.

Linearity means that sequential increases in mAs should produce the same sequential increase in the exposure measured. In other words, if factors of 70 kVp and 10 mAs were to produce 50 mR of exposure on a dosimeter, then factors of 70 kVp and 20 mAs on the same x-ray generator should produce an exposure of 100 mR if the mA station and timer are accurate. ● *Any variation must be within ± 10%.* This can be evaluated in a manner similar to reciprocity.

Procedure

1. Place the dosimeter on the x-ray table on a lead apron, just as in the reciprocity procedure.

2. Make four exposures using 70 kVp, 0.1 second (100 ms) and mA stations of 50, 100, 200, and 400. This yields mAs values of 5, 10, 20, and 40 (each exposure twice the previous one). These factors can be modified if the x-ray generator does not have these mA stations.

3. Record each reading, and determine the mR/mAs for each exposure, along with the maximum, minimum, and average mR/mAs values, which are then placed into the following equation:

$$\text{Linearity variance} = \left(\frac{[\text{mR/mAs}_{max} - \text{mR/mAs}_{min}]}{\text{mR/mAs}_{average}}\right) \div 2$$

Adequate linearity exists when the variance is less than 0.1 (10%). (This variance can also be determined without a dosimeter, using a step-wedge or homogenous phantom and a standard cassette. Expose the phantom using the above factors and compare the optical density readings of the same area to see if they are within 10%.) Problems in the x-ray generator, such as the mA selector, timer circuitry, or rectifier failure, can cause the linearity variance to exceed accepted limits.

Focal Spot Size

The area of the anode that is bombarded by projectile electrons is called the *focal spot*. Because these projectile electrons lose their kinetic energy at this point, this is also the source of x-rays. This area can be viewed from two perspectives: the actual rectangular surface on the target where electrons strike, called the **actual focal spot**, and the actual focal spot viewed from the perspective of the image receptor, called the **effective** (apparent or projected) **focal spot**. The effective focal spot always appears smaller than the actual focal spot because of the angle of the **line focus principle** (Figure 6-21). This effect is the result of the angle of the anode surface (the smaller the anode angle, the smaller the effective focal spot size). The effective focal spot size has a significant impact on the recorded detail of a radiographic image, because this value decreases as the focal spot size increases. Therefore focal spot size should remain relatively constant over the life of the x-ray tube. However, focal spot size can increase with age and use and with increases in the mA station selected. This phenomena is known as **focal spot blooming**. To evaluate the degree of focal spot blooming, several performance tests can be used.

Pinhole Camera. As shown in Figure 6-22, a pinhole camera is made up of a plate of gold platinum alloy with a tiny hole of a specified shape and size cut into its center. A

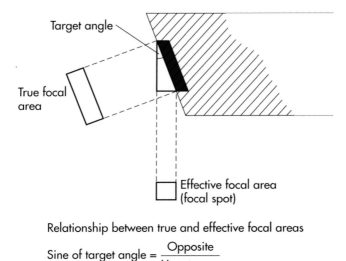

FIGURE 6-21
Line focus principle.

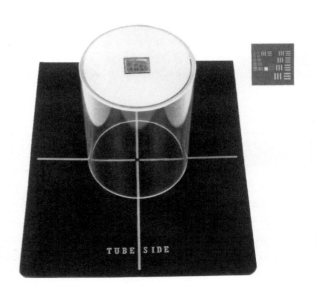

FIGURE 6-23
Image from the focal spot test tool. (Courtesy Nuclear Associates, Carle Place, N.Y.)

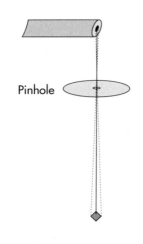

FIGURE 6-22
Concept of the pinhole camera.

0.03-mm hole is used for measuring focal spots smaller than 1 mm. A 0.075-mm hole is used for focal spot sizes from 1 to 2.5 mm, and a 0.1 mm hole is used for focal spot sizes greater than 2.5 mm. When placed on a stand over an image receptor (preferably a fine-grain film placed in a non-screen holder or an extremity cassette) and then exposed, an image of the focal spot is projected on the film and can be measured with a ruler or micrometer after processing. This can then be compared with the stated, or nominal, focal spot size that is supplied by the x-ray tube manufacturer.

Procedure

1. Place the pinhole camera stand on the x-ray tabletop and align with the central ray and image receptor.

2. Adjust the pinhole-to-image receptor distance and SID to obtain the proper enlargement factor. For focal spots less than 2.5 mm, an enlargement factor of 2 should be selected. This means that the pinhole-to-image receptor distance should be 60 cm, and the x-ray source-to-pinhole distance should be 30 cm. For focal spots larger than 2.5 mm, the enlargement factor should be 1. This is obtained by using a source-to-pinhole distance of 40 cm and a pinhole-to-image receptor distance of 40 cm.

3. Expose the image receptor to 75 kVp and 50 mAs (100 mAs if a non-screen image receptor is used). This should yield an optical density of between 0.8 and 1.2 on the resulting image.

4. Measure the pinhole image on the processed film with a ruler or calipers in both the X and Y axis (with the long axis of the x-ray table and transverse to the long axis of the x-ray table).

5. Divide the measurements by the enlargement factor obtained in step 2 to obtain the dimensions of the focal spot.

Focal Spot Test Tool. As shown in Figure 6-23, an image of this test tool is obtained and the resulting image is

Table 6-2   Accompany Focal Spot Test Tool

Smallest group resolved	1 p/mm of group	Dimension of effective focal spot
1	0.84	4.3 mm
2	1.00	3.7 mm
3	1.19	3.1 mm
4	1.41	2.6 mm
5	1.68	2.2 mm
6	2.00	1.8 mm
7	2.38	1.5 mm
8	2.83	1.3 mm
9	3.36	1.1 mm
10	4.00	0.9 mm
11	4.76	0.8 mm
12	5.66	0.7 mm

The accuracy of this test is limited to 16% because the group sizes change by steps of 16%.

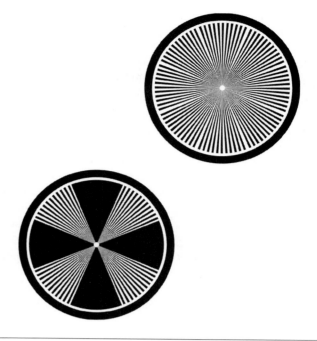

FIGURE 6-24
Star resolution patterns.

compared with a chart supplied by the manufacturer (Table 6-2).

Resolution Chart. Resolution charts are tools that project a chart pattern of various shapes or lines onto a film when radiographed, which can be used to estimate focal spot size. The two basic types are star and slit charts (Figure 6-24). When using a star pattern resolution chart, the pattern is imaged on a fine-grain film (preferably in a non-screen holder) and the image diameter (D_i) is measured from the resulting film (see Figure 6-18). When this is compared with the actual diameter of the star pattern (D_o), the magnification factor (M) can be calculated using the following equation:

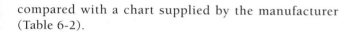

$$M = \frac{D_i}{D_o}$$

The diameter of the blur zone, or zero contrast band, in mm is measured from the image using a ruler (the diameter measured in both the X and Y dimensions can be used to obtain the exact dimensions of the focal spot). This is the diameter of the center of the pattern where the lines appear blurred. A smaller focal spot size should be able to image lines that are closer together (such as in the center of the star pattern), so the blur zone will be smaller in diameter. Once the diameter of the blur zone is ob-

Table 6-3   Values for Nominal Focal Spot Size Variation

Stated focal spot size	Percentage of focal spot blooming variation allowed
0.8 mm or less	50%
0.8 mm to 1.5 mm	40%
1.6 mm or greater	30%

tained, the following equation can be used to calculate the focal size:

$$\text{Focal spot size in mm} = \frac{\theta D}{(M - 1)}$$

where θ is the spoke angle of the star pattern in radians (radians = degrees $\times$ $\pi/180$) obtained from the star pattern. D is the diameter of the blur zone, and M is the magnification factor. Both the X and Y dimensions of the focal spot size should be calculated.

The focal spot size should be determined upon acceptance and then evaluated annually. The amount of focal spot blooming that is acceptable is determined by the National Electronics Manufacturers Association (NEMA). The values for nominal focal spot size variation are listed in Table 6-3.

For example, if a focal spot size is stated to be 0.5 mm by the manufacturer but measures 0.75 mm during an evaluation test, is it within the NEMA guidelines? The answer is yes. Because its stated size is 0.5 mm, it is allowed up to a 50% variation, and 50% of 0.5 mm is 0.25 mm. Therefore the maximum focal spot size would be 0.75 mm, which would be just within the variation allowed.

Beam Restriction System

The beam restriction system is responsible for regulating the size of the x-ray field area. It therefore plays a significant role in patient dosage (because it controls the amount of patient anatomy that is exposed to radiation) and image contrast (because an increase in the area of field increases the production of scattered radiation). Performance of this system should be evaluated upon acceptance and then every 6 months or whenever work is performed on the system. The factors to evaluate within the beam restriction system include light field-radiation field congruence, image receptor-radiation field alignment, accuracy of the *X-Y* scales, and illuminator bulb brightness.

Light Field–Radiation Field Congruence. The light field-radiation field congruence value measures how well the collimator regulates the field size and if the area illuminated by the positioning light and the area exposed by x-rays are the same. The collimator is made up of two sets of lead shutters that can be opened and closed, along with a small light bulb mounted on the outer edge and a mirror mounted in the center to reflect the light from the bulb through the shutter opening (Figure 6-25). Over time, this mirror may shift or the

mechanism that moves the shutters can malfunction, causing improper performance. This can lead to higher patient dosage and repeat images. ⬤ *The light field and radiation field must be congruent to within ±2% of the source-image-distance (SID). Evaluation can be performed using either a collimator test tool* (Figure 6-26) *using the manufacturer's instructions or the eight penny (or nine penny) test* (Figure 6-27).

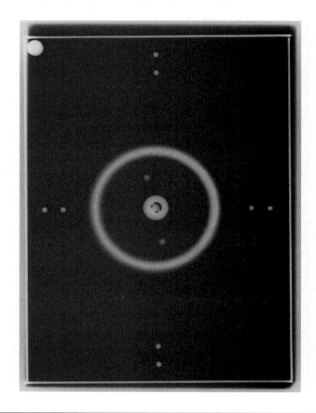

FIGURE 6-26
Image obtained with a collimator test tool showing collimator is within accepted limits.

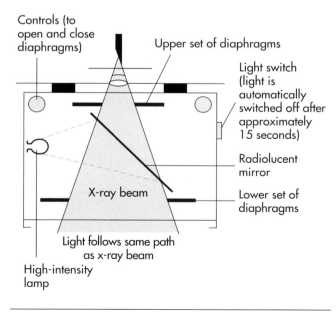

FIGURE 6-25
Schematic of variable aperture collimator.

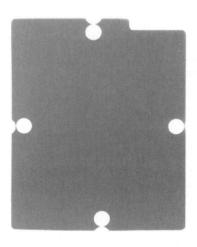

FIGURE 6-27
Image obtained with the eight penny test.

The collimator test tool requires a cassette. The tool is placed on the cassette, and the field size is adjusted with the collimator and then exposed to technical factors specified by the manufacturer. The resulting image is analyzed visually to determine the light field-radiation field congruence.

The eight penny test involves laying eight pennies on a 10- × 12-inch (25 × 35 cm) cassette placed on a tabletop but collimated to an 8- × 10-inch field size at a 40-inch SID. Four of the pennies are placed on the inside edge of the light field at the center of each dimension, and the other four are placed on the outside edge in contact with the inner pennies, meeting at the edge of the light field. When a radiograph is made and the film processed, the collimation line of the x-ray field should also fall in between the pairs of pennies or at least within the shadow of the pennies, because the diameter of a penny is 0.8 inches (which is exactly 2% of 40 inches).

Image Receptor–Radiation Field Alignment. The image receptor-radiation field alignment value must be determined for x-ray units equipped with positive beam limitation (PBL) or automatic collimation. These systems have sensors in the Bucky tray that detect the size of the image receptor and then automatically adjust the collimator shutters to match. Malfunctions in this system can occur with age and use and can be evaluated with the eight penny test or collimator test tool mentioned previously. ● *Variation between the x-ray field and image receptor size must be within ±3% of the SID.* An override switch should be in place to disconnect the PBL in case of malfunction. ● *The sum of the x-ray field and image receptor misalignment should be no more than ±4% of the SID used in taking the measurement.*

Accuracy of the X-Y Scales. Modern collimators have two knobs or dials on the front that allow the radiographer to control the x-ray field size during manual collimation. These knobs also have some type of indicator that shows the size of the X and Y dimensions of the x-ray field. ● *The indicated size on the collimator of the X and Y dimensions and the actual field size measured at the film must correspond to within ±2% of the SID.* This can be tested using a collimator test tool or by taking a 14- × 17-inch (36 cm × 45 cm) cassette and placing it at 40-inches SID tabletop.

Procedure

1. Set the *X-Y* control knobs on the collimator to a 10- × 12-inch field size (25 × 33 cm) and expose.

2. Process the film and use a ruler to measure the black rectangle in the center of the image. The dimensions should be within 0.8 inch of 10 × 12 inches.

Illuminator Bulb Brightness. The beam restriction system must be equipped with a positioning light and mirror, according to the Center for Devices and Radiological Health (CDRH). The light bulb to center of mirror distance should equal the distance from the x-ray tube focal spot to the center of the mirror. ● *The illumination of the light source must be at least 15 ft-c (160 lux) when measured at a 100-cm (40 inch) distance.* A photometer such as the one used in Chapter 2 for evaluation of view box brightness should be used. Measurements should be made in the approximate center of each quadrant of the light field. An illuminator bulb with an inadequate level of brightness may lead to positioning errors and subsequent repeat images. This problem is usually corrected by replacing the light bulb and/or cleaning the mirror inside of the collimator.

Beam Alignment

The x-ray beam must be mounted properly in its metal housing and aligned to the Bucky tray. This alignment should be evaluated upon acceptance and then annually with a beam alignment test tool (Figure 6-28). Items to evaluate in this category include perpendicularity and x-ray beam–Bucky tray alignment.

Perpendicularity. ● *The x-ray tube must be mounted in its housing so that the x-ray beam is within 1 degree of perpendicular.* If not, the image will be distorted. Rough handling of the housing during x-ray examinations could cause the x-ray tube to shift slightly. An image of the test

FIGURE 6-28
Beam alignment tool.

tool is made, and then the alignment is determined according to the manufacturers instructions.

X-ray Beam–Bucky Tray Alignment or Central Ray Congruency. The center of the Bucky tray and the center of the x-ray beam must be aligned to avoid clipping important anatomy and to avoid grid cutoff. ● *X-ray beam-Bucky tray alignment must be within 1% of the SID.* The same beam alignment tool used to determine perpendicularity can also be used to evaluate this alignment. The tool consists of a plastic cylinder with a metal washer on top (Figure 6-29).

Procedure

1. With the x-ray tube centered using the centering detent lock, place a film in the Bucky tray and slide it into its proper place.

2. Position the test tool so that the metal washer is in the exact center of the x-ray field, using the crosshairs from the positioning light, and expose the film.

3. Process the film and visually analyze the resulting image. The image of the washer should be in the center of the film or within 0.4 inch (or approximately 1 cm) of the center. A service engineer should be called if the alignment is off by more than this amount.

SID Indicator

All medical x-ray units must be equipped with an SID indicator, according to the CDRH, because the SID influences patient dose, optical density, recorded detail, and size distortion. ● *The indicator must be installed so that it is accurate to within ±2% of the SID.* This accuracy is determined using a simple tape measure or the triangular method and should be checked upon acceptance and then annually or when service is performed on the x-ray tube. When evaluating using the triangulation method use the following procedure.

Procedure

1. Place a radiopaque object (such as a metal plate about 2 inches long) at a distance from the focal spot mark on the x-ray tube housing.

2. Using a 40-inch SID, make an image of the object using a cassette.

3. Process the film and measure the size of the radiopaque object recorded in the image. These values are then placed into the following equation:

$$\frac{\text{Image size}}{\text{Object size}} = \frac{(\text{SID} + y)}{(\text{SOD} + y)}$$

Using similar triangles, the focal spot will be the distance (*y*) above the reference mark.

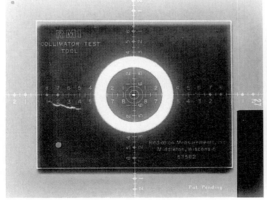
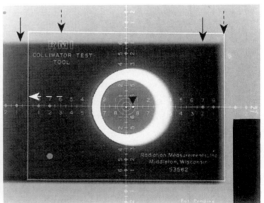

FIGURE 6-29

A, Acceptable beam perpendicularity and beam-light field alignment. **B,** Unacceptable beam perpendicularity and beam-light alignment. Radiation beam (*arrows*) does not agree with collimator light field (*broken arrows*). Perpendicularity is out of alignment. Note top head is shifted to the right (*arrowhead*). (From Ballinger PW: *Merrill's atlas of radiographic positions and radiologic procedures,* ed 8, St Louis, 1995, Mosby.)

Overload Protection

Most x-ray generators are equipped with an overload protection mechanism to prevent excessive temperatures inside the x-ray tube during a single exposure. ● *The overload protection mechanism should not permit an exposure that would exceed 80% of the tube capacity for a single exposure.* This exposure level can be determined by selecting a kVp and mAs combination that would exceed this 80% limit and then engaging the rotor button. This should cause a tube overload indicator light to appear on the control panel; some systems will not allow the rotor to engage in this situation. Should either of these fail to occur, call a service technician to repair the system. Do *not* engage the expose button, because serious x-ray tube damage could result if the overload protection system is malfunctioning. The overload protection mechanism should be evaluated upon acceptance and then annually or when service is performed on the x-ray generator.

X-ray Tube Heat Sensors

As mentioned above, most x-ray generators are equipped with overload protection circuits to prevent excessive tube heat in a single exposure. They generally do not protect against cumulative heat build-up that can occur when several exposures are made within a relatively short period. To guard against this accumulated heat, radiographers can rely on anode cooling charts or housing cooling charts supplied by the tube manufacturer. This is especially critical during fluoroscopy and angiography, in which considerable heat can be produced very quickly. Many newer units are equipped with x-ray tube heat sensors that provide an LED readout of the percentage of heat capacity remaining inside of the x-ray tube housing. ● *Heat sensors should provide a warning when anode heat reaches 75% of maximum.* These devices should be checked upon acceptance and then every 6 months. This involves taking several exposures at a known heat unit value and then comparing the total with the known maximum heat capacity of the x-ray tube provided by the manufacturer.

SUMMARY

Through visual inspections, environmental inspections, and performance testing, variation in the functioning of radiographic equipment can be kept to a minimum. This should increase department efficiency, lower the repeat rate, and reduce unnecessary exposure.

Review Questions

1. Which type of x-ray generator has the least amount of voltage ripple?
   a. single-phase, half-wave rectified
   b. single-phase, full-wave rectified
   c. three-phase, six-pulse
   d. three-phase, 12-pulse

2. A three-phase x-ray generator can operate at a maximum of 100 kVp and 500 mA at 100 ms. What is the kilowatt rating of this generator?
   a. 5 kW
   b. 35 kW
   c. 50 kW
   d. 500 kW

3. A single-phase generator can operate at the same maximum values as the unit in question 2. What is its kilowatt rating?
   a. 5 kW
   b. 35 kW
   c. 50 kW
   d. 500 kW

4. How large of an arc appears during a spinning top test of a three-phase x-ray generator at 50 ms?
   a. 18 degrees
   b. 20 degrees
   c. 36 degrees
   d. 90 degrees

5. A quality control program for radiographic equipment should include:
   1. visual inspection
   2. environmental inspection
   3. performance testing
   a. 1 and 2 only
   b. 2 and 3 only
   c. 1 and 3 only
   d. 1, 2, and 3

6. The minimum half value layer for x-ray units operating at 80 kVp is _____ mm of aluminum.
   a. 1.3
   b. 1.5
   c. 2.3
   d. 2.5

7. The maximum variability allowed for the reproducibility of exposure is ± _____ %.
   a. 2
   b. 5
   c. 10
   d. 20

8. Any variations between the stated kVp on the control panel and the measured kVp must be ± _____ %.
   a. 2
   b. 5
   c. 10
   d. 20

9. The variability allowed for timer accuracy in exposures less than 10 ms is ± _____ %.
   a. 2
   b. 5
   c. 10
   d. 20

10. The variability allowed for mA and time linearity is ± _____ %.
   a. 2
   b. 5
   c. 10
   d. 20

Student Experiment 6.1   Radiographic Unit Visual Check

PURPOSE

To ensure that the components in an x-ray room are present and functioning according to accepted parameters.

EQUIPMENT NEEDED

1. Checklist
2. Tape measure
3. Protractor
4. Photometer

PROCEDURE

Using a checklist, check the following items. Indicate a pass by a check mark and a fail by an F.

1. SID indicator: Check accuracy of SID using a tape measure. Remember to measure from the focal spot.
2. Perpendicularity: Stand at the end of the table and see if the tube and collimator are perpendicular to the tabletop.
3. Angulation indicator: Use a protractor to verify the accuracy of the indicator.
4. Locks: Check the function of all locks.
5. Field light: Determine whether the field light is functioning and whether it is of sufficient brightness using a photometer.
6. Bucky center light: Verify that the light is centered to the Bucky.
7. High-tension cables: Check all cables for frayed coverings, discolored insulation, tight bends, and unsupported areas.
8. Overhead tube crane movement: Move the crane system and make sure that it moves without obstruction.
9. Bucky lock: Ensure that the lock is functioning.
10. Cassette lock: Verify that the cassette lock holds the cassette firmly.
11. Measuring caliper: Check caliper with ruler to verify accuracy.
12. Handswitch placement: Should be mounted in fixed position behind barrier.
13. Panel switches, lights, and meters: Check for proper functioning and accuracy.
14. Technique charts: Ensure that technique charts are present.
15. Overload protection: Verify the function of the technique overload system by attempting to make an exposure at maximum kVp, mA, and time factors.

ANALYSIS

1. Comment on the information gathered from the checklist. Indicate any conditions that fail and describe how they would affect both radiation safety and radiographic quality.
2. Give any recommendations for improvement of the conditions in the radiographic room that were evaluated with the checklist.
3. Submit the checklist with the analysis.

 **Student Experiment 6.2**   Half-Value Layer Measurement and Filtration

PURPOSE

To verify that the radiographic unit has sufficient filtration to meet federal guidelines and guarantee patient safety. Because the half-value layer measures beam quality, a check of this quantity can also be accomplished.

EQUIPMENT NEEDED

1. Aluminum attenuators
2. X-ray generator
3. Pocket or digital dosimeter
4. Graph paper

PROCEDURE

Part 1 HVL Measurement

1. Center the x-ray tube to the table and set the SID at 40 inches tabletop. Place a sheet of lead vinyl on the table and set the dosimeter in the center. Collimate to an area just slightly larger than the dosimeter.
2. Take a series of exposures using 80 kVp, 200 mA, and 1 second. The aluminum attenuators can be placed on top of the dosimeter for each exposure. Record the readings below.

    0 mm _____ mR   5 mm _____ mR
    1 mm _____ mR   6 mm _____ mR
    2 mm _____ mR   7 mm _____ mR
    3 mm _____ mR   8 mm _____ mR
    4 mm _____ mR

Part 2 Filtration Check

1. Set the x-ray tube, SID, lead vinyl, and collimator exactly the same as in Part 1 on this experiment.
2. Make an exposure of the dosimeter using 80 kVp and 50 mAs. Record the reading obtained.
3. Place a 2.3-mm aluminum attenuator on top of the dosimeter and make a second exposure using the same factors as in step 2. Record the reading obtained.

ANALYSIS

Part 1 HVL Measurement

1. Using the graph paper provided, plot the dosimeter readings in mR on the y axis and the thickness of aluminum absorber on the x axis. Connect all of the points to form an attenuation curve.
2. Determine the HVL and compare to the CDRH recommendation of 2.3 mm Al.
3. Determine the second HVL from the graph and calculate the homogeneity coefficient using the following equation:

$$\frac{\text{First HVL}}{\text{Second HVL}}$$

4. Is the coefficient within acceptable limits (less than 1)? If not, what are the possible explanations? Which should be greater, the first or the second HVL? Why?
5. Submit the graph and sample calculations with the analysis.

Part 2 Filtration Check

1. Using the readings obtained in Part 2, determine if the filtration is sufficient.
2. What explanation can you give for filtration values that are not within the accepted guidelines?
3. What is the effect of filtration on x-ray quantity and quality?

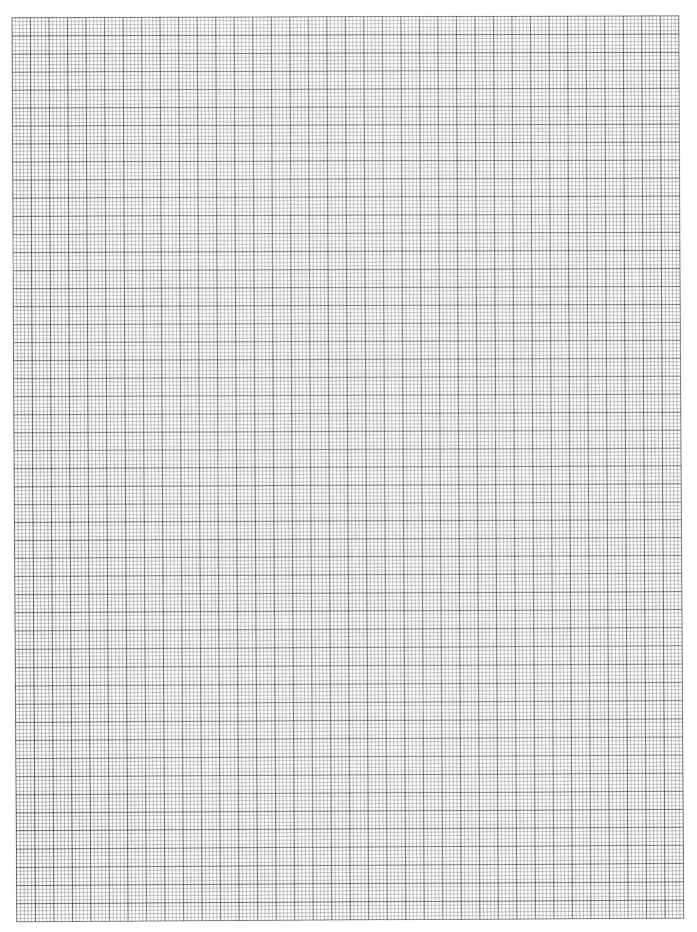

(FIGURE 6-30)

PURPOSE

To check the mA and time station linearity of an x-ray generator. With the kVp constant and either the mA or time altered in even multiples ($2\times$, $4\times$, etc.), the output of radiation (measured in mR) should experience the same multiple change to within $\pm10\%$ to the variable of mA or time being tested.

EQUIPMENT NEEDED

1. X-ray generator
2. Digital dosimeter
3. Sheet of lead vinyl

PROCEDURE

Part 1 Timer Linearity

1. Place the x-ray tube at 40 inches SID tabletop.
2. Place the sheet of lead vinyl on the tabletop, directly under the x-ray tube.
3. A series of four exposures at 70 kVp will be made of the dosimeter (remember to reset to zero each time) using the factors listed below. Complete the rest of the chart with the dosimeter results.

mA	Sec	mAs	mR	mR/mAs
100	0.4	40	—	—
100	0.2	20	—	—
100	0.1	10	—	—
100	0.05	5	—	—
—	—	—	Average	—

Part 2 mA Linearity

1. Keep the x-ray tube, lead vinyl sheet, and kVp exactly the same as in Part 1.
2. Make a series of four exposures using the factors listed below. Complete the chart with the dosimeter results.

mA	Sec	mAs	mR	mR/mAs
50	0.2	10	—	—
100	0.2	20	—	—
200	0.2	40	—	—
400	0.2	80	—	—
—	—	—	Average	—

ANALYSIS

Part 1 Timer Linearity

1. Using the information from the chart in Part 1, determine the timer linearity variance by using the following formula:

$$\text{Variance} = \frac{[(\text{mR/mAs}_{max}) - (\text{mR/mAs}_{min}) \div 2]}{\text{mR/mAs}_{average}}$$

2. Is your variance within accepted limits (less than 0.1)? Give some possible explanations for a variance that is not within accepted limits.

PART 2 mA Linearity

1. Using the information from the chart in Part 2, determine the mA linearity variance by using the same equation from Part 1.
2. Is the variance within accepted limits (less than 0.1)? Give some possible explanations for a variance that is not within accepted limits.
3. Discuss the importance of proper mA and time linearity for an x-ray generator.

Student Experiment 6.4   Reproducibility, mAs Reciprocity, and mR/mAs

PURPOSE

To ensure that mAs reciprocity (mAs and kVp are held constant using different combinations of mA and time) and reproducibility (mA, time and kVp are kept constant) are within acceptable limits.

EQUIPMENT NEEDED

1. X-ray generator
2. Pocket or digital dosimeter
3. Lead vinyl

PROCEDURE

Part 1 mAs Reciprocity

1. Set the x-ray tube for 40 inches SID tabletop.
2. Place a sheet of lead vinyl in the center of the x-ray table and set the detector in the center.
3. Make a series of four exposures at 80 kVp using the factors listed below. Complete the rest of the chart using the dosimeter results.

mA	Sec	mAs	mR	mR/mAs
50	0.4	20	—	—
100	0.2	20	—	—
200	0.1	20	—	—
400	0.05	20	—	—
—	—	—	Average	—

Part 2 Reproducibility

1. Keep the x-ray tube and lead vinyl the same as in Part 1.
2. Make five separate exposures of the dosimeter and record each reading in the chart. The exposure factors to use are 100 mA, 0.1 sec, and 80 kVp.

Exposure 1	mR
Exposure 2	mR
Exposure 3	mR
Exposure 4	mR
Exposure 5	mR

ANALYSIS

Part 1 mAs Reciprocity

1. Using the information from the chart in Part 1, determine the reciprocity variance using the following equation:

$$\text{Variance} = \frac{[(\text{mR/mAs}_{max}) - (\text{mR/mAs}_{min}) \div 2]}{\text{mR/mAs}_{average}}$$

2. Is the variance within accepted limits (less than 0.10)? Give some possible explanations for variance that is not within accepted limits.
3. If the mAs reciprocity variance is outside accepted limits, what effect could this have on radiographic quality and patient dose?

Continued

Student Experiment 6.4   Reproducibility, mAs Reciprocity, and mR/mAs—cont'd

Part 2 Reproducibility

1. Using the information from the chart in Part 2, determine the reproducibility variance using the following equation:

$$\frac{(mR/mAs_{max} - mR/mAs_{min})}{(mR/mAs_{max} + mR/mAs_{min})} = VARIANCE$$

2. Is the variance within accepted limits (less than 0.05)? Give some possible explanations for a variance that is not within accepted limits.
3. If the reproducibility variance is not within accepted limits, what effect could this have on radiographic quality and patient dose?

Student Experiment 6.5   Collimation and Beam Alignment

PURPOSE

To ensure that the x-ray field and the light field are congruent and that the collimation is within accepted limits.

EQUIPMENT NEEDED

1. Beam alignment tool
2. Collimator test tool
3. 10- × 12-inch cassette

PROCEDURE

1. Place the cassette on the tabletop and adjust the SID to 40 inches.
2. Place the tools in the proper position on the cassette and make an exposure at 60 kVp and 3 mAs. Process the film.
3. Adjust the SID to 40-inches Bucky and place the test cassette in the Bucky. Place the alignment tools carefully in the center of the table over the cassette. Make another exposure at 60 kVp and 15 mAs and process the film.

ANALYSIS

1. On the tabletop film, compare the placement of the steel ball in relation to the metal washer on the image. If the image of the steel ball appears within the center of the washer, the central ray is within 0.5 degrees of perpendicular. If it is superimposed on top of the washer, it is about 1.5 degrees from perpendicular. Should it appear outside the shadow of the washer, it is greater than 3 degrees out of alignment.
2. Compare the alignment of both the tabletop and Bucky films. Were their images within 1 degree of perpendicular according to CDRH recommendations? If not, approximately how far out of alignment is the x-ray tube?
3. Were the collimators aligned to within 2% of the SID according to CDRH recommendations? If not, how far out of alignment are they?
4. Discuss the importance of proper alignment of both the x-ray tube and collimators in terms of image quality and patient exposure.

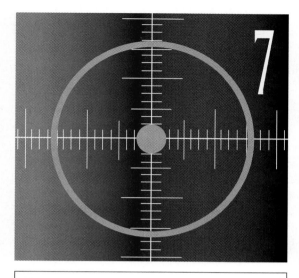

7 Radiographic Ancillary Equipment

Objectives

At the completion of this chapter the reader will be able to do the following:

- List the main components of an AEC system
- Perform quality control testing of various AEC parameters
- Describe the quality control parameters for conventional tomographic systems
- Explain the factors affecting screen speed
- Describe the importance of spectral matching of intensifying screens and film
- Describe the different types of screen resolution
- Discuss the importance of grid uniformity and alignment on image quality
- Explain the quality control tests performed on mobile equipment

Key Terms

automatic exposure control
comparator
contrast resolution
edge spread function
grid latitude
homogenous phantom
intensification factor
ion chamber
Law of Reciprocity
line spread function
linear tomography
mobile x-ray generator
modulation transfer function
objective plane
photodetector
pluridirectional tomography
point spread function
portable x-ray generator
quantum mottle
relative speed
reproducibility
screen speed
sensor
solid-state detector
spatial resolution
spectral matching

The creation of diagnostic radiographs in a modern radiology department requires more than just an x-ray generator, x-ray tube, and x-ray table. Several types of ancillary equipment are also involved in the imaging chain to help create or enhance the radiographic image, regulate x-ray production, and protect the patient and radiographer. These include automatic exposure control systems, tomographic systems, film/screen image receptors, grids, and mobile X-ray systems. Because variation in this equipment can occur during use, quality control protocols must be in place to minimize repeat examinations.

AUTOMATIC EXPOSURE CONTROL SYSTEMS

The **automatic exposure control** (AEC) system has been in use in radiography since the 1960s and functions to regulate the exposure time. These systems involve some type of radiation detection device that measures the quantity of x-rays received by the patient or image receptor. When this exposure reaches a level corresponding to a predetermined value, the system causes the x-ray generator to terminate the exposure. This value is set by a service engineer, based on the image receptor system used in the department. There are two main parts to an automatic exposure control system, the sensor and the comparator.

Sensor

The **sensor** is a radiation detector that monitors the radiation exposure at or near the patient and produces a corresponding electric current that is proportional to the quantity of x-rays detected. Sensors are sometimes referred to as *cells* or *chambers*. Normally, three sensors are available for use by the radiographer, one in the midline and one on either side of the midline (Figure 7-1). Units are also available with only one or two sensors. Three different types of radiation detectors have been used in AEC systems: photodetectors, ion chambers, and solid-state detectors.

Photodetectors

The **photodetector**, or photocell, uses a scintillation crystal (usually sodium iodide) coupled with a photomultiplier tube (Figure 7-2). When radiation interacts with the crystal, light is created, which enters the photomultiplier tube. This light then releases electrons through the process of photoemission. These electrons multiply in number and form an electric current that is proportional to the original amount of x-rays. The photodetector was the original detector used as a sensor and was marketed under the name "phototimer." This name is still commonly used to describe AEC systems, even though the photodetector is seldom used in modern systems. These sensors are placed behind the image receptor to measure the exposure, because they are not radiolucent. Care must be taken with these systems so that the lead in the back of the cassettes (normally present to control backscatter) is not excessive.

Ion Chambers

The **ion chamber** (discussed in Chapter 6) consists of a gas-filled chamber. It is smaller than a photocell and can be made of a radiolucent material. This allows it to be placed between the grid and the front of the image receptor, so that any type of cassette design can be used. This is the most common type of sensor found in current AEC systems. It is often marketed under the name "ionomat."

Solid-State Detectors

The **solid-state detector** uses a small silicon or germanium crystal, which is more sensitive but also more expensive than photocells or ion chambers. The crystals are radiolucent and can be placed between the grid and image receptor. The solid-state detector is often marketed under the name "autotimer."

Comparator

The **comparator** is an electronic circuit that receives the current signal sent by the sensor. An internal capacitor stores a voltage as long as this current is flowing. When the

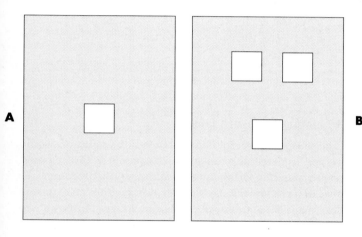

A   B

FIGURE 7-1
Sensor cell location for AEC systems. A, Single cell option. B, Three-sensor option.

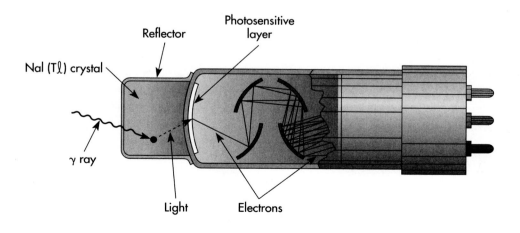

FIGURE 7-2
Schematic for photomultiplier tube and scintillation crystal.

voltage (V) in the capacitor becomes the same as a preset reference voltage (V_r), a switch is opened, which terminates the exposure. Changing the density selector switch changes this reference voltage and therefore the quantity of x-rays produced by the generator. Each step on the density selector should change the radiation exposure by 25% to 30%. Typical selector settings are shown in Figure 7-3. The radiographer must also select the proper chamber, kVp, and mA; verify that the patient and x-ray tube are properly positioned; and verify backup time in case of system failure.

AEC Testing

It is becoming more common for radiographic examinations to be performed using AEC systems. It is estimated that over 60% of all hospital radiology departments have radiographic equipment that uses AEC systems or anatomically programmed units (which contain a microprocessor circuit with preprogrammed technical factors). The advantage of AEC is that it delivers consistent optical density on radiographs over a wide range of patient thickness and kVp settings. Proper system performance should therefore be monitored through quality control procedures upon acceptance and then semiannually or whenever work is performed on the system. Items that should be monitored include backup, or maximum exposure time and minimum exposure time.

Backup, or Maximum Exposure, Time

Because the exposure is controlled by the sensor and comparator combination instead of a conventional timer, care must be taken to avoid excessive patient exposure and heat in the x-ray tube in the case of system failure or when an extremely large patient is being studied. This is accomplished by setting a backup timer on the control unit. ● *The backup timer should terminate the exposure within 6 seconds or 600 mAs, whichever comes first.* This can be checked using the following procedure.

Procedure

1. Place a lead apron over the sensor cells and make an exposure at 70 kVp and 100 mA.

2. Watch the mAs meter on the control panel, in addition to using a stopwatch, to see if the backup system terminates the exposure within the specified parameters. If not, release the expose button so the x-ray tube is not damaged.

Minimum Exposure Time

The sensor and comparator combination requires a certain period to detect the radiation, compare it with the preset value, and then terminate the exposure (usually around 10 ms). If a particular x-ray examination requires an exposure less than this amount, the AEC system will not be able to respond in time and the resulting image will be overexposed. For this reason, distal extremity radiographs are generally not performed using AEC. The manufacturer's literature should be checked as to the minimum exposure time available, and then the technologists should be instructed as to which radiographic examinations and kVp and mA combinations can and cannot be used with AEC.

AEC Quality Control

Consistency of Exposure with Varying mA

The AEC system should be able to adjust the exposure time and maintain optical density with any changes in mA on the control panel. ● *Any variation cannot exceed ±10%.* To evaluate this parameter, use the following procedure.

Procedure

1. Obtain a **homogenous phantom** made of Plexiglas or Lucite acrylic of at least 10 cm in thickness.

2. Make a series of four radiographs of the phantom on a 10- × 12-inch (25 × 30 cm) cassette using 70 kVp, 40-

	Density setting
Weak, very young Very old, debilitated	−2
Thin Easy to penetrate	−1
Average Normal build	0/Neutral
Muscular	+1/+2

FIGURE 7-3
AEC density selector settings.

inch SID Bucky, and normal density setting, with each at a different mA station.

3. Process each film and use a densitometer to measure the optical density of the center of each image. ● *The optical density values should measure the same or be within an optical density of ±0.2.* If not, inconsistent optical density in the resulting radiographs can occur, leading to repeat exposures. This is usually the result of a malfunctioning comparator.

Consistency of Exposure with Varying kVp

The AEC system should be able to adjust the exposure time and maintain optical density with any changes in kVp on the control panel. This can be evaluated using the same homogenous phantom mentioned earlier.

Procedure

1. Make four exposures of the phantom on a 10- × 12-inch cassette, using 100 mA, normal density setting, and 40-inch SID Bucky and using kVp values of 60, 70, 80, and 90.

2. Process the four films and take density readings of the center of each image. ● *The optical density values should measure the same or be within an optical density of ±0.2.*

Consistency of Exposure with Varying Part Thickness

The AEC system should be able to adjust the exposure time and maintain optical density with any changes in part thickness. System evaluation will again employ a homogenous phantom.

Procedure

1. Make three exposures on separate 10- × 12-inch cassettes at 70 kVp, 100 mA, normal density setting, and 40-inch SID Bucky. Make each exposure with a phantom thickness of 10 cm, 20 cm, and 30 cm.

2. Process each film and take density readings of the center. ● *The optical density values should measure the same or be within an optical density of ±0.2.*

Consistency of Exposure with Varying Field Sizes

AEC systems should also be able to compensate for changes in the area of field, provided the chamber remains in the field. Radiographs of the homogenous phantom can also be used to evaluate this parameter.

Procedure

1. Make a series of three exposures of the phantom, using factors of 70 kVp, 100 mA, normal density settings, and 40-inch SID.

2. Each exposure is made using a different field size of 6- × 6-inch, 10- × 10-inch, and 14- × 14-inch, with an appropriate cassette size. Be sure that the x-ray beam is centered to the sensor chamber.

3. Process the films and record the optical density from the center of each. ● *The optical density values should measure the same or be within an optical density of ±0.1.*

Consistency of Sensor Chambers

Most AEC systems use a configuration of three chambers. Each chamber should provide the same exposure or exposure time as the other two. For evaluation use the following procedure.

Procedure

1. Make a series of three radiographs of the homogenous phantom, each using a different chamber selection. Be sure that the phantom is placed over the appropriate chamber. Use exposure factors of 70 kVp, 100 mA, normal density setting, and 40-inch SID Bucky.

2. Process the films and compare the density readings from the center of each image. ● *The optical density values should measure the same or be within an optical density of ±0.2.*

Reproducibility

Exposures made at the same kVp and mA stations of the same phantom thickness should produce the same optical density on the resulting image. This is referred to as **reproducibility.**

Procedure

1. Make three exposures of the homogenous phantom using 80 kVp, 200 mA, normal density setting, 10- × 12-inch cassette size, and 40-inch SID Bucky.

2. Process each radiograph and compare the optical density readings taken from the center of each image. ● *The readings should be within an optical density of ±0.10 of each other.*

An alternative method of evaluating reproducibility is to make the same three exposures but do not use a cassette to record an image. Instead, place a radiation detector and homogenous phantom over the appropriate sensor chamber and record the readings obtained in each exposure. For valid results be sure that the radiation detector is radiolucent. The reproducibility variance can then be calculated using the equation found in Chapter 6. ● *The reproducibility variance must be within ±0.05 (5%).*

Density Control Function

The density selector switch should allow for changes in radiation exposure of 25% to 30% for each increment. The accuracy of this system can be evaluated by the following procedure.

Procedure

1. Make a series of five radiographs of the homogenous phantom using 70 kVp, 100 mA, and 40-inch SID Bucky and at the density selector settings of normal (0/neutral), +1, +2, −1, and −2 (these settings will vary according to manufacturer). Be sure to mark each image with a lead number or some other identifier.

2. Take density readings from the center of each of the processed films and compare. Each should increase in optical density by a value of 0.2 to 0.25, from the lowest to the highest density setting (−2 to +2).

Reciprocity Law Failure

The **Law of Reciprocity** states that the same amount of radiation should be created at any mAs value, regardless of the mA/time combination used. Therefore the optical density of any resulting image should also be the same. Film/Screen image receptor systems can experience reciprocity failure at very short exposure time values (less than 10 ms) and very long exposure time values (greater than 1 second).

- Phantom images of either a homogenous phantom or an anthropomorphic (lifelike) phantom should be made at 70 kVp, normal density setting, 40-inch SID Bucky, and the lowest mA station possible on the control panel (so that a long exposure time is made).
- Another image should be made using the highest mA station available (to yield a short exposure time).
- Optical density readings should be obtained from the center of each image and compared. If reciprocity failure exists, the optical density of the films will vary by more than a value of ±0.2.

CONVENTIONAL TOMOGRAPHIC SYSTEMS

Many radiographic units are equipped with a conventional tomographic system, which is used to image certain "slices" of the body while all other slices are blurred. This helps remove superimposition and improve the radiographic contrast in the area of interest. There are two basic types of conventional tomography, linear tomography and pluridirectional tomography.

In **linear** (sometimes called *rectilinear*) **tomography** the x-ray tube and image receptor move longitudinally in opposite directions during the exposure (Figure 7-4). The plane through the fulcrum or pivot point remains in focus, and structures above and below this plane are blurred by the motion of the tube and film. This plane is called the ob-

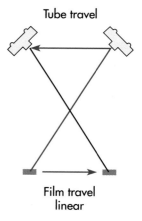

Tube travel

Film travel linear

FIGURE 7-4

Principle of linear tomography.

jective plane or tomographic section. The fulcrum level determines the level of the objective plane and is measured from the x-ray tabletop upward. For example, a 5-cm tomographic section means that the objective plane is 5 cm above the tabletop. The thickness of the tomographic section is determined by the tomographic angle. This is the angle between the central ray at the beginning of the exposure and at the end of the exposure. The greater the tomographic angle, the thinner the tomographic section because of the greater motion of the tube and film (Figure 7-5).

In **pluridirectional tomography** the x-ray tube and film move in a variety of patterns, such as circular, elliptical, hypocycloidal, and trispiral (Figure 7-6). These units produce sharper images than rectilinear units because of the increased motion of the tube and film. Because of this complexity of motion, pluridirectional units are usually dedicated to only tomographic imaging.

Because tomography involves motion of the x-ray tube and image receptor, considerable variation can occur in the performance of these systems with age and use. Mechanical instabilities can manifest in the tube system as a result of the large mass of the x-ray tube and housing. This can cause inconsistencies in the exposure and asymmetry in tube motion, leading to poor image quality. Therefore specific quality control tests should be performed upon acceptance and then annually. Specialized test tools and phantoms should be used for these evaluations (Figure 7-7). Factors to evaluate include section level, section thickness, level incrementation, exposure angle, spatial resolution, section uniformity and beam path, and patient exposure.

Section Level

⬤ *The level of the tomographic section (fulcrum level) that is indicated on the equipment and the actual level of the tomographic section that is imaged above the tabletop should be the same or within ±5 mm (some manufacturers suggest ±1 mm for pluridirectional units).* Evaluation is made using a test tool that has a series of lead numbers at various depths that are imaged on the film (Figure 7-8).

Section Thickness

The thickness of the tomographic section is dependent on the tomographic angle. Table 7-1 lists the section thickness at various tomographic angles. Evaluation is made using a special test tool according to manufacturer's instructions.

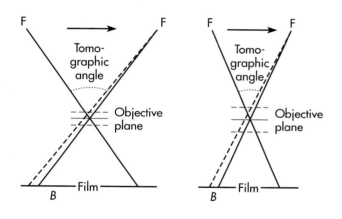

FIGURE 7-5

Effect of tomographic angle on section thickness.

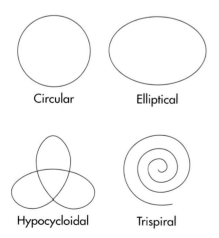

FIGURE 7-6

Pluridirectional tomographic patterns.

FIGURE 7-7

Tomographic test tool. (Courtesy Gammex/RMI, Middleton, Wis.)

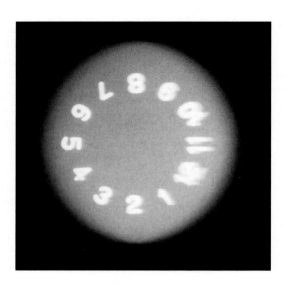

FIGURE 7-8

Image from tomographic test tool indicating the level of tomographic section.

Table 7-1   Section Thickness at Various Tomographic Angles

Tomographic angle	Section thickness (mm)
50 degrees	1.1
40 degrees	1.4
30 degrees	2.0
10 degrees	6.0
5 degrees	11.0
0 degrees	—

Level Incrementation

All tomographic units have some type of ruler or other device to indicate the level of the tomographic section. ● *A ruler should be constructed so that changing from one tomographic section to the next is accurate to within ±2 mm.* Evaluation can be accomplished using the same test phantom and procedure used in section level determination.

Exposure Angle

The exposure angle determines the thickness of the tomographic section. ● *It is important that the value indicated on the equipment and the actual angle are the same or within ±5 degrees for units operating at angles greater than 30 degrees. For exposure angles less than 30 degrees, the variation is ±2 degrees.* Accurate measurement of this vari-

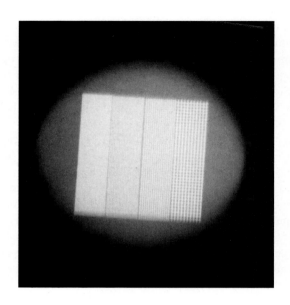

FIGURE 7-9

Image from tomographic test tool indicating the resolution pattern.

able is difficult and is best accomplished by evaluating the section thickness with the appropriate phantom. Variations in section thickness are usually the result of improper exposure angles.

Spatial Resolution

The structures within the tomographic section must be demonstrated with sufficient spatial resolution to make an accurate diagnosis possible. Figure 7-9 shows an image of a tomographic resolution test tool with wire mesh patterns of 20 holes/inch (0.8 holes/mm), 30 holes/inch (1.2 holes/ mm), 40 holes/inch (1.6 holes/mm), and 50 holes/inch (2.0 holes/mm). Most tomographic units should be able to resolve at least a 40 hole/inch mesh screen pattern. Variations in resolution usually are due to asymmetry in tube motion.

Section Uniformity and Beam Path

The amount of radiation emitted should be consistent throughout the tomographic exposure, so that the optical density of the image is uniform. This can be evaluated using a test tool consisting of a lead aperture (Figure 7-10). When an exposure is made on a linear tomographic unit, a thin line should appear on the resulting image (Figure 7-11). Optical density readings should be taken throughout the line and compared. ● *Any variation should be within an optical density value of ±0.3.* This same device also can be used for evaluation of beam path. Any asymmetry in motion or inconsistencies in the exposure could alter the nor-

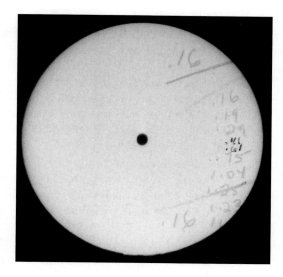

FIGURE 7-10

Lead aperture of tomographic test tool.

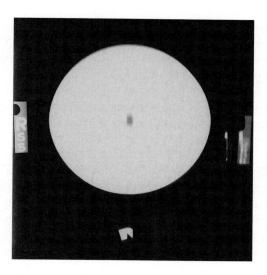

FIGURE 7-11

Image of lead aperture with linear tomography.

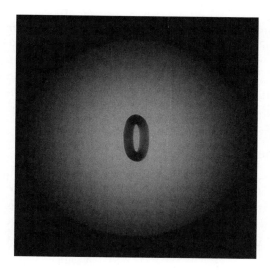

FIGURE 7-12

Image of lead aperture with elliptical motion. (Courtesy DuPage Hospital, Winfield, Ill.).

mal shape of the beam path. Linear units should demonstrate a straight line, as in the image shown in Figure 7-11. Pluridirectional units should create images that are appropriate to the pattern selected. Figure 7-12 shows an image created with an elliptical pattern. ● *Path closure in pluridirectional units should be within ±10% of the path length.*

Patient Exposure

As the x-ray tube and film move in opposite directions during tomography, different patient thicknesses exist at vari-

ous points within the exposure. Therefore the mAs is greater during conventional tomography than with conventional radiography of the same view. The tomographic exposure should not exceed 2 times the nontomographic exposure for the same part. For example, if 50 mAs is required for an AP view of the kidneys, an AP tomographic cut of the same kidneys should be obtained at 100 mAs or less. For departments equipped with more than one tomographic unit, patient exposure should not vary by more than 20% if the units have comparable x-ray tubes and generators.

FILM/SCREEN IMAGE RECEPTORS

Most of the images recorded during conventional radiography are obtained with film/screen combination image receptors. Thomas Edison developed intensifying screens in 1896, and Michael Pupin first used a film/screen combination in radiography later that same year. The x-rays exiting the patient energize the phosphor crystals, resulting in the emission of light, called *luminescence.* This light is used to expose the film, creating 95% to 98% of the optical density, rather than x-ray interaction. This results in lower patient exposure, because only a relatively small number of x-rays are necessary for the screens to emit a relatively large quantity of light. Proper application of intensifying screens are necessary to create adequate images. Because considerable variation can occur with the use of screens, proper quality control protocols should be in place. Several intensifying screen variables are discussed below.

Intensifying Screen Speed

Intensifying **screen speed** refers to the amount of light emitted by the screen for a given amount of x-ray exposure. A screen that is designated as fast creates more light than a screen designated as slow when both are exposed to identical kVp and mAs factors. Screen speed can be measured by intensification factor, relative name, or speed value.

Intensification Factor

The exposure required to create a certain optical density without a screen (direct exposure) is divided by the exposure required with a screen to create the same optical density, which determines the **intensification factor.**

$$\text{Intensification factor} = \frac{\text{Exposure without screens}}{\text{Exposure with screens}}$$

For example, if 100 mAs creates an optical density of 1 on a direct exposure film and 5 mAs creates the same value using a film/screen combination, then that screen will have an intensification factor of 20. The larger this value, the faster the speed of the screen.

Relative Speed Value

Relative speed is the most common method of designating screen speed and is used for all screens using rare earth phosphors. A mathematic number that is a multiple of 100 is used, with a larger number designating a faster speed. When changing from one speed to another, a change in mAs is required to maintain optical density. This can be calculated by using the following equation:

$$\text{New mAs} = \frac{\text{Old mAs} \times \text{Old relative speed value}}{\text{New relative speed value}}$$

For example, if 10 mAs is used with a 100 speed screen, then 5 mAs are used with a 200 speed screen.

Name of Screen

Older, non–rare earth screens use specific names, such as *fast* or *slow,* to designate screen speed. A listing of these older names, along with their relative speed values is presented in Table 7-2.

Factors Affecting Screen Speed

Type of Phosphor Material. Many different phosphor materials have been used in screens since 1896. They are generally divided into two categories, rare earth and non–rare earth phosphors. The non–rare earth phosphors are the original type of screen material and emit light in the blue-violet portion of the color spectrum (see Chapter 2). Examples include calcium tungstate, barium strontium sulfite, and barium fluorochloride. The rare earth phosphors were developed in the early 1970s and are currently the most common type of intensifying screen material. The name *rare earth* comes from the fact that these materials have atomic numbers ranging from 57 through 71 and are known as the *lanthanide,* or *rare earth,* series from the periodic table of elements. These materials possess a greater quantum detection efficiency (QDE) (the ability to interact with x-rays) and greater conversion efficiency (the ability of screens to convert x-ray energy into light energy). The older calcium tungstate screens have a conversion efficiency of 4% to 5%, whereas the newer rare earth screens have values ranging from 15% to 25%. This makes the rare earth phosphors faster in speed than the non-rare earth phosphors. Table 7-3 presents the more common rare earth phosphors and the color of light emitted.

The rare earth phosphors are mixed with materials called *activators* (the elements terbium, niobium, or thulium), which help determine the intensity and color of the emitted light.

Thickness of Phosphor Layer. A thicker layer of phosphor material causes the screen to emit more light, because the extra material can absorb more x-rays. This decreases the resolution of the resulting image because of increased light diffraction or diffusion (Figure 7-13). Rare earth screens generally demonstrate better resolution than non-rare earth screens because they have greater conversion efficiencies and therefore do not have to be placed in as thick a layer. The average range of phosphor thickness is from 150 to 300 μm.

Table 7-2 Older Names for Screen Speed

Name of screen	Relative speed value
Ultra high or hi-plus	300
High or fast	200
Medium, par or standard	100
Detail, slow or high resolution	50
Ultra-detail	25

Table 7-3 Common Rare Earth Phosphors

Rare earth phosphor	Color of emission
Gadolinium oxysulfide	Green
Lanthanum oxysulfide	Green
Yttrium oxysulfide	Blue-green
Yttrium tantalate	Blue-green
Lanthanum oxybromide	Blue
Lutetium tantalate	Blue

Size of Phosphor Crystals. Using larger-size phosphor crystals increases the speed of the screen but decreases image resolution because of light diffusion.

Reflective Layer. When x-rays interact with the phosphor material of a screen, light is emitted isotropically (in all directions). Because the film is only on one side of the screen, light traveling away from the film would normally be lost to the imaging process. Faster-speed screens add a layer of titanium dioxide to reflect light back toward the film. This increases the speed but decreases the resolution because of the angle of the reflected light.

Light-Absorbing Dyes. Slower speed screens have light-absorbing dyes added to the phosphor layer to control reflected light (Figure 7-14). This dye decreases speed but increases image resolution.

Ambient Temperature. When the ambient temperature of an intensifying screen increases significantly above room temperature (above 85° F [30° C]), the screen may behave slower than normal. The higher temperature gives the phosphor crystal more kinetic energy. This additional energy does not cause more light to be emitted but rather increases the energy (and therefore the color) of the light emitted. Because the film may not be sensitive to this new color, the resulting radiograph will appear underexposed.

kVp Selection. The phosphor material in a screen must interact with the x-ray photon for luminescence to occur. The greatest absorption of x-rays occurs when the x-ray photon energy and the binding energy of the K-shell electron are almost the same. This is called the *K-edge effect*. Because the kVp setting on the control panel regulates the x-ray photon energy and the phosphor material used controls the K-shell binding energy, care must be taken to match the kVp used in technique selection. For example, a dedicated mammography cassette usually will have a lower K-edge value (15 to 20 keV), because lower kVp techniques are employed. If one of these cassettes is used at 100 kVp instead, it behaves much more slowly than if used at its proper kVp. Table 7-4 indicates the K-shell binding energies for different phosphor materials.

Quality Control Testing of Screen Speed

Quality control testing of screen speed should occur upon acceptance and then yearly. First evaluate whether similar cassettes marked with the same relative speed are the same by the following procedure.

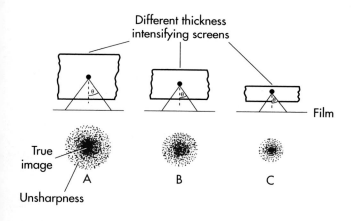

FIGURE 7-13
Effect of screen active layer on light diffusion and image sharpness.

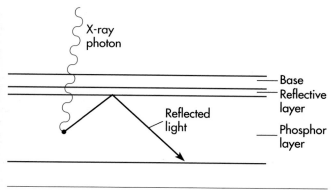

FIGURE 7-14
Reflected light within phosphor layer.

Procedure

1. Expose a step-wedge or homogenous phantom on a cassette so that the center of the image has an optical density of about 1.5.
2. Expose each cassette to the same technique.
3. Process each radiograph and take optical density readings of the same center area in each. If the cassettes are all the same relative speed, the optical density readings should not vary by more than a value of ±0.2.

Table 7-4 K-Shell Binding Energies for Some Phosphor Materials

Element	Atomic number	K-shell binding energy in keV
Yttrium	39	17.05
Barium	56	37.40
Lanthanum	57	38.90
Gadolinium	64	50.20
Tungsten	74	69.50

Cassettes should also be evaluated to be sure that the screen speed is uniform throughout the entire surface.

Procedure

1. Expose a homogenous phantom on a cassette, which yields an optical density of 1.5.

2. Process the film and take density readings in the center and in each of the four quadrants of the image. These values should not vary by an optical density value of more than ±0.05.

Spectral Matching

In Chapter 2, we mentioned that various films were sensitive to specific colors of light and therefore required special colored safelights to illuminate the darkroom. Because intensifying screen phosphors emit either blue, blue-green, or green light, the film used inside the cassette should be sensitive to the corresponding color. This is known as **spectral matching**. Any blue-violet-emitting screen phosphor should be used with monochromatic blue-violet film, and green-emitting phosphors must be used with orthochromatic film. The non–rare earth screen phosphors tend to emit a broad band of light (Figure 7-15), whereas rare earth phosphors emit specific colors of light, also known as *line emission* (Figure 7-16).

Screen Resolution

Intensifying screens should be able to demonstrate clear images of patient anatomy so that the proper diagnosis can be obtained. The ability of an imaging system to accurately display these images is known as *resolution*, of which there are two types, contrast resolution and spatial resolution.

Contrast Resolution

Contrast resolution is the ability of an imaging system to distinguish structures with similar x-ray transmission as separate entities. In other words, separate shades of gray (contrast) should appear, so that one structure stands out from the other. Contrast resolution is affected by the sensitivity of the image receptor (speed) and the amount of radiographic mottle (also called *noise*). If the radiographic mottle is increased, the contrast resolution decreases. The radiographic mottle is determined by film graininess (also called *random* or *stochastic noise*), the uniformity of the screen phosphor layer (also called *structured or nonstochastic noise*), and **quantum mottle** (also called *quantum noise*), which is the statistical fluctuation in the number of photons per unit area that contribute to image formation. The quantum noise that is perceived in the image is normally stated as a percentage and determined by the following equation:

$$\frac{\text{Quantum}}{\text{noise}} = 100 \times \frac{\sigma}{N}$$

N is the mean number of photons per unit area and σ is the standard deviation that measures the width of the distribution about that mean and is equal to the square root of N. For example, if a mean of 100 photons exposes a film, the σ is 10 and the quantum noise is 10%. If a mean of 100,000 photons exposes a film, the σ is 316, but the quantum noise is only 0.3%. Therefore, as the total number of photons increases, the quantum noise perceived in the image decreases. Care must be taken with very fast speed screens, because lower mAs values are required. This decrease in the number of photons increases the quantum noise, which will manifest as a blotchy appearance to the image and decreased contrast resolution. Contrast resolution is often measured using a value known as the *signal-to-noise ratio (SNR)*.

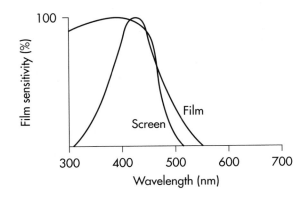

FIGURE 7-15
Broad-brand spectrum from non–rare earth screen phosphor.

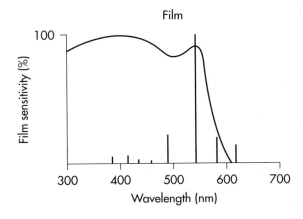

FIGURE 7-16
Line spectrum from rare earth screen phosphor.

$$SNR = \frac{Signal}{Noise}$$

The signal in diagnostic imaging is the contrast, or gray scale, of the image. Because we want this value to be relatively large and the noise to be relatively small, a large SNR will indicate high-contrast resolution. The SNR value is more commonly used when describing television and computerized images.

Spatial Resolution

Spatial resolution is the ability of an imaging system to create separate images of closely spaced objects. In other words, will the two objects appear sharp and clear or will they blur together? This is determined by the amount of light diffusion that occurs between the screen and film, which is in turn affected by the screen thickness, phosphor crystal size, and film/screen contact. The most common method of measuring spatial resolution is to use a value known as *spatial frequency*. The unit of spatial frequency is the line pair per millimeter (lp/mm) and is obtained with a resolution chart (Figure 7-17). A line pair is a space and a line, each being 0.1 mm wide. The greater the line pair per millimeter value, the smaller the object that can be imaged and the better the spatial resolution. The resolving power of the unaided human eye at normal reading distance is about 5 lp/mm. Most film/screen systems cannot provide quite this level of spatial resolution. Other methods of measuring spatial resolution include PSF, LSF, ESF, and MTF.

Point Spread Function. Point spread function (PSF) is a graph that is obtained using a pinhole camera and a mi-crodensitometer. The pinhole camera creates a black dot in the center of a film, and a microdensitometer is used to take readings of this point. These values are plotted on a graph versus the distance from the center of the point, as shown in Figure 7-18. The narrower the peak on the graph, the better the spatial resolution and image quality.

Line Spread Function. Line spread function (LSF) is graph that is more accurate and easier to obtain than the PSF graph. It requires an aperture with a slit that is 10 μm wide instead of the pinhole camera. The density readings are taken of the center line and plotted (Figure 7-19).

Edge Spread Function. Edge spread function (ESF) requires a sheet of lead to be placed on a cassette and exposed. Density readings are taken at the border between the black and white areas and plotted on a graph (Figure 7-20).

Modulation Transfer Function. Modulation transfer function (MTF) is a numeric value that is used to measure the spatial resolution and is obtained from the LSF graph

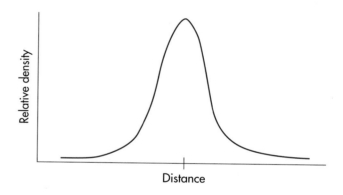

FIGURE 7-18
Point spread function graph.

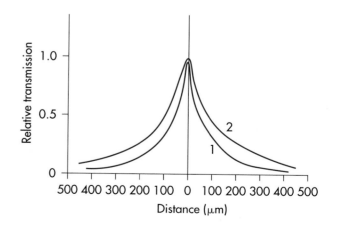

FIGURE 7-19
Line spread function graph.

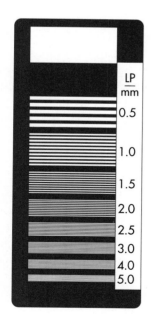

FIGURE 7-17
Line pair per millimeter resolution chart.

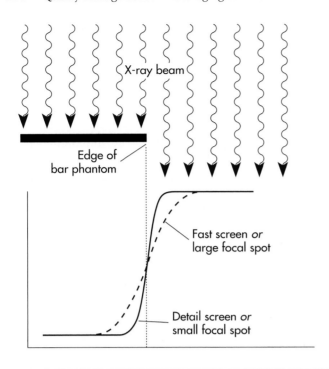

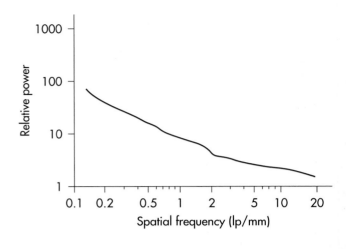

FIGURE 7-21

Weiner spectrum indicating the modulation transfer function.

FIGURE 7-20

Edge spread function graph.

using a mathematic process known as *Fourier transformation*. Just as a mathematic number (slope) can be obtained from a linear graph, Fourier transformation can obtain a number from a curve. This number ranges from 0 to 1 (0 to 100%), with 1 being the maximum spatial frequency. An easier way to think of MTF is demonstrated by the following equation:

$$MTF = \frac{Information \ recorded \ in \ an \ image}{Information \ available \ in \ the \ part}$$

If all of the patient information is recorded in the image, a value of 1 is obtained. An MTF value of 0.5 would indicate that 50% of the patient's anatomy is recorded, and so on. The total MTF of an imaging system is obtained by combining all of the component MTF values.

$$MTF_{total} = MTF_1 \times MTF_2 \times MTF_3, \text{ and so on}$$

For example, if a film can demonstrate 80% of the patient anatomy on an image (MTF = 0.8) and a screen can demonstrate 70% (MTF = 0.7), the total system MTF equals 0.8 × 0.7, or 0.56. A Weiner spectrum graph is sometimes used to demonstrate the relationship of MTF and spatial frequency (Figure 7-21).

The resolution test tool (see Figure 7-17) can be imaged with a cassette upon acceptance and then yearly to evaluate any variation. One variable that can affect resolution is the film/screen contact. Because poor film/screen contact

increases light diffusion (Figure 7-22) and therefore decreases resolution, a wire mesh test should be performed at least annually (more often with larger cassette sizes, because they are more prone to develop poor contact).

Procedure

1. Expose the wire mesh test tool that is placed on the cassette front, using exposure factors of 50 kVp and 5 mAs tabletop.

2. Process the film and evaluate the resulting image. Areas of poor contact appear as localized blurring (Figure 7-23). Bent or warped cassettes, warped screens, and foreign objects inside of the cassette are the most common cause of poor contact.

Screen Condition

Intensifying screens must be free of dirt, stains, and defects to properly image anatomic structures. A regular schedule (at least every 6 months) of screen cleaning with an antistatic solution should be standard department policy, because artifacts can mimic certain pathologies. An ultraviolet (UV) lamp can be used in the darkroom to examine the surface condition of the screens. Be sure to remove the film from the cassette before turning on the UV lamp.

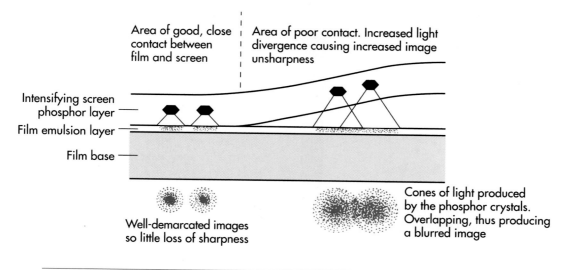

Area of good, close contact between film and screen

Area of poor contact. Increased light divergence causing increased image unsharpness

Intensifying screen phosphor layer

Film emulsion layer

Film base

Well-demarcated images so little loss of sharpness

Cones of light produced by the phosphor crystals. Overlapping, thus producing a blurred image

FIGURE 7-22

Effect of film/screen contact on light diffusion.

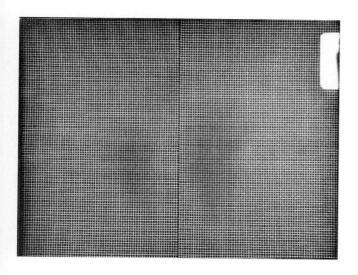

FIGURE 7-23

Wire mesh image.

GRIDS

The grid is the most common device for controlling scattered radiation (assuming collimation to the appropriate field size has been performed). Improper use of a grid can cause grid cutoff (resulting in an underexposed radiograph) or grid artifacts (grid lines, moiré patterns, etc.). These artifacts are discussed in detail in Chapter 11. Grid artifacts can also occur from imperfections during the manufacturing process or from mishandling during clinical use (dropping the grid). Barium or other contrast media can also create artifacts and must be

removed. Grid variables that should be checked upon acceptance and then annually are grid uniformity and grid alignment.

Grid Uniformity

All of the lead strips in the grid must be uniformly spaced or a mottling effect may appear in the image, which can mimic pathology. Nonuniformity can occur from manufacturing defects or by dropping a grid on its edges. To evaluate grid uniformity, the following procedure may be used.

Procedure

1. Place a film under a grid and make an image of a homogenous phantom (made of either aluminum Lucite, or a pan of water), using a kVp comparable for use with the grid ratio and enough mAs to create an optical density of 1.5.

2. After processing, take density readings of the center and the four quadrants (and any suspicious areas) and compare. ● *All density readings should be within an optical density value of ±0.10 for proper uniformity.* Stationary grids on grid cassettes may require more frequent evaluation.

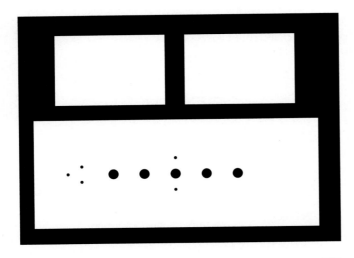

FIGURE 7-24
Grid alignment tool. (Courtesy Nuclear Associates, Carle Place, N.Y.)

Grid Alignment

Grids that are misaligned attenuate more of the primary x-ray beam, which results in a loss of image quality and higher patient dosage. Proper alignment refers to the centering of the x-ray field with the focused grid, as well as proper grid focusing distance. Alignment is more critical with higher grid ratios, such as 10:1, 12:1, and 16:1, because grid latitude is less. **Grid latitude** is the margin of error in centering the x-ray beam to the center of the grid before significant grid cutoff appears in the resulting image. The alignment must be within the grid latitude specified by the manufacturer (usually within 1 inch). The grid latitude value can be found either on the grid front or with the literature supplied by the manufacturer. A grid alignment tool is commercially available (Figure 7-24) and should be used according to the manufacturer's specifications.

PORTABLE AND MOBILE X-RAY GENERATORS

Many radiographic examinations must be performed with **mobile x-ray generators** in hospitals and medical centers, because patient condition may prevent them from being transported to the main x-ray department. Most of the variables mentioned in Chapter 6, such as reproducibility, linearity, focal spot size, and so on, can be tested using the same test tools and procedures used for standard radiographic equipment. Testing should occur upon acceptance and then annually or when service is performed. Electrical safety and grounding are critical for safe operation of mo-

bile equipment. A distinction should be made between portable and mobile x-ray generators.

Portable X-ray Generator

A **portable x-ray generator** is small enough to be carried from place to place by one person. It consists of an oil-filled metal tank or casing that contains a stationary anode x-ray tube and transformers. A smaller control unit containing the exposure switch and timer circuit attaches to the casing via a 6-foot (1.8 m) cord. A metal stand or tripod holds the casing in place. The maximum output for portable units is 75 kVp and 15 mA, so use is generally confined to chest and extremity examinations in nursing homes, battlefield use by the military, and field veterinary use.

Mobile X-ray Generator

A **mobile x-ray generator** is a smaller version of radiographic unit that is mounted on wheels and pushed from one location to the next. Mobile units are most often found in hospitals for examination of patients that are too ill or injured to be brought to the main x-ray department. Mobile units often are mistakenly called "portables." There are several types of mobile x-ray generators (Table 7-5).

Direct-Power Units

Direct-power units are usually equipped with stationary anode x-ray tubes and have a plug that is placed into a standard 110/120-volt outlet. The maximum output for most of these units is 100 kVp and 15 mA. These units are subject to power fluctuations in line voltage.

Capacitor Discharge Units

Capacitor discharge units are equipped with a high-tension capacitor that must be precharged before each exposure. To operate, the unit is plugged into the main power supply and the appropriate kVp and mAs are selected. A charge button is then activated on the control panel, which allows the capacitor to charge up to the selected value. This normally takes about 10 seconds, and then a green light indicates a full charge. The x-ray exposure should be made immediately after the indicator light appears, because the charge on the capacitor will begin to leak. If the kVp drops below 2 kVp of the selected value, the green light deactivates and no exposure can be made until the unit is recharged. Because the voltage drops during the exposure (at about 1 kV/mAs), the exposure time should be kept short to keep the kVp at the desired level. This effect also makes testing for kVp variation difficult for these units; therefore an average kVp/mAs value should be established upon acceptance and then maintained throughout the life

Table 7.5   Comparison of Mobile Radiographic Units

Direct power	Capacitor/discharge	Battery powered	High frequency
Single-phase output	Constant potential (x-ray production constant)	Constant potential (x-ray production constant)	Constant potential (x-ray production constant)
Limit of 15 mA	Limited to short exposure time	Unit is relatively large and heavy	Unit is small and light weight
Subject to power fluctuations	No power fluctuation	No power fluctuation as long as batteries are charged	High kVp and mAs available
Requires standard outlet in immediate area of operation	Requires standard outlet in immediate area of operation	No need for outlet in immediate area of operation	Requires standard outlet in immediate area of operation

of the unit. ● *Any variation of kVp/mAs value must be within ±5%. X-ray output is constant, much like that of a three-phase or high-frequency x-ray generator.*

Cordless, or Battery-Powered, Mobile Units

Cordless, or battery-powered, mobile units use a series of lead or nickel-cadmium wet-cell batteries (usually three) that must be kept charged when the unit is not in use (using a built-in charger that is plugged into the main power supply). The batteries are used to power a drive motor that propels the unit and a polyphase electric generator that produces the electric current that energizes the x-ray tube. These units can usually attain a maximum output of 100 kVp and 25 mA, with a constant x-ray output. The batteries should be removed from the unit, cleaned, completely discharged, and then recharged every 6 months to maintain a continued optimum charge.

High-Frequency Mobile Units

Like their large counterparts, these mobile units are equipped with a microprocessor circuit that increases the frequency of the alternating current to create a nearly constant potential. They are plugged into a standard outlet and can achieve up to 133 kVp and 200 mAs with a minimum exposure time of 3 ms.

SUMMARY

Ancillary equipment used in conjunction with radiographic units must function within specific parameters to obtain consistent and acceptable quality images. Therefore quality control testing is also required to monitor this level of performance.

Review Questions

1. A major problem with automatic exposure control is:
   a. backup timing often interferes with the exposure
   b. it is inefficient when high mAs is used
   c. it does not work well at short exposure times
   d. positioning of the part is critical

2. Each step on the density selector switch on an AEC system should change the exposure by:
   a. 10% to 20%
   b. 25% to 30%
   c. 40% to 50%
   d. 50% to 75%

3. The backup timer for an AEC system should terminate the exposure at _____ seconds or _____ mAs, whichever comes first.
   a. 1; 100
   b. 3; 300
   c. 6; 600
   d. 9; 900

4. The normal number of sensors available in a typical radiographic AEC systems is:
   a. 1
   b. 2
   c. 3
   d. 4

5. Which type of tomographic motion yields the greatest degree of resolution?
   a. rectilinear
   b. curvilinear
   c. circular
   d. hypocycloidal

6. The indicated level of the tomographic section and the actual level of the section must correspond to within ± _____ mm.
   a. 2
   b. 5
   c. 10
   d. 15

7. The amount of light emitted by a screen for a given amount of x-ray exposure is referred to as screen:
   a. speed
   b. sensitivity
   c. lag
   d. resolution

8. The most common method of designating screen speed is:
   a. intensification factor
   b. relative speed
   c. name of speed
   d. none of the above

9. The ability of a screen material to convert x-ray energy into light energy is termed:
   a. screen speed
   b. quantum detection efficiency
   c. conversion
   d. resolution

10. The ability of an imaging system to create separate images of closely spaced objects is known as:
    a. screen speed
    b. spatial resolution
    c. contrast resolution
    d. quantum mottle

Student Experiment 7.1   Automatic Exposure Control Reproducibility

PURPOSE

To ensure that the exposure is being terminated at the proper time after a predetermined quantity of radiation has been detected.

EQUIPMENT NEEDED

1. 200-speed or faster camera
2. Abdomen or knee phantom
3. Densitometer

PROCEDURE

1. Place the phantom over the center cell and select the kVp and mA normally used for this part at your hospital. Set the density control to normal. Place the cassette in the Bucky and make an exposure. Process the film.
2. Place a fresh cassette in the Bucky and make a second exposure using a different mA station but keep all other factors the same. Process the film.
3. Place a fresh cassette in the Bucky and make a third exposure using a different kVp but the same mA station as the first film. Process the film.
4. Take an optical density reading from the same part of each image and record.

ANALYSIS

1. Were the optical density readings from all three images within the acceptable range (±0.2)? What are possible explanations for any variation that may have occurred?
2. What factors must be taken into consideration by the radiographer when using an automatic exposure control technique system?
3. Submit all films and data with this analysis.

Student Experiment 7.2   Automatic Exposure Control and Patient Positioning

PURPOSE

To determine the effect of positioning errors on the image quality of radiographs taken with automatic exposure control.

EQUIPMENT NEEDED

1. X-ray generator with AEC
2. Automatic processor
3. 14- × 17-inch cassette, suitable for AEC
4. Abdomen phantom

PROCEDURE

1. Set the tube to a 4-inch SID and center to the table. Position the phantom for a lateral lumbar spine and place a 14- × 17-inch cassette in the Bucky.
2. Select the normal density setting for the AEC system and use the mA station that is normally used for this examination. Make an exposure using 80 kVp and the center chamber. Process the film.
3. Make a second exposure using the same factors but with the phantom moved 2 inches posteriorly. Process the film.
4. Produce a third radiograph using the same factors but with the phantom moved 2 inches anteriorly. Process the film.
5. Review the three radiographs with respect to optical density and contrast.

ANALYSIS

1. Which image exhibits the best image quality? Why? Which image exhibits the worst film quality? Why?
2. What would have caused any variation among the three radiographs taken?
3. Submit all films with this analysis.

 **Student Experiment 7.3**   Measurement of Spatial Frequency and Grid Alignment

Part 1: Measurement of Spatial Frequency

PURPOSE

To measure the spatial frequency of various image receptors.

EQUIPMENT NEEDED

1. Resolution chart test tool
2. 400-speed cassette
3. 200-speed cassette
4. Cardboard cassette

PROCEDURE

1. Bring a 400-speed cassette and the resolution chart into a radiographic room and make a tabletop exposure at 60 kVp, 5 mAs, and 40-inch SID.
2. Repeat the above procedure using a 200-speed cassette and 60 kVp and 10 mAs exposure factors.
3. Repeat using the 100-speed cassette at 60 kVp and 20 mAs.
4. Repeat using the cardboard cassette at 60 kVp and 160 mAs.
5. Process each film.

Part 2: Grid Alignment

PURPOSE

To test the alignment of the radiographic grid with respect to the central ray of the x-ray tube.

EQUIPMENT NEEDED

1. Grid alignment tool
2. 10- × 12-inch cassette

PROCEDURE

1. Position the test tool on top of the table so its long dimension is perpendicular to the grid lines. Center the middle hole of the tool in the optical crosshairs of the collimator light field.
2. Make an exposure at 60 kVp, 4 mAs, and 40-inch SID.
3. Process the test film and measure the optical density of each hole.

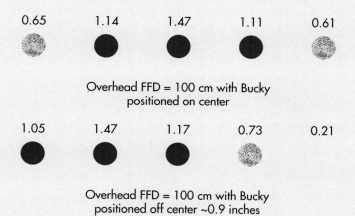

Continued

Student Experiment 7.3   Measurement of Spatial Frequency and Grid Alignment—cont'd

ANALYSIS

Part 1: Spatial Frequency

1. Examine each of the images and determine the spatial frequency in line pairs per millimeter for each image receptor and record below.
2. Which image receptor displayed the greatest resolution? Explain why this occurred.
3. Which image receptor displayed the poorest resolution? Explain why this occurred.
4. What considerations are necessary for deciding the type of image receptor to be used for various radiographic procedures?

Part 2: Grid Alignment

1. Did the middle hole display the highest optical density? (If yes, the grid is properly aligned within ±0.5 inches)
2. Was the optical density fall off pattern symmetric?
3. What effect would a misaligned grid have on radiographic image quality?

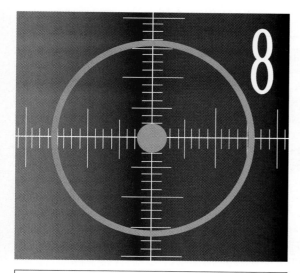

8 Quality Control of Fluoroscopic Equipment

Key Terms

automatic brightness control
automatic brightness stabilization
automatic gain control
brightness gain
charge-coupled device
cinefluorography
flux gain
high-contrast resolution
image intensifier
image lag
low-contrast resolution
minification gain
multifield image intensifier
orthicon
photoemission
photofluorospot
pincushion distortion
plumbicon
relative conversion factor
S distortion
veiling glare
vidicon
vignetting

Fluoroscopic imaging is widely used in radiology to visualize the dynamics of internal structures and fluids. The image produced is a dynamic, or real time, image compared with conventional radiography, which creates a static image. Because of the real time image created, fluoroscopy is widely used for gastrointestinal studies, vascular and cardiac studies, and interventional procedures. Many of these studies and procedures involve a considerable length of x-ray exposure time for the patient. For this reason, fluoroscopy is considered the principle source of medical radiation to the population of the United States.

Strict quality control guidelines and protocols should be in place to minimize variation in equipment performance, so that patient dosage is as low as possible. Federal guidelines for fluoroscopic equipment can be found in 21 CFR sub-chapter J, which uses input from the American College of Radiology, the American Association of Physicists in Medicine and various other groups. Many states have or will be adopting fluoroscopic protocols developed by the NEXT (Nationwide Evaluation of X-ray Trends) committee of the Conference of Radiation Control Program Directors (CR-CPD). This chapter contains many of the above guidelines and protocols, but regulations in the state of practice must also be checked.

INTRODUCTION TO FLUOROSCOPIC EQUIPMENT

The three main parts of a typical fluoroscopic unit are the x-ray tube and generator, the image intensifier, and the video monitoring system. The x-ray generators in modern fluoroscopic units are either three-phase or high-frequency units, for maximum efficiency. Fluoroscopic units equipped with cinefluorography require fast exposure times, on the order of 5 to 6 ms for a framing rate of 48 frames/sec. Therefore the x-ray generators must offer a high output, on the order of 130 to 200 kW power rating. The x-ray tubes are usually higher-capacity tubes (at least 500,000 heat units) than general radiographic tubes (about 300,000 heat units). The x-ray tube and generator must generally perform to the same standards as radiographic units and are evaluated in a similar way. Factors such as filtration (HVL), focal spot size, x-ray tube heat sensors, overload protection, kVp accuracy, reproducibility, linearity, output waveforms, AEC (for spot film devices), and grid uniformity and alignment should all be tested at least every 6 months using the methods and test tools discussed in previous chapters.

Image Intensifiers

Components

Modern fluoroscopic systems use image intensifiers, which electronically brighten the image obtained during fluoroscopy by converting a low-intensity full-size image into a high-intensity minified image. This was first developed by Coltman in 1948 using similar technology to an electron microscope (Figure 8-1). The essential parts of an image intensifier are the glass envelope, input phosphor, photocathode, electrostatic focusing lenses, anode, and output phosphor.

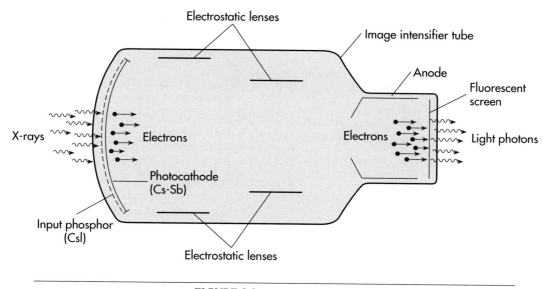

FIGURE 8-1

Schematic of image intensifier tube.

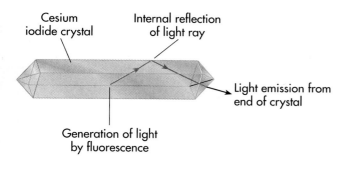

FIGURE 8-2

Cesium iodide light pipe.

Glass Envelope. An image intensifier is a vacuum tube that allows the free flow of electrons from one side of the device (photocathode) to the other (anode). The glass envelope is necessary to contain this powerful vacuum, which can experience as much as a ton of force from the outside air pressure pushing against it. Breakdown of the vacuum integrity is the usual cause of limited life of the image intensifier.

Input Phosphor. Upon entry into the image intensifier, the x-rays strike the input phosphor, which absorbs them and converts their energy into visible light. The image intensifier ranges in diameter from 6 inches to 16 inches (15 to 40 cm) and is curved to maintain an equal distance between all points on the input and output phosphors. An input phosphor consists of either a glass or thin aluminum base (used in most newer input phosphors) with a coating of sodium-activated cesium iodide crystals placed in a layer

from 0.1 to 0.2 mm thick. The crystals form long, needle-like shapes that act as light pipes to emit light with minimal divergence (Figure 8-2). The light emitted has a wavelength of about 4200Å (420 nm), placing it in the blue portion of the color spectrum.

Photocathode. Light photons from the input phosphor immediately strike the photocathode, which is a thin layer of antimony and cesium compounds. The light photons release electrons from the photocathode through the process of **photoemission.**

Electrostatic Focusing Lenses. Electrostatic focusing lenses are positively charged metal plates that focus and accelerate the electrons as they travel toward the output phosphor.

Anode. The anode is a positively charged electrode that attracts the electrons toward the output phosphor. The potential difference between the anode and photocathode is 25 to 35 kV.

Output Phosphor. Output phosphor is usually a piece of glass or aluminum about 1 inch (2.54 cm) in diameter and coated with a thin layer (4 to 8 μm) of zinc cadmium sulfide (also known as *P20*). When electrons from the photocathode strike these crystals, light is emitted with wavelengths of between 5000 and 6500Å (500 to 650 nm), placing it in the yellow-green portion of the color spectrum. Because the light is placed in the approximate center of the visible light spectrum, video cameras (and the human eye) can easily detect this light.

Image Brightness

The **image intensifier** increases the brightness of the image by the following two processes:

- The image from the larger input phosphor is condensed onto the smaller output phosphor. Because the image is emitted from a smaller area, it will appear to be brighter. This increase in brightness is known as **minification gain**, and can be calculated by the following equation:

$$\text{Minification gain} = \frac{\text{Input diameter}^2}{\text{Output diameter}^2}$$

- A high voltage accelerates the electrons from the photocathode, increasing their kinetic energy. This increase in energy releases many times more light photons from the output phosphor surface. This increase in brightness is known as the **flux gain**. At 25 kV, one electron incident on the output phosphor will release 50 light photons. The flux gain would then be considered 50 times.

The total **brightness gain** is determined by multiplying the minification gain by the flux gain. Brightness gain may be referred to as the amount of brightness of an image-intensified image vs. a non–image-intensified fluoroscopic image. The brightness level of a fluoroscopic image is affected by mA, kVp, **automatic brightness control**, kVp, variable tube current, and variable pulse width, as shown in Box 8-1.

Box 8-1   Factors Affecting Brightness of Fluoroscopic Images

mA

An increase in the fluoroscopic x-ray tube mA increases the number of x-ray photons incident upon the image intensifier and therefore increases image brightness.

kVp

An increase in the fluoroscopic x-ray tube potential difference increases the number of x-ray photons reaching the image intensifier, which also increases image brightness.

PATIENT THICKNESS AND TISSUE DENSITY

An increase in these factors reduces the number of x-ray photons reaching the image intensifier, thereby decreasing the image brightness.

AUTOMATIC BRIGHTNESS CONTROL OR AUTOMATIC BRIGHTNESS STABILIZATION (ABS)

Automatic brightness control (ABC), or **automatic brightness stabilization** (ABS), allows the fluoroscopic unit to automatically maintain the brightness level of the image for variations of patient thickness and attenuation. This can be accomplished by one of the following three methods, depending on the manufacturer.

- *Variable kVp.* Variable kVp uses a motor-driven autotransformer that varies the kVp in response to brightness-sensing electrodes. These electrodes can monitor the output phosphor directly or use a signal generated by a video camera. This method can cover a wide range of patient thicknesses; however, it is slow, and the images may demonstrate quantum noise and low contrast at high kVp values.
- *Variable tube current.* This system varies mA or tube current and requires a large-capacity x-ray generator.
- *Variable pulse width.* In the variable pulse width method the x-ray output is pulsed with a grid-controlled x-ray tube at a sequence rapid enough to avoid image flicker. A faster-pulsing sequence increases image brightness.

Multifield Image Intensifiers

The **multifield image intensifier** allows the fluoroscopic image to be magnified electronically. This is accomplished by changing the voltage on the electrostatic focusing lenses, which decreases the amount of the input phosphor image sent to the output phosphor. The resulting image is then magnified (Figure 8-3). Because the minification gain becomes decreased, the mA must be increased to maintain image brightness. This results in significantly increased pa-

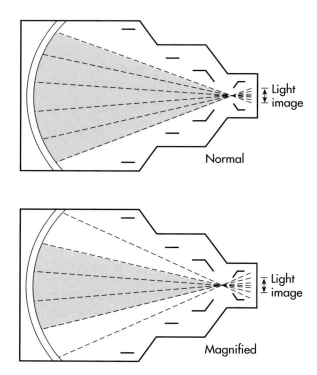

FIGURE 8-3

Multifield image intensifier showing normal and magnification modes.

tient dose. Another disadvantage is that the field of view is decreased. This type of image intensifier is used in digital fluoroscopic units and interventional, vascular, and cardiac studies.

The two basic types of multifield image intensifiers are dual focus and trifocus.

Dual Focus. The dual focus multifield image intensifier allows for a choice of two different fields of view to be used. The most common dual focus option is called the *9/6*, which means that the input phosphor can vary from a 9-inch diameter for a normal field of view to a 6-inch diameter for a magnified field of view (also called *23/15* for centimeter diameter measurement).

Trifocus. The trifocus option allows the user a choice of three input phosphor diameters, the most common of which is the 10/7/5 (in inches) or the 25/18/12 (in centimeters).

Image Intensifier Artifacts

The use of image intensifiers in fluoroscopic systems may lead to four basic types of artifacts.

Veiling Glare, or Flare. Veiling glare, or flare, is caused by light being reflected from the window of the output phosphor, which reduces image contrast. This most often occurs when moving from one portion of the patient's anatomy to another (such as when imaging the chest and moving down into the abdominal area), causing a sudden increase in image brightness. Most manufacturers incorporate designs to reduce veiling glare to minimize this effect.

Pincushion Distortion. Also known as *barrel distortion*, **pincushion distortion** is caused by projecting an image from a curved surface (input phosphor) onto a flat surface (output phosphor). This effect is similar to that of a carnival mirror that distorts appearance and is greater toward the lateral portions of the image (Figure 8-4).

Vignetting. Vignetting is a decrease in image brightness at the lateral portions of the image and is caused by a combination of pincushion distortion and the coupling of the TV camera to the output phosphor.

S Distortion. An **S distortion** artifact is a warping of the image along an **S**-shaped axis and is the result of strong magnetic fields changing the trajectory of the electrons moving across the image intensifier tube.

Image Monitoring Systems

Because the output phosphor is only 1 inch (2.54 cm) in diameter, the image projected is relatively small and must therefore be magnified and monitored by an additional system. The main methods used include mirror optics, closed-circuit television monitoring, cinefluorography, photofluorospot, and film/screen spot devices.

Mirror Optics

Mirror optics is the oldest method of monitoring the image from an image intensifier. It uses a system of mirrors and lenses. The final image is projected onto a 6-inch-diameter mirror mounted on the side of the image intensifier tower. The field of view is small, so only one person can view the

Test object

Image displaying "S" distortion

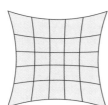
Test object

Image displaying "pin-cushion" distortion

FIGURE 8-4
Pincushion and **S** distortion.

image at a time. Image resolution of this system is on the order of 3 to 4 lp/mm.

Closed–Circuit Television Monitoring

Closed–circuit television monitoring (CCTV) is the most common method for monitoring the fluoroscopic image. A television camera is focused onto the output phosphor and then displayed on a monitor. The components necessary for television monitoring are a television camera, the camera to output phosphor linkage, and a television monitor.

Television Camera. The television camera converts visible light images into electronic signals. There are four basic types of television cameras that have been in use over the years, namely the orthicon, plumbicon, vidicon, and charge-coupled device.

ORTHICON. The **orthicon** is the largest and most sensitive type of television camera. Image quality is excellent; however, it is expensive and requires a long warm-up time.

PLUMBICON. The **plumbicon** camera uses lead oxide as the target phosphor and often is used in digital fluoroscopy because of its short lag time.

VIDICON. The **vidicon** camera is currently the most common type of video camera in fluoroscopic systems. Target material in the camera is antimony trisulfide, which has a relatively long lag time (helpful in GI studies) to help reduce image noise.

CHARGE-COUPLED DEVICE. The **charge-coupled device** (CCD) does not use a photoconductive target inside of a glass tube to convert light images into electronic signals (as in the first three types of cameras). Instead, an array of several hundred thousand tiny (5 to 20 µm) photodiodes on a solid-state computer chip form pixels (usually 512 × 512) to create the signal. Most home video cameras use CCD technology. More fluoroscopic units are being equipped with CCD cameras, a trend that should increase

as the number of pixels increases (which increases resolution). The CCD camera exhibits virtually no lag and very low electronic noise.

Television Camera to Output Phosphor Linkage. The television camera must be coupled, or linked, to the output phosphor, so that image quality is maintained. This can be accomplished by one of two methods, fiber optics and lens coupling.

FIBER OPTICS. Fiber optics linkage uses flexible glass or plastic fibers where the total internal reflection takes place (Figure 8-5). This method is small, rugged, and relatively inexpensive but cannot accommodate auxiliary devices such as cine or spot film cameras.

LENS COUPLING. The lens coupling method uses a system of lenses and mirrors to split the image, so that auxiliary devices can view the image simultaneously with the television camera (Figure 8-6).

Television Monitor. The television monitor in most fluoroscopic systems uses the Electronics Industries Association's RS-170 standard for closed-circuit black and white television, which uses 525 lines/frame, with 30 separate frames appearing each second. To avoid flicker, standard monitors use a method called *interlaced horizontal scanning*. This involves scanning the odd-numbered lines in the first half of the frame and the even-numbered lines during the second half, rather than all 525 at once. This type of monitor can resolve between 2 and 2.5 lp/mm. Noninterlaced, or progressive, scan monitors are also available and are used in most personal computer displays. These monitors are

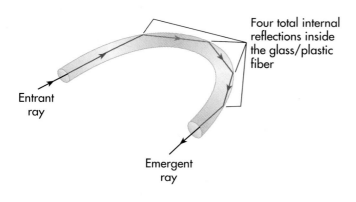

FIGURE 8-5
Principle of fiber optics.

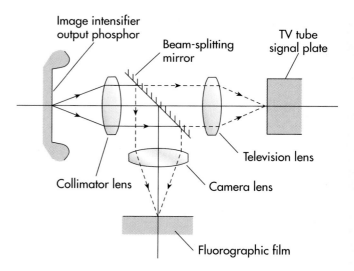

FIGURE 8-6
Split mirror for monitoring fluoroscopic images.

preferred in angiographic and interventional procedures because of their reduced flickering. High-resolution monitors using 1023 lines/frame are available and demonstrate 2.5 to 3 lp/mm. As high-definition television systems (HDTV) are developed, they eventually will replace current monitors.

Cinefluorography

With the **cinefluorography** method, a motion picture camera is used to monitor the image from the output phosphor. This high-speed motion picture camera records the image of fast-moving objects, making it ideal for cardiac catheterization studies (95% of all cine studies involve cardiac studies). The film employed is either 16 mm or, most often, 35 mm (98% of all cine studies) black-and-white motion picture film. The larger size yields better image quality but requires a higher patient dose. The camera is capable of recording framing frequencies of 7.5, 15, 30, 60, and 120 frames/second, depending on the motion of the object. The greater the framing frequency, the greater the ability to freeze motion, but with increased patient dose. The x-ray beam is pulsed using a grid-controlled x-ray tube to match the framing frequency. Quality control tests on cine equipment are discussed in Chapter 9.

Photofluorospot, or Spot Film, Camera

The **photofluorospot**, or spot film, method employs a spot film camera that takes a static photograph of the fluoroscopic image using a lens coupling device. The lens has a longer focal length than cine cameras to cover a larger film format. These cameras use either 70-mm, 90-mm, 100-mm, or 105-mm roll or cut film sizes. The larger the film format, the better the image quality but with a higher patient dose. The patient dose with this method is lower than with film/screen spot filming, as is the cost of film and processing. Quality control tests on these cameras are discussed in Chapter 9.

Film/Screen Spot Film Devices

Film/Screen spot film devices do not monitor the fluoroscopic image from the image intensifier but rather use the fluoroscopic x-ray tube to create a radiograph on a standard cassette. This cassette is routinely kept in a lead-shielded compartment until the spot film device is activated. It will then be placed into the x-ray beam path behind a grid, and a field format is selected (1 on 1, 2 on 1, etc.) (Figure 8-7). The fluoroscopic x-ray tube is then changed from approximately 3 mA to as much as 1000 mA, and the exposure is made and then controlled with an AEC

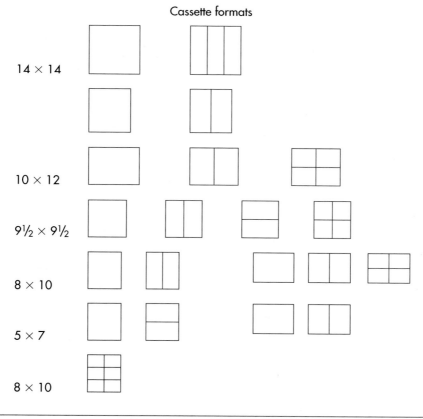

Cassette formats

14 × 14

10 × 12

9½ × 9½

8 × 10

5 × 7

8 × 10

FIGURE 8-7
Film/Screen spot film formats.

system. The images created with this method have higher contrast and spatial resolution than photofluorospot images. Spot film devices are preferred for most angiographic procedures, air contrast GI examinations, ERCP, arthrography, and sialography.

QUALITY CONTROL OF FLUOROSCOPIC EQUIPMENT

The procedure for evaluation of fluoroscopic systems involves much the same process as evaluation of radiographic systems, using the components of visual inspection, environmental inspection, and performance testing.

Visual Inspection

A fluoroscopic system visual inspection should be performed at least every 6 months using a checklist. A sample checklist is found in Appendix B. The following should be included in the checklist:

- *Fluoroscopic tower and table locks.* Manually operate all locks to verify function.
- *Power assist.* The tower should move smoothly over the tabletop when the power assist is activated.
- *Protective curtain.* A protective curtain or drape must be in place and move freely so that it can be placed between the patient and any personnel in the fluoroscopic room. This curtain must contain at least 0.25 mm lead equivalent, which should be verified upon acceptance. This can be accomplished by exposing the lead curtain to 100-kVp x-rays and taking radiation measurements on either side. The reading behind the lead curtain should be about 50% of the input reading (because the HVL of lead at 100 kVp is 0.24 mm).
- *Bucky slot cover.* When the Potter-Bucky diaphragm is moved to the far end of the examination table, a metal cover should move in place and must attenuate the equivalent of at least 1 TVL (about 0.5 mm Pb). Radiation readings on either side of the cover should be taken, with the amount outside of the cover being 10% of the input exposure, and should be verified upon acceptance. Operation of the cover should be verified every 6 months.
- *Exposure switch.* All fluoroscopic system exposure switches must be a dead man type of switch, which requires continuous pressure for activation, and should be verified upon acceptance. Subsequent visual inspections should focus on sticking or malfunction of this switch.
- *Fluoroscopic timer.* A 5-minute reset timer is required for monitoring the length of time that the fluoroscopic x-ray tube is energized. An audible signal should sound at the

end of 5 minutes. The timer accuracy can be verified using a stopwatch.
- *Lights/Meter function.* All indicator lights and meters should function as specified by the manufacturer.
- *Compression device, or spoon, observation.* The compression device, or spoon, should move easily and be free of any splatters of contrast media.
- *Park position interrupt.* When the tower is in the parked position, it should not be possible to energize the x-ray tube. This may be checked while wearing a lead apron and depressing the fluoroscopic exposure switch to see if the system is activated.
- *Primary protective barrier.* The entire cross-section of the useful beam should be intercepted by a primary protective barrier at all SIDs. This is usually built into the tower assembly for units in which the image intensifier is above the x-ray table. With the tower at the maximum SID and the shutters wide open, the exposure rate above the tower should not exceed 2 mR/hr for every R/min measured at tabletop. This can be evaluated using a dosimeter with a homogenous phantom made of 15 cm of acrylic in place or with the shutters completely closed to protect the image intensifier.
- *Collimation shutters.* ◗ **When the adjustable collimators are fully open, the primary beam should be restricted to the diameter of the input phosphor and must be accurate to within ±3% of the SID.** This can be verified using a commercially available template consisting of ruler increments, which is placed on the face of the image intensifier. When the image is observed, the ruler markings should indicate the size of the input phosphor that is being irradiated.
- *Monitor brightness.* A penetrometer should be placed on a homogenous phantom (6 to 10 inches of water in a plastic bucket, 15 cm of Lucite, or 1.5-inch-thick block of aluminum). The brightness and contrast controls on the monitor should be adjusted to show as many of the steps as possible.
- *Table angulation and motion.* The table should move freely to the upright position and stop at the appropriate spot. The table angle indicator and the actual table angle should coincide within 2 degrees.
- *Lead aprons and gloves.* Lead apparel should be exposed under remote fluoroscopy at 100 kVp, with the image observed on the TV monitor for the presence of any cracks or irregularities. Otherwise, radiographs of the apron should be made to reduce operator exposure.

Environmental Inspection

Environmental inspections are essentially the same in fluoroscopic units as in radiographic units and should be performed at least every 6 months. Generally, these can be performed at the same time as the visual inspection of many of the items included on the checklist. Condition of high-tension cables and mechanical condition of the image intensifier tower and table are especially important.

Performance Testing

As with radiographic units, performance testing of fluoroscopic units is critical to avoid variation in system performance. Many states have strict guidelines for fluoroscopic systems and mandate performance testing as conditions for granting the license to operate such equipment. Because of the potentially high patient dosage in fluoroscopic procedures, these tests should be performed at least every 6 months or as indicated by state law.

Reproducibility of Exposure

Procedure

1. Place a homogenous phantom on the fluoroscopic tabletop, and place a dosimeter between the phantom and the image intensifier input phosphor.

2. Depress the expose button for 10 seconds (use a stopwatch) and record the reading.

3. Clear the dosimeter and repeat this procedure twice.

4. Compare the readings and calculate the reproducibility variance using the equation from Chapter 6. ● *The reproducibility variance must be less than 0.05 (5%).*

Focal Spot Size

Procedure

1. Place the same focal spot test tools used in Chapter 6 on top of a homogenous phantom and expose a film.

2. If a photofluorospot or cine monitoring system is used, tape a nonscreen film to the bottom of the image intensifier tower.

3. After the film is processed, calculate the focal spot size according to the instructions with the test tool. Focal spot blooming should conform to the NEMA guidelines discussed in Chapter 6.

Table 8-1 Half-Value Layer Valves for Common Fluoroscopic kVps

Fluoroscopic kVp	Minimum HVL in mm of aluminum
80	2.3
90	2.5
100	2.7
110	3.0
120	3.2
130	3.5
140	3.8
150	4.1

Filtration Check

Procedure

1. Use the aluminum plates and a dosimeter to measure the half-value layer (HVL), using the same procedure as in Chapter 6.

2. Because fluoroscopic kVp values are usually higher than those in radiography, the HVL should be determined using the most common kVp used for that unit. For example, if a particular fluoroscopic unit is used mostly for upper GI examinations at 100 kVp, then calculate the HVL for 100 kVp. Table 8-1 contains the HVL values for common fluoroscopic kVps.

kVp Accuracy

The kVp test cassette or digital kVp meter can be used as described in Chapter 6. ● *The measured kVp and the value indicated on the control should coincide within ±5%.*

mA Linearity

A dosimeter and stopwatch are used with a homogenous phantom in place.

Procedure

1. With the dosimeter placed between the phantom and the image intensifier, make a 10-second exposure at 0.5 mA.

2. Record the reading and calculate the mR/mAs value.

3. Repeat at 1 mA and then 2 mA.

4. Determine the mR/mAs values for each and then calculate the linearity variance from the equation in Chapter 6.
● *The linearity variance should be within 0.1 (10%).*

X-ray Tube Heat Sensors

X-ray tube heat sensors can be tested using the same basic procedure used in Chapter 6, but with a stopwatch and a homogenous phantom to determine the exposure time.

Procedure

1. Calculate the heat units for a 30-second exposure at the maximum fluoroscopic kVp and mA and compare this to the maximum tube limit stated in the manufacturer's specifications.
2. Now look at the LED readout on the sensor to see if the values coincide. If necessary, continue fluoroscopy until 75% of the maximum is achieved to see if an alarm is activated. If it does not, contact a service engineer.

Grid Uniformity and Alignment

Follow the same procedure as discussed in Chapter 7 for grid uniformity, using a spot film for evaluation.

Procedure

1. For grid alignment, tape the test tool to the bottom of the image intensifier and image with a homogenous phantom in place.
2. Alignment is then determined according to the instructions with the test tool.

Voltage Waveform

An x-ray output detector can be attached to an oscilloscope, and the voltage waveform of the x-ray generator can be displayed as discussed in Chapter 6.

Automatic Brightness Stabilization Systems

The automatic brightness stabilization (ABS) system should automatically adjust the technical parameters (kVp, mA, and pulse width) for changes in part thickness. A dosimeter and homogenous phantom of varying thickness should be in place.

Procedure

1. Place the dosimeter between the phantom and the x-ray source, using a phantom of 7.5-cm thick Lucite.
2. Expose for 10 seconds and record the reading.
3. Add another 7.5-cm thickness and repeat. The dosimeter reading should be approximately double the 7.5-cm reading, if the system is functioning properly.

Automatic Gain Control

Some fluoroscopic systems are equipped with **automatic gain control** to maintain image brightness. These systems vary the gain of the video system rather than adjust the technical factors.

Procedure

1. Place a dosimeter under the 7.5-cm homogenous phantom and expose for 10 seconds, watching the monitor for image brightness.
2. Repeat the procedure for a 15-cm thickness. The radiation readings and the image brightness should be the same for both exposures.

Maximum Exposure Rate

● *The intensity of the x-ray beam at tabletop should not exceed 10 R/min (2.6 mC kg^{-1}min^{-1}) for units equipped with ABS and 5 R/min (1.3 mC kg^{-1}min^{-1}) for units without ABS.*

Procedure

1. Place a dosimeter on the tabletop along with two 3-mm thick lead sheets that are placed in front of the image intensifier. For units in which the image intensifier is under the table and the x-ray tube is over the table (Figure 8-8) the dosimeter should be placed 30 cm above the tabletop.
2. Expose for 30 seconds using the maximum kVp and mA available.

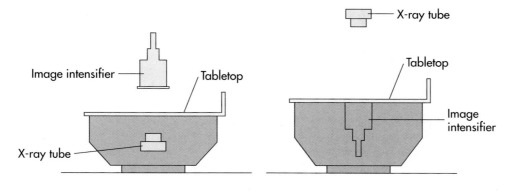

FIGURE 8-8
Diagram of fluoroscopic units with the image intensifier mounted above or below the tabletop.

3. Record the dosimeter reading in roentgens (or C kg^{-1}) and multiply by 2 to obtain the R/min (or C kg^{-1}min^{-1}) value; compare with the above-mentioned limits.

Magnification studies using multifield image intensifiers (specially activated fluoroscopy) and cine systems have no federally mandated limits as of this writing. The Food and Drug Administration (FDA) and CRCPD are investigating these studies, and possible limits may be forthcoming. These fluoroscopic units are required to have a separate exposure switch or pedal, and an audible sound must be emitted by the system when delivering high-intensity fluoroscopy.

Standard Entrance Exposure Rates

The Joint Commission the Accreditation of Healthcare Organizations (JCAHO) requires that standard or typical exposure rates be monitored, because the maximum values do not represent typical usage. A 15-cm Lucite homogenous phantom and a dosimeter should be used.

Procedure

1. Place the dosimeter between the x-ray source and the phantom, either on the tabletop for tower image intensifiers or at 30 cm above the tabletop for image intensifiers mounted under the tabletop.

2. The exposure should be made at the standard kVp and mA levels for that unit for 30 seconds.

3. Record the reading in roentgens or mC kg^{-1} and multiply by 2 to determine the R/min or mC kg^{-1} min^{-1} value. Exposure values should range from 1 to 3 R/min (0.3 to 0.5 mC kg^{-1} min^{-1}) for typical use. Grid exposures may be 1.5 to 2 times greater.

For photofluorospot cameras, the entrance exposure should be monitored with a dosimeter and a homogenous phantom at an exposure that creates an optical density of between 0.8 to 1.2 on the resulting film. The exposure should be in the range of 50 to 200 μR/image (13 to 52 nC kg^{-1}/image). For cine film exposures, the Inter-Society Commission for Heart Disease Resources (ICHD) recommends a minimum entrance exposure of 15 μR/frame (4 nC kg^{-1}frame^{-1}) for 9-inch (23 cm)-diameter image intensifiers and 35 μR/frame (9 nC kg^{-1} frame^{-1}) using the 6-inch (15 cm) mode.

Standard entrance exposure rate should remain constant for a single room each time this test is performed (every 6 months). When comparing different rooms, any variation exceeding ±25% should be investigated.

High-Contrast Resolution

High-contrast resolution is the ability to resolve small, thin black and white areas. A test tool for high-contrast resolution consists of copper mesh patterns of 16, 20, 24, 30, 35, 40, 50, and 60 holes/inch (Figure 8-9). An image intensifier with a 9-inch input phosphor should be able to resolve at least 20 to 24 holes/inch in the center of the image and 20 holes/inch at the edge when monitored with a CCTV system. The same image intensifier monitored with a cine camera or photofluorospot camera should demonstrate at least 40 holes/inch at the center and 30 holes/inch at the edge of the image. The test tool is taped to the bottom of the image intensifier and imaged at the lowest possible kVp setting and 1 mA.

Low-Contrast Resolution

Low-contrast resolution is the ability to resolve relatively large objects that differ slightly in radiolucency from the surrounding area. A low-contrast resolution tool consists of two 1.9-cm thick aluminum plates and a 0.8-mm aluminum sheet with two sets of holes of 1.5 mm, 3.1 mm, 4.7 mm, and 6.3 mm (Figure 8-10).

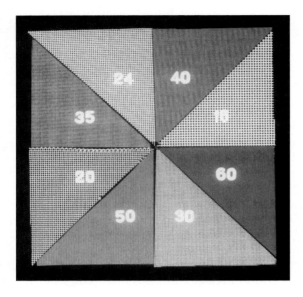

FIGURE 8-9

Image of fluoroscopic high-contrast resolution test tool.

FIGURE 8-10

Low-contrast resolution test tool.

Procedure

1. Insert the 0.8-mm aluminum sheet between the two heavy aluminum plates placed midway between the focal spot and the image intensifier.

2. Expose at 100 kVp and observe the image on the monitor. The contrast between the holes and the surrounding area is 2%. All fluoroscopic systems should image the two largest holes clearly, and the third largest (3.1 mm) holes should just barely be visible. Better systems are able to image the smaller holes.

Spatial Resolution

Various resolution test patterns are available for evaluating the spatial resolution of fluoroscopic systems. These test patterns are similar to those used in film/screen systems that should yield values of lp/mm. Most image intensifiers can image 5 lp/mm; however, CCTV systems reduce this value to less than 3 lp/mm because of the television monitor. Most of these are taped to the bottom of the image intensifier with a homogenous phantom in place while the image is observed under fluoroscopy. Cine and spot film exposures can also be made using this process and should be able to create 4 to 5 lp/mm.

Source-to-Skin Distance

The minimum source-to-skin distances (SSD) for fluoroscopic units are established by the FDA as follows:

Fixed or stationary units: 38 cm or 15 inches
Mobile units: 30 cm or 12 inches
Specialized units*: 20 cm or 8 inches

In units in which the fluoroscopic x-ray tube is above the tabletop, a simple tape measure can be used to measure SSD. For units in which the x-ray tube is under the table, two metal plates can be used, one 4 inches long and the other 2 inches long.

Procedure

1. The 4-inch plate is taped to the bottom of the image intensifier, and the 2-inch plate is placed on the tabletop. A homogenous phantom of 15-cm Lucite is placed on top of the 2-inch plate to protect the image intensifier. The long axis of the two plates should be in the same direction, with both centered to the central ray of the x-ray beam.

2. Under fluoroscopy, the height of the image intensifier should be adjusted until the outer edges of the plates coincide. Under these conditions, the distance between the tabletop and the 4-inch strip is equal to the target-to-tabletop distance (and therefore the SSD). An alternative is to use the similar triangle method discussed in

*Such as a hand-held fluoroscopic unit.

Chapter 6. For mobile C-arm fluoroscopic units, a cone or spacer frame should be permanently attached to maintain a 12-inch or 30-cm SSD.

Distortion

A wire mesh pattern (similar to that used for film/screen contact) is taped to the bottom of the image intensifier, and a homogenous phantom is placed on the x-ray table. Under fluoroscopy, the image of the wire mesh is observed for any signs of pincushion or S distortion (see Figure 8-4). If present, consult a service engineer.

Image Lag

Image lag is defined as a continuation or persistence of the image and can blur objects as the image intensifier is moved over the patient. This can be evaluated by the following procedure.

Procedure

1. Place a metal washer with a ¼-inch (6 mm) hole (or lead diaphragm with a similar-size hole) in the center of a homogenous phantom.

2. Perform fluoroscopy on the phantom while moving the image intensifier back and forth and observe the image for lag. Some amount of lag is inherent in the system, with vidicon camera tubes demonstrating more than the other types of cameras. ●*The maximum amount of lag should be less than 10% for cardiac, vascular, and interventional studies, because a 0.014-inch moving guidewire must be visualized. For GI studies, lag times up to 20% are acceptable.* If excessive lag is present, a service engineer should be consulted to adjust the system or possibly replace the camera.

Image Noise

Most noise in fluoroscopic images results from either quantum mottle or electronic noise. To determine the specific nature of the noise, first observe the monitor with no fluoroscopic image. If noise is present, it will be electronic in nature and a service engineer should be contacted to correct the problem, usually by reducing the gain of the video amplifier. Once this is corrected, use the following procedure.

Procedure

1. Place a homogenous phantom on the fluoroscopic table and expose at the lowest possible mA and 80 kVp.

2. Gradually increase the mA to the maximum value. If the amount of noise decreases with increased mA, the noise is quantum mottle. To compensate, increase the mA until the noise is at an acceptable level.

Relative Conversion Factor

The **relative conversion factor** measures the amount of light produced by the output phosphor per unit of x-radiation incident upon the input phosphor. This can be measured in the following units:

$$\frac{\text{Candela/m}^2}{\text{mR/sec}} \quad \text{or} \quad \frac{\text{Nit}}{\mu\text{C kg}^{-1}\text{sec}^{-1}}$$

A dosimeter measures the amount of x-radiation at the entrance to the input phosphor, and a photographic light meter measures the light emitted from the output phosphor. This should be measured at 80 kVp and the same fluoroscopic mA each time. A homogenous phantom should be placed in the beam path to protect the image intensifier. This value should be recorded and compared with all future values. Image intensifiers can potentially deteriorate at a rate of 10% per year, which is reflected by the resultant values. Once the values have degraded by more than 50% from the value at acceptance, a service engineer should be consulted, because image quality will become poor and patient dose will significantly increase.

Veiling Glare, or Flare

As previously mentioned, veiling glare, or flare, is defined as scattered or reflected light, usually within the linkage between the output phosphor and the television camera, which reduces image contrast. To evaluate for flare, two methods may be employed. The first involves a homogenous phantom and a small lead disk of 1 to 2 cm in diameter. A photo fluorospot or cine film image should be obtained, along with optical density values of the center of the disk area and the area outside of the disk. These optical density values can then be used to calculate the contrast modulation of the system, using the following equation.

$$\text{Contrast modulation} = \frac{(\text{OD}_{max} - \text{OD}_{min})}{(\text{OD}_{max} + \text{OD}_{min})} \times 100$$

OD_{max} is the optical density of the film outside of the image of the lead disk, and OD_{min} is the optical density in the center of the lead disk. This value should be at least 70% for most fluoroscopic applications.

Another method of measuring flare involves a video waveform monitor attached to the camera output video cable (most easily accessed by disconnecting it from the back of the TV monitor). The same setup using the lead disk and homogenous phantom is used, but no spot films are taken. Instead, the disk is imaged under fluoroscopy and the voltage waveform pattern is observed on the waveform monitor, which plots voltage versus time (Figure 8-11). The voltage measurements from the area behind the disk and outside of the disk are compared and used to calculate the contrast using the following equation.

$$\% \text{ Contrast} = 1 - \left(\left[\frac{\text{Voltage behind lead strip}}{\text{Peak white voltage}}\right]\right) \times 100\%$$

● *Video signal levels should be within ±5% of those specified in the RS 170 standards.* This procedure is described in detail elsewhere.*

Video Monitor Performance

The final fluoroscopic image is usually displayed on a television monitor, even though this is the weakest link in the imaging chain in terms of loss of resolution. To evaluate proper monitor performance, a multiformat test generator is required, which creates a test pattern designed by the Society of Motion Picture and Television Engineers (SMPTE) in accordance with SMPTE Recommended Practice RP

---

*Gray J, Winkler N, Stears J, et al: *Quality control in diagnostic imaging,* Baltimore, 1983, University Park Press.

133-1986, "Medical Diagnostic Imaging Test Pattern for Television Monitors and Hard Copy Recording Cameras" (Figure 8-12).

Procedure

1. Remove the input cable from the TV monitor and replace it with the output cable from the test pattern generator.

2. Once the image is displayed, evaluation of resolution, geometry, contrast, aspect ratio, uniformity, brightness, and gray scale can be determined and compared with the manufacturer's specifications. All of the 10% steps of the test pattern should be visible.

SUMMARY

Fluoroscopic examinations can potentially administer high dosages of x-radiation, particularly if the equipment is not functioning within accepted guidelines. To minimize this risk, quality control protocols for this equipment are essential for diagnostic radiology departments.

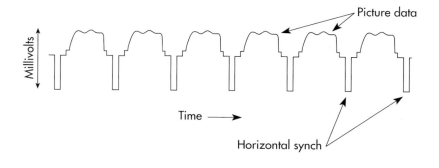

FIGURE 8-11

Video waveforms.

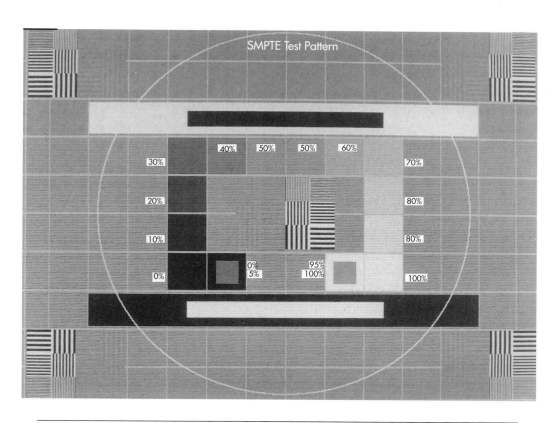

FIGURE 8-12

SMPTE test pattern.

Review Questions

1. Which of the following is not normally part of an image intensifier tube?
   a. filament
   b. photocathode
   c. anode
   d. output phosphor

2. Which material is most often used in the input phosphor of an image intensifier?
   a. calcium tungstate
   b. cesium iodide
   c. zinc cadmium sulfide
   d. lanthanum oxybromide

3. The increase in image brightness resulting from the difference in size between the input and output phosphors is termed:
   a. brightness gain
   b. flux gain
   c. minification gain
   d. resolution gain

4. Which of the following will increase the brightness of a fluoroscopic image?
   1. increase kVp
   2. increase mA
   3. increase pulse width
   a. 1 and 2
   b. 2 and 3
   c. 1 and 3
   d. 1, 2, and 3

5. The main advantage of using a multifield image intensifier is that:
   a. the field of view is increased
   b. the image brightness is increased
   c. a magnification option is available
   d. the patient dose is decreased

6. The type of image intensifier artifact that results from projecting an image onto a flat surface is called:
   a. veiling glare
   b. pincushion distortion
   c. vignetting
   d. S distortion

7. Which of the following is not a "tube" type of television camera?
   a. orthicon
   b. plumbicon
   c. vidicon
   d. CCD

8. The primary beam should be restricted to the diameter of the input phosphor to within ± _____ % of the SID.
   a. 2
   b. 3
   c. 4
   d. 5

9. The video monitor of a fluoroscopic system should be evaluated using a test pattern created by:
   a. NEMA
   b. AAPM
   c. SMPTE
   d. ASRT

10. The intensity of the x-ray beam at tabletop should not exceed _____ R/min for units that are equipped with automatic brightness stabilization.
    a. 3
    b. 5
    c. 10
    d. 20

Student Experiment 8.1   Fluoroscopic Exposure Levels

PURPOSE

To ensure long-term consistency of the exposure rate and to establish and maintain the lowest reasonable exposure rate.

EQUIPMENT NEEDED

1. Pocket dosimeter of digital dosimeter with probe
2. Abdomen phantom
3. Fluoroscopic unit

PROCEDURE

1. Place the abdomen phantom in the center of the x-ray table and insert the dosimeter or probe under the phantom, closest to the x-ray tube. Pull the image intensifier over the phantom and energize the fluoroscopic system for 1 minute. Record the reading (this will be the tabletop intensity in R/min).
2. Place the dosimeter or probe on top of the phantom (closest to the image intensifier). Energize the fluoroscopic system again for 1 minute and record the reading.

ANALYSIS

1. What was the output intensity at tabletop in R/min? Is this within acceptable limits?
2. What is the output intensity in R/mA/min? Is this within acceptable limits?
3. What difference was measured between the input exposure to the phantom and the output exposure? Why did this occur?
4. What is the importance of proper output intensity for fluoroscopic units in terms of image quality and patient safety?

Student Experiment 8.2   Image Resolution of a Fluoroscopic System

PURPOSE

To ensure that the image resolution of a fluoroscopic system is within accepted guidelines.

EQUIPMENT NEEDED

1. High-Contrast Resolution Test Tool Model 141
2. Fluoroscopic unit

PROCEDURE

1. Determine the size of the input phosphor of your fluoroscopic unit by asking the administrative technologist or supervisor.
2. Tape the test tool to the face of the image intensifier if possible. Otherwise, tape it to the bottom of the changer assembly. For Siemens fluoroscopic units with the image intensifier under the examination table, the test tool can be placed directly on the tabletop.
3. Set the fluoroscopic unit to 80 kVp and 1 mA.
4. Observe the image on the monitor and note the minimum number of holes per inch that are visible in the center and at the edge of the image. The image should resemble that shown in Figure 8-9.
5. If the fluoroscopic unit is equipped with a multifield image intensifier, select a different field size and repeat the above procedure.
6. Make a radiograph of the test tool by placing it on a cassette and making an exposure at 80 kVp and 10 mAs. Process the film.

ANALYSIS:

1. How many holes per inch were visualized in the center and at the edge of each image? How does this compare to the accepted values listed below?

Input Phosphor Size	Holes/Inch (Center)	Holes/Inch (Edge)
9 inches (22.9 cm)	at least 24	at least 20
6 inches (15.2 cm)	at least 30	at least 24

2. Was there a difference between the resolution in the center of the image versus the resolution observed at the edges of the image? If so, explain why this would occur.
3. How does the television monitor resolution compare with that of the radiograph made with a film/screen combination? (See Figure 8-9.) Explain why this might occur. To help answer this question, the following chart may be helpful.

Holes/Inch	Line Pair/Millimeter Resolution
20	0.8
24	1.0
30	1.25
40	1.6
50	2.0
60	2.5

Student Experiment 8.3   Fluoroscopic Image Noise

PURPOSE

To help isolate the cause of troublesome noise (static, extra grayness, blurring, or quantum mottle) in televised fluoroscopic systems.

EQUIPMENT NEEDED

1. Fluoroscopic unit with television monitor
2. Abdomen phantom

PROCEDURE

1. Set the fluoroscopic unit to 90 kVp and the mA normally used for an abdomen.
2. Observe the monitor with no fluoroscopic image. Any noise present will be electronic in nature.
3. Place an abdomen phantom on the tabletop and energize the fluoroscopic unit. Observe the image on the television monitor for noise.
4. Select a higher fluoroscopic mA and repeat step 3.
5. Return to the original fluoroscopic mA and select 120 kVp and repeat step 3.

ANALYSIS

1. Was any noise visible with the fluoroscopic x-ray beam off? If so, what might be the cause?
2. Was any noise visible when the fluoroscopic x-ray beam was energized? If so, what might be the cause?
3. Did the amount of noise change when the fluoroscopic mA was increased? If so, what might be the cause?
4. Did the amount of noise change when the kVp was increased? If so, what might be the cause?
5. Why is noise undesirable in fluoroscopic images?

 **Student Experiment 8.4**   Fluoroscopic Automatic Brightness Control

PURPOSE

To demonstrate the basic function of a fluoroscopic brightness control system.

EQUIPMENT NEEDED

1. Energized fluoroscopic unit
2. Lead apron
3. Abdomen phantom

PROCEDURE

1. Wearing a lead apron, place the phantom at the center of the fluoroscopic unit and move the carriage into the operating position.
2. Energize the fluoroscopic unit and observe the image of the phantom on the monitor. Start in the center of the phantom and gradually move the unit from the top to the bottom of the phantom and from the left to the right of the phantom. Observe the image and note any differences in image brightness that may occur.

ANALYSIS

1. Describe how the image brightness changes as the fluoroscope moves from a thick portion to a thinner portion. Explain why this may have occurred.
2. List the three main types of fluoroscopic automatic brightness control systems.

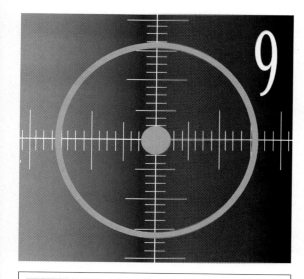

9 Advanced Imaging Equipment

Objectives

At the completion of this chapter the reader will be able to do the following:

- Describe the basic principle of digital radiography
- State the advantages and disadvantages of digital radiography versus conventional film/screen radiography
- Discuss the quality control procedures for evaluating digital radiographic systems
- Describe the basic principle of digital fluoroscopy
- Explain how digital subtraction angiography is performed
- Discuss the quality control procedures for evaluating digital fluoroscopy
- Describe the basic principle of image production from multiformat cameras, laser cameras, cathode ray tube cameras, videotape and videodisc recorders, and cinefluorographic equipment and discuss the quality control procedures for each
- Explain the basic image archiving and management networks and discuss the applicable quality control procedures

Outline

In recent years, diagnostic imaging has undergone an explosion in technology with the advent of computerized imaging, magnetic resonance imaging (MRI), and digital archiving and retrieval systems. All of these technologies are now commonplace in diagnostic imaging departments and can be subject to variations with age and use. Therefore quality control protocols should be in place to monitor for these variations so that they can be kept to a minimum.

DIGITAL RADIOGRAPHIC SYSTEMS

Digital radiography (DR), or computerized radiography (CR), is a digital image acquisition and processing system for producing static radiographs. It was developed in 1981 by Fuji Corporation, with the first clinical application in 1983 (Figure 9-1). This system uses standard x-ray tubes and generators but requires specialized image receptors and processing.

Components

Digital radiography systems consist of the image receptors, CR reader unit, and workstation. The image receptor does not contain intensifying screens and film but instead contains an imaging plate made of metal or plastic and coated on one side with photostimulable phosphors in a layer less than 1 mm thick. The phosphor material is barium fluorobromide doped with europium (Ba Fb R: Eu^2 +). When these crystals are exposed to x-rays, they are energized (up to 6 hours) until they are exposed to light. This light causes the crystals to release the extra energy in the form of visible light, which can be scanned and used to create an image. Once an imaging plate is exposed to x-rays, a latent image is present. The exposed image receptor is placed into a slot in the front of a CR reader unit that will remove the plate. The phosphors are stimulated by a scanning helium-neon laser, causing the crystals to release light, which is detected by a photocell and sent to a computer for interpretation (Figure 9-2). After the image is obtained from the imaging plate, it is transferred to another part of the CR

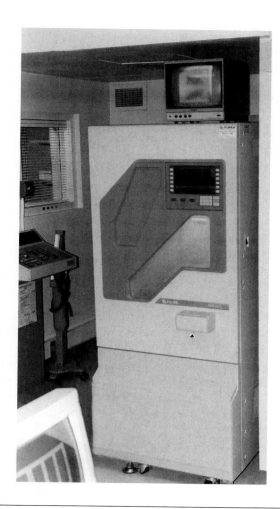

FIGURE 9-1

Digital radiographic unit. (Courtesy Good Samaritan Hospital, Downers Grove, Ill.)

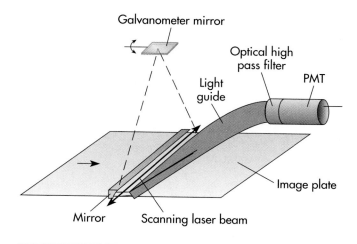

FIGURE 9-2

Schematic diagram of a digital radiography reader system.

Table 9-1	Percentage Dose Reduction for Various Radiographic Examinations	
Examination	**Decrease in patient dose**
Upper Gi	5%
Pelvis	12%
Chest	14-20%
IVP or IVU	50%

reader unit, where a high-intensity sodium discharge lamp erases any residual image so that it can be reused. These plates are kept in a storage bin until needed, at which time they can be transferred back into the image receptor. Most current systems can process about 110 imaging plates per hour. A workstation consisting of a computer console at which the final image can be manipulated is the final component. The workstation functions include:

- Gradational enhancement (contrast)
- Spatial frequency enhancement (recorded detail)
- Subtraction/Addition option
- Image magnification
- Region of interest (ROI) display
- Statistical analysis used for calculation of surface areas and estimating volumes or changes in tissue density.
- Database functions

These functions are used for storage and display, hard copy images, and edge-enhanced image option.

The image is created using a 2048 × 2048 matrix. Hard copy images are created with a laser camera.

Advantages of Computerized Radiography Versus Conventional Radiography

CR has several advantages over conventional radiography, including the following:

1. Lower patient dose as a result of the higher quantum detection efficiency (up to 50%) of the imaging plate phosphors. Table 9-1 lists the percentage dose reduction for various radiographic examinations.
2. Lower repeat rate because of improper technical factors.
3. Higher-contrast resolution and wider exposure latitude than with radiographic film emulsion. This can be demonstrated using a sensitometric curve (Figure 9-3). The response of the CR imaging plate is linear over an x-ray exposure range of four orders of magnitude between

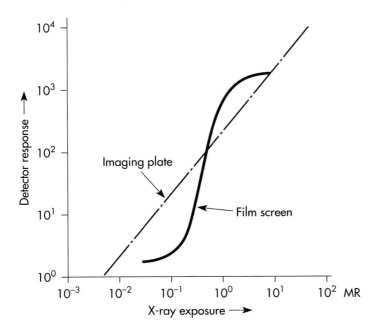

FIGURE 9-3

Plot of system response of film/screen imaging system and digital radiographic imaging plate.

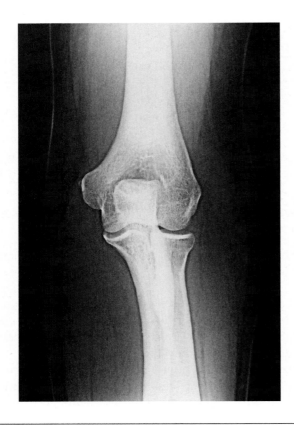

FIGURE 9-4

Digital radiographic image with artifact caused by dirt on plate.

5 μR to 50 mR. The film/screen combination is limited to about two orders of magnitude and a sigmoidal response. This means that at high and low exposures, the contrast is greatly reduced; a linear response exists only for about one order of magnitude in exposure.

4. No darkroom or film costs (unless hard copy images are desired).
5. Edge-enhanced images.
6. Easy image storage through either hard copy or electronic storage.
7. Easy interface with PACS or IMACS system.

Disadvantages of Computerized Radiography

The disadvantages of CR include the following:

1. High capital costs for image receptors, CR reader unit, and workstation hardware and software.
2. Small image size. Most current CR systems produce images that have about two thirds reduction in image size from a standard 14- × 17-inch image.
3. Lower spatial resolution. Spatial resolution is controlled by the dimension of the crystals in the imaging plate, the size of the laser beam in the CR reader unit, and the matrix size. Film screen combinations can resolve 3 to 5 lp/mm compared with 2 to 4 lp/mm for CR systems. This can make visualization of linear fractures in bone difficult. Better computer software yielding larger matrix sizes is forthcoming and should improve image resolution.
4. Collimation and centering of the part is critical for the computer to determine the proper optical density and contrast.

Quality Control of Digital Radiography Units

Because the image is created digitally, variation in system performance is less than with film/screen systems. The image plate loading and unloading mechanisms in the CR reader unit must be cleaned and lubricated regularly. Care must be taken to avoid dirt or dust on the image plates to prevent artifacts on the final image, which can mimic pathologic conditions (Figure 9-4). A resolution test tool indicating line pairs/millimeter should be imaged regularly (every 6 months) and compared with previous test images and manufacturers' specifications. Changes in image quality should be brought to the attention of a service engineer.

DIGITAL FLUOROSCOPY

Digital fluoroscopy (DF), or computerized fluoroscopy (CF), was developed during the 1970s at the University of

Wisconsin and the University of Arizona. Standard fluoroscopic units feed the image from the television camera directly to the monitor for immediate viewing. In digital fluoroscopy, the analog signal from the camera is first sent through an analog-to-digital converter (ADC) and then through a microprocessor circuit that processes the image (Figure 9-5). This digital computer carries out two forms of image processing before display on the monitor: image enhancement and image resolution.

Image Enhancement

The computer allows image improvement or **image enhancement** of structures of interest in the image through various means. The image contrast can be manipulated by controlling window width and window level. **Window width** selects the width of the band of values in the digital signal, which can be represented as gray tones in the image. This provides a means of compressing or expanding image contrast. The **window level** selects the level of the displayed band of values within the complete range. This allows for contrast manipulation on different parts of the image to optimize image quality.

Image Restoration

The computer allows **image restoration** to correct for distortion and vignetting that may occur in the image intensifier.

The digitally generated image can be displayed on the monitor using either monochrome gray-scale images, in which each pixel produces a certain gray tone (most common), or with bistable images, in which the pixel is either black or white with no intermediate gray tones. This is generally used in radionuclide imaging. The monitor can use several scan modes for image display, including continuous fluoroscopy mode, pulsed interlaced scan mode, pulsed progressive scan mode, and slow scan mode.

Continuous Fluoroscopic Mode

A standard 525-line monitor is used with continuous fluoroscopy at a low mA value (less than 5 mA). With this lower mA value, quantum mottle and low signal-to-noise ratio is a problem; therefore the computer uses as many as 20 to 30 separate frames to produce a single image.

Pulsed Interlaced Scan Mode

In the pulsed interlaced scan mode, the x-ray tube delivers radiation in short, high-intensity pulses at about one per second. This reduces quantum mottle and increases resolution and signal-to-noise ratio. This pulsed mode can also reduce patient dose and is more commonly employed than continuous fluoroscopy.

Pulsed Progressive Scan Mode

In the pulsed progressive scan mode, the x-ray beam is pulsed but the monitor scans the lines in natural order rather than interlaced. This reduces image flicker and improves resolution but requires a 1023-line monitor.

Slow Scan Mode

In slow scan mode, seven and one half 1050-line frames are scanned per second, which doubles image resolution.

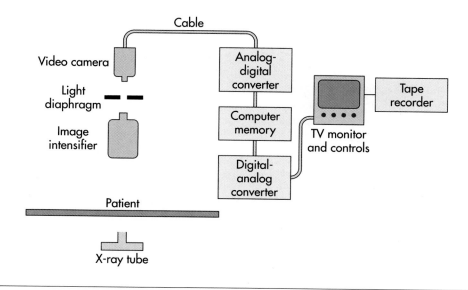

FIGURE 9-5
Block diagram of digital fluoroscopic system.

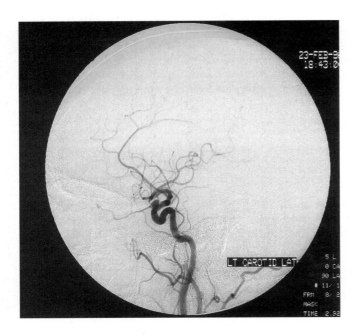

FIGURE 9-6
Image obtained during digital subtraction angiography.

All modes have a freeze frame and last image recall option that allow the image to remain on the monitor even though no fluoroscopy is currently taking place. This function reduces patient dose.

Digital Subtraction Angiography

The main application for DF systems is for **digital subtraction angiography** (DSA). This involves removing or subtracting background structures from an image so that only contrast media–filled structures remain (Figure 9-6). Before DSA, radiographs were taken before the administration of contrast media. Because a standard radiograph is a photographic negative, a positive of this image, called a *mask film,* is then created. When a second radiograph is taken with contrast media present (again, a photographic negative), it is combined with the mask film to create the subtraction image. This method is time-consuming and cumbersome. DSA involves imaging the patient before the arrival of contrast media; the computer stores the image as the mask. When the image with the contrast media is created, the computer stores it in a separate area and then combines it with the mask to create the subtracted image. Figure 9-7 shows a block diagram of this process. The advantages of DSA over the film method include wider exposure latitude, computerized enhancement of image contrast, and quick image acquisition. The main disadvantages are small field of view (because it is limited by the input phosphor size) and lower spatial resolution (because of pixel size and the

limitation of the monitor). A laser camera should be used to create hard copy images. There are several types of DSA, including temporal mask subtraction, time-interval difference subtraction, and dual-energy subtraction.

Temporal Mask Subtraction

Temporal mask subtraction is the standard type of DSA described earlier, in which the computer uses a noncontrast mask with the contrast media image to create the subtracted image. Patient motion must be avoided between the two images, or image noise and degradation will result.

Time-Interval Difference Subtraction

In the process of time-interval difference subtraction, a series of images are obtained at equally spaced times after injection of contrast media. Each image is subtracted from the next to form new subtraction images. This helps identify certain pathologies in the vasculature that inhibit the flow of contrast media over time.

Dual-Energy Subtraction

In dual-energy subtraction, two different qualities (energies) of x-ray beam are used, one at just below 33 keV and one at just above this value. This is because the K-edge of iodine is at 33 keV, so the images created at each different energy are compared by the computer to create the subtracted image.

Quality Control of Digital Fluoroscopy Units

The nondigital functions of DF units should be checked using the conventional fluoroscopic methods described in Chapter 8. Once these have been evaluated and are performing within specified parameters, then the DF functions should be checked upon acceptance and then every 6 months or when service is performed on the system. This requires a phantom that conforms to the recommendations found in Report No. 15 by the American Association of Physicists in Medicine (AAPM) Digital Radiography/Fluorography Task Group of the Diagnostic Imaging Committee (Figure 9-8). The phantom evaluates the variables of high- and low-contrast resolution, spatial resolution, subtraction effectiveness, image uniformity, amplifier dynamic range, registration (to detect any changes in pixel position between the test image and the mask image), and linearity. Linearity in this context refers to changes in iodine content (measured in mg/cm^2) within a specific area, which should change the pixel shade or tone accordingly. For example, if an image is obtained of two iodine-filled vessels, one with an iodine content of 1 mg/cm^2 and the other 2 mg/cm^2, then the shade or tone of the pixel should differ by a factor of 2. Some phantoms also have components that simulate blood vessels and aneurysms of various sizes.

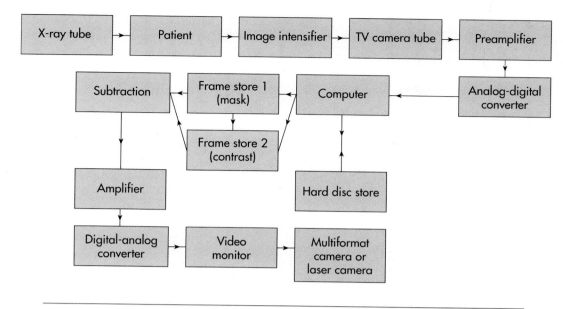

FIGURE 9-7

Block diagram of digital subtraction angiography.

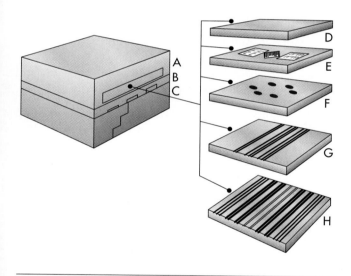

FIGURE 9-8

Digital subtraction angiography phantom. *A,* Slot block. *B,* Bone block. *C,* Step-wedge. *D,* Block insert. *E,* High contrast resolution pattern insert. *F,* Linearity insert. *G,* Low-contrast artery insert. *H,* Low-contrast iodine line pair insert. (Courtesy Nuclear Associates, Carle Place, N.Y.)

MULTIFORMAT CAMERAS

Most diagnostic imaging modalities (with the exception of conventional radiography, fluoroscopy, cinefluorography, and photofluorography) do not automatically create a hard copy of the final image. Instead, the image is stored in computer hardware or created on some form of cathode ray tube. Therefore an electronic device is required to transfer the image onto film or other storage medium. One such device is the multiformat camera, so-called because each film can be formatted or divided up into as many as 25 separate images (Figure 9-9). This is a useful and cost-effective method of recording hard copy images from computed tomography (CT), MRI, ultrasound, and DSA.

Components

The video signal from the respective modality is fed into the camera, where it is displayed on a cathode ray tube. The front of the cathode ray tube is flat, as opposed to the curved face on standard television monitors, to avoid pincushion distortion. These tubes use a 525- or 1023-line raster pattern, and the screen phosphors are commonly P11 (blue-emitting) or P45 (blue-green–emitting). Standard fluoroscopic monitors (and black and white televisions) use P4 phosphors, which emit white light. The image from the screen is reflected through a series of mirrors and lenses onto a film platform (Figure 9-10). Depending on the manufacturer, the cathode ray tube, film platform, optical system, or combinations of the above move to format the film. Most multiformat cameras have three parameters on the unit control panel to control image quality: brightness, contrast, and exposure time.

Brightness Adjustment

When the brightness level of the cathode ray tube increases, the optical density of the resulting image increases, especially in images with an optical denisty less than 1.

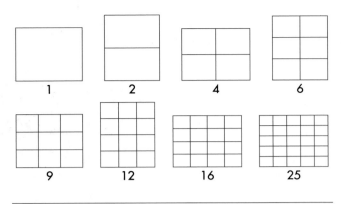

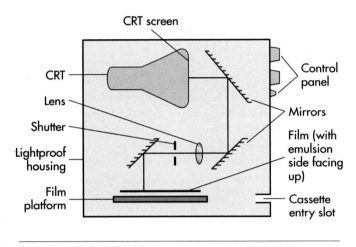

FIGURE 9-9
Format patterns for multiformat cameras.

FIGURE 9-10
Schematic diagram of multiformat camera.

Contrast Adjustment

If the cathode ray tube's contrast level increases, the maximum optical density values (those above 2) in the image increase as well. Very little difference is seen in the lower values. Conversely, reducing the contrast level decreases maximum density.

Exposure Time Adjustment

When the amount of time that the film is being exposed increases, the optical densities of the resulting image increase in all regions.

Quality Control of Multiformat Cameras

To evaluate the performance of a multiformat camera, it is necessary to use a multiformat test-pattern generator that creates a Society of Motion Picture and Television Engineers (SMPTE) test pattern (described in Chapter 8), as shown in Figure 9-11.

Procedure

1. With the image of the test pattern on the cathode ray tube, the brightness, contrast, and exposure time should be adjusted to optimum levels and a hard copy image should be created. This image is used to evaluate such parameters as resolution, contrast gray scale, and so on.

2. A densitometer should be used to record the following areas of the hard copy SMPTE film:

   40% Patch: This value determines the level of the mid-density or speed indicator, which should be approximately 1.15.

   10% and 70% Patches: The optical density of these two regions are subtracted from each other to yield the contrast indicator, which should be approximately 1.2.

   90% Patch: This value is just above the base + fog and should be about ±0.1 of 0.25.

3. The brightness, contrast, and exposure time settings should be recorded on the film for future reference. This test should be performed upon acceptance and then should be performed daily if possible (or at least weekly). The films created each time should be compared with the original for signs of variation. The image screen of the cathode ray tube has an electrostatic charge that attracts dust particles. The screen should be cleaned at least monthly to prevent dust from producing artifacts on the recorded image. A regular preventive maintenance program should be established with a qualified service engineer and should include proper lubrication of moving parts, cleaning of mirrors and optical lenses, and verification of proper alignment of all internal components. A checklist should be used to verify completion of the preventive maintenance program.

LASER CAMERAS

Also known as a *laser imager,* the laser camera is used for providing hard copy images from CT, MRI, CR, and DSA (Figure 9-12).

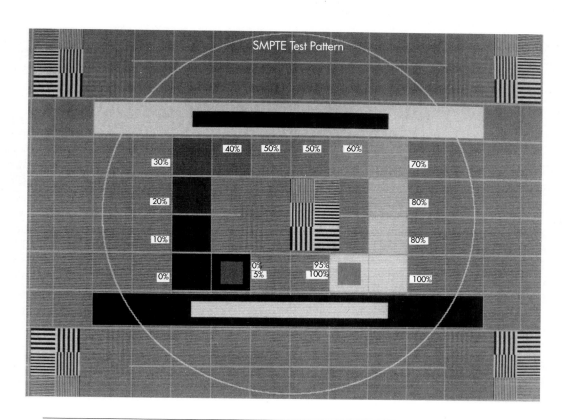

FIGURE 9-11

SMPTE test pattern.

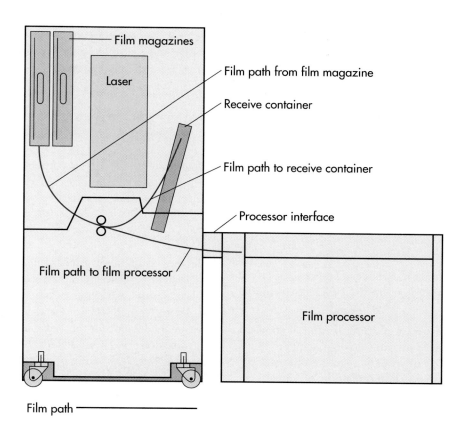

FIGURE 9-12

Schematic diagram of laser camera.

Components

Instead of using a cathode ray tube, a thin (85 μm) laser beam rapidly scans the film (at about 600 lines/second). The intensity of the laser beam light modulates in proportion to the intensity of the signal received from the original image to regulate the optical density of the final image. The laser used in most of these units emits light in the red portion (7500 to 8500 Å), requiring special film. An optical system composed of a rotating polygonal mirror and lenses focuses the laser onto the film. Because the laser produces a coherent light source that is very intense and not divergent (light photons are perfectly parallel), image resolution is very high (about 20 times better than a 1023-line cathode ray tube monitor). Usually no phosphor or electronic noise is associated with laser cameras. Other advantages include multiple inputs (so that many modalities can interface with the same unit), improved contrast or gray scale, clear or black border option, positive or negative images, up to 20 image formats, and remote control. The main disadvantages of laser cameras are higher cost compared with multiformat cameras, longer exposure time (20 to 30 seconds versus 1 to 5 seconds for multiformat cameras), and lower resolution when multiformatting small size images. In this case, each individual small image is created using the same number of scan lines as in a full-size image. With multiformat cameras, the optical system changes the image size, whereas the cathode ray tube uses the same number of scan lines as for a full-size image to form the smaller image. An automatic processor is usually directly linked to the laser camera for direct access to images.

Quality Control of Laser Cameras

Evaluation of laser cameras or printers is similar to that of multiformat cameras.

Procedure

1. A multiformat test generator should be used to create an SMPTE test pattern.

2. Hard copy images should be produced and analyzed using the same standards that are used for multiformat camera images.

3. If an automatic processor is linked to the unit, it should be evaluated and serviced the same way as a standard film processor. Regular preventive maintenance is critical and the maintenance program should include cleaning and lubricating of the internal components and the assessment of laser function.

CATHODE RAY TUBE CAMERAS

Components

Cathode ray tube (CRT) cameras consist of a single lens that connects to the front of a CRT screen and a "back" to hold the film. The most common back is called the *Shackman;* it holds an 8- × 10-inch cassette. Up to six images can be formatted on one sheet of film at a much lower cost compared with a laser or multiformat camera. CRT cameras are often found in nuclear medicine and ultrasound equipment. Operation of a CRT camera requires focusing of the camera lens, setting the aperture size (measured in *f* numbers ranging from *f* 1.9 to *f* 11; the smaller the *f* value, the larger the aperture opening) and setting the exposure time. The exposure time should be longer than 1/30 second because of the interlacing in a 525-line cathode ray tube monitor. The screen material found on the cathode ray tube monitor is usually a P11 (blue-emitting) or P24 or P31 (green-emitting).

Quality Control of Cathode Ray Tube Cameras

CRT cameras have fewer moving parts than multiformat or laser cameras but still require maintenance. The CRT screen should be cleaned weekly, and the back should also be cleaned regularly. Evaluation should take place upon acceptance and then daily. An image should be created using a test pattern generator or special imaging phantom specific to the modality in which the camera is used. The resulting image should be analyzed for variation in image quality from the manufacturer's specifications.

VIDEOTAPE, VIDEODISC, AND DIGITAL RECORDERS

Videotape and videodisc recorders are used in certain applications to record fluoroscopic images, especially in GI studies and cardiac imaging.

Components

Videotape units involve recording the image on magnetic tape contained inside of a plastic cassette. Video cassettes for home units use either 8-mm (used in video cameras) or 13-mm (½-inch VHS or Beta) tape. These smaller tape sizes are inadequate for most diagnostic imaging because of excessive noise and a bandwidth that is too narrow. At least a 20-mm (¾-inch U-matic) or, preferably, a 25-mm (1 inch) tape size should be used for proper image quality. Analog videodisc recorders use a disc (similar to a computer disc) to record images and yield superior quality "stop action" or "freeze frame" images compared with videotape. This makes them useful for mobile C-arm fluoroscopic units, in which a "last-image-hold" feature often is incorporated. When the fluoroscopic switch is released, the last image will be frozen and remain on the screen until the switch is again depressed. Framing rates for videodisc units vary from 1 image/second to 30 frames/second. Videotape and videodisc recorders have many advantages over cinefluorography, including immediate playback, no separate film processor, no special viewer or projector, reusable tape, and contrast and brightness adjustment on the video monitor. Perhaps the greatest advantage is lower patient dose. The entrance skin dose is approximately 0.01 to 0.04 rad per frame (0.1 to 0.4 mGy) for cinefluorography, whereas video recording delivers only 0.025 to 0.1 rad (0.25 to 1.0 mGy) per second. A 10-second image recording time for each delivers about 10 rads (100 mGy) with cinefluorography compared with only 1 rad (10 mGy) with video recording. The disadvantages of video recording include a lower image resolution than in cine film images and poor quality still frame images with videotape recording.

Digital image recorders have replaced videotape and videodisc recorders in many newer applications. These units store the image in a digital form via computer hardware and software until needed. The image can then be recalled onto a video monitor or hard copies may be generated using a laser camera. Images can be stored on computer discs. Digital image recorders also allow images to be enhanced or manipulated for better visualization of anatomic structures but currently record only a few frames in their memory circuits.

QUALITY CONTROL OF ANALOG AND DIGITAL RECORDERS

Analog videotape and videodisc recorders should be evaluated upon acceptance and then at least every 6 months. Variation in performance is usually caused by the build-up of dirt on the recording heads, tape guides, and drive system, which can alter tape or disc speed and image quality.

Procedure

1. A multiformat test generator that creates a SMPTE test pattern should be used for evaluation of these units. If this is not available, a videotape or videodisc of the test pattern is available from various distributors at a much lower cost.

2. When the test pattern image is recorded and evaluated, the image should display all of the 10% patches and dis-

tortion should be minimal. The contrast or gray scale on the recorded image should be the same as on the original image.

A regular preventive maintenance program should be in place to clean and evaluate the internal components. Digital recorders have fewer moving parts and are not subject to as much variation as analog units. The SMPTE test pattern can be used to evaluate the performance of these units in the same way as with analog units. Digital units generally perform correctly or not at all because of the solid-state nature of the equipment.

CINEFLUOROGRAPHY AND PHOTOFLUOROGRAPHY

As discussed in Chapter 8, the camera used for **cinefluorography** uses black and white motion picture film to record the motion of fast-moving objects, such as in cardiac catheterization studies. When framing rates in excess of 16 frames/second are used, the human eye perceives the successive images as continuous. In addition to a lens, shutter, and aperture, the camera also contains a variable-speed motor to advance the film and control the framing rate, along with a film magazine containing a film supply spool and a take-up spool (Figure 9-13). The x-ray gener-

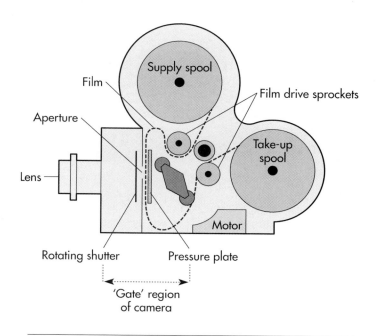

FIGURE 9-13
Diagram of cine camera.

ator and camera are synchronized so that that x-rays are emitted only when the film frame is in place. This pulsed operation greatly reduces patient dose. Photofluorographic cameras create static images at slower framing rates than cine cameras using larger format film.

Quality Control of Photofluorospot Cameras and Cine Equipment

Cinefluorography produces relatively high patient dosage under normal operating conditions. These units are also susceptible to variations in performance, which can degrade image quality and increase patient dosage. Therefore periodic evaluation (at least every 6 months) of these units should take place, along with a preventive maintenance program to clean the optical system. High- and low-contrast resolution can be evaluated with test tools similar to those used for evaluating image intensifiers. The high-contrast tool should have a fine copper mesh pattern ranging from 60 to 150 holes/inch. A special cine-video quality control phantom is available from various distributors. This phantom contains a high-resolution test pattern, a step-wedge for optical density and contrast measurement, and a mesh screen to test uniformity of focus (Figure 9-14). Some of these phantoms also provide patient identification information so that they may be imaged at the beginning of the study, before the patient is placed on the table. In this way, quality control is continuous and provides immediate feedback on system performance. Photofluorospot cameras can be evaluated with the same phantom.

Films recorded on cine film require an automatic processor to convert the latent image into a manifest image (Figure 9-15). These processors are equipped with a processor-loading cassette that removes the exposed film from its magazine. The film then is advanced through the processor onto a take-up spool, where it is ready for viewing. These processors should be monitored in the same way as standard processors, using the sensitometric tests and procedures discussed in Chapter 3. The film advance drive motor requires a few drops of light machine oil in the gear case every 6 months.

Following processing, the cine film is viewed on a cine projector, which must function according to manufacturers' specifications to demonstrate proper image quality. Most units use a 500-watt quartz-iodine lamp to project the image onto a viewing screen. The light output should be at least 16 ft-cd at the viewing screen and should be checked periodically with a photometer. Routine maintenance should include cleaning of the film advance claw and optical elements. Projector image quality is evaluated using a cine image of the SMPTE test pattern, which should demonstrate all of the resolution elements in the test film. Maintenance and test strip evaluation should take place at least every 6 months.

FIGURE 9-14

Cine-video quality control phantom. (Courtesy Nuclear Associates, Carle Place, N.Y.)

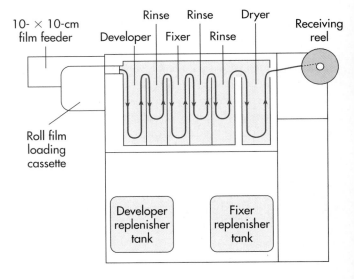

FIGURE 9-15

Diagram of cine film processor.

IMAGE ARCHIVING AND MANAGEMENT NETWORKS

A recent trend in diagnostic imaging is the storage of images into a central computer system for retrieval at a later date. This reduces the space required for film storage and increases the speed and accuracy of retrieval. The computer system allows remote access of patient images and other pertinent information from within the hospital itself and from physicians offices and clinics several miles away and even around the world as a result of satellite transmission of digital data. The two most common systems are Picture Archiving and Communication System (**PACS**), which stores images and Image Management And Communication Systems (**IMACS**), which include images as well as all other patient medical records. Digital images can be easily downloaded into these systems from their original units. Conventional film images (which are analog in nature) must be converted to digital data using film digitization scanners that are similar to scanners used with personal computers to enter pictures or data. Most scanners use a CCD digitizer or a laser to scan the image and convert it to digital form. The resolution created by these scanners is less than the original film image, because the pixel size used is larger than the silver grains that are found in the film.

Quality Control of Archiving Systems

Because archiving systems are digital, variation in system performance is relatively rare. However, a quality control mechanism should be in place to guarantee optimum performance. Film digitization scanners should be kept clean and free of dust or debris to avoid artifacts on the downloaded images.

Procedure

1. An image of an SMPTE test pattern or a special PACS test pattern (Figure 9-16) consisting of horizontal, vertical, and diagonal lines should be digitized and displayed on the monitor.

2. Image resolution should conform to the manufacturer's specifications. Laser printers, which are used to make hard copy images from these systems, should be evaluated, as previously discussed.

MISCELLANEOUS SPECIAL PROCEDURES EQUIPMENT

Many diagnostic imaging departments contain a so-called special procedures laboratory or area in which angiographic, cardiac, and interventional procedures are performed. These types of procedures require additional equipment that is not normally found in standard radiographic and fluoroscopic suites, including pressure injectors for administration of contrast media, film changers, electrocardiographic units, physiologic monitors, and recorders. Proper functioning of this equipment is critical to a successful procedure and patient well-being. Therefore proper quality control testing should be performed at least semiannually. However, this equipment varies greatly, and there are currently no uniform national protocols for quality control testing. Therefore the operating manual for the equipment supplied by the manufacturer should be consulted for this testing, or a procedure should be developed by a medical physicist and the service representative for the equipment. Some suggested guidelines follow.

FIGURE 9-16

PACS test pattern. (Courtesy of Nuclear Associates, Carle Place, N.Y.)

Film Changers

Film changers are available in many different formats, but most transport the film through a pair of intensifying screens, where it is exposed and the image is recorded. Film-to-screen contact is critical for proper image resolution, just as it is in standard screen cassettes. This can be tested using the wire mesh test tool described in Chapter 7. Images of the test tool should be obtained during dynamic conditions (when rapid filming is taking place) and compared with an image obtained during static conditions (when just a single exposure is made). These images should demonstrate no significant differences in a properly functioning film changer.

Another variable that should be tested with film changers is the uniformity of optical density during dynamic imaging. Because film changers produce a series of images in rapid sequence, each image should not vary in optical density from the others obtained during the same run. An anthropomorphic phantom or high-contrast resolution fluoroscopic test phantom should be imaged during rapid filming using technical factors that create optical densities in the diagnostic range of 0.25 to 2.5. The optical densities of these images should be compared for uniformity. These values should not vary by more than an optical density of ±0.2.

Film changers should also be evaluated for low- and high-contrast resolution, similar to fluoroscopic x-ray units. A low- and high-contrast fluoroscopic test tool (discussed in Chapter 8) can be used for this evaluation. Image each type of test tool during static and dynamic imaging and compare the images. They should not vary significantly in a properly functioning film changer.

Pressure Injectors

Pressure injectors are used to administer contrast media into vascular or lymphatic vessels during many diagnostic procedures. Variables such as injected volume and injection time should be tested so that what is selected on the programmer is exactly what is administered to the patient. This usually involves the selection of a specific catheter and contrast media (usually the type most commonly used by the facility) and having the injector administer the material into a beaker or other graduated container. The volume in this container can then be compared with the control panel for variation. This procedure can also be timed with a stopwatch so that the administration time can be compared with the value set on the unit.

SUMMARY

Advanced imaging systems are commonplace in most diagnostic imaging departments. A current trend in diagnostic imaging is emphasis toward digital imaging and away from conventional film images to reduce department costs. This should increase the use of these devices in the future. Therefore proper quality control protocols must be in place to ensure that this equipment is operating within accepted guidelines.

Review Questions

1. Which of the following is found inside of the image receptor used for digital radiographic systems?
   a. intensifying screen
   b. duplitized film
   c. imaging plate
   d. all of the above

2. Which of the following are advantages of computerized radiography versus conventional radiography?
   a. lower patient dose
   b. higher-contrast resolution
   c. edge enhancement
   d. all of the above

3. Which of the following are true in comparing computerized radiography versus conventional radiography?
   a. CR has greater spatial resolution than conventional
   b. CR has a lower capital cost than conventional
   c. collimation and part centering are critical for CR images
   d. CR demonstrates larger image size than conventional

4. The fluoroscopic scan mode by which the x-ray tube delivers radiation in short, high-intensity pulses is:
   a. continuous fluoroscopic mode
   b. pulsed interlaced scan mode
   c. slow scan mode
   d. all of the above

5. The standard black and white television monitor will scan _____ horizontal lines per frame.
   a. 125
   b. 325
   c. 525
   d. 1025

6. Types of digital subtraction angiography include:
   1. temporal mask subtraction
   2. time-interval difference subtraction
   3. dual-energy subtraction
   a. 1 and 2
   b. 2 and 3
   c. 1 and 3
   d. 1, 2, and 3

7. The type of device in which a hard copy image is transferred from a cathode ray tube onto a hard copy film is a:
   a. laser camera
   b. multiformat camera
   c. photofluorospot
   d. cine camera

8. When the framing rate of a cine camera exceeds _____ frames/second, the human eye perceives the images as continuous.
   a. 4
   b. 8
   c. 12
   d. 16

9. The laser used in most laser cameras emits light in the _____ portion of the color spectrum.
   a. red
   b. green
   c. blue-violet
   d. all of the above

10. Which of the following are components of a computerized radiographic system?
    1. image receptors
    2. reader unit
    3. workstation
    a. 1 and 3
    b. 2 and 3
    c. 1 and 3
    d. 1, 2, and 3

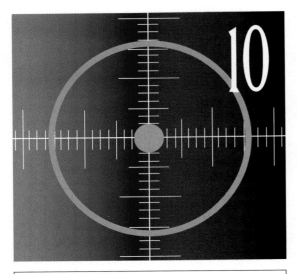

10 Additional Quality Management Procedures

Objectives

At the completion of this chapter the reader will be able to do the following:

- Describe the three main components of a quality management program
- List and define the basic terms used in statistical analysis
- Determine the repeat rate of a diagnostic imaging department
- Identify artifacts that may appear on diagnostic images
- Explain the difference between the concepts of accuracy, sensitivity, and specificity
- List the basic administrative responsibilities of a quality management program
- Describe the radiation safety protocols for patients and radiation personnel

Outline

Outline—cont'd

Water spots
Wet-pressure sensitization
Hyporetention
Insufficient optical density
Excessive optical density
Exposure artifacts
  Motion
  Patient artifacts
  Improper optical density
  Improper patient position or missing anatomy of interest
  Quantum mottle
  Poor film-to-screen contact
  Double exposure
  Grid artifacts
Handling and storage artifacts
  Light fog
  Age fog
  Safelight fog
  Radiation fog
  Pressure marks
  Static
  Crescent, or crinkle, marks
  Scratches
  Cassette marks
Accuracy, Sensitivity, and Specificity Analysis
Accuracy
Sensitivity
Specificity
Miscellaneous Administrative Responsibilities
Threshold of acceptability
Communication network
Patient comfort
Personnel performance
Record-keeping system
Corrective action
Radiation Safety Program
Patient radiation protection
  High kVp and low mAs exposure factors
  Fast-speed imaging systems
  Proper filtration
  Smallest field size plus proper collimation
  Gonadal shielding
Personnel protection
  Time
  Distance
  Shielding
Summary

A comprehensive quality management program should consist of the following three main components:

- *Equipment quality control.* This involves evaluation of equipment performance to ensure proper image quality.
- *Administrative responsibilities.* This involves data collection and analysis, educating personnel, repeat analysis, cost control, and other activities.
- *Radiation safety program.* This is to ensure that patient exposure is kept **As Low As Reasonably Achievable (ALARA)** and to ensure protection of department personnel, medical staff, and members of the general public.

The preceding chapters of this book primarily have dealt with equipment quality control. This chapter concentrates on some of the more important administrative procedures and the radiation safety program.

BASIC STATISTICS

An important aspect of administering a quality management program is the ability to analyze data. Statistical analysis of precise records allows quantification and measurement of improvement. A basic knowledge of terminology used in statistical analysis is needed so data can be incorporated into the appropriate processes. These terms are defined in Box 10-1.

REPEAT ANALYSIS

An important aspect of a quality management program is a retake, or **repeat analysis**, procedure. This is a systematic process of cataloging rejected films and determining the nature of the repeat so that it can be minimized or eliminated in the future. Repeat analysis provides important data concerning equipment and accessory performance, departmental procedures, and the skill level of the technical staff. With this knowledge, solutions can be found to minimize repeats and also document the effectiveness (or lack thereof) of quality control and quality assurance protocols.

Advantages

The main advantages of lower department repeat rates are improved department efficiency, lower department costs, and lower patient dosage.

Improved Department Efficiency

By keeping the number of repeats low, the amount of time that patients must spend undergoing diagnostic procedures decreases. This increases patient (customer) satisfaction and allows the department to service more patients in the same period.

Lower Department Costs

By reducing the number of repeats, the costs associated with film, processing, labor, and depreciation of the equipment decrease significantly. Food and Drug Administration (FDA) studies estimate the average cost of a repeat radiograph to be about $25.00 per film (based on a 14- × 17-inch sheet of film at a unit cost of $2.00) when the above-mentioned factors are considered. If a department averages 20 repeats per day for one year, the department will waste over $182,000 (which would pay the annual salaries of six technologists or equip an x-ray room with a new x-ray tube and generator).

Lower Patient Dosages

A lumbar spine series performed on a 200-speed imaging system yields an entrance skin exposure of approximately 600 millirads (6 mGy). A repeat study obviously doubles the above values.

Causal Repeat Rate

In repeat analysis studies performed on departments without quality control procedures for the darkroom, processor, and equipment, 75% of all repeats were caused by improper optical density of the radiographic images. With quality control protocols in place, studies have demonstrated that most repeats are the result of positioning errors. Table 10-1 indicates nationwide averages of repeat causes for departments with quality control procedures.

To perform a repeat analysis study, a worksheet such as the one included in Figure 10-1 for radiographic imaging departments should be used, so that the proper statistical information is obtained and recorded. Because reject films are saved for silver reclamation purposes, it is easiest to sort them daily and record the data on the worksheet. Most departments tabulate the data monthly to obtain a large enough statistical sample (at least 250 patients) for reliability. The worksheet should include the radiographic procedures performed in the department, along with the possible causes of rejects, such as positioning, overexposure, underexposure, motion, artifacts, and miscellaneous causes. Once the data has been recorded for the specified period, the causal repeat rate and the total department rate should be determined. The causal repeat rate is the percentage of repeats from a specific cause and is calculated using the following equation:

$$\text{Causal repeat rate} = \frac{\text{Number of repeats for a specific cause}}{\text{Total number of repeats}} \times 100$$

Box 10-1 Terminology Used in Statistical Analysis

Population

A **population** comprises the entire set or group of items that are being measured.

Sample

A **sample** is the number of items that are actually measured from a population.

Frequency

Frequency is the number of times a particular value of a variable occurs.

Central Tendency

The **central tendency** is the central position of a sample frequency. In statistics, there are several averages, or measures, of central tendency in common use, three of which are the mean, the median, and the mode.

Mean

The **mean** is the average set of observations and is denoted by either $\bar{X}$ or M.

$$\text{Mean} = \frac{\text{Sum of observed values}}{\text{Total number of values}} \text{ or } \frac{\Sigma}{N}$$

For example, if values of 7, 3, 6, and 4 are observed, the mean is determined by $20 \div 4$, which yields a mean of 5.

Median

The **median** is a point on a scale of measurement above which are exactly one half of the values and below which are the other half. For example, if values of 4, 6, 8, 10, and 12 are observed, the median is 8.

Mode

The **mode** is the one value that occurs with the most frequency. For example, for the series of values 2, 3, 4, 4, 4, 5, 5, the mode is 4.

Standard Deviation

The **standard deviation** is the range of variation surrounding the mean. This may be symbolized by the capital letters *SD* or the small Greek letter *sigma* (σ).

$$SD = \sqrt{\frac{\Sigma x^2}{N}}$$

Where small letter x is the amount of a value X deviates from the mean ($\bar{X}$). $x = \bar{X} - X$. For example, using the values of 7, 3, 6, and 4, the mean is 5.

$$SD = \frac{\sqrt{(7-5)^2 + (3-5)^2 + (6-5)^2 + (4-5)^2}}{5} = 1.41$$

An alternative method of calculating standard deviation can be borrowed from nuclear counting methods. According to Poisson statistics, the standard deviation can be estimated by taking the square root of the mean. For example, if a sample set has a mean of 144, the standard deviation is 12.

Variance

Variance is the square of the standard deviation and is used to determine if the separate means of several groups differ significantly from each other (e.g., between male and female patients, different age groups, etc.).

Continuous Variables

Continuous variables have an infinite range of mathematical values (e.g., age, weight, time, etc.).

Dichotomous Variables

Dichotomous variables have only two values or choices (e.g., on/off, male/female, etc.).

Table 10-1   Nationwide Averages of Repeat Causes for Departments with Quality Control Procedures

Category	% Repeat
Positioning	30
Light films	14
Miscellaneous (artifacts, etc.)	14
Dark rooms	11
Black films	9
Tomo scouts	8
Fog	5
Patient motion	5
Mechanical problems	4

For example, if a radiology department has a total of 185 repeat films during a 1-month period, and 67 of the 185 are the result of positioning errors, then the percent of repeats caused by positioning error is 36%.

Total Repeat Rate

The total department repeat rate is determined using the following equation:

$$\text{Total repeat rate} = \frac{\text{Number of repeat films}}{\text{Total number of views taken}} \times 100$$

For example, if a department performs a total of 1160 views during a 1-month period, and 132 are rejected and must be repeated, then the total department repeat rate is 11.4%. Many factors influence this rate, such as the quality of the equipment, competence of the technical staff, patient population, and how particular the radiologists are in accepting images presented to them for diagnosis.

Data from the repeat analysis is used to identify which of these factors is a major contributor to the overall repeat rate. If a particular piece of equipment is often identified as being at fault for repeat images, data from the repeat analysis can be used to justify repair or replacement costs. If certain employees demonstrate an abnormally high number of repeats, additional inservice education or other corrective action can be used to help alleviate the problem. ● *Department repeat rates should not exceed 4% to 6% and should be less than 2% for mammographic procedures.* However, this may not be practical in all departments, considering the amount of variation in the previously mentioned factors affecting the repeat rate. Any repeat rates ex-

ceeding 10% to 12% should be examined seriously, because these departments are inefficient and contribute to high patient dosage.

ARTIFACT ANALYSIS

One of the causes of rejected images listed in the repeat analysis worksheet is the presence of image artifacts. These can contribute significantly to the total repeat rate; therefore a thorough knowledge of artifacts and their possible causes is necessary so that corrective action can be taken. Image artifacts can be placed into one of three categories: processing artifacts, exposure artifacts, and handling and storage artifacts.

Processing Artifacts

Processing artifacts are caused by or occur during the processing of diagnostic images.

Emulsion Pickoff

In emulsion pickoff, the emulsion is removed or "picked off" of the base of the film. This occurs when two films are stuck together before or during processing and then pulled apart afterward. It also occurs with single sheets of film that are processed in underreplenished developer, which causes glutaraldehyde failure. The emulsion is removed from the film and deposited on the rollers.

Gelatin Build-up

Emulsion that has been removed from prior films and either stuck on processor rollers or dissolved in the developer solution can be deposited on subsequent films. The primary cause is underreplenished developer solution or failure of the developer circulation system filter.

Curtain Effect

Solution dripping, or "running down," a film can form patterns on the film that resemble a lace curtain (Figure 10-2). This is more common in manually processed films but can occur in automatically processed films if the wash water is dirty or if a film has jammed and has to be removed from the processor before passing through the dryer section.

Chemical Fog

Chemical fog is an overdevelopment of the film that results in excessive base + fog and D_{min} values with sensitometry films and excessive optical density with radiographic images (Figure 10-3). The main cause is developer temperature, time, pH, or concentration that exceed recommended limits, or overreplenishment.

REPEAT ANALYSIS WORKSHEET

SURVEY PERIOD _____ to _____   LOCATION _____

REPEAT CATEGORY EXAMINATION	POSITION	OVER-EXPOSED	UNDER-EXPOSED	MOTION	ARTI-FACTS	OTHER	TOTAL	%
Chest								
Ribs								
Shoulder								
Humerus								
Elbow								
Forearm								
Wrist								
Hand								
C-Spine								
T-Spine								
L-Spine								
Skull								
Facial								
Sinuses								
Abdomen								
Pelvis								
Hip								
Femur								
Knee								
Lower leg								
Ankle								
Foot								
UGI								
LGI								
IVP								
Other								
Total								
%								

FIGURE 10-1

Repeat analysis worksheet.

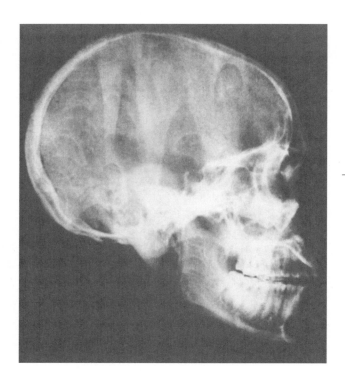

FIGURE 10-2
Curtain effect.

Normal fog

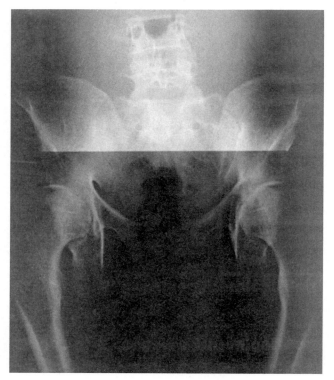

FIGURE 10-3
Chemical fog.

Severe fog

Guide Shoe Marks

Guide shoe marks are scratches on films made by the jagged edges of the guide shoes because of improperly seated transport racks or rollers (Figure 10-4). These scratches run in the same direction the film travels.

Pi Lines

Pi lines is an artifact that occurs relative to the circumference of a roller and so occurs at regular intervals (Figure 10-5). These marks run perpendicular to the direction of film travel.

Dichroic Stain

The term *dichroic* refers to "two colors," brown and greenish-yellow. The presence of brown stains on a radiograph could indicate a film processed in oxidized developer or hyporetention that has been present during several years of storage. The greenish-yellow type of stain indicates the presence of unexposed and undeveloped silver halide crystals remaining on the film after processing and is caused by incomplete fixation.

Reticulation Marks

Uneven solution temperatures can cause excessive expansion and contraction of the film emulsion during processing, which results in a network of fine grooves in the film surface.

Streaking

Streaking is uneven development of the image that can be caused by failure to agitate in manual processing or the failure of the circulation system in automatic processing (Figure 10-6).

Hesitation Marks

Hesitation marks are stripes of decreased optical density where transport rollers are left in contact with the film, which prevent further development (Figure 10-7). This artifact occurs when the processor is turned off or loses power while the film is in the developer section or if the film becomes jammed while in the developer section.

Water Spots

Should water or other liquid come in contact with an unprocessed image, a pattern of increased optical density will appear following processing (Figure 10-8).

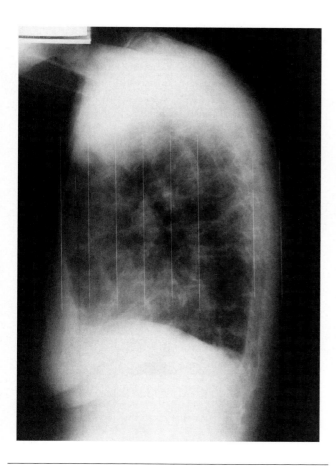

FIGURE 10-4
Guide shoe marks.

Direction of film transport

FIGURE 10-5
Pi lines.

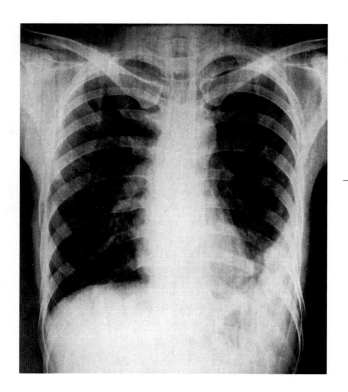

FIGURE 10-6
Streaking.

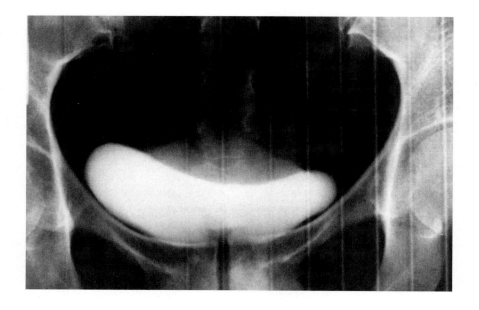

FIGURE 10-7
Hesitation marks.

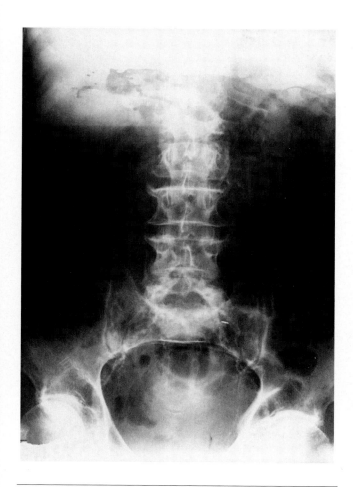

FIGURE 10-8
Water spots.

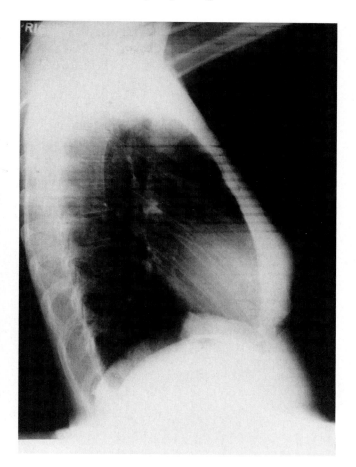

FIGURE 10-9
Wet-pressure sensitization.

Wet-Pressure Sensitization

The entrance rollers on most processors are made of soft rubber rollers with grooves on the surface to grab the film from the feed tray. Should these rollers or the film become wet before the film is introduced, the combination of the pressure and the water marks form a series of dark stripes that match the grooves on the rollers (Figure 10-9). These marks run in the same direction as film travel.

Hyporetention

Hyporetention is a white, powdery residue remaining on the film surface as a result of incomplete washing (Figure 10-10). This residue forms when the fixer chemicals crystallize as the film dries.

Insufficient Optical Density

Images that lack sufficient optical density as a result of processing problems can occur because of the following conditions: developer temperature that is below accepted limits, insufficient developer time, underreplenishment of

developer solution, contamination of the developer by fixer, developer pH that is too low, or insufficient developer concentration.

Excessive Optical Density

Images with excessive optical density as a result of processing problems can occur because of the following conditions: developer temperature that exceeds accepted limits, excessive developer time, overreplenishment, developer pH that is above accepted limits, or excessive developer concentration.

Exposure Artifacts

Exposure artifacts are caused by the patient, the technologist, or the equipment during a diagnostic procedure.

Motion

A motion artifact is a blurring of the image caused by the motion of the patient, x-ray source, or image receptor.

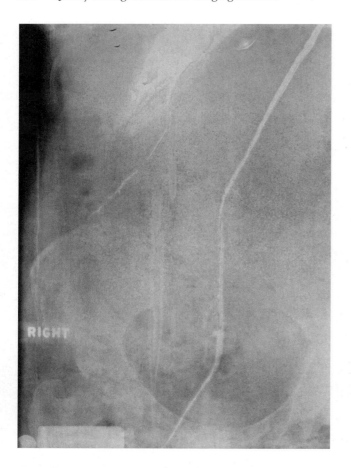

FIGURE 10-10
Hyporetention.

FIGURE 10-11
Grid lines.

Patient Artifacts

Patient artifacts are caused by items that are either on or within the patient when a diagnostic procedure is performed. Examples of patient artifacts include buttons, snaps, necklaces, earrings, hairpins, wet hair, body piercing, and so on.

Improper Optical Density

Improper selection of technical factors by the technologist or improper cell selection with automatic exposure control results in improper optical density.

Improper Patient Position or Missing Anatomy of Interest

Improper patient position or missing of anatomy of interest is the result of improper patient, x-ray tube, or image receptor positioning by the technologist or improper collimation, which can clip the anatomy of interest.

Quantum Mottle

Quantum mottle is a blotchy appearance in a radiograph that is caused by statistical variations in the number of x-ray photons covering a specific area. This usually is present when very low mAs exposure factors (less than 2 mAs) are used.

Poor Film-to-Screen Contact

Poor film-to-screen contact results in localized blurring of the radiographic image, which may also demonstrate slightly increased optical density in these regions.

Double Exposure

Double exposure occurs when a cassette is exposed twice before the film is processed.

Grid Artifacts

Improper use of a grid causes grid artifacts, which include grid lines, grid cutoff, and moiré effect.

    Grid Lines. Grid lines are shadows of the lead strips, which appear on the resulting image and are caused by failure of the grid to move during the exposure, improper grid-focusing distance, improper angulation of the central ray with respect to the grid lines, or improper centering (Figure 10-11).

FIGURE 10-12
Grid cutoff.

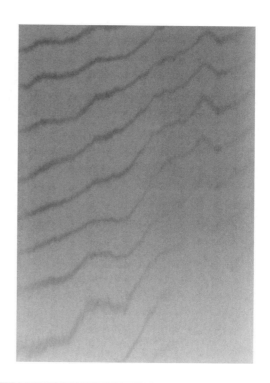

FIGURE 10-13
Moiré effect, or zebra pattern, artifact.

Grid Cutoff. Grid cutoff is a decrease in optical density caused by primary radiation being absorbed by (or cutoff by) the grid (Figure 10-12). Any improper use of a grid can cause grid cutoff.

Moiré Effect. Moiré effect, or zebra pattern artifact, is a double set of grid lines caused by placing a grid cassette in a Bucky (Figure 10-13).

Handling and Storage Artifacts

Handling and storage artifacts occur during darkroom handling or during storage before use.

Light Fog

Any light of improper color that strikes the film before development will fog the film, lowering the image contrast.

Age Fog

A film that has been exposed and processed beyond the expiration date or has been stored in a warm, humid environment will demonstrate age fog, which results in lower image contrast.

Safelight Fog

Safelight fog is caused by an improper safelight filter, cracks or pinholes in the safelight filter, incorrect wattage of the safelight bulb, incorrect distance between the safelight and work surfaces, or sodium vapor lamp shutters that are open too wide.

Radiation Fog

Film that has been exposed to ionizing radiation before development will demonstrate radiation fog.

Pressure Marks

Excessive pressure, such as a heavy object placed on the film before development, will cause pressure marks, which are areas of increased optical density. Pressure marks occur because the pressure can split the bond between the silver and the halide ion in the film emulsion, resulting in the presence of black metallic silver after processing. Film should be stored vertically to minimize the risk of pressure artifacts.

Static

The sparks from static electricity will expose film and produce three types of static artifacts: tree static, crown static, and smudge static (Figure 10-14).

Tree Static. Tree static resembles trees or bushes without leaves and is usually caused by low humidity conditions in the film processing area.

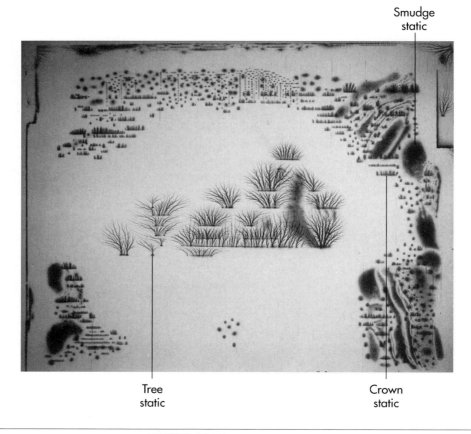

FIGURE 10-14

Image demonstrating static artifacts.

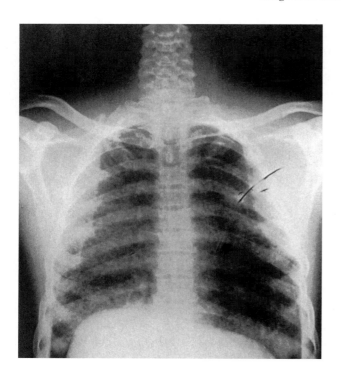

FIGURE 10-15

Crescent marks.

Crown Static. Crown static marks radiate in one direction so that they resemble a crown. Excessive friction from the pulling of the film (such as in a daylight system, in which the film is "squeezed" too tightly between the intensifying screens) can produce these marks.

Smudge Static. Smudge static is dark areas where excessive amounts of light have exposed the film and is usually caused by rough handling in the film processing area.

Crescent, or Crinkle, Marks

Crescent, or crinkle, marks are black, half-moon-shaped marks caused by bending of the film before processing (Figure 10-15).

Scratches

Scratches are areas where the emulsion has been removed by a sharp object, such as fingernails or sharp points on surfaces.

Cassette Marks

Cassette marks are white specks on the image caused by dirt or debris that is inside the cassette. This foreign mat-

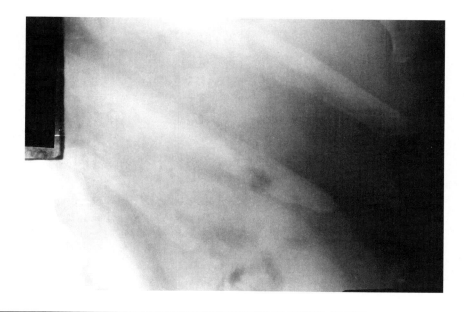

FIGURE 10-16
Cassette marks.

ter blocks the light from the screen from reaching the film. Regular cleaning of the screens with an anti-static cleaner can minimize these artifacts (Figure 10-16).

ACCURACY, SENSITIVITY, AND SPECIFICITY ANALYSIS

The main outcome of a diagnostic imaging examination is an accurate diagnosis of patient condition so that proper treatment can be administered. This is affected by factors such as image quality (for which the technical staff is responsible) and the competency of the radiologist to interpret the image (determining if the anatomy demonstrated in the image is healthy or not). In images of certain anatomic structures, the distribution of normal healthy patients follows a bell-shaped normal distribution. The distribution of diseased patients also follows a normal distribution but with a different mean value (which can be larger or smaller depending on the patient population studied). Figure 10-17 demonstrates the distribution of these two groups. The two means are relatively far apart, so it should be easy to distinguish between the two. The region where the two groups overlap indicates less of a distinction between them, and accurate diagnosis is more difficult. A diagnostic cutoff level is placed to distinguish healthy from diseased diagnosis. Patients that have been diagnosed with the disease are considered positive. If a biopsy reveals that the diagnosis is correct, a designation of *true positive (TP)* is given. If further study indicates that the patient does not have the disease despite the positive finding from the image, it is des-

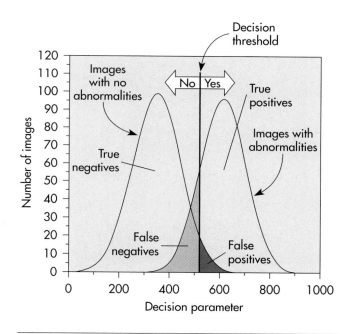

FIGURE 10-17
Graph showing diseased versus normal patients.

ignated as *false positive (FP)*. Healthy patients with no disease present are considered negative. If a diagnosis of negative is determined from an image and supported by follow-up studies, it is designated as *true negative (TN)*. If a negative diagnosis is given to a patient who is later found to have the disease, then a *false negative (FN)* designation is assigned. This information can be obtained from patient medical records and should be determined

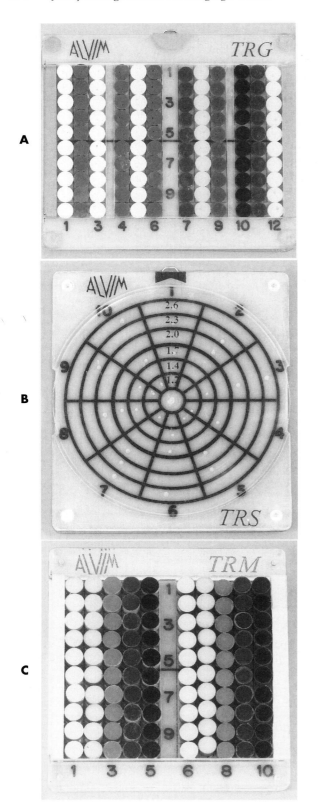

for high-risk studies, such as mammography images. From this information, the values of accuracy, sensitivity, and specificity can be obtained.

Accuracy

Accuracy is the percentage of cases that are diagnosed correctly; it can be determined by the following equation:

$$Accuracy = \frac{(N_{TP} + N_{TN})}{N_{Total}} \times 100$$

N designates the number of cases. For example, if 210 mammograms are performed in 1 month, and the number of true negatives is 167 and the number of true positives is 36, then the accuracy rate of image diagnosis is 0.967, or 96.7%.

Sensitivity

Sensitivity is also referred to as the *true-positive fraction* and indicates the likelihood of obtaining a positive diagnosis in a patient with the disease. Sensitivity is determined by the following equation:

$$Sensitivity = \frac{N_{TP}}{(N_{TP} + N_{FN})}$$

If a department demonstrates 36 true-positives and 3 false-negatives, then the sensitivity is 0.92, or 92%.

Specificity

Specificity is also known as the *true-negative fraction* and indicates the likelihood of a patient obtaining a negative diagnosis when no disease is present. Specificity is determined by the following equation:

$$Specificity = \frac{N_{T}}{(N_{TN} + N_{FP})}$$

A department receiving 167 true negatives and 4 false positives will have a specificity of 0.97, or 97%.

An ideal for all of the above values is 100%. A diagnostic imaging department is responsible for establishing its own threshold of acceptability for each value, with both internal and external factors being considered (see Chapter 1). Departments wishing to improve accuracy, sensitivity, and specificity can use special statistical phantoms for radiographic, mammographic, and fluoroscopic analysis (Figure 10-18).

MISCELLANEOUS ADMINISTRATIVE RESPONSIBILITIES

In Chapter 1, a distinction between quality assurance (which deals with human factors) and quality control (which deals

FIGURE 10-18

Statistical phantoms for **A**, radiographic; **B**, mammographic, and **C**, fluoroscopic images. (Courtesy Nuclear Associates, Carle Place, N.Y.)

Box 10-2 Administrative Procedures

Establish thresholds of acceptability.
Establish an effective communication network.
Provide for patient comfort.
Ensure accepted performance of diagnostic imaging personnel.
Develop a record-keeping system.
Establish corrective action procedures.

Box 10-3 Quality Management Technologist Duties

1. Performs acceptance testing on new equipment.
2. Implements quality control testing for x-ray generators and fluoroscopic systems.
3. Supervises image processor maintenance and quality control.
4. Monitors performance of silver reclamation equipment.
5. Prepares and updates technique charts for each x-ray room.
6. Monitors the status of equipment repairs and preventive maintenance, gathers data on equipment malfunction and associated downtime, and documents the effects of these on patient care.
7. Maintains and evaluates all accessory equipment.
8. Disseminates department and institution policies, procedures, and regulations and ensures personnel compliance.
9. Maintains knowledge of, observes, and enforces the practice of standard precautions.
10. Gathers data and participates in the department's quality assessment and improvement plan to achieve a defined level of quality and appropriateness of patient care services.

Data from *Scopes of Practice for Health Care Professionals in the Radiologic Sciences,* Albuquerque, 1989, American Society of Radiologic Technologists.

with equipment factors) is made. Merging these entities in a total quality management program requires certain administrative procedures (Box 10-2) to be implemented by radiologists, department administrators, quality control technologists (Box 10-3), and quality control committees. Some of the important administrative procedures follow.

Threshold of Acceptability

The threshold of acceptability includes levels of accuracy, sensitivity, and specificity. It should also include such items as the number of radiographs per examination, the amount of radiation per examination, and the performance thresholds of the equipment. These should be established according to both external factors, such as federal and state guidelines or professional and accrediting agencies, and in-

ternal factors, which are based on the needs and resources of the individual department.

Communication Network

Proper communication between all members of a diagnostic imaging department is essential for quality management. Items such as the proper radiographic examination ordered for a particular patient must be supplied to the technologist from the ordering physician and office support staff. Patient history and proper film identification and marking must be communicated by the technologist to the radiologist. Administrative personnel and radiologists must then communicate with technologists as to proper procedures and guidelines for patient care and image parameters. Diagnostic imaging departments should also have proper communication with other departments within the health care setting, such as the emergency room or floor nurses, so that the patient can be properly cared for. Proper communication also includes report dictation, transcription, and distribution to the ordering physician and other interested parties.

Patient Comfort

Patient comfort, convenience, and privacy should be provided for within reasonable limits in diagnostic imaging departments. Factors such as patient scheduling, preparation, waiting time, ambient room temperature, and politeness and consideration of personnel should be monitored regularly. This is best accomplished by a patient survey or questionnaire, which should be sent to patients between 3 and 7 days after the procedure for maximum reliability.

Personnel Performance

Policies should be developed to ensure that diagnostic personnel are performing their duties within accepted professional standards for areas such as proper equipment operation, critical thinking, and interaction with patients and other personnel. Information obtained from repeat analysis studies and patient surveys can be useful in assessing performance. Documentation of data, periodic review of this data, and corrective actions taken should also be included.

Record-Keeping System

A record-keeping system is necessary to document that quality control procedures are being implemented and that they are in compliance with accepted norms. Items that should be included are processor control charts, equipment checklists, examination requisitions, room logs, incident reports, film badge reports, and image interpretation reports.

Corrective Action

If equipment or personnel are not performing to accepted standards, corrective action must be taken and documented. Equipment downtime and failure should be documented in a log book. Inservice education or other corrective action procedures may be necessary for department personnel. A flowchart is a useful tool in demonstrating corrective actions for possible problems.

RADIATION SAFETY PROGRAM

Diagnostic imaging procedures (with the exception of magnetic resonance imaging [MRI] and sonography) contribute the largest single exposure to artificial (man-made) radiation (greater than 90%) in the United States. The average effective dose equivalent for diagnostic x-rays is 39 mrem (0.39 mSv) and for nuclear medicine procedures is 14 mrem (0.14 mSv). This is in addition to the 140 mrem (1.4 mSv) per year that is received from natural sources, such as cosmic radiation (from outer space), terrestrial radiation (from the earth, air, and drinking water), and internal radiation (from our own body tissues). One of the goals of a quality management program is to keep patient dose as low as reasonably achievable during diagnostic imaging procedures, as well as to minimize any exposure to department personnel and the general public. Therefore a radiation safety program should be in place to accomplish this goal. One aspect of the program that will benefit the patient as well as the technologist is the proper design and manufacture of the equipment. The Food and Drug Administration (FDA) through its sub-branch, the Center for Devices and Radiologic Health (CDRH) has established regulations that equipment manufacturers and distributors must follow. These regulations are contained in Title 21 of the Code of Federal Regulations Part 1020 (21 CFR 1020). Consideration of the risk of a diagnostic procedure versus the benefit to the patient should take place before an examination is ordered. Unnecessary examinations, such as routine employment or hospital admission screenings, should be eliminated, as indicated in the Consumer-Patient Radiation Health and Safety Act. Only properly qualified staff should be allowed to operate the equipment, and routine quality control testing on the equipment should be performed at specified intervals.

Patient Radiation Protection

High kVp and Low mAs Exposure Factors

The use of high kVp and low mAs exposure factors is the most effective method of reducing patient exposure.

Fast-Speed Imaging Systems

The second most effective method of patient radiation protection is the use of fast-speed imaging systems, because these systems require lower mAs values to obtain a diagnostic image.

Proper Filtration

Beam filtration in appropriate amounts can reduce the patient skin dose by as much as 90%.

Smallest Field Size Plus Proper Collimation

Use the smallest field size possible, along with proper collimation. The effect of field size can be seen by calculating a value known as the *dose area product (DAP)*, which incorporates the total dosage of radiation and the area of field that is being used. The units used to measure this value are either roentgen (R) $\times$ cm^2 or C/kg $\times$ cm^2. For example, a field size of 5 cm $\times$ 5 cm (25 cm^2) can receive a dosage of 4 R, yielding a DAP of 100 R $\times$ cm^2. A field size of 20 cm $\times$ 20 cm (400 cm^2) can receive only 0.25 R but still yields the same DAP of 100 R $\times$ cm^2.

Gonadal Shielding

For gonadal shielding, a lead shield with at least 0.5-mm lead equivalence should be in place whenever the gonads are within 5 cm of the collimation line and would not interfere with the anatomy of interest.

Personnel Protection

Personnel who perform diagnostic procedures using ionizing radiation have the potential of receiving significant amounts of radiation and must therefore use radiation safety practices. ● *Radiation safety practices should guarantee effective dose equivalent of under 5 rem (50 mSv) per year for whole body exposure.* Examinations using mobile equipment, fluoroscopy, cardiac catheterization, and interventional procedures pose a higher risk than conventional radiography. Medical facilities must have an orientation program on radiation safety for newly employed technologists, as well as a continuing education program to update the skills of all department personnel. Periodic surveys using properly calibrated instruments such as GM counters and ionization chambers should be performed to assess that radiation in the workplace does not exceed accepted standards. ● *Warning signs should be posted for any areas where dosage can exceed 5 mR/hr.* All personnel must wear a monitoring device, such as a film badge, thermoluminescent dosimeter (TLD), or pocket ionization chamber. The three main principles of radiation protection (time, distance, and shielding) should be followed to reduce exposure to personnel.

Time

Keep the time of exposure to radiation as short as possible, because the amount of exposure is directly proportional to the time of exposure, as indicated in the following equation:

$$\text{Exposure} = \text{Exposure rate} \times \text{time}$$

The exposure rate is the output of radiation from the source per unit time.

Distance

Always maintain as large a distance as possible between the source of radiation and the personnel administering the radiation. This is because radiation continually diverges from its source, so as distance is increased, less radiation exists per unit area. Reduction in radiation intensity with distance follows an inverse square relationship and can be determined from the following equation:

$$\frac{\text{New intensity}}{\text{Old intensity}} = \frac{\text{Old distance}^2}{\text{New distance}^2}$$

For example, if the radiation intensity at 90 cm is 1.3 R/min, then at 270 cm it would be reduced to an intensity of only 0.14 R/min.

Shielding

Any material that can be placed between you and a source of radiation is considered shielding. Materials with a high atomic number, such as lead, are best for shielding, because the greatest amount of photoelectric absorption will occur. Shielded booths are required for housing the control panel of radiographic units. The walls of the examination room are designed to protect personnel, other hospital employees, and the general public from unnecessary exposure. Lead aprons and gloves must be provided to employees who must be outside of the control booth during diagnostic procedures. ● *Lead aprons must have a minimum lead equivalent thickness of at least 0.5 mm, and lead gloves must be of at least 0.25 mm lead equivalence.* Technologists should not have the responsibility of routinely holding patients during diagnostic procedures and must wear protective apparel if such an event occurs.

SUMMARY

Implementing a quality management program requires more than just equipment monitoring and maintenance. A basic knowledge of statistics and data collection, artifact analysis, administrative responsibilities, and radiation safety practices are essential characteristics of quality management technologists.

Review Questions

1. The entire set or group of items that are being measured are called the:
   a. population
   b. sample
   c. frequency
   d. central tendency

2. The average set of observations is known as the:
   a. mean
   b. median
   c. mode
   d. variance

3. Variables that have only two values or choices are termed:
   a. continuous variables
   b. dichotomous variables
   c. stochastic variables
   d. statistical variables

4. In departments with a quality management program in place, the greatest number of repeat images are due to:
   a. mechanical problems
   b. dark room fog
   c. patient motion
   d. positioning error

5. If a department performs a total of 1160 views during a 1-month period and 132 are repeated, the department repeat rate is:
   a. 9.5%
   b. 10.7%
   c. 11.4%
   d. 14.8%

6. Any repeat rate exceeding _____ % should be seriously examined.
   a. 2 to 4
   b. 4 to 6
   c. 6 to 8
   d. 10 to 12

7. Which of the following processing artifacts run in the same direction as film travel?
   a. Pi lines
   b. guide shoe marks
   c. hesitation marks
   d. chemical fog

8. A white, powdery residue on a film after processing normally is due to:
   a. static electricity
   b. wet-pressure sensitization
   c. hyporetention
   d. water spots

9. The types of static artifacts include:
   1. tree
   2. crown
   3. smudge
   a. 1 and 2
   b. 2 and 3
   c. 1 and 3
   d. 1, 2, and 3

10. The likelihood of obtaining a positive diagnosis in a patient with the disease actually present is termed:
    a. sensitivity
    b. specificity
    c. variance
    d. frequency

Student Experiment 10.1   Reject-Repeat Analysis

PURPOSE

To provide a method for the analysis of the rejected radiographs in a radiology department. The results of such an analysis provide information concerning those aspects of radiologic imaging that require the most attention.

EQUIPMENT NEEDED

1. Rejected radiographs and a count of the total number of films consumed during the survey period.
2. A quality control technologist and, preferably, a radiologist.

PROCEDURE

1. Clean out all rejected film bins in the department and collect rejects for a 2-week period.
2. Establish the total number of films taken for the same 2-week period.
3. Analyze, with a radiologist if possible, all of the rejected films and determine the reason that they were rejected.
4. Classify the rejects into the categories of positioning error, technique error, processing error, patient motion, and handling and storage artifacts and record this information on a data page (copy and use Figure 10-1).
5. Determine the causal repeat rate for each of the above categories.

ANALYSIS (INCLUDE DATA SHEET, FIGURE 10-1)

1. What is the overall department repeat rate? Is it within acceptable limits?
2. What is the causal repeat rate for each of the following: positioning error, technique error, processing error, patient motion, and handling and storage artifacts?
3. What are some recommendations to help reduce the repeat rate in each category?

PURPOSE

To accurately determine the attenuation or transmission of radiation under critical conditions and evaluate the effect of different combinations of factors on reducing patient exposure.

EQUIPMENT NEEDED

1. Pocket dosimeter or digital dosimeter with probe
2. X-ray generator
3. Pelvis or abdomen phantom
4. Lead vinyl

PROCEDURE

1. Place the phantom on the tabletop and set the x-ray tube to 40-inch SID Bucky.
2. A series of exposures will be taken with the dosimeter on top of the gonadal area of the phantom, unshielded by lead vinyl (entrance dose); on top of the gonadal area but under a gonadal shield (shielded dose); and beneath the phantom, unshielded (exit dose).
3. Set the field size to 14 × 17 inches, and make a series of exposures using 70 kVp and 120 mAs. Record the following values:
   Entrance dose _____ mR
   Exit dose   _____ mR
   Shielded dose _____ mR
4. Repeat the above exposures using 90 kVp and 30 mAs.
   Entrance dose _____ mR
   Exit dose   _____ mR
   Shielded dose _____ mR
5. Add an additional 2 mm of aluminum filtration to the bottom of the collimator, and record the readings taken at 70 kVp and 120 mAs.
   Entrance dose _____ mR
   Exit dose   _____ mR
   Shielded dose _____ mR
6. Keep the 2-mm filtration in place and expose at 90 kVp and 30 mAs.
   Entrance dose _____ mR
   Exit dose   _____ mR
   Shielded dose _____ mR
7. Remove the additional filtration, and adjust the collimator to a 5- × 5-inch field size, centered to the gonadal area. Make a series of exposures at 70 kVp and 120 mAs.
   Entrance dose _____ mR
   Exit dose   _____ mR
   Shielded dose _____ mR
8. Repeat the 5- × 5-inch field size exposures using 90 kVp and 30 mAs.
   Entrance dose _____ mR
   Exit dose   _____ mR
   Shielded dose _____ mR

ANALYSIS

1. Compare the entrance dose, exit dose, and shielded dose values for the 70 kVp and 90 kVp exposures in steps 3 and 4. What are some explanations for the results obtained?
2. Compare the values obtained with the additional filtration in place from steps 5 and 6 with those with no additional filtration in place from steps 3 and 4. How can any differences be explained?
3. Compare the values obtained from the 5- × 5-inch field size from steps 7 and 8 with those obtained with the 14- × 17-inch field size from steps 3 and 4. How can any differences be explained?
4. Based on the data, which combination has the greatest impact on patient exposure?
   a. High kVp, low mAs factors
   b. Additional filtration
   c. Reduction in field size
Support the chosen combination with data.

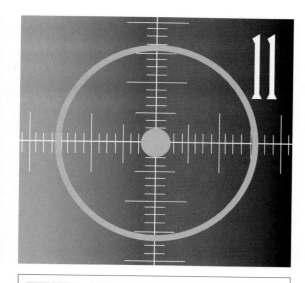

11 Mammographic Quality Standards

Mammography is soft tissue radiography of the breast. It requires different equipment and techniques from conventional radiography because of the close similarities between anatomic structures (low subject contrast). Low kVp in the 20- to 30-kVp range must be deployed to maximize the amount of photoelectric effect and enhance differential absorption. The side effect of these low kVp exposure factors are correspondingly higher mAs values, which increase the total radiation dosage to the patient. Because the glandular tissue of the breast is inherently radiosensitive, care must be taken to minimize radiation exposure through dedicated equipment and quality control procedures.

DEDICATED MAMMOGRAPHY EQUIPMENT

X-Ray Generator

The x-ray generators used in mammographic studies should be dedicated solely to mammographic imaging (Figure 11-1). All current mammographic x-ray generators are either three-phase or, more commonly, high-frequency, to reduce the space requirement of the unit. The kVp range available on most units is between 20 and 35 kVp. All systems must be equipped with an automatic exposure control (AEC) system consisting of 2 to 3 sensors to regulate the optical density of the resulting image.

X-ray Tube

Modern mammographic x-ray units use rotating anode x-ray tubes just as conventional radiographic units do. However, some significant differences are present, including the x-ray tube window, target composition, focal spot size, and source-to-image distance (SID).

X-ray Tube Window

X-ray tubes used in conventional radiographic, fluoroscopic, and computed tomography units incorporate a window made primarily of glass (which is essentially silicon with an atomic number of 14). Because relatively high kVp exposure factors are used in these studies, absorption of lower-energy x-rays in the window material is acceptable and actually desired. Mammographic x-ray tubes use a thinner glass window or a **beryllium window** (atomic number of 4), which is less likely to absorb the low kVp x-rays used in mammographic procedures. The inherent filtration of the beryllium is about 0.1 mm Al equivalent compared with 0.5 mm Al equivalent for standard radiographic tubes.

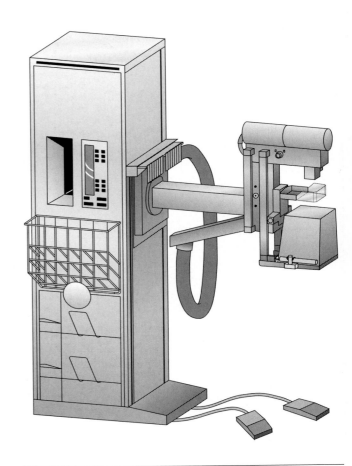

FIGURE 11-1
Dedicated mammographic unit.

Target Composition

Conventional radiographic x-ray tubes use a **target composition** of a tungsten-rhenium alloy. A mixture of x-rays produced by both bremsstrahlung (the slowing down of the projectile electron causing a wide range of x-ray energies) and characteristic radiation (x-rays created by electron transitions between orbits resulting in specific or discrete energies). This effect can be demonstrated using an x-ray **emission spectrum** graph (Figure 11-2). This wide band of energies may be desirable in conventional radiography but is not desirable in mammography because of the low subject contrast. Factors affecting the x-ray emission spectrum graph include mA, kVp, added filtration, target material, and voltage waveform/ripple.

mA. The factor of mA changes the amplitude of the curve (height of the Y axis) but not the shape of the curve (Figure 11-3).

kVp. The factor of kVp changes both the amplitude and the position of the spectrum curve. An increase in kVp shifts the spectrum to the right, indicating higher energy values (Figure 11-4).

Added Filtration. Because filtration affects x-ray quality, the effect on the x-ray emission spectrum is similar to that of kVp. If filtration is increased, the amplitude decreases and the spectrum shifts slightly to the right (Figure 11-5).

Target Material. The amplitude and shape of the emission spectrum changes with any changes in the atomic number of the target material. If the atomic number increases, the continuous portion of the spectrum (bremsstrahlung) increases slightly in amplitude, especially to the high-energy side, whereas the discrete portion of the spectrum (characteristic x-rays) shifts to the right (Figure 11-6). The target materials used in mammographic x-ray

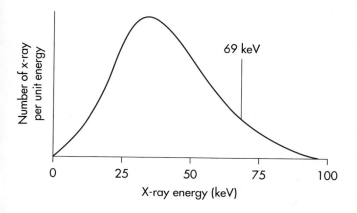

FIGURE 11-2

Emission spectrum for tungsten-rhenium target.

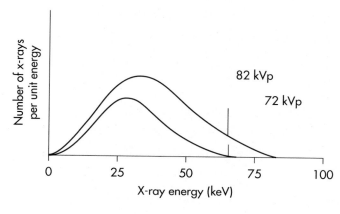

FIGURE 11-4

Effect of kVp on emission spectrum.

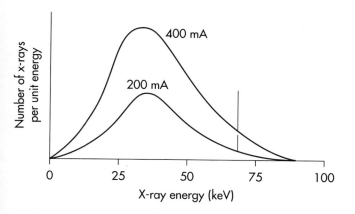

FIGURE 11-3

Effect of mA on emission spectrum.

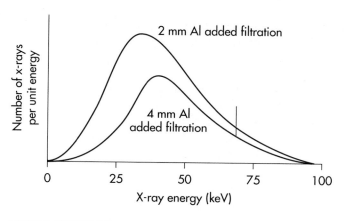

FIGURE 11-5

Effect of added filtration on emission spectrum.

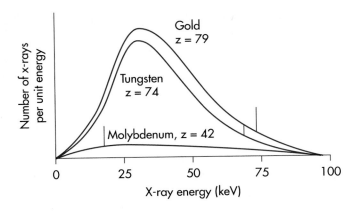

FIGURE 11-6

Effect of target material on emission spectrum.

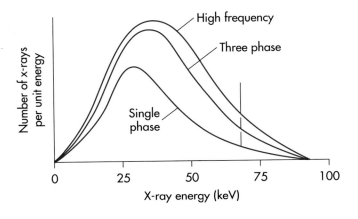

FIGURE 11-7

Effect of voltage waveform on emission spectrum.

tubes can include tungsten, molybdenum, rhodium, or a combination of these.

TUNGSTEN (ATOMIC NUMBER, 74). Tungsten produces a wide band of x-ray energies, including some that are not useful in mammographic imaging. The emission spectrum is then shaped using filters of either aluminum, molybdenum, or rhodium.

MOLYBDENUM (ATOMIC NUMBER, 42). The lower atomic number significantly reduces the number of bremsstrahlung x-rays, so that virtually all of the x-rays exiting the x-ray tube housing are characteristic x-rays of approximately 17.5 keV (well within the K-edge of the image receptor being used). A 30- to 50-μm molybdenum filter is added to further eliminate any bremsstrahlung x-rays. This target material is commonly used for normal or fatty breast composition.

RHODIUM (ATOMIC NUMBER, 45). Rhodium creates an emission spectrum similar to that of molybdenum. The characteristic x-rays have an energy of about 23 keV (slightly higher than molybdenum, making it better for

more dense breast tissue), and more bremsstrahlung x-rays are created. A 50-μm rhodium filter is used.

MOLYBDENUM-RHODIUM-TUNGSTEN ALLOY. Molybdenum-Rhodium-Tungsten alloy target material exhibits a mixed emission spectrum with characteristics of each element. By selecting either aluminum, rhodium, or molybdenum filters, the emission spectrum can be shaped to fit the image receptor that is employed.

Voltage Waveform/Ripple. Three-phase and high-frequency x-ray generators create x-rays with a higher average energy (quality) and in greater number (quantity) than single-phase x-ray generators. Therefore the amplitude and relative position of the spectrum are different. With the three-phase and high-frequency generators, the amplitude increases and the spectrum shifts to the right, indicating higher average energy (Figure 11-7).

Focal Spot Size

The spatial resolution required in mammographic images is greater than that of conventional radiography because of the need to demonstrate microcalcifications. This must be accomplished using a small focal spot, ranging in size from 0.1 to 0.6 mm. Some manufacturers tilt the x-ray tube toward the cathode side, which reduces the effective focal spot size even further.

Source-to-Image Distance

The source-to-image distance (SID) used in dedicated mammographic units ranges from 50 to 80 cm. Effective October 1, 2000, the Food and Drug Administration (FDA) will require that the minimum SID shall be at least 55 cm.

Compression

All modern mammographic units must be equipped with a **compression** device, usually made of radiolucent plastic. This is used to gently compress the breast tissue using a force of up to 45 lb. An automatic adjust and release mechanism is found on most systems. The advantages of breast compression are shown in Box 11-1.

Grids

To help increase image contrast, fiber-interspaced grids are often used. The grid ratios range from 3:1 to 5:1, and the grid frequency is 30 lines/cm and focused to the x-ray source. Uniformity of construction and motion are paramount.

Image Receptors

The majority of mammographic examinations currently performed use film/screen combinations as the primary

Box 11-1 Advantages of Breast Compression

1. Immobilization of the part, which reduces motion blur.
2. More uniform part thickness, which manifests as more uniform optical densities in the final image.
3. All object structures are brought closer to the image receptor, which reduces geometric unsharpness and improves spatial resolution.
4. The part is thinner, which reduces patient dosage and scattered radiation.

image receptor. The film is most often single-emulsion, to eliminate any parallax effect, and spectrally matched to the screen. Rare-earth phosphors (often containing yttrium) are used in the intensifying screens to help reduce patient dose and increase image contrast. Digital image receptors using charge-coupled devices (discussed in Chapter 8) or imaging plates similar to those used in digital radiography are becoming more common.

Film Processors

Mammographic images should have a dedicated film processor for conversion of the latent image into a manifest image. A common option for processing mammographic images is **extended processing**, which extends the standard cycle of a 20-second developing time to a cycle of 40 seconds. The developer temperature, concentration, and composition remain unchanged. The main advantages of extended processing are greater image contrast (approximately 15%), increased image receptor sensitivity (about 30%), and reduced patient dose (about 30%). These improvements occur only when single-emulsion films are used.

MAMMOGRAPHIC QUALITY ASSURANCE

The importance of mammography in the early diagnosis of breast cancer has been well demonstrated. Mammograms can detect breast cancer as early as 2 years before a lump can be felt during manual examination. To accomplish this, the images must be of the highest quality and the interpreting physician must be highly trained. This means that a detailed quality management program must be in place to minimize any variations, which are even more detrimental to image quality in mammography because of the low subject contrast.

Mammography Quality Standards Act

Before 1992, quality standards for mammography were the responsibility of individual state agencies. The American College of Radiology (ACR) began a voluntary Mammography Accreditation Program (MAP) in 1987, which required specific quality control and quality assurance procedures for equipment and personnel. Approximately 30% of facilities that initially applied for ACR accreditation failed on their first attempt. Because so few facilities voluntarily sought and obtained ACR accreditation, concern of mammographic image quality prompted the U.S. Senate Committee on Labor and Human Resources to hold hearings on breast cancer in 1992. This committee discovered many problems with mammographic procedures in the United States, including poor-quality equipment, a lack of quality assurance procedures, poorly trained interpreting physicians, and no consistent oversight or facility inspections. This led to the enactment of Public Law 102-539, better known as the **Mammography Quality Standards Act** (MQSA), which passed on October 27, 1992. This law requires that all facilities (except for those of the Department of Veterans Affairs) be accredited by an approved accreditation body and certified by the Secretary of Health and Human Services to legally provide mammography services after October 1, 1994. The Secretary of Health and Human Services delegated the authority to approve accreditation bodies and to certify facilities to the FDA.

The main provisions of MQSA include the following:

- Accreditation of mammography facilities by private, nonprofit organizations (such as the ACR) or state agencies that have met the standards established by the FDA (including Iowa, Arkansas, and California) and have been approved by the FDA.
- An annual mammography facility physics survey, consultation, and evaluation performed by a qualified medical physicist.
- Annual inspection of mammography facilities performed by FDA-certified federal and state inspectors. To date, the District of Columbia, Puerto Rico, New York City, and all states except New Mexico are approved to perform these inspections.
- Establishment of initial and continuing qualification standards for interpreting physicians, radiologic technologists, medical physicists, and mammography facility inspectors.
- Specification of boards or organizations eligible to certify the adequacy of training and experience of mammography personnel.
- Establishment of quality standards for mammography equipment and practices, including quality assurance and quality control programs.
- Establishment of a National Mammography Quality Assurance Advisory Committee (NMQAAC) to advise the FDA of appropriate quality standards.
- Standards governing record keeping for examinee files and requirements for mammography reporting and ex-

aminee notification by physicians. Images must be kept no less than 5 years and no more than 10 years if no additional mammograms are performed at the facility.

Interim regulations enacted in 1992 served as a temporary and streamlined process that made it possible for mammography facilities to meet the October 1, 1994, deadline. Final regulations were developed in 1996 and implemented in 1997. The new requirements emphasize performance objectives rather than specifying the behavior and manner of compliance. The new requirements include the following:

- Specific regulations for accrediting bodies.
- General facility provisions, such as requirements for the content and terminology in the mammography report, specific guidelines for mammography reports, definition of the responsibilities of facility personnel, review of mammography medical outcomes audit data at least every 12 months, standards for examinees with breast implants, requiring of facilities to develop a system for collecting and resolving serious consumer complaints.
- Personnel regulations for interpreting physicians, medical physicists, and mammographers.
- New equipment requirements, which will phase in over a 10-year period, to reduce the cost of replacing or retrofitting equipment before its normal replacement date.

Quality Control Responsibilities

MQSA designates specific responsibilities for various members of the diagnostic imaging department.

Radiologist (Interpreting Physician)

The primary responsibility for mammography quality control is the lead interpreting physician or radiologist. Minimum qualifications include a license to practice medicine and certification by the American Board of Radiology (ABR), the American Osteopathic Board of Radiology (AOBR), or the Royal College of Physicians and Surgeons of Canada (RCPSC) or at least 2 months of documented full-time training in the interpretation of mammograms. They must also continue to read and interpret at least 40 patients per month over 24 months and obtain at least five continuing education units (CEUs) per year in mammography. These individuals also have the responsibility of following up any patient with a positive diagnosis.

Medical Physicist

Medical physicists are responsible for the quality control evaluation of the mammographic equipment. They must have a license or state approval or be certified by an FDA-

approved accrediting body. They must also obtain at least five CEUs per year in mammography. Specific areas on the equipment to inspect include the following:

- Visual inspection of mammographic assembly.
- Collimation assessment, which must be accurate to within ±2% of the SID.
- Focal spot size, which must conform to NEMA standards.
- kVp accuracy, which is checked semiannually with a digital kVp meter and must be accurate to within ±1 kVp (5%).
- kVp reproducibility, which can be evaluated with a dosimeter or phantom image, with a maximum variance of ±5% on a semiannual basis.
- Beam quality assessment. The minimum acceptable half-value layer is 0.3 mm aluminum equivalent. This is determined using the procedure outlined in Chapter 6 and is performed semiannually. Effective October 1, 2000, systems with variable filtration type or thickness shall be interlocked to prevent exposure if the selected filtration material is inappropriate for the target material chosen.
- Timer accuracy. The timer must be accurate to within ±5% and evaluated semiannually.
- AEC systems. An image of an approved homogenous phantom (Figure 11-8) should be created daily using the AEC system. The optical density of the film at the center shall not change from the established operating level by a value of more than ±0.2. This established level should be at least 1.2. The mAs shall not change by more than 10% from the established value corresponding to the operating level optical density.
- Uniformity of screen speed. The intensifying screen speed must be uniform throughout the entire surface and evaluated using the procedure outlined in Chapter 7.
- Breast entrance exposure. This must be determined at least annually using an approved phantom designed to simulate a breast made of 50% glandular and 50% adipose tissue that has been compressed to a 4.5-cm thickness. Measurement is obtained using a thermoluminescent dosimeter (TLD) or ion chamber, using the appropriate technique for the phantom size, and usually will range from about 300 mR to 800 mR per view.
- Average glandular dose. This value is derived from the breast entrance dose measurement (usually about 15% of this value) and should never exceed 400 mR.
- Image quality evaluation. Image quality is assessed by imaging an ACR mammography phantom that includes simulated microcalcifications, fibrils, and nodules. Microcalcifications of 320 μm, fibrils of 750 μm, and nodules of 1 mm must be visible in the final image.
- Artifact evaluation. Any artifacts should be identified on a daily basis using phantom and reject images so that corrective action can be immediately taken.

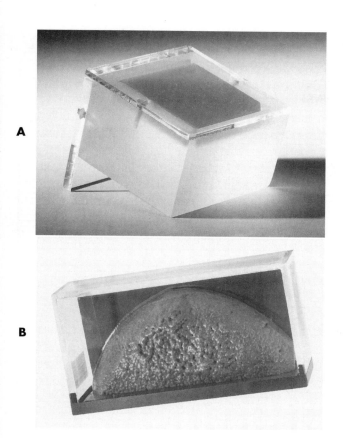

A

B

FIGURE 11-8

Conventional mammographic phantom (**A**) and anthropomorphic (lifelike) phantom (**B**). (Courtesy Nuclear Associates, Carle Place, N.Y.)

- Collimation. The light field/x-ray field alignment must be within ±2% of the SID. Effective October 1, 2005, all systems shall be interlocked to prevent exposure, unless appropriate combinations of beam limitation and image receptor size are selected.

Radiologic Technologist (Mammographer)

Technologists who perform mammograms must have at least 40 hours of training in mammography and be licensed by the individual state and/or certified by an approved agency (e.g., the ARRT) to verify competency in radiography. Technologists also should obtain five CEUs per year in mammography or as individual state guidelines dictate. Quality control duties are specified for technologists at daily, weekly, monthly, quarterly, and semiannual intervals.

Daily Duties

DARKROOM CLEANLINESS. The floor, countertops, processor feed tray, and passboxes should be cleaned with a damp cloth to remove any loose dirt that could get into the cassette and cause artifacts. Safelights and overhead air vents should be cleaned weekly.

PROCESSOR QUALITY CONTROL. The processor must be cleaned daily and must be operating according to manufacturer's specifications. Variations in developer temperature cannot exceed ±0.5° F (0.3° C) and must be checked only with a digital thermometer. Film immersion time should not vary by more than ±2% from manufacturer's specifications. After it has been determined that the processor is operating within accepted parameters, a sensitometric strip should be created and analyzed. The sensitometer should be spectrally matched with the type of film used (usually orthochromatic). If a single-sided film is used, then the sensitometer should be a single-sided device. For dual-emulsion film, a dual-sided device should be used. The exposed sensitometric film should always be processed in the same manner each day, usually first thing in the morning before any mammograms. The least exposed end should be fed into the processor first, and the same side of the feed tray should be used, with the emulsion side down to avoid bromide drag and location effect (see Chapter 4). The optical densities of the processed strip should be measured immediately and the following values determined:

- Base + Fog (B + F). The density of the clear portion of the film and must not vary by more than ±0.03 from the initial control value.
- D_{min}, or L. The optical density of the step closest to 0.25 above the B + F and should not vary by more than ±0.05 from the accepted value.
- Speed indicator, or medium density. This is the optical density of the step closest to 1 above the B + F and cannot vary by more than ±0.15 from the accepted value. If this variance occurs, all mammogram procedures must be halted and the cause of the variation must be found and corrected.
- D_{max}, or H. This is the optical density of the step closest to 2 above the B + F, and it cannot vary by more than ±0.15 from the accepted value.
- Contrast indicator, or density difference (DD). This value is obtained by subtracting the D_{min} from the D_{max}. The result should not vary by more than ±0.15 from the accepted value.

The B + F, speed indicator, and contrast indicator are plotted daily on a control chart (Figure 11-9).

During MQSA inspections, the inspector performs the Sensitometric Technique for the Evaluation of Processing (STEP) test on the processor. This involves comparing the optical densities of FDA control film processed in the facility processor to the same film developed in an FDA processor. If the optical densities of the two films are the same, a relative processing speed of 100 is given for stan-

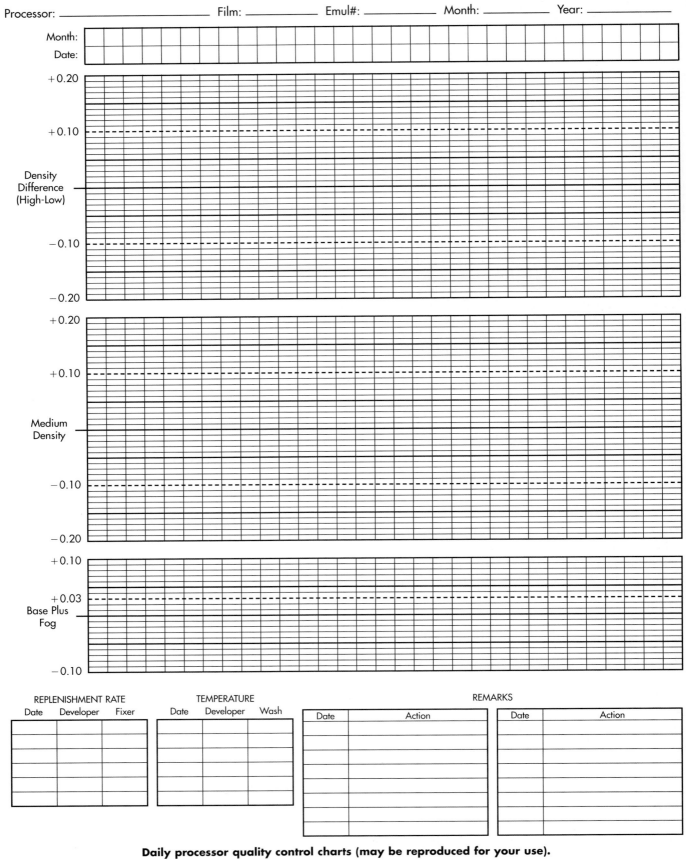

Daily processor quality control charts (may be reproduced for your use).

FIGURE 11-9

ACR processor control chart.

dard cycle and between 130 and 140 for extended cycles. Standard cycles with a speed of less than 80 or an extended cycle with a speed of less than 100 are cited as a Level 2 noncompliance.

Weekly Duties

SCREEN CLEANLINESS. Intensifying screens should be cleaned at least weekly or as needed. This can be accomplished using a screen cleaner recommended by the screen manufacturer and a lint-free gauze pad. Screens should be allowed to air dry while standing vertically before use. Alternate cleaning methods include the use of compressed air (available in cans from a photographic supply store) or dusting with a camel's hair brush.

VIEWBOXES AND VIEWING CONDITIONS. Viewbox fronts should be cleaned and free of any marks. The viewbox brightness level, color temperature, and ambient light conditions should be monitored using the equipment and procedures outlined in Chapter 2. Light output should be about 3500 nit, and ambient light should be 50 lux or less. Fluorescent bulbs should be replaced at least every 2 years. Figures 11-10, *A*, and 11-10, *B*, are checklists to document daily and weekly responsibilities.

Monthly Duties

PHANTOM IMAGES. Phantom images are taken to assess optical density, contrast, uniformity, and image quality. An ACR accreditation or equivalent phantom is required, along with an acrylic disk that is 4 mm thick and 1 cm in diameter (Figure 11-11). A magnifying glass, densitometer, and specialized control chart (Figure 11-12) are also required.

Procedure

1. Place the phantom on the cassette holder and position it so that the edge of the phantom is aligned with the chest wall side of the image receptor. Place the acrylic disc on the top of the phantom but position it so that it will not obscure details of the phantom.

2. Next, bring the compression device into contact with the phantom. If the AEC system is used, the same sensor should be used for each phantom image and the phantom must completely cover the sensor. If manual technique is used, select the appropriate mA and exposure time.

3. Make the exposure at 28 kVp (or the most commonly used clinically) and record the mAs from the display on the control panel onto the control chart. This value should stay within a range of ±15%.

4. After the film is processed, measure the optical density of the film in the area of the disc and in the background directly adjacent to the disc. This should be to the left or right of the disc, perpendicular to the anode-cathode axis. The background density should be greater than 1.2, with an allowed range of ±0.2 on all subsequent images. Plot this value on the control chart.

5. The optical density from under the disc is then subtracted from the background density to determine the density difference. This value should be approximately 0.4, with an allowed range of ±0.05. The density difference is also plotted on the control chart.

6. Next, determine the total number of simulated masses, speck groups, and fibers visible in the image. A mass is counted as 1 point if a density difference is seen at the correct location, with a circular border, and 0.5 points if it is visible, but the shape is not circular. A fiber is counted as 1 if its entire length is visible at the correct location and with correct orientation. If one half or more of its length is visible, a value of 0.5 is assigned. Less than one half is assigned a value of zero. The speck groups should be viewed with a magnifying glass, and, if four or more of the six groups are visible, a value of 1 is assigned. If at least two of the six groups are visible, a value of 0.5 is given. Each score should be plotted on the control chart. The minimum score required to pass ACR accreditation is four fibers, three speck groups, and three masses, for a total of 10 objects. The score of phantom objects on subsequent images should not decrease by more than 0.5.

VISUAL INSPECTION. A visual inspection of the mammographic unit (similar to those described for radiographic units in Chapter 6) should be performed using a checklist (see Figure 11-13). Specific items of note include the following:

- SID indicator. The SID indicator must be accurate to within ±2% of the source-to-image distance.
- Angulation indicator. The system should provide a visual indication of the gantry angle to within ±5°. This will become mandatory effective October 1, 2005.
- Field light. The field light should provide an average illumination of not less than 160 lux (15 ft-cd) at 100 cm or the maximum SID, whichever is less. This is evaluated with a photometer.
- Compression. All mammographic systems should incorporate a compression device. The following are effective October 1, 2000:

Text continued on p. 184

Mammography Quality Control Checklist

Mammography Quality Control Checklist

Department of Diagnostic Radiology

Daily and Weekly Checks

Year																															
Month																															
Date																															
Initials																															
Darkroom cleanliness																															
Processor quality control																															
Screen cleanliness																															
Viewboxes and viewing conditions																															

A

Year																															
Month																															
Date																															
Initials																															
Darkroom cleanliness																															
Processor quality control																															
Screen cleanliness																															
Viewboxes and viewing conditions																															

Year																															
Month																															
Date																															
Initials																															
Darkroom cleanliness																															
Processor quality control																															
Screen cleanliness																															
Viewboxes and viewing conditions																															

FIGURE 11-10

ACR daily **(A)** and weekly checklists. **B,** Monthly, quarterly, and semiannually checklists.

Mammography Quality Control Checklist
Department of Diagnostic Radiology

Monthly, Quarterly, and Semiannual Checks

Mammography
Quality Control
Checklist

Year											
Month											
Date											
Initials											
Phantom images											
Visual checklist											
Repeat analysis											
Fixer retention											
Darkroom fog											
Screen-film contact											
Compression											

B

FIGURE 11-10, cont'd
For legend see opposite page.

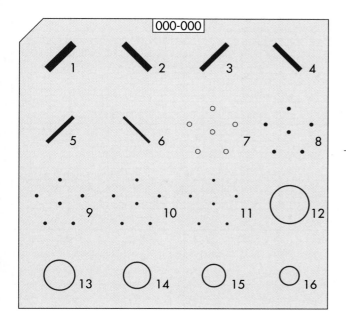

FIGURE 11-11
ACR accreditation phantom.

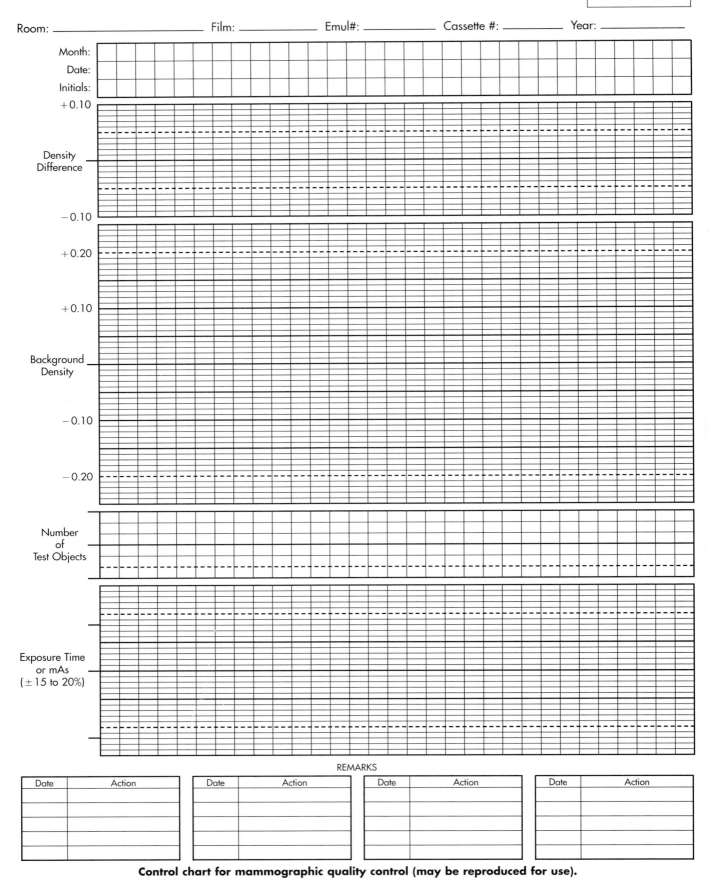

Control chart for mammographic quality control (may be reproduced for use).

FIGURE 11-12

ACR phantom control chart.

Mammography Quality Control Visual Checklist

Visual Quality Control Checks

Building: _____ Room No: _____ Tube: _____

C-Arm	SID indicator or marks																
	Angulation indicator																
	Locks (all)																
	Field light																
	High tension cable/other cables																
	Smoothness of motion																
	_____																
Cassette holder	Cassette lock																
	Compression device																
	Compression scale																
	Amount of compression: Automatic																
	Manual																
	Grid																
	_____																
Control booth	Hand switch placement																
	Window																
	Panel switches/lights/meters																
	Technique charts																
	_____																
Other	Gonad shield/aprons/gloves																
	Cones																
	Cleaning solution																
	_____																
	_____																
	_____																

Pass = ✓
Fail = F
Does not apply = NA

Month:

Date:

Initials:

Visual checklist (may be reproduced for use).

FIGURE 11-13
ACR visual checklist.

- Power-driven compression activated by foot controls operable from both sides of the examinee shall be provided, along with fine-adjustment compression controls.
- The compression device shall provide a maximum compression for the power drive between 25 lb (111 N) and 45 lb (200 N).
- A manual emergency compression release that can be activated in the event of power failure or equipment malfunction shall be provided.
- Grids. The grid motion shall not be impeded when a breast is subjected to compression during mammography.

Quarterly Duties

REPEAT ANALYSIS. All rejected films should be collected, examined for the specific cause, and recorded on a repeat analysis form (Figure 11-14). At least 250 patients are needed for valid results. The total repeat rate and causal repeat rate should be calculated using the equations listed in Chapter 10. The overall repeat should be less than 2%, and the causal repeat rate in any one category should not exceed 5%.

ARCHIVAL QUALITY. The amount of hyporetention in mammographic films should be evaluated using a test kit such as the one described in Chapter 3.

Procedure

1. Place a drop of solution on a sheet of unexposed but processed film and allow it to stand for 2 minutes.
2. Remove the excess solution and compare the stain on the film with the test strip supplied by the manufacturer (Figure 11-15). If the amount of hyporetention exceeds 0.05 g/m², the processor should be inspected and the reason for the discrepancy investigated.

Semiannual Duties

DARKROOM FOG. Inspection should be performed semiannually to ensure that darkroom safelights and other light sources do not fog mammographic films (because this would reduce contrast). Safelight filters and bulb wattage should be inspected and proper distance from work surfaces verified. The personnel performing the inspection should turn off all lights in the darkroom and remain in the dark for 5 minutes to allow the eyes to become adjusted to minimal light conditions. Observe and correct any obvious light leaks, especially around doors,

passboxes, processors, or ceiling. Turn on all fluorescent lights in the darkroom for 2 minutes and then turn them off. Observe any obvious afterglow (greater than 1 minute).

Procedure

1. Expose a film from the bin with a sensitometer on the right side and then the left side of the sheet of film and place it on the countertop.
2. Cover the image on the right side with a piece of cardboard or other opaque material and leave the left side uncovered. Turn on all safelights, let the film lay on the countertop for 2 minutes, and then process the film.
3. Find the step having an optical density closest to 1.4 on the covered strip and then take a density reading of the same step from the uncovered strip. The difference between the two values should not exceed an optical density value of 0.02. If the difference does exceed this value, corrective action must be taken.

FILM-SCREEN CONTACT. Mammographic image receptors must provide spatial resolution of at least 11 lp/mm (significantly greater than conventional image receptors). To maintain this level of spatial resolution, the contact between the film and screen must be as close as possible. A mammography film-screen contact test tool consisting of a copper screen with at least 40 wires per inch is required (Figure 11-16). This is usually laminated in plastic with the equivalent density of 4 cm of acrylic.

Procedure

1. Place the contact tool over the cassette, move the compression device as close as possible to the x-ray tube, and expose at 28 kVp and enough mAs to produce an optical density between 0.7 and 0.8 when measured over the mesh area near the chest wall side of the film.
2. After processing, place the film on a viewbox and look for clarity and nonuniformity in optical density. Dark or "fuzzy" areas indicate poor film-screen contact. Areas greater than 1 cm or more than two areas less than 1 cm should not be tolerated.

Mammography Repeat Analysis

Repeat
Analysis

From _____ To _____

Cause	Number of Films	Percentage of Repeats
1. Positioning		
2. Patient motion		
3. Light films		
4. Dark films		
5. Black film		
6. Static		
7. Fog		
8. Incorrect patient ID or double exposure		
9. Mechanical		
10. Miscellaneous (?)		
11. Good films (no apparent problem)		
12. Clear film		
13. Wire localization		
14. QC		

Totals

Rejects (all; 1-14)	%	
Repeats (1-11)	%	

Total film used [   ]

Form for repeat analysis data collection (may be reproduced for use).

FIGURE 11-14
ACR repeat analysis form.

COMPRESSION. For adequate compression of the breast, the compression force should range from 25 to 45 lb in both manual and power-drive modes; hold this compression for at least 15 seconds. This can be evaluated using a scale placed directly under the compression device. Any compression greater than 45 lb is dangerous to the patient.

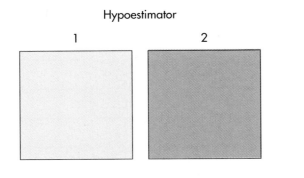

FIGURE 11-15
Hyporetention estimator test strip.

If the power drive fails to cease compression when greater than 45 lb is measured, then a service engineer is required.

FDA Inspection

As a result of the MQSA, only FDA-certified facilities may lawfully conduct mammography. To maintain its certified status, each facility must do the following:

- Have an annual survey performed by a qualified medical physicist.
- Undergo periodic audits and/or clinical image reviews by the accreditation body.
- Undergo annual inspection by an FDA-certified inspector.
- Pay an inspection fee and/or reinspection fee if necessary.
- Correct any deficiencies found during the inspections.

The FDA-MQSA inspection covers equipment performance, technologist and physicist quality control tests, medical audit and outcome analysis records, medical records (mammography reports and films), and personnel qualification records. Approximately 6 hours are required to complete an inspection of a facility with a single mammographic unit.

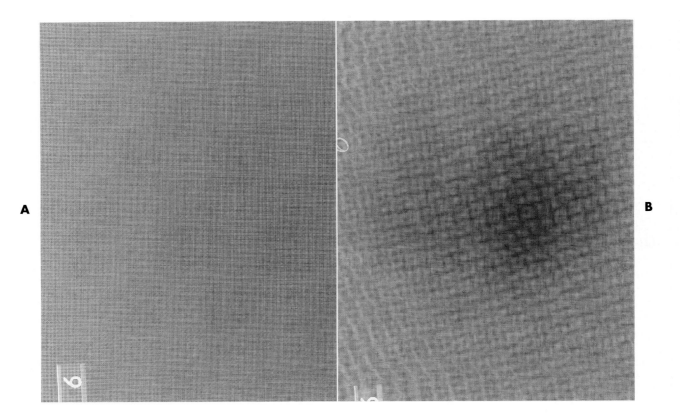

FIGURE 11-16
Wire mesh test images showing **(A)** good and **(B)** poor film screen contrast. (Courtesy Sharon Glaze; from Bushong SC: *Radiologic science for technologists,* ed 6, St Louis, 1997, Mosby.)

Equipment Performance

For equipment performance, the inspector assesses the following:

- Collimation system (x-ray field/image receptor and image receptor/compression device alignments).
- Entrance skin exposure and exposure reproducibility.
- Beam quality (HVL) measurement.
- Phantom image quality evaluation (including phantom scoring).
- Processor evaluation and darkroom fog measurement.

Records

The records that the inspector will ask to review include the following:

- Records for the previous 12 months for the 11 technologist quality control tests/tasks mentioned previously.
- Actual sensitometric film strips for the previous 30 days of mammographic film processing and charting of the strips for the previous 12 months.
- Images from film-screen contact and darkroom fog tests for the previous 12 months.
- Phantom images and charting for the previous 12 months.
- Annual medical physicist's report for each x-ray unit.
- Quality assurance/quality control documentation forms.
- Personnel orientation program for technologists.
- Procedures for equipment use and maintenance.
- Mammographic technique charts, including information pertinent to optimizing mammographic quality, such as positioning and compression.
- Radiation safety policy and responsibilities.
- Medical audit and outcomes analysis. This is a system to track positive mammograms and a process to correlate the findings with the surgical biopsy results obtained.
- Examinee permanent records, which include the actual film images and the mammography report of the interpreting physician.

Inspection Report

Following the inspection, a report summarizing the inspection findings will be sent to the institution. The findings will fall into one of the following categories.

Level 1. A Level 1 finding is a deviation from MQSA standards that may seriously compromise the quality of mammography services offered by a facility. A warning letter will be sent if this type of finding exists, to allow the facility to correct the problem before any enforcement action is implemented.

Level 2. A Level 2 finding is not as serious a deviation from MQSA standards as a Level 1 finding, but it still may compromise the quality of a facility's mammography program and should be corrected as soon as possible. Facilities with these findings are rated "acceptable" but must submit an acceptable corrective action plan to the FDA.

Level 3. A Level 3 finding is a minor deviation from MQSA standards. Facilities with only Level 3 findings are rated "satisfactory" but should institute policies and procedures to correct these conditions.

No Findings. A report of no findings shows that the facility has met all requirements of the MQSA.

SUMMARY

Quality control and quality assurance for mammographic equipment and procedures are mandatory for compliance with MQSA. Proper documentation of these procedures is essential for a facility to remain accredited to perform mammographic procedures.

Review Questions

1. What kilovoltage range should be used during film/screen mammography?
   a. 15 to 20 kVp
   b. 20 to 28 kVp
   c. 30 to 40 kVp
   d. 40 to 50 kVp

2. The focal spot size for most mammographic x-ray tubes ranges from:
   a. 0.1 to 0.6 mm
   b. 0.6 to 1.0 mm
   c. 1.0 to 1.5 mm
   d. 1.5 to 2.5 mm

3. Which type of filter material should be used with a molybdenum target x-ray tube?
   a. aluminum
   b. copper
   c. rhodium
   d. molybdenum

4. Which of the following will not change the shape of the x-ray emission spectrum?
   a. mA
   b. kVp
   c. exposure time
   d. target material

5. What is the usual range of force for mammographic system compression devices?
   a. 5 to 20 lb
   b. 15 to 30 lb
   c. 25 to 40 lb
   d. 45 to 60 lb

6. Which of the following is not an advantage of extended film processing in mammography?
   a. greater image contrast
   b. increased image receptor sensitivity
   c. reduced patient dose
   d. increased recorded detail

7. The light field/x-ray field alignment for mammographic units must be accurate to within ± _____ % of the SID.
   a. 2
   b. 3
   c. 4
   d. 5

8. The base + fog value of a mammographic sensitometry film should not vary by more than ± _____ from the initial control value.
   a. 0.02
   b. 0.03
   c. 0.05
   d. 0.10

9. The contrast indicator, or density difference, of mammographic sensitometry films should not vary by more than ± _____ from the initial control value.
   a. 0.03
   b. 0.05
   c. 0.10
   d. 0.15

10. Phantom images with an ACR accreditation phantom should be obtained at least:
    a. daily
    b. weekly
    c. monthly
    d. yearly

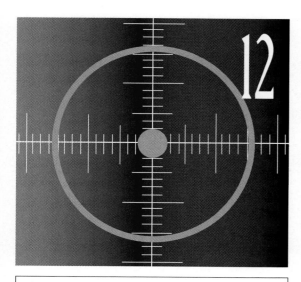

12

Quality Control in Computed Tomography

• Lorrie Kelly

Objectives

At the completion of this chapter the reader will be able to do the following:

• Differentiate between high- and low-contrast resolution
• Describe how basic quality control tests for computed tomography are conducted
• Describe the selection factors for quality control measurements
• Identify the parameters under technologist control that influence noise and spatial resolution

Outline

Acceptance Testing
Routine Testing
Couch incrementation
Contrast scale and the mean computed tomography number of water
High-contrast spatial resolution
Low-contrast resolution
Laser light accuracy
Noise and uniformity
Slice thickness
Linearity
Patient dose
Summary

Key Terms

acceptance testing
contrast scale
high-contrast spatial resolution
linearity
low-contrast resolution
mean CT number
noise
phantoms
region of interest
standard deviation

The goal of any quality control program is to ensure that the imaging equipment is producing the best possible image quality with a minimal radiation dose to the patient. The image quality in computed tomography can be difficult to maintain because of the complex nature of image acquisition and display. A contemporary computed tomography (CT) system is composed of numerous electronic parts and computers that generate and process huge amounts of data. Because of the system's complexity, a quality assurance program is essential to ensure optimal system performance and image quality with the least amount of radiation dose to the patient. Quality assurance programs in CT are designed to provide certain performance parameters that allow for performance comparisons between two scanners and help determine whether a newly installed unit meets the specifications set by the vendor.

ACCEPTANCE TESTING

Typically, the installation of most CT units is immediately followed by extensive **acceptance testing** by qualified physicists. The purpose of the acceptance tests is to ensure that the equipment is performing according to the manufacturer's specifications before it is released for clinical use. Acceptance testing consists of measuring radiologic and electromechanical performance, analyzing image-performance, and evaluating the system components. The results of the acceptance tests are used to identify system components that may need only slight adjustments and defective parts that should be replaced. At the conclusion of the acceptance testing, scans are taken of standard objects so that their images, CT numbers, and **standard deviations** can be recorded as a baseline for future measurements of the system's performance.

ROUTINE TESTING

To establish more consistency in the performance measurements of CT scanners, federal performance standards state that the vendors of CT systems manufactured after September 1985 are required to supply the following: instructions for performing quality control tests, a schedule for testing, allowable variations for the indicated parameters, a method to store and record the quality assurance data, and dose information in the form of a CT dose index. In addition, each vendor is required to supply **phantoms** capable of testing the following parameters: contrast scale, noise, slice thickness, spatial resolution capabilities for both high- and low-contrast objects, and the **mean CT number** of water or other reference material. Most routine quality control testing can be performed by a CT technologist. In most instances, vendors specify the test conditions

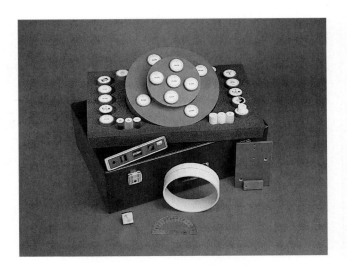

FIGURE 12-1

This CT phantom is used to evaluate noise, spatial resolution, contrast resolution, slice thickness, linearity, and uniformity. (From Bushong S: *Radiologic science for technologists,* ed 6, St Louis, 1997, Mosby.)

for evaluating their system's performance. Therefore specific procedures for evaluating a system's performance may vary among manufacturers. Also, there is some disagreement among manufacturers regarding the proper monitoring frequency for high- and low-contrast resolution, alignment, contrast scale, and slice thickness. Until a standard for monitoring frequency can be agreed upon it is best to follow the manufacturer's recommendations.

The performance of CT scanners is evaluated using a phantom as a test object. The phantoms that are supplied by the manufacturer can vary among vendors because of the differing requirements for performance evaluations and quality control testing. However, a typical phantom used to assess the performance of a CT system is multisectioned, which enables the separate evaluation of different parameters (Figures 12-1 and 12-2). In general, a phantom is constructed from plastic cylinders, with each section filled with water and/or other test objects to measure specific parameter performance. Some phantoms are designed so that numerous parameters can be evaluated with a single scan.

The commonly recommended quality control tests for routine performance evaluation of a CT system include contrast scale and mean CT number of water, high-contrast resolution, low-contrast resolution, laser light accuracy, noise and uniformity, slice thickness, and patient dose.

All quality control tests described in this chapter should be performed according to the following three basic tenets of quality control:

- The quality control tests should be performed on a regular basis

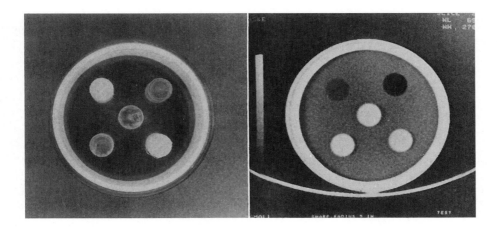

FIGURE 12-2

Photograph *(left)* and CT image *(right)* of the five-pin test phantom designed by the American Association of Physicists in Medicine. The attenuation coefficient for each pin is known precisely and the CT number computed. (From Bushong S: *Radiologic science for technologists,* ed 6, St Louis, 1997, Mosby.)

- All quality control test measurements should be documented using the data form provided by the manufacturer (Figure 12-3).
- The quality control test should indicate whether the tested parameter is within specified guidelines.

If quality control tests are not being performed according to these tenets, notify the appropriate personnel, such as the service engineer or the department physicist, so corrective action can be taken. In addition, the quality control tests described in this chapter should be considered generic only. They are intended to provide a basic guide for testing specific performance parameters (Table 12-1). It is always advisable to follow the instructions and specifications for quality control testing that are set by the manufacturer.

Couch Incrementation

Because the couch (table) moves through the gantry for CT examinations, the couch incrementation must be precise to ensure accurate patient position. All that is needed for this test is a measuring tape. An optional method uses a single piece of covered x-ray film.

Procedure

The first method can be performed during a routine patient examination.

1. Before scanning the patient, note the starting position of the couch.

2. Scan the patient as usual and note the end position of the couch.

3. Using the measuring tape, measure the distance the couch moved and compare with the intended couch movement.

The optional method uses the covered x-ray film.

1. Place the x-ray film lengthwise on the couch and tape into place.

2. To simulate the weight of a patient, place a phantom or other source weighing approximately 100 lb on the couch.

3. Using as small a collimation as possible, perform a series of 10 to 12 scans, with each scan separated by 10 mm. This test creates narrow bands of exposure on the covered film.

4. After processing the film, use a ruler to measure the distance between the exposed bands. This measurement should be compared with the intended movement of the couch between exposures.

Measured couch incrementation should be within ±2 mm of the intended couch movement. A couch incrementation test should be performed on a monthly basis.

Contrast Scale and the Mean Computed Tomography Number of Water

Contrast scale is defined as the change in linear attenuation coefficient per CT number relative to water. The con-

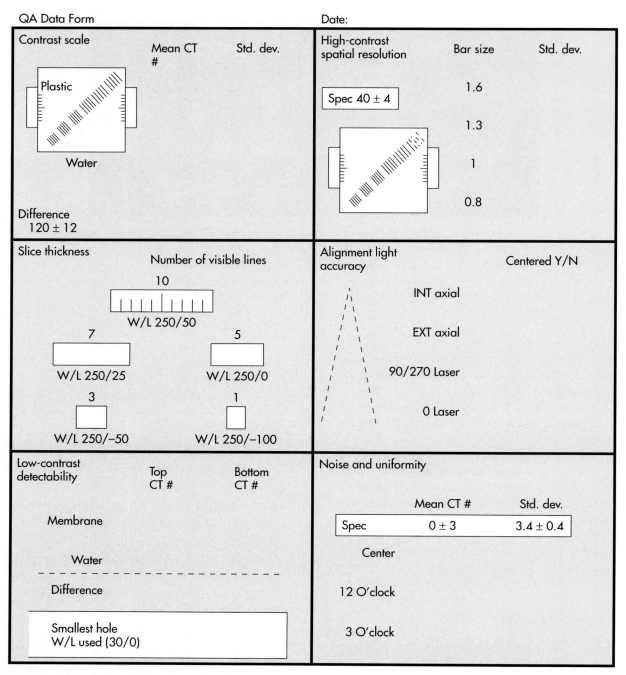

FIGURE 12-3

Sample quality assurance data form.

Table 12-1 Quality Control Tests for Specific Performance Parameters

Quality control test	Result	Frequency
Contrast scale and the mean CT number of water	CT number of water should not deviate more than ±3 CT numbers from 0; CT number of air should not deviate more than ±5 CT numbers from −1000	Weekly
High-contrast spatial resolution	0.45-1.5 lp/mm	Monthly
Low-contrast resolution	3-mm objects with density differences of 0.5% or less	Monthly
Laser light accuracy	Light and radiation fields should coincide with in 2 mm	Semiannually
Noise and uniformity	Noise should not exceed ±10 HU; uniformity should not vary more than ±2 HU between center and periphery	Weekly
Section thickness	If >5 mm, should not vary more than ±1 mm; if <5 mm, should not vary more than ±0.5 mm	Semiannually
Patient dose	Values should remain within ±10% of the manufacturer's specifications	Semiannually

trast scale is determined by the CT numbers for air (−1000 HU) and water (0 HU). In CT, the scanner assigns CT numbers to the attenuation values of x-rays passing through tissue. This test is done to determine if the scanner is assigning CT numbers that correspond to the appropriate tissue. This is important because many radiologists use CT numbers to identify suspected pathology in the image. To measure contrast scale it is necessary to calculate the CT number of known materials.

Water is the reference material used to determine CT numbers because it constitutes up to 90% of soft tissue mass, is easy to obtain, and is completely reproducible. Because water has a CT number value of zero, tissues with densities greater than water will have positive CT numbers, and those with densities less than water will have negative CT numbers.

A plastic, water-filled phantom is commonly used to measure the contrast scale of a CT system.

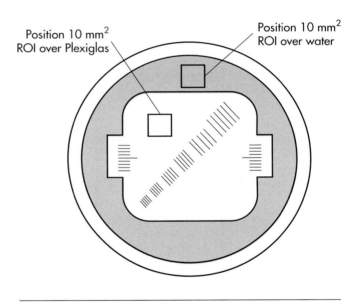

FIGURE 12-4
Test for contrast scale.

 Procedure

1. Using a specific technique, take a single scan through the phantom.

2. On the reconstructed image, select a 2- to 3-cm area in the center of the phantom and perform a **region of interest** (ROI) measurement (Figure 12-4).

3. From the pixels located within the ROI calculate the two parameters, the mean CT number and the standard deviation of the CT numbers.

4. On a monthly basis move the cursor outside of the phantom on the reconstructed image and perform the ROI function over air.

The contrast scale can vary with different x-ray energies. Therefore, for quality control testing, each test should be repeated at the same kVp setting. For optimal performance evaluation, measurements should be made for each kVp setting that is used clinically.

For consistent results, it is important to use the same cursor size and location each time the test is performed.

The acceptable limit for the CT number of water should not deviate more than ±3 CT numbers from zero. The acceptable limit for the CT number of air should not deviate more than ±5 CT numbers from −1000. When measurements of the contrast scale are compared, they can provide an indication of the low-contrast capabilities of a CT system on a day-to-day basis.

This quality control test should be performed on a weekly basis.

High-Contrast Spatial Resolution

High-contrast spatial resolution is described as the minimum distance between two objects that allows them to be seen as separate and distinct. The parameters that influence the high-contrast spatial resolution of a CT scanner include (1) scanner design (focal spot size, detector size and spacing, magnification); (2) image reconstruction (pixel size, reconstruction algorithm, slice thickness); (3) sampling (number of rays per projection and number of projections); and (4) image display capabilities (display matrix).

There are two procedures that can be used to evaluate the spatial resolution capabilities of a CT scanner. In the first method an edge is measured to determine the point spread function (PSF). The PSF is then mathematically transformed to obtain the modulation transfer function (MTF). This process takes considerable time and is usually completed by the physicist. The second method uses a bar or hole pattern to determine the spatial resolution. This method is commonly performed by the CT technologist and is explained in the following procedure.

Measurements of high-contrast spatial resolution are determined by using a phantom with test objects having contrast differences of 10% or greater. Typically, the quality control phantom contains rows with a set number of equally spaced squares or holes that have been drilled in plastic. Within each row, the holes will be of equal diameter; however, the diameter of the holes decreases from one row to the next (Figure 12-5).

Procedure

1. Take a single scan through the test object.

2. On the resultant image determine which row has the smallest set of holes in which all the holes can be clearly identified. This is known as the *limiting resolution* of the CT scanner.

Additionally, placing the cursor over a single- or multiple-bar pattern gives an ROI measurement that provides the standard deviation of the pixel values. This measurement is a quantitative method for assessing changes in the system resolution.

The limiting high-contrast spatial resolution of a CT scanner is measured in line pairs per centimeter. The range of 0.45 to 1.5 lp/mm represents the typical high-contrast resolution of CT scanners used today. Even though many modern scanners have the ability to resolve holes as small as 0.3 mm, the spatial resolution of CT scanners is still much lower than that of conventional radiography. The lower spatial resolution of CT is primarily a result of the spacing between the detectors. The results of this test can be compared with the baseline measurement of the scanner collected during optimal system performance or compared with the manufacturer's specifications. Comparative measurements over time provide an index of the performance reproducibility of the CT system.

It is recommended that this test be performed on a monthly basis.

Low-Contrast Resolution

Low-contrast resolution refers to the capability of the CT system to demonstrate subtle differences in tissue densities from one region of anatomy to another. Compared with conventional radiography, CT provides superior low-contrast resolution. Typically, contrast resolution is expressed in one of two ways: the smallest diameter of an object with a specific contrast that can be detected or the smallest difference in x-ray attenuation that can be discriminated for an object of a specific diameter.

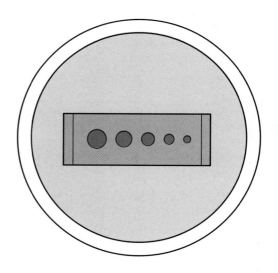

FIGURE 12-5

Phantom with equally spaced holes drilled in the plastic, used to measure high-contrast spatial resolution. (Courtesy GE Medical Systems.)

A phantom consisting of test objects, such as holes drilled into plastic, is used for this test. The rows of holes should be of varying sizes and filled with a liquid that has a CT number that differs from the CT number of the plastic by approximately 0.5% (Figure 12-6).

Procedure

1. Scan the phantom and determine the smallest row of holes that can be seen clearly.
2. Current CT scanners are capable of displaying 3-mm objects with density differences of 0.5% or less.

The primary factor limiting low-contrast resolution in CT is image noise caused by quantum mottle. As noise increases in an image, edge definition of anatomic borders and subtle differences in attenuation between tissues decreases (Figure 12-7).

This test should be performed on a monthly basis.

Laser Light Accuracy

Internal and external laser lights are used extensively for patient positioning and alignment. Accurate laser light performance is critical during stereotactic and interventional procedures.

Measurements to determine laser light accuracy can be made using the manufacturer's specific phantoms or a piece of covered, unexposed x-ray film.

Procedure

1. Tape the unexposed x-ray film securely to the CT table.
2. To measure the accuracy of the internal laser lights, turn on the internal laser lights and poke two small holes through the wrapper and x-ray film at the exact location of the light field. One hole should be near the right edge of the film, and the second hole should be near the left edge of the film.
3. Perform a scan through the location specified by the internal laser lights.
4. To measure the accuracy of the external laser lights, turn on the external laser lights and poke two small holes through either edge of the film at the exact location of the external light field.
5. Advance the table so it is in position to scan and perform a scan at that location.

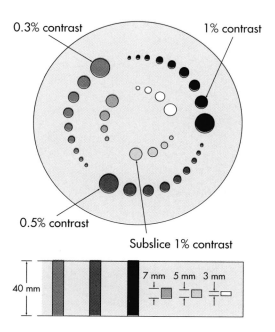

FIGURE 12-6

Drawing of a low-contrast CT phantom. (Modified from Bushong S: *Radiologic science for technologists,* ed 6, St Louis, 1997, Mosby).

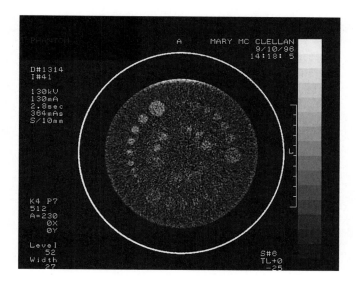

FIGURE 12-7

Image generated by using a phantom similar to the one demonstrated in Figure 12-6. (From Bushong S: *Radiologic science for technologists,* ed 6, St Louis, 1997, Mosby).

After processing the x-ray film, the two sets of holes represent the internal and external light fields and the two dark bands from radiation exposure represent the radiation field. To measure the accuracy of the laser lights, check to see if the dark bands of exposure fall directly over the associated holes. For optimal performance the light field should coincide with the radiation field to within 2 mm.

An alternative method to measure laser light accuracy is to scan the phantom and place a grid over the resultant image. Check to see if the grid lines up accurately with the lines on the phantom.

This test should be performed semiannually.

Noise and Uniformity

Noise represents the portion of the CT image that contains no useful information. It is defined as the random variation of CT numbers about a mean value when an image of a uniform object is obtained. The contrast resolution of a CT system is primarily determined by the amount of noise in the images. Noise produces a "salt-and-pepper" appearance or grainy quality in the image. The sources of noise in a CT image include quantum (statistical) noise, electronic noise, object size, reconstruction algorithms, and artifacts. Of these, the predominant source of noise is quantum noise, which is defined as the statistical variation in the number of photons detected.

Factors under the influence of the technologist that affect the amount of noise in an image are pixel size, slice thickness, and technique factors. Methods to minimize noise and help provide uniform images include tube warm-ups and daily system calibrations. Because the amount of noise contained in an image is inversely proportional to the total amount of radiation absorbed, noise can be measured by obtaining the mean and standard deviation of the CT numbers within an ROI.

Uniformity refers to the ability of the CT scanner to yield the same CT number regardless of the location of the ROI within a homogenous object.

A simple 20-cm water phantom can be used to measure noise and uniformity in CT.

Procedure

1. Take a scan through the water phantom, and position a cursor over the resultant image in three different locations.

2. The cursor should be positioned in the center, at the top, and at the side of the image (Figure 12-8).

3. At each cursor location, take an ROI measurement and record the standard deviation and mean CT number.

For noise measurements, the noise in a CT system should not exceed ±10 HU. However, if the scanner is used for quantitative CT, tighter specifications might be necessary.

For uniformity measurements, the uniformity (of the CT number of water) should not vary more than ±2 HU from the center of the phantom to the periphery.

These tests should be performed on a weekly basis.

Slice Thickness

The slice thickness in CT is determined primarily by the collimators. The position of the collimators determines the width of the slice that falls within the view of each detector. Another factor affecting slice thickness is focal spot size. The focal spot size can influence the penumbra, or sharpness of the edge of the x-ray beam, which can cause the edge of the slice to spread. Focal spot size in CT is determined by the technique factors and/or algorithm selected for the scan parameters.

Measurements of slice thickness are determined using a phantom that includes a ramp, spiral, or step-wedge in the test objects. The test objects have known measurements

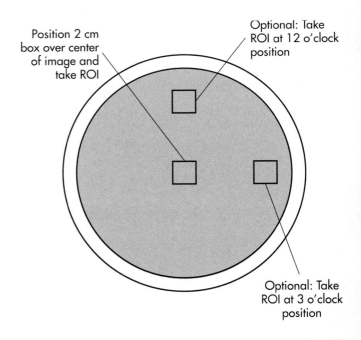

FIGURE 12-8

Test for noise and uniformity.

and provide a standard to compare with the scanner. Typically, the test objects are aligned obliquely to the scan plane (Figure 12-9).

Procedure

1. Perform three separate scans through the test object, each with a specified thickness (10 mm, 5 mm, 1 mm).

2. Display the images using the manufacturer's recommendations.

3. If a ramp is used, the length of the resultant image gives the slice width. For a spiral test object, the resultant image will contain an arc, with the arc length giving the slice width. When a step-wedge is used, the slice width can be determined by the number of steps that are imaged.

For a slice thickness of 5 mm or greater, the slice thickness should not vary more than ±1 mm from the intended slice thickness. For a slice thickness of 5 mm or less, the slice thickness should not vary more than ±0.5 mm.

This test should be performed semiannually.

Linearity

Linearity refers to the relationship between CT numbers and the linear attenuation values of the scanned object with a particular kVp value. When linearity is present within an image, it is an indication that subject contrast is constant across the range of CT numbers within the image.

A standard phantom containing materials with known physical and x-ray absorption properties is used for this test.

Procedure

1. Take a single scan through the appropriate phantom.

2. Plot the average CT numbers as a function of the attenuation values corresponding to the materials within the phantom.

Over time, these values can vary because of changes in system components. Daily calibrations help maintain image quality by compensating for changes in detector channel variations and responses.

The plotted values should demonstrate a straight line between the average CT numbers and the linear attenuation coefficients (Figure 12-10). Any deviation from the straight

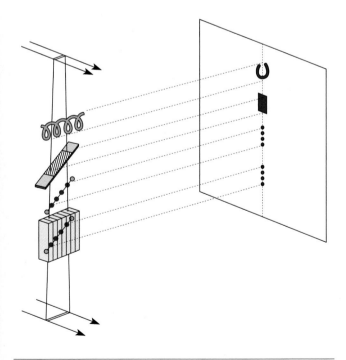

FIGURE 12-9

Test objects used for determining slice thickness. (From Marshall C: *The physical basis of computed tomography,* St Louis, 1982, Warren H Green.)

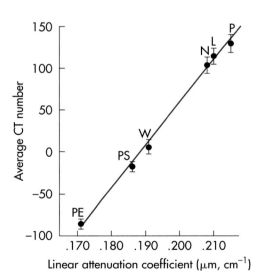

FIGURE 12-10

Graph demonstrating CT linearity. (From Bushong S: *Radiologic science for technologists,* ed 6, St Louis, 1997, Mosby.)

line could indicate that inaccurate CT numbers are being generated or the scanner is malfunctioning.

Linearity should be measured on a semiannual basis.

Patient Dose

It is important that personnel monitor the amount of radiation to which patients and staff are exposed. It is equally important for a CT technologist to realize that the patient dose can increase with changes in slice thickness, kVp, and mAs. In addition, if it is necessary for ancillary personnel to remain within the scan room, all CT technologists should be able to direct them to the safest location within the room to avoid unnecessary radiation exposure. Figure 12-11 provides representative isodose curves for a typical CT scanner.

Specially designed ionization chambers or thermoluminescent dosimeters (TLD) are used to measure the radiation dose. These specially designed radiation detectors are capable of providing measurements from which the dose can be calculated for the exposure factors used (slice thickness, mAs, and kVp).

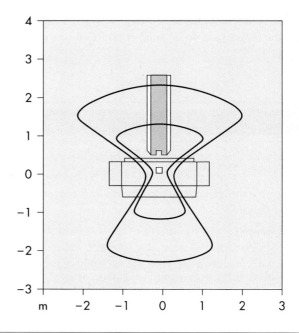

FIGURE 12-11

Isodose curves for a typical CT scanner. (From Wegener, OH: *Whole body computed tomography,* Cambridge, Mass, 1992, Blackwell Scientific.)

Procedure

1. Along with a standard phantom, position the radiation detecting device at the location and intervals of the desired radiation measurements.

2. Initiate the appropriate scans at the selected locations and measure the resultant radiation dose. Some facilities prefer to take two scans at each location, but with a change in the technique factors to simulate the difference between head and body examinations. This gives a more reliable dose estimate for a particular CT examination.

There are no acceptable maximum levels of radiation specified for the permissible dose to a patient during a CT procedure. In addition, the results can vary according to patient location and distance from the x-ray source. However, most experts agree that the values should remain within ±10% of the manufacturer's specifications when using a fixed technique.

This test should be performed semiannually or annually by the department physicist.

SUMMARY

An effective quality assurance program provides a method for systematic monitoring of the CT system's performance and image quality. The collected data is beneficial in identifying specific problems or malfunctions. Increasingly, it is becoming the responsibility of the CT technologist to perform and document the routine quality control tests. However, more extensive quality assurance procedures should be performed periodically by the department physicist and/or service engineer.

Review Questions

1. What is used as the reference material for CT number calibrations?
   a. bone
   b. liver
   c. water
   d. lung

2. Which of the following is the expected result of a CT number calibration test?
   a. 0 ± 5
   b. 1000 ± 5
   c. 0 ± 3
   d. 1000 ± 3

3. Which of the following is the primary determination of slice thickness?
   a. spacing between detectors
   b. collimators
   c. focal spot size
   d. field of view (FOV)

4. Which term describes the ability of a CT scanner to differentiate objects with minimal differences in attenuation coefficients?
   a. spatial resolution
   b. contrast resolution
   c. linearity
   d. modulation

5. Which of the following factors can affect the accuracy of a density (Hounsfield) measurement in a CT image?
   a. system calibration
   b. window width setting
   c. window level setting
   d. display field of view

6. Spatial resolution can be improved by increasing the:
   a. FOV
   b. matrix
   c. pixel size
   d. slice thickness

7. The main limiting factor for contrast resolution is:
   a. noise
   b. pixel depth
   c. voxel volume
   d. focal spot size

8. The modulation transfer function (MTF) is one method of measuring:
   a. low-contrast resolution
   b. high-contrast spatial resolution
   c. attenuation
   d. section thickness

9. A contemporary CT system should be able to detect 3-mm objects with density differences of:
   a. 0.05%
   b. 0.5%
   c. 1.0%
   d. 1.5%

10. What is the tolerance limit for noise in a CT image?
    a. ±3
    b. ±5
    c. ±10
    d. ±15

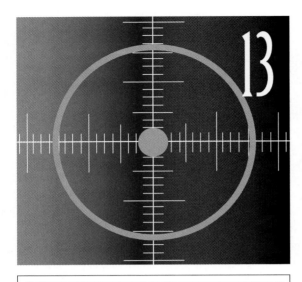

13

Quality Control for Magnetic Resonance Imaging Equipment

● Luann Culbreth

Objectives

At the completion of this chapter the reader will be able to do the following:

- Describe the various types of phantoms used in MR imagers
- Understand the frequency of quality control testing of various MR parameters
- Describe the concept of signal-to-noise ratio
- Understand the concept of resonant frequency
- Perform quality control testing for image uniformity, spatial linearity, slice position, and spatial resolution

Key Terms

image uniformity
signal-to-noise ratio
slice position
spatial linearity
spatial resolution
resonance frequency

Outline

Quality assurance procedures for magnetic resonance imaging (MRI) equipment are designed to establish a standard of measurement for daily system performance and the documentation of any variance thereof. Although the definition of "standard" varies from scanner to scanner, the goal of quality control is to detect any changes or potential changes in the system performance. Documentation of daily quality control measurements is considered an essential part of the MRI quality control program and must be done properly. The ultimate goal is to maintain high image quality.

PHANTOMS

Typically, the phantoms for routine quality control tests are provided by the MR system manufacturer. A users manual and charts for documenting standardized tests are also provided. Use of the equipment can easily be taught to the technologists during the site installation. The specific actions for obtaining and documenting quality control results vary among manufacturers.

Generally, quality control phantoms are a paramagnetic material in an oil or water solution. Ions such as copper, aluminum, manganese, and nickel are often used. The materials used are designed to mimic biologic tissues and/or shorten T1 relaxation times for strong MR signals. The relaxation rates vary with each material, B0 field strength, and temperature. Other considerations for materials are minimal chemical shifts and thermal and chemical stability. For the sake of the scan time when performing quality control tests, the T1 of the phantom material should be compatible with a short TR, and the T2 should be long enough for any TE value obtainable. Figure 13-1 demonstrates a copper (II) sulfate ($CuSo_4$) phantom used daily at a clinical site.

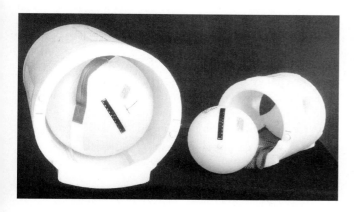

FIGURE 13-1

Left, Body coil phantom and holder. *Right,* Head coil phantom and holder.

Quality control phantoms are designed with various shapes, sizes, and geometric variables. The same type of phantom may be used for signal-to-noise ratio (SNR) and resonant frequency tests; whereas a different phantom is required for spatial resolution and linearity. Regardless of the type of test is being performed, it is important that any quality control phantom be placed in the magnet at isocenter, unless specified otherwise. It is also important to document the scanning parameters used, that is, TR, TE, flip angle, slice thickness, matrix, coil, and so on.

PRIMARY QUALITY FACTORS

Quality control tests should be performed daily by the MR technologist and monthly, quarterly, and semiannually by a service engineer. Planning and preparing for the quality control tests should be a part of the site installation process. A medical physicist, service engineer, system manufacturer specialist, and site technologists should discuss goals and potential outcomes for regular quality control tests. It can then be decided which tests should be performed at certain intervals and by which personnel. Although all of the tests are important, all are not required daily. Think of it as monitoring essential fluids in a car. The windshield washer fluid may be checked infrequently, the oil checked more regularly, and the gasoline monitored daily. The factors listed here are unanimously believed to be essential indicators of MR system performance.

Signal-to-Noise Ratio

The **signal-to-noise ratio** (SNR) has many varying definitions. Although some describe it in complicated mathematical calculations, others simplify it into a measure of the graininess of the image. The simplest form seems to be the signal, which is the mean intensity within a uniform phantom region-of-interest (ROI), divided by the noise, which is the standard deviation within an ROI in the background. Most MR systems have a means to calculate the SNR automatically. It is important to be aware that ROIs with apparent artifacts impede SNR calculation.

Several factors can influence the SNR. Radio frequency (RF) shielding, scanning parameters, field strength, RF coil, and general calibration of the system contribute to variations in SNR (Figure 13-2). It is important that the phantom consist of a uniform material and occupy at least 80% of the field of view (FOV). It should be positioned consistently from day to day. Once moved to isocenter, the fluid should not be moving during the scan, because this motion can induce artifacts. A specific quality control protocol should be set up so that the scanning parameters are chosen consistently. Again, the choice of parameters is quite

FIGURE 13-2
RF interference from a steady carrier frequency source. A strong signal from the nitrogen fill–monitor circuit is detected within the pass-band of the MRI receiver. It is displayed as a full vertical column perpendicular to the *x* coordinate that corresponds to the frequency of the spurious signal. The receiver performance overall is degraded by intermodulation distortion, causing the background noise level to rise in comparison with the signal of the phantom. (From Ros PR, Bidgood WD: *Abdominal magnetic resonance imaging,* St Louis, 1993, Mosby.)

flexible. However, it is important that they are not changed, because this will change the SNR outcomes.

Remember, it is not how the SNR test is done but that it is done consistently that is paramount. Following the manufacturer's suggested guidelines for daily SNR tests and documenting the results will give the earliest information about equipment performance. Most malfunctions in the MR scanner affect the SNR. The SNR should be as high as possible. If an SNR test fails when outside of the control amount, the test should be repeated to determine if any transient artifact affected the original calculation. If the test fails again, the service engineer should be contacted and a plan to continue operating evaluated. Figure 13-3 demonstrates phantom images acquired during an SNR test.

Resonance Frequency

The resonant frequency for an MR scanner is calculated by using the Larmor equation:

$$B0 \times 1H \text{ gyromagnetic ratio} = \text{Resonant frequency}$$

Examples:
$$1.5T \times 42.57 \text{ MHz/T} = 63.86 \text{ MHz}$$
$$1.0T \times 42.57 \text{ MHz/T} = 42.57 \text{ MHz}$$
$$0.5T \times 42.57 \text{ MHz/T} = 21.29 \text{ MHz}$$
$$0.3T \times 42.57 \text{ MHz/T} = 12.77 \text{ MHz}$$

The term **resonance frequency** is used interchangeably with center frequency and Larmor frequency. Like SNR, the value for resonance frequency should be recorded daily. Conveniently, the resonant frequency can be obtained during the prescan mode of the SNR test. Most manufacturers provide an automated way to determine the resonance frequency.

If a notable change in the resonance frequency occurs, the service engineer should be notified. As determined by the Larmor equation above, a change in the resonance frequency is an indication that there is a change in the

strength of the main magnetic field, B0. This could be a result of cryogen boil off, external ferromagnetic materials (i.e., construction), shim coil failure, and other potential effects on the main windings current.

In a superconducting magnet, it is important to routinely monitor the cryogen levels. Although most systems have a cryogen alarm if the levels are too low, it is best to monitor this to avoid an urgent situation (similar to running out of gas in your car!). If the superconductor uses liquid helium and liquid nitrogen, both should be monitored. It is important to notify the service organization if the cryogens seem to be decreasing more than normal between replenishments.

Significant changes in the resonance frequency indicate changes in the SNR.

Procedure

1. Use the same phantom that is generally used in the SNR test.

2. Perform a test prescan and record the value obtained.

3. Note changes that occur in spatial linearity because the gradients are interacting with an inhomogeneous magnetic field. In general, the resonant frequency is an indirect measure of the main magnetic field strength and its stability.

Image Uniformity

Image uniformity is the ability of the MR scanner to produce the same signal intensity from the same structure at different locations within the imaging volume. This directly applies to transmit-receive coils, such as the head or

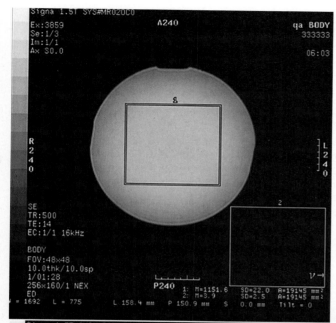

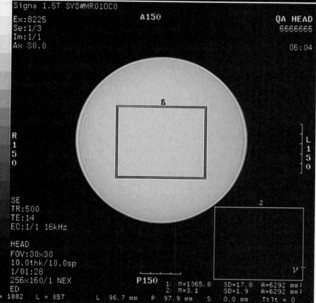

FIGURE 13-3

A, SNR test performed with the body coil phantom. B, SNR test performed with the head coil phantom. Note that the head coil yields a higher SNR.

body coils. Surface coil signals vary depending on the coil size and obtainable FOV.

Fortunately, the same phantom used for SNR and resonance frequency can also be used for image uniformity. However, it may be necessary to perform this quality control test only on a monthly basis, quite possibly during the preventive maintenance done by the service engineer.

Box 13-1   Image Uniformity Calculation

To calculate the image uniformity simply, a multislice acquisition (~3) is done with a large slice gap and an FOV slightly larger than the phantom. Once the chosen image is displayed, the ROI should be approximately 75% of the center phantom area. Determine the maximum and minimum intensities within the ROI using the display window. The following equation can then be used:

$$U = \frac{(1 - [I_{max} - I_{min}])}{(I_{max} + I_{min})} \times 100\%$$

where U = uniformity and I = intensity. Although ideal uniformity is 100%, large fields of view yield less uniformity. In general, uniformity should be above 80%.

Procedure

1. Use a phantom consisting of uniform material and occupying at least 80% of the FOV.

2. Evaluate image uniformity (Box 13-1) in all three orthogonal directions: sagittal, transverse, coronal.

3. Images in these three directions have similar uniformity in the body coil; however, depending on the design of the head coil, the uniformity is likely to vary. In either case, significant changes from the baseline should be assessed. Nonuniformity could indicate inhomogeneities in the main magnetic field, nonuniformity in the RF coil, or failure of the image display processor (Figure 13-4).

Spatial Linearity

Spatial linearity refers to the amount of geometric distortion in the image (Figure 13-5). This is affected by the homogeneity of the main magnetic field and the gradient magnetic fields. The geometric distortion is best determined using a large FOV and a high-resolution square matrix. SNR parameters (TR, TE, NSA) should not affect the spatial linearity.

Procedure

1. Use a different phantom than those used in the previous procedures. The most useful phantoms are gridlike, with an array of holes, tubes, rods, or so on. If a grid phantom is not available, position smaller phantoms of different sizes on a holder and center them at isocenter.

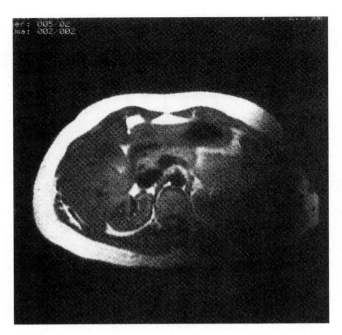

FIGURE 13-4

Nonuniformity of image intensity produced by RF field inhomogeneity. Note the region of hypointensity in the left flank. The cause in this case is improper setting of active shim coil current, producing an unwanted focal gradient in the main magnetic field. (From Ros PR, Bidgood WD: *Abdominal magnetic resonance imaging,* St Louis, 1993, Mosby.)

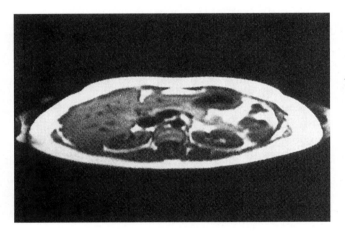

FIGURE 13-5

Example of gradient amplitude falloff resulting in A-P minification of a T1W axial image of the upper abdomen. (From Ros PR, Bidgood WD: *Abdominal magnetic resonance imaging,* St Louis, 1993, Mosby.)

In either case, the phantom should occupy a large portion of the largest FOV obtainable.

2. Position the objects in the grid so that their size and location space can be measured (Figure 13-6).

3. Measure the objects in the phantom and the distance between them to determine their true size.

4. Obtain a multislice acquisition, with slices at the phantom center and outer edges. Do this in all three orthogonal planes.

5. Use high spatial resolution (2562 or 5122) to minimize pixel size errors.

6. Measure the phantom object sizes and their distances on the acquired images. These measurements can be done either on the viewing monitor or the hard copy film. It is considered best to do both, because differences could be seen on the hard copy from filming systems versus just the magnet system.

7. Calculate the percentage of distortion. Use the following formula for calculating the percentage of distortion (D):

$$D = \frac{(\text{Object true size} - \text{image measured size})}{\text{object true size}} \times 100\%$$

Obviously, the percent distortion should be as small as possible. The greatest amount of distortion is seen near the edges of the FOV. Although these edge distortions are commonly expected, consideration should be given to MR image-guided procedures, such as surgical and treatment planning, in which distance measurements are critical.

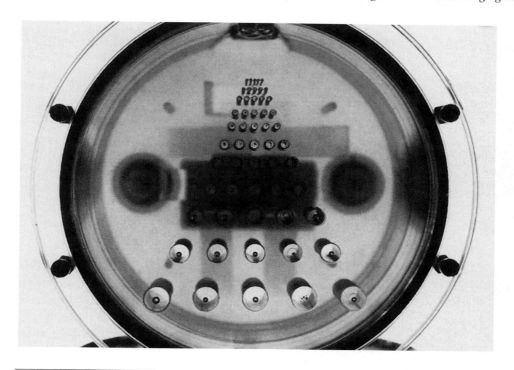

FIGURE 13-6

Multipurpose phantom. Plastic rods of known size and separation provide standard scan targets for measurement of spatial resolution. (From Ros PR, Bidgood WD: *Abdominal magnetic resonance imaging,* St Louis, 1993, Mosby.)

Spatial linearity tests are often performed by the site engineer during the system preventive maintenance. The distortion percentage may require reshimming the magnet or simply removing lost ferromagnetic objects (i.e., paper clips, coins, bobby pins) from the magnet bore.

Slice Position

The **slice position** test is performed to ensure that the landmarking location is actually centered to the magnet bore. Misalignment could simply be due to mechanical problems with the table, positioning devices, or lighting beams.

Procedure

1. Use any signal-generating phantom for this test, provided it has a landmark indicator.

2. Once the localizing light has been aligned with the phantom landmark, move it to isocenter and obtain a single slice acquisition. A slice obtained along the long axis of the magnet (either sagittal or coronal) is best for measuring positioning accuracy. The FOV should be larger than the phantom.

3. If the MR system has a positioning coordinate grid option, choose this and superimpose it over the acquired image. This will immediately show any deviation in the slice position both top to bottom and side to side. If this option is not available, measure the distances from the phantom edge to the FOV edge to demonstrate position deviation.

4. The actual slice position deviation should not be more than 2 mm. If so, contact the service engineer for repairs.

Spatial Resolution

Spatial resolution is the ability of the MR system to show the separation of small objects, particularly when there is minimal noise. The phantom used for this test is unlike those discussed earlier. It should consist of an array of either pegs, bars, or rods that produce a signal. The space between them should be twice the dimension of the bar or diameter of the rod. (The space should be non–signal producing.) A typical spatial resolution phantom may have an array of varying element sizes.

The scanning sequence can be any multislice sequence, as long as SNR parameters are chosen to minimize noise.

The testing parameters are those that affect pixel size, slice thickness, matrix, and FOV. A two-dimensional pixel size can be determined by dividing the acquisition matrix into the FOV.

$$\text{Examples:} \quad \frac{200\text{-mm FOV}}{128\ x\ \text{and}\ y\ \text{encodes}} = 1.56\text{-mm}^2\ \text{pixel}$$

$$\frac{400\text{-mm FOV}}{256\ x\ \text{and}\ y\ \text{encodes}} = 1.56\text{-mm}^2\ \text{pixel}$$

$$\frac{200\ \text{mm FOV}}{256\ x\ \text{and}\ y\ \text{encodes}} = 0.78\text{-mm}^2\ \text{pixel}$$

$$\frac{400\ \text{mm FOV}}{192\ x\ \text{and}\ y\ \text{encodes}} = 2.08\text{-mm}^2\ \text{pixel}$$

Box 13-2   Quality Control Tests Performed By a System Engineer

Receiver Setting

The receiver setting is the amount by which MR signals are amplified before digitization.

Transmitter Setting

The transmitter setting is a number expressed in decibels that influences the flip angle of each RF pulse.

Coil Q

Known as the *quality factor*, coil Q describes the performance of a coil used to receive MR signals.

Ghost Intensity

Ghost intensity is an expression of the intensity of background ghosts relative to the intensity of a phantom.

RF Shielding Effectiveness

The RF shielding effectiveness test verifies that the RF shield is attenuating radio waves originating from outside the scan room.

Surface Coil Performance

To check surface coil performance a separate test is done on each surface coil to determine the SNR and image uniformity.

Slice Thickness

Slice thickness is the full width at half-maximum of a slice profile, the region from which MR signals are emitted.

Maximum Gradient Strength

The maximum gradient strength determines if gradients are still achieving the maximum amplitude specified by the manufacturer and originally measured.

Specific Absorption Rate Monitor

The specific absorption rate (SAR) monitor verifies that the imaging procedures would not cause excessive RF power to be deposited into a patient.

Although resolution is traditionally known as *lines pairs per millimeter,* here it is determined by pixel size and what the human eye can resolve on the image. Resolution is determined by the smallest array element (bar, rod, etc.) visible but completely separated from the adjacent element. The calculated pixel size is then compared with the smallest resolvable element.

This quality control test is another that may be routinely performed by the site engineer during the system preventive maintenance. This test is likely to fail in conjunction with the spatial linearity test. Gradient amplitude and duty cycle, as well as reconstruction filters, could easily affect the spatial resolution.

Secondary Quality Factors

As stated previously, all quality control measurements are considered to be an essential part of overall system performance. Listed in Box 13-2 are abbreviated definitions of tests that should be performed by a system engineer not only on an agreed upon scheduled basis but whenever there are changes to the site scanner and environment, such as hardware and software upgrades, magnet quench, or facility construction.

SUMMARY

Quality control procedures for MRI are becoming more prevalent because of the introduction of the American College of Radiology (ACR) MR Site Accreditation program in the spring of 1997. The ACR has a dedicated quality control component to the application for accreditation process. A specific phantom must be used; information about the entire process can only be obtained by contacting the ACR.

Many sites that did not routinely perform quality control are now having to educate themselves on the various quality factors. Although some sites do just what is necessary to get by, other sites with dedicated quality assurance departments likely have a comprehensive program for each imaging modality. In MRI this could include assessment of warning signs placement, fire alarms and extinguishers, magnet quench procedures, computer room air conditioners, patient/technologist intercom, resetting of halon systems, start-up and shut-down of MR systems, and even clearing jams in the camera and processor.

Training and competency assessment of new and existing MR personnel will help maintain the overall quality of the facility. With a limited operating budget, the MR technologists is often called upon to do a lot of error troubleshooting before calling for service. Ironically, productivity issues may drive quality assurance programs, whereas quality assurance should be thought of as enhancing productivity.

Review Questions

1. Phantoms for MRI quality control tests are made with which material?
   a. aluminum
   b. copper
   c. manganese
   d. all of the above
2. Daily quality control tests should be performed by which personnel?
   a. medical physicist
   b. MR technologist
   c. service engineer
   d. system specialist
3. When performing the SNR test, changing the imaging parameters will not affect the resulting SNR.
   a. false
   b. true
4. Which equation is used to calculate the system's resonance frequency?
   a. Bloch
   b. Fourier
   c. Larmor
   d. Plank
5. Image uniformity values should range between:
   a. 20% to 40%
   b. 40% to 60%
   c. 60% to 80%
   d. 80% to 100%

6. The phantom used for the spatial linearity test can be the same as the phantom for the resonance frequency test.
   a. false
   b. true
7. The quality control test performed to ensure that the landmarking location is at isocenter is:
   a. slice position
   b. slice thickness
   c. slice uniformity
   d. spatial localization
8. An acquisition with a 20-cm FOV and a 1282 matrix will yield what size pixel?
   a. 0.78 mm^2
   b. 1.56 mm^2
   c. 1.92 mm^2
   d. 2.56 mm^2
9. What term is used to describe the quality factor of the coil used to receive signals?
   a. coil Q
   b. receiver setting
   c. resonance frequency
   d. SNR
10. Which of the following personnel is considered key to a good quality control MR program?
    a. medical physicist
    b. MR technologist
    c. service engineer
    d. all of the above

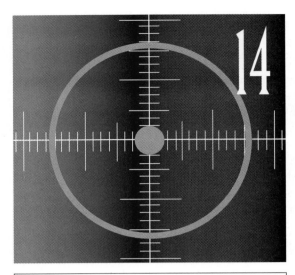

14 Ultrasound Equipment Quality Assurance

● James A. Zagzebski

Objectives

At the completion of this chapter the reader will be able to do the following:

- Discuss the importance of quality assurance for ultrasound equipment
- Describe the various phantoms used in ultrasound quality assurance
- Identify the basic quality control tests for ultrasound
- Explain the importance of documentation of quality assurance testing
- Describe the basic quality control testing for Doppler color flow equipment

Outline

Outline—cont'd

In an imaging facility, quality assurance is a process carried out to ensure that equipment is operating consistently at its expected level of performance. During routine scanning every sonographer or ultrasound technician is vigilant for equipment changes that could lead to suboptimal imaging and might require service. Thus, in some ways, ultrasound equipment quality assurance is carried out every day, even when not identified as a process in itself.

Quality assurance steps to be discussed here go beyond judgments of scanner performance that are made during routine ultrasound imaging. They involve prospective actions to identify problem situations, even before obvious equipment malfunctions occur. Quality assurance testing provides confidence that image data, such as distance measurements and area estimations, are accurate and that image quality is the best possible from the imaging instrument.

COMPONENTS OF AN ULTRASOUND QUALITY ASSURANCE PROGRAM

Quality Assurance and Preventive Maintenance

Various approaches are used by ultrasound facilities when setting up a quality assurance program for their scanners. Sometimes these programs include both preventive maintenance procedures performed by trained equipment service personnel and in-house testing of scanners using phantoms and test objects. Some facilities rely on only one of these measures. For preventive maintenance, emphasis usually is given to electronic testing of system components, such as voltage measurements at test points on the scanner. Sometimes preventive maintenance also involves an assessment of the imaging capability by scanning a normal subject or a phantom.

In-house scanner quality assurance programs usually involve imaging phantoms or test objects and assessing the results. The in-house tests might be performed by sonographers, physicians, medical physicists, clinical engineers, or equipment maintenance personnel. Detailed recommendations from professional organizations and experts in ultrasound on establishing an in-house quality assurance program are available elsewhere.[2,11,15]

Tissue-Mimicking Phantoms

In-house scanner quality assurance tests are most often performed using tissue-mimicking phantoms. In medical ultrasound a phantom is a device that mimics soft tissues in its ultrasound transmission characteristics. **Phantoms** represent "constant patients," enabling images taken at different times to be closely compared. Penetration capabilities, for example, are readily evaluated for changes over time when images of a phantom are available for comparison. Phantoms also have targets in known positions, so images can be compared closely with the region scanned. Examples include simulated cysts, echogenic structures, and thin "line targets."

Tissue Properties Represented in Phantoms

Tissue transmission characteristics mimicked by commercially available phantoms are the speed of sound, ultrasonic attenuation, and, to some degree, echogenicity, that is, the ultrasonic scattering level. It should be mentioned that phantoms cannot exactly replicate the acoustic properties of soft tissues. This is partially because of the complexity and variability of tissues. Instead, phantom manufacturers construct these objects to have average acoustic properties that are representative of tissues. Sometimes the term *tissue-equivalent* is used when describing phantoms. However, this term should not be interpreted literally because most phantom materials are not acoustically equivalent to the tissues they represent.

Typical Quality Assurance Phantom Design

An example of a general purpose ultrasound quality assurance phantom is shown in Figure 14-1. Such phantoms are scanned with scanner settings very similar to settings used in scanning patients. B-mode images have gray-scale char-

acteristics that are analogous to characteristics of organs, although the actual structures are not anatomically represented.

Figure 14-1, *B*, is a schematic showing details of the phantom. The tissue-mimicking material within the phantom consists of a water-based gelatin in which microscopic graphite particles are mixed uniformly throughout the volume.[5,6] The speed of sound in this material is about 1540 ms, the same speed assumed in the calibration of ultrasound instruments. The ultrasonic attenuation coefficient

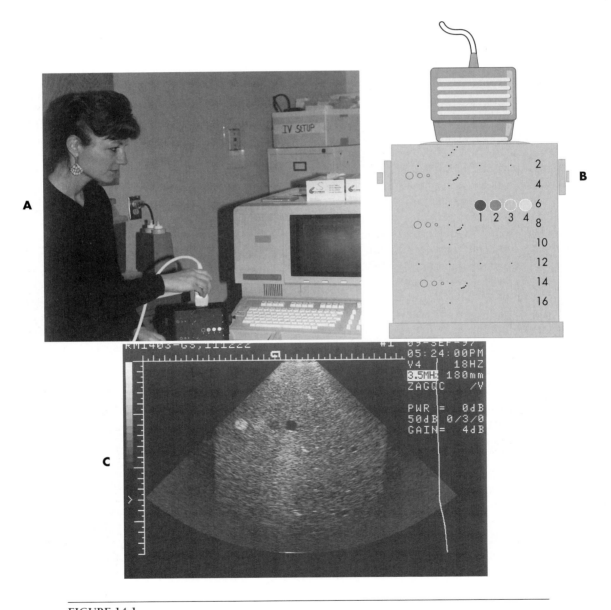

FIGURE 14-1

Example of a general purpose quality assurance phantom. **A**, Phantom being imaged with an ultrasound scanner. **B**, Schematic drawing. **C**, B-mode image of the phantom. (Courtesy Gammex/RMI, Middleton, Wis.)

versus frequency is one of two values: either 0.5 dB/cm MHz or 0.7 dB/cm MHz (Box 14-1). Some users prefer the lower attenuating material because they find it easier to image objects in the phantom. However, standards groups recommend the higher attenuation because it challenges machines more thoroughly.

Attenuation in the gel-graphite material in the phantom is proportional to the ultrasound frequency, mimicking the behavior in tissues. Other types of materials have been used in phantoms, but only water-based gels laced with powder have both speed of sound and attenuation with tissuelike properties.[5,6]

Small scatterers are distributed throughout the tissue-mimicking material. Therefore the phantoms appear echogenic when scanned with ultrasound imaging equipment (Figure 14-1, C). Many phantoms have simulated cysts, which are low-attenuating, nonechogenic cylinders. These should appear echo-free on B-mode images and should exhibit distal echo enhancement. Some tissue phantoms provide additional image contrast by having simulated masses of varying echogenicity. Such objects are evident in the image in Figure 14-1.

Most quality assurance phantoms also contain discrete reflectors, such as nylon-line targets, to be used mainly for evaluating the distance measurement accuracy of a scanner. Tests of the accuracy of distance measurements rely on the manufacturer of the phantom to have filled the device with a material with a sound propagation speed of 1540 ms or at least close enough to this speed that no apprecia-ble errors are introduced in calibrations. These phantoms also rely on the manufacturer having defined the reflector positions accurately.

Phantoms often contain a column of reflectors, each separated by 1 or 2 cm, for vertical measurement accuracy tests. One or more horizontal rows of reflectors are used for assessing **horizontal measurement accuracy**. Additional sets of reflectors may be found for assessing **axial resolution** and **lateral resolution** of scanners.

Cautions Regarding Phantom Desiccation

When using phantoms made of water-based gels, loss of water and shrinking of the scanning window may become a problem as the phantom ages. Occasionally, water losses become so problematic that air enters the phantom window, leading to inability to image the phantom effectively. Users should follow the instructions given by the phantom manufacturer to avoid significant desiccation losses. For example, some recommend storage in a humid, air-tight container, and this practice should be adhered to if so stated.

Desiccation is not a problem with rubber-based phantom materials produced by one manufacturer (Figure 14-2). These phantoms can be stored with the tissue-mimicking material directly exposed to the environment, which

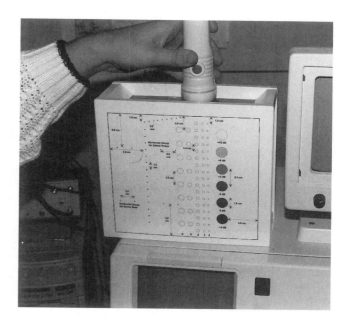

FIGURE 14-2

Rubber-based tissue-mimicking phantom. Although the acoustic properties are not as precise as the water-based phantoms, less care is required during manufacturing and with on-site storage to minimize changes over time. (Courtesy ATS Laboratories, Bridgeport, Conn.)

 Box 14-1 Tissue Attenuation Coefficients

Attenuation coefficients normally are specified in dB/cm. To include the dependence of attenuation on frequency, phantom manufacturers divide the attenuation coefficient by the frequency at which the measurement is done. This yields units of dB/cm MHz. Strictly speaking, this approach should be used only when attenuation is directly proportional to the frequency, as we often assume for tissues. The value of 0.7 dB/cm MHz is representative of the attenuation coefficient in difficult-to-penetrate fatty liver.* The depth that structures can be visualized within tissue-mimicking material having this amount of attenuation more closely correlates with clinical penetration.

*Lu ZF, Lee FT, Zagzebski JA: *Ultrasonic backscatter and attenuation in diffuse liver disease,* manuscript submitted for publication; *Performance criteria and measurements for Doppler ultrasound devices,* Laurel, Md, 1993, American Institute of Ultrasound in Medicine.
From Zagzebski J: Acceptance tests for Doppler ultrasound equipment. In Goldman L, Fowlkes B, editors: *Medical CT and ultrasound: current technology and applications,* Madison, Wis, 1995, Advanced Medical Publishers.

can be an advantage compared with water-based gels. The primary disadvantage of rubber materials is that their speed of sound is lower than 1540 ms (about 1450 ms in some rubber-based phantoms) and their attenuation is not proportional to the ultrasound frequency. Therefore they may not be as effective when imaging over a large frequency range as water-based gel phantoms.

BASIC QUALITY ASSURANCE TESTS

A recommended set of instrument quality assurance tests[2,14] includes checks for consistency of instrument sensitivity, evaluation of image photography and image uniformity, and checks of both vertical and horizontal distance measurement accuracy. This group of tests can be done by a sonographer in 10 to 15 minutes, including time for recording the results on a worksheet or in a notebook.

Transducer Choice

Results of some test procedures depend on which transducer assembly is used with the instrument. On systems in which several transducer assemblies are available it may be inconvenient to do routine tests with more than one probe. If this is the case, choose a transducer assembly that will become a standard for all test procedures. A good choice is the transducer assembly used most frequently in clinical scanning. Be sure to record all necessary transducer assembly identification information, including the frequency, size, and serial number, so future tests will be conducted with the same probe.

System Sensitivity

The **sensitivity** of an instrument refers to the echo signal level that can be detected and displayed clearly enough to be discernible on an image. Most scanners have controls that vary the receiver amplification (gain) and the transmit level (e.g., output or power). These are used to adjust the sensitivity during clinical examinations. When the controls are positioned at the maximum practical settings, we refer to the *maximum sensitivity* of the instrument. Often the maximum sensitivity is limited by electrical noise appearing on the display when the receiver gain is at maximum levels. The noise may be generated externally, for example, by electronic communication networks or computer terminals. More commonly it arises from within the instrument itself, such as in the first preamplification stage of the receiver amplifier.

Concerns during quality assurance tests are usually centered around whether notable variations in sensitivity have occurred since the last quality assurance test. Such varia-

tions might result from a variety of causes, such as damaged transducers, damaged transducer cables, or electronic drift in the pulser-receiver components of the scanner. Sometimes questions related to the sensitivity of a scanner occur during clinical imaging; a quick scan of the quality assurance phantom and comparison with results of the most recent quality assurance test help determine whether there is cause for concern.

A commonly used technique for detecting variations in maximum sensitivity is to measure the maximum **depth of visualization** for signals from scattered echoes in the tissue-mimicking phantom.[2,11,14,15]

Procedure

1. Adjust the output power transmit levels and receiver sensitivity controls so that echo signals are obtained from as deep as possible into the phantom. This means that the output power control is positioned for maximum output and the receiver gain adjusted for the highest values without excessive noise on the display. (Experience helps in establishing these control settings; they should be recorded in the quality control worksheet, described below.)

2. Scan the phantom and estimate the maximum depth of visualization of texture echo signals (Figure 14-3).

In the examples in Figure 14-3, the maximum depth of visualization is 15.2 cm at 4 MHz; it is 16.8 cm at 3.5 MHz, reflecting the lower attenuation as frequency is reduced. With a 2.5-MHz mode, it could not be measured with this phantom.

To interpret the results of the test, a comparison is made with maximum visualization results from a previous test, perhaps 6 months earlier. Results should agree to within 1 cm. Normal trial-to-trial variations in scanning and interpretation prohibit making closer calls than this. These errors might be several millimeters, so penetration cannot be judged any better than this. However, using hard copy images and records of maximum depth of visualization tests, it should be possible to ascertain whether a scanner/transducer combination has drifted significantly over time in echo detection capabilities.

In addition to doing this measurement using the standard transducer, it is useful to perform the test occasionally using different transducers. For example, the test can be done with all transducers that are available for each in-

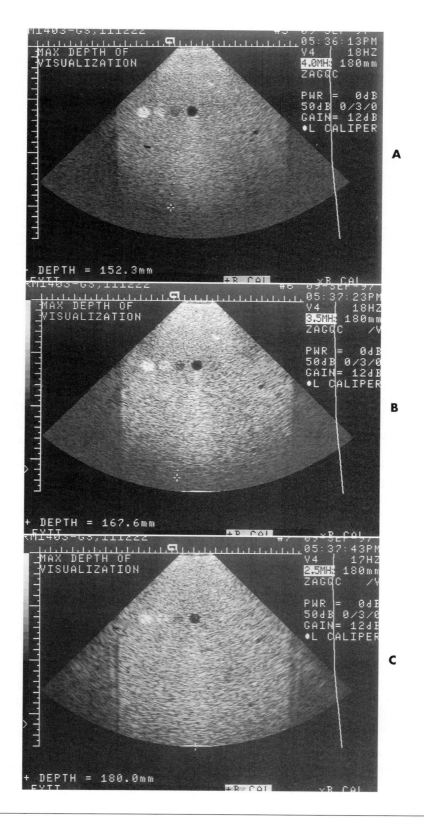

FIGURE 14-3

Images obtained for the maximum depth of visualization quality assurance test with a multifrequency array transducer. The phantom has an attenuation coefficient of 0.7 dB/cm MHz. **A,** At 4 MHz the maximum depth of visualization is 15.2 cm. **B,** At 3.5 MHz it is 16.8 cm. **C,** At 2.5 MHz the maximum depth of visualization cannot be determined with this phantom, because visualization remains excellent all the way to the bottom of the phantom.

strument when quality control tests are first established and semiannually thereafter. This helps pinpoint the source of any decrease in the maximum sensitivity or at least determine whether the standard transducer is at fault.

Photography and Gray-Scale Hard Copy

Perhaps the most frequent source of ultrasound instrument variability over time is related to image photography. All too often drift in the imaging instrument, in the hard copy cameras, or in film processing reduces image quality to the point that significant amounts of detail related to echo signal amplitude variations are lost on hard copy B-mode images. However, if image viewing and recording monitors are set up properly and if sufficient attention is given to photography during routine quality control, these problems can be reduced.

Setting Up Monitors and Recording Devices

Most instruments provide both an image display monitor, which is viewed during scan build-up, and an image recording device. As a general rule the display monitor should be set up properly first, and then adjustments made, if necessary, to multiformat cameras or other hard copy recording devices to produce acceptable gray scale on hard copy images. It is expected that establishing proper settings is only done during installation of a scanner, during major upgrades, or when image problems are detected. Image display settings should not be shifted routinely. Many facilities go so far as to remove the control knobs on image monitors once the contrast and brightness are adjusted to an acceptable level, removing the temptation to change settings casually.

An effective method for setting up both viewing and hard copy monitors has been described by Gray.[8] This author recommends that adjustments be done using an image containing a clinically representative sampling of gray shades.

Procedure

1. First attend to the display monitor viewed during scan build-up. With the contrast settings of the monitor initially set at minimum settings, adjust the brightness to a level that just allows television raster lines to be discernible.

2. Once this is done, adjust the monitor contrast until a clinically acceptable image is obtained. After the viewing monitor is properly adjusted, make provisions to prevent casual changes in settings by department personnel.

3. Adjust the image recording device to obtain the same gray shades that appear on the display monitor. This may require several iterations, varying the contrast and the overall brightness, until satisfactory results are obtained.

Routine Quality Assurance of Image Recording

Routine quality assurance checks should be performed of the quality of gray-scale photography or other hard copy recording media. Photography and processing should always be such that all brightness variations in the viewing monitor image are successfully recorded on the hard copy image.

Images of a tissue-mimicking phantom, along with the gray bar pattern appearing on the edge of most image displays, can be used for routinely assessing photography settings.

Procedure

1. On an image of a tissue-mimicking phantom (or of a patient), check to see whether weak echo signal dots appearing on the viewing monitor are successfully recorded on film.

2. Determine whether the entire gray bar is visible and whether all gray levels are distinguishable. For example, for a scanner whose gray bar includes 15 levels of gray, along with the background, the hard copy image should portray distinctions between all of the different levels.

3. The entire length of the gray bar pattern displayed on the viewing monitor should be visible on the final image (see Figure 14-3). For multiple images on a single sheet of film or paper, all images should have the same background brightness and display the gray bar pattern in the same manner. This may be verified from clinical images taken on the same day the quality assurance tests are taken or from the quality assurance films themselves.

Scan Image Uniformity

Ideally, when a uniform region within a phantom is scanned, and the machine's gain settings are adjusted properly, the resultant image has a uniform brightness throughout, or **scan image uniformity** (Figure 14-4, *A*). Nonuni-

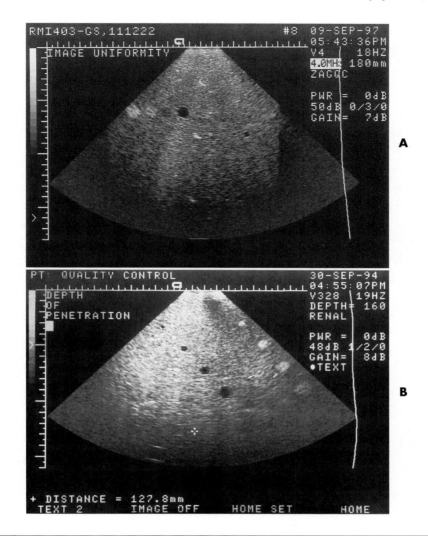

FIGURE 14-4

Image uniformity tests. **A**, Good uniformity. **B**, Results with a transducer that should be repaired or replaced.

formities caused by the ultrasound imager can occur as a result of the following situations:

- Bad elements in a linear or curved array or loose connections in beam former board plug-ins can lead to vertically oriented nonuniformities (Figure 14-4, *B*) (boards can be loosened if the scanner is wheeled over bumps or if it is transported by van to other hospitals).
- Inadequate side-to-side image compensation in the machine can lead to variations in brightness from one side of the image to another.
- Inadequate blending of pixel data between transmit and receive focal zones can lead to horizontal or curved streaks parallel to the transducer surface. Quality assurance testing is an ideal time to assess whether such faults are noticeable. An image is taken of a uniform region in the quality assurance phantom, and the image is inspected for these problems.

Distance Measurement Accuracy

Instruments used for measuring structure dimensions, organ sizes, and areas should be tested periodically for accuracy of distance indicators. Distance indicators usually include l-cm depth markers on M-mode and B-mode scanning displays and digital calipers on B-mode scanning systems. Calipers on workstations that are part of computer archiving systems and therefore also should be checked for accuracy.

The principal distance measurement tests are separated into two parts: one used for measurements along the sound beam axis, which is referred to as the **vertical distance measurement** test, or the axial distance measurement test, and a second that is used for measurements taken perpendicular to the sound beam axis, which is called the **horizontal distance measurement** test.

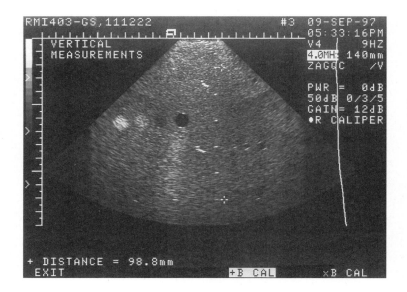

FIGURE 14-5

Vertical distance measurement check. The caliper reading (9.9 cm) is compared with the actual (10 cm) separation between pins positioned along a vertical column in the phantom. Shorter distances should be used when high-frequency transducers are evaluated.

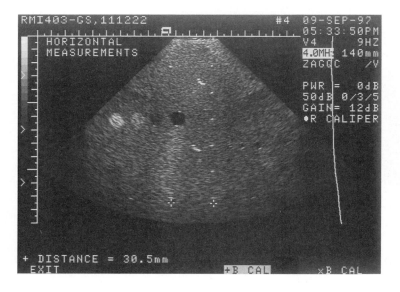

FIGURE 14-6

Horizontal distance measurement check. The caliper reading (30.5 mm) is for a measurement taken horizontally on the image and compared with the actual pin separation (30 mm).

Vertical Distance Measurements

Vertical distance measurement accuracy is also called *depth calibration accuracy* in some texts.

Procedure

1. To evaluate a scanner's vertical distance measurement accuracy, scan the phantom, ensuring that the vertical column of reflectors in the phantom are clearly imaged (Figure 14-5).

2. Position the digital calipers to measure the distance between any two reflectors in this column.

   A. Correct caliper placement is from the top of the echo from the first reflector to the top of the echo from the second reflector or from any position on the first reflector to the corresponding position on the second reflector.

   B. When testing general-purpose scanners, choose reflectors separated by at least 8 to 10 cm for this test. Most laboratories also measure a closer spacing, such as 4 cm. For small parts scanners and probes, use a distance of approximately 1 or 2 cm.

3. Determine that the measured distance agrees with the actual distance given by the phantom manufacturer to within 1 mm or 1.5%, whichever is greater. If a larger discrepancy occurs, consult with the ultrasound scanner manufacturer for possible corrective measures.

Horizontal Distance Measurements

Horizontal measurement accuracy should be checked similarly. Measurements obtained in this direction (Figure 14-6) are frequently less accurate because of beam width effects and scanner inaccuracies. Nevertheless, results should agree with the phantom manufacturer's distances to within 3 mm or 3%, whichever is greater. Correct caliper placement for this test is from the center of one reflector to the center of the second reflector. For the example in Figure 14-6, measurement results are within 1 mm of the actual distance between the reflectors examined. This is well within the expected level of accuracy.

Other Important Instrument Quality Assurance Tasks

During routine performance testing it is a good idea to perform other equipment-related chores that require occasional attention. These include cleaning air filters on instruments requiring this service (most do!); checking for loose and frayed electrical cables; looking for loose handles or control arms on the scanner; checking the wheels and wheel locks, and performing recommended preventive maintenance of photography equipment, which may include dusting or cleaning of photographic monitors and maintenance chores on cameras.

DOCUMENTATION

An important aspect of a quality assurance program is keeping track of the results of tests. Most laboratories will want to adopt a standardized worksheet to write down the test results. The worksheet helps the user carry out the tests in a consistent manner by having enough information to facilitate recall of transducers, phantoms, and machine settings. It also includes blank spaces for recording the results. An example is given in Box 14-2.

SPATIAL RESOLUTION TESTS

Some laboratories include spatial resolution in their quality assurance testing. Measurements of spatial resolution generally require more exacting techniques to achieve results

Box 14-2 Ultrasound Quality Control Results

Machine: <u>Acuson 128</u>   Room: <u>E3 315</u>
Tranducer assembly: I.D.: <u>V4</u>   Serial no: <u>555-1212</u>
Date: <u>9/09/97</u>   Phantom: <u>RMI 403GS</u>
Instrument settings: Power <u>0</u> dB
                      Dynamic range: <u>50</u> dB
                      Pre <u>0</u>/Persis <u>3</u>/Post <u>0</u>
                      Gain: <u>12</u> dB
                      Transmit focus: <u>16 cm</u>
                      Image magnification: <u>18 cm</u>

1. Depth measurement accuracy
   Electronic calipers
      Measured distance .... <u>98.8</u> mm
      Actual distance .... <u>100</u> mm
      Error .... <u>1.2</u> mm
2. Horizontal measurement accuracy
   Electronic calipers
      Measured distance .... <u>30.5</u> mm
      Actual distance .... <u>30</u> mm
      Error .... <u>0.5</u> mm
3. Depth of penetration (4 MHz)
      Measured distance .... <u>152</u> mm
      Baseline distance .... <u>150</u> mm
      Variation from baseline .... <u>2</u> mm
4. Image uniformity

Significant nonuniformity			Excellent uniformity	
1	2	3	④	5

5. Photography
   Gray bars
      Number of gray bars visible .... <u>13</u>
      Number of gray bars visible on baseline .... <u>15</u>
      Variation .... <u>2</u>
   Low-level echoes
      All echoes diplayed on viewing monitor also seen
         on film: Yes <u>x</u> No <u>   </u>
   Contrast and brightness
      Level of agreement between contrast and brightness on
        viewing monitor and film:

Poor			Excellent	
1	2	3	④	5

6. Filters
   Clean <u>   </u>   Dusty <u> x </u>

that allow intercomparisons of scanners. Therefore many centers do not do such performance tests routinely, but may do so only during equipment acceptance tests.[4,15] Common methods for determining axial resolution, lateral resolution, and focal lesion resolution are discussed in this section.

Axial Resolution

Axial resolution is a measure of how close two reflectors can be to one another along the axis of an ultrasound beam and

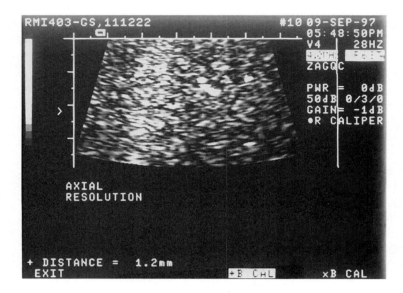

FIGURE 14-7

Axial resolution measurement. The thickness of the pin target is 1.2 mm. In the axial resolution target set (vertical separation 2 mm, 1 mm, 0.5 mm and 0.25 mm) the 2-mm pair is separated a sufficient distance vertically that there is no vertical overlap of the images of these two targets, whereas the 1-mm pair would overlap if the two targets were on a vertical line; the axial resolution is just over 1 mm, in agreement with the estimate made from the thickness of the single target image.

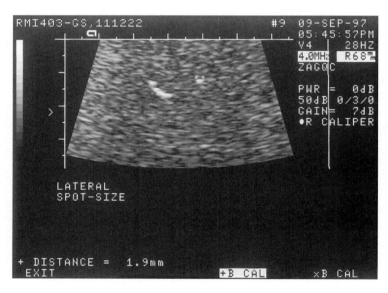

FIGURE 14-8

Lateral resolution measurement. The horizontal size of the pin target is 1.2 mm.

still be resolved as separate reflectors. Axial resolution also is related to the crispness of the image of a reflector oriented approximately perpendicularly to the ultrasound beam.

Axial resolution may be estimated by measuring the thickness of the image of a line target in the quality assurance phantom. Alternatively, some phantoms contain sets of reflectors for axial resolution testing. Both approaches are shown in Figure 14-7. The axial separations between successive targets in this phantom are 2 mm, 1 mm, 0.5 mm, and 0.25 mm. The targets are offset horizontally to minimize effects of shadowing of deeper targets by shallow ones. The pair most closely spaced yet still clearly distinguishable indicates the axial resolution. Often, as in this phantom, the target pair separations are not finely spaced

enough to allow a good measure of axial resolution; that is, the 1-mm pair in this example is not clearly resolved, whereas the 2-mm pair certainly is. The vertical thickness of a single target (1.2 mm in this case) is sometimes used to obtain more detailed indication of the axial resolution.

Lateral Resolution

Lateral resolution is a measure of how close two reflectors can be to one another perpendicular to the beam axis and still be distinguished as separate reflectors on an image. One approach that is used for lateral resolution tests is to measure the width on the display of a pointlike target, such as a line target inside a phantom. For example, Figure 14-

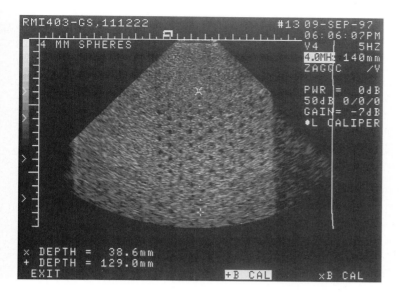

```
RMI403-GS,111222          #13 09-SEP-97
                               06:06:07PM
4 MM SPHERES              V4       5HZ
                          4.0MHz 140mm
                          ZAGQC    /V

                    X     PWR  =   0dB
                          50dB 0/0/0
                          GAIN= -7dB
                          •L CALIPER

                    +

x  DEPTH =    38.6mm
+  DEPTH =   129.0mm
EXIT              +B CAL       xB CAL
```

FIGURE 14-9

B-mode image of a phantom containing 4-mm low-scattering spheres mimicking cysts. The spheres are centered in a regular array within a plane, and the scanning plane is carefully aligned to coincide with the plane containing the spheres. They can be visualized from depths of 3.8 through 12.9 cm with this transducer.

8 demonstrates such a measurement. The cursors indicate that the displayed width is 1.2 mm for this case. The displayed response width is related to the lateral resolution at the depth of the target. By imaging targets at different depths it is easy to see that the lateral resolution usually varies with depth for most transducers.

Cautions Regarding Resolution Tests with Discrete Targets

The lateral, as well as axial, dimensions of the displayed image of a pointlike target depend on the power and gain settings on the machine. This is one of the difficulties of adopting such tests in routine testing. Quantitative results for axial and lateral resolution have been obtained by measuring the dimensions of pointlike targets when they are imaged at specified sensitivity levels above the threshold for their display.

Procedure

1. Obtain an image with the sensitivity of the scanner set so that the target is barely visible on the display.

2. Next, obtain a second image, with the scanner sensitivity increased 20 dB above the setting for display threshold.

3. Set the calipers to measure the lateral resolution at this scanner setting. Additional information is available elsewhere.[1,3]

Spherical Object Phantom

Another phantom becoming increasingly popular for spatial resolution tests is one that has simulated focal lesions embedded within echogenic tissue-mimicking material.[1,2,7] Different simulated lesion sizes and different object contrast levels (i.e., relative echogenicity) have been tried.[12] An example is presented in Figure 14-9, in which the phantom imaged contained 4-mm diameter, low-echo masses. The centers of the masses are coplanar and distributed in a well-defined matrix.

A test of the ultrasound imaging system is used to determine the "imaging zone" for detection of masses of a given size and object contrast.[2] The 4-MHz phased array used for Figure 14-9 can successfully detect the masses over a 3.8-cm to 13-cm depth range. The **slice thickness**[13] is too large for this transducer to pick up these structures at more shallow depths.

A particularly useful aspect of spherical mass phantoms is that they present realistic imaging tasks that readily demonstrate resolution capabilities in terms of resolution. For spherical targets the resolution is a combined, effective resolution, made up of axial and lateral, as well as slice, thicknesses. If cylindrical objects are used as phantoms, only two dimensions, usually axial and lateral, are involved in their visualization. Because slice thickness usually is the worst measure of spatial resolution with array transducers, cylindrical objects can be misleading in terms of translating minimum sizes resolved into resolution of actual focal masses. The spherical lesion phantom is superior in this regard.

DOPPLER TESTING

Limited evaluations of Doppler and color flow equipment also can be done in the clinic. A number of devices, including string test objects, flow velocity test objects, and flow phantoms are available to clinical users for carrying out tests of Doppler equipment.[8,16]

String Test Objects

String test objects consist of a thin string wound around a pulley and motor-drive mechanism. The string is echogenic, so it produces echoes that are detected by an ultrasound instrument. The drive moves the string at precise velocities, either continuously or following a programmed waveform. This provides a way to evaluate the velocity measurement accuracy of Doppler devices. String test objects also may be used to evaluate the lateral and axial resolution in Doppler mode and can be used to determine the accuracy of gate registration on duplex Doppler systems.[8]

The advantage of the string test object is that it provides a small target moving at a precisely known velocity. The disadvantages are (1) the echogenic characteristics of the string are not the same as blood, and (2) actual blood flow,

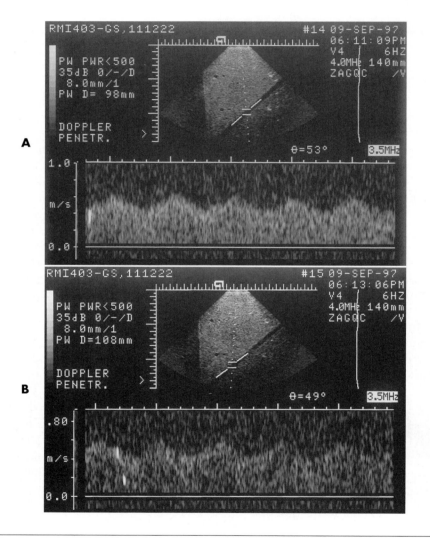

FIGURE 14-10

B-mode and spectral Doppler display of a flow phantom for evaluating Doppler penetration. **A,** A strong Doppler signal and good signal-to-noise ratio is obtained when the sample volume is at a depth of 9.8 cm. **B,** The Doppler signal is just detectable above the electronic noise when the sample volume is at a depth of 10.8 cm. The maximum depth of detection of the Doppler signal in this case is 10.8 cm.

with its characteristic distribution of velocities across the vessel, is not mimicked.

Doppler Flow Phantoms

Doppler flow phantoms (Figures 14-10 and 14-11) consist of one or more hollow tubes coursing through a block of tissue-mimicking material. A blood-mimicking fluid is pumped through the tube(s) to simulate blood flowing through vessels in the body. Usually the blood-mimicking fluid is made of a water and glycerol solution that has small plastic particles suspended in it. The blood-mimicking material should provide the same echogenicity as whole human blood at the ultrasound frequencies of the machine, and reasonable representative blood-mimicking materials now are available for use in these phantoms. If the tissue-mimicking material in the body of the phantom has a representative amount of beam attenuation, the depth-dependent echogenicity of the fluid within the phantom will be representative of signal levels from actual vessels in vivo.

Doppler flow phantoms are used for the following types of tests of Doppler and flow imaging equipment.[8,9]

* The maximum depth at which flow waveforms can be detected in the phantom has been used to assess whether

the Doppler sensitivity has varied from one quality assurance test to another.* This is illustrated in Figure 14-10. Penetration in this case is 10.8 cm.

* Alignment of the pulsed Doppler sample volume with the volume indicated on a duplex B-mode image.
* Volume flow accuracy. Some Doppler flow phantoms have precise volume flow measuring equipment. A flow phantom can thus be used in assessments of the accuracy of flow measuring algorithms on Doppler devices.
* Velocity accuracy. If the velocity of the fluid within the phantoms can be determined accurately, then this can be used to evaluate velocity displays on Doppler and color flow machines.
* Color flow penetration (Figure 14-11). System sensitivity settings are at their maximum levels without excessive electronic noise. The maximum depth at which color data can be recorded in the flow phantom is noted. Any changes over time, such as greater than 1 cm, indicate a change in the sensitivity of the instrument.

---

*This measurement may be useful for consistency checks, which are an essential part of quality assurance, in attempting to verify that equipment is operating at least as well as when it was delivered or last upgraded. As an absolute measure of Doppler sensitivity, it is controversial because many factors are involved in the concept of Doppler sensitivity.[15]

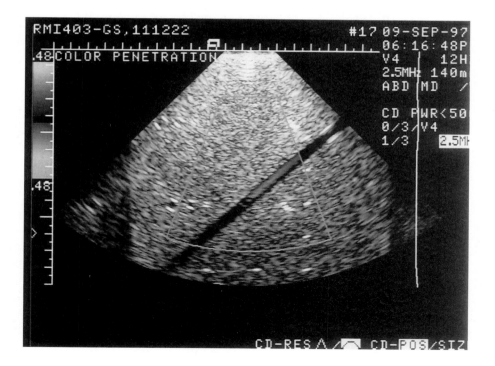

FIGURE 14-11

An example of a color flow image of a Doppler flow phantom used to determine the maximum penetration in color.

- Alignment of color flow image with B-mode image (image congruency test). This test checks whether the color flow image and B-mode image are aligned so that they agree spatially. Color images of vessels should be completely contained within the B-mode image of the vessel. Sometimes bleeding out occurs, and this can be easily corrected by equipment service personnel.

References

1. *AAPM quality assurance manual,* College Park, Md, 1995, American Association of Physicists in Medicine.
2. *AIUM quality assurance manual,* Laurel, Md, 1995, American Institute of Ultrasound in Medicine.
3. *AIUM standard methods for measuring performance of ultrasound pulse-echo equipment,* Laurel, Md, 1990, American Institute of Ultrasound in Medicine.
4. Burlew M et al: A new ultrasound tissue-equivalent material with a high melting point and extended speed of sound range, *Radiology* 134:517, 1980.
5. Carson P, Goodsitt MM: Acceptance testing of pulse-echo ultrasound equipment. In Goldman L, Fowlkes B, editors: *Medical CT and ultrasound: current technology and applications,* Madison, Wis, 1995, Advanced Medical Publishers.
6. Carson P, Zagzebski J: *Pulse-Echo ultrasound imaging systems: performance tests and criteria, AAPM Report No 8,* New York, 1980, American Institute of Physics.
7. Goldstein A: Slice thickness measurements, *J Ultrasound Med* 7:487, 1988.
8. Gray J: Test pattern for video display and hard copy cameras, *Radiology* 154:519, 1985.
9. Hoskins PR, Sheriff SB, Evans JA, editors: *Testing of Doppler ultrasound equipment,* Rep No 70, York, UK, 1994, The Institute of Physical Sciences in Medicine.
10. Lu ZF, Lee FT, Zagzebski JA: Ultrasonic backscatter and attenuation in diffuse liver disease, manuscript submitted for publication, 1993.
11. Madsen EL et al: Tissue mimicking material for ultrasound phantoms, *Med Phys* 5:391, 1978.
12. Madsen EL et al: Ultrasound lesion delectability phantoms, *Med Physics* 18:1771, 1991.
13. Maklad N, Ophir J, Balara V: Attenuation of ultrasound in normal and diffuse liver disease in vivo, *Ultrason Imaging* 6:117, 1984.
14. NCRP Report 99: *Quality assurance for diagnostic imaging equipment,* Bethesda, Md, 1988, National Council on Radiation Protection and Measurements.
15. *Performance criteria and measurements for Doppler ultrasound devices,* Laurel, Md, 1993, American Institute of Ultrasound in Medicine.
16. Zagzebski J: Acceptance tests for Doppler ultrasound equipment. In Goldman L, Fowlkes B, editors: *Medical CT and ultrasound: current technology and applications,* Madison, Wis, 1995, Advanced Medical Publishers.

Review Questions

1. Routine tests done to determine that an ultrasound scanner is operating at its expected level of performance is referred to as:
   a. equipment acceptance tests
   b. general equipment maintenance
   c. quality assurance
   d. instrument upgrades

2. Which one of the following statements is true regarding quality assurance tests of ultrasound scanners?
   a. They require expertise of a hospital engineer or physicist.
   b. Quality assurance for each scanner takes around 2 hours per week.
   c. Good record-keeping is an essential component.
   d. Quantitative results are generally not necessary.

3. In-house quality assurance programs usually involve all of the following except:
   a. tests using phantoms
   b. inspection and cleaning of air filters
   c. records and worksheets showing test results
   d. voltage measurements at specified points

4. Material making up the body of a typical quality assurance phantom is "tissuelike" in terms of its _____ properties.
   a. attenuation and perfusion
   b. sound speed and attenuation
   c. sound speed and reflector location
   d. echogenicity and reflector location

5. To be used for tests of geometric accuracy, the _____ and _____ in a phantom must be precisely specified.
   a. echogenicity and reflector location
   b. sound speed and reflector location
   c. attenuation and reflector location
   d. echogenicity and attenuation

6. If the actual distance between two reflectors in a phantom is 4 cm, but the digital caliper readout indicates it is 3.8 cm, the percentage error in the caliper readout is:
   a. less than 1%
   b. 1.5%
   c. 5%
   d. 10%

7. On the slice thickness phantom the slice width is estimated from the _____ of the image of the scattering plane.
   a. axial extent
   b. lateral margins
   c. brightness
   d. amount of shadowing

8. A string phantom is useful for measuring:
   a. maximum depth of Doppler signal detection
   b. velocity accuracy in spectral Doppler
   c. axial resolution in B-mode
   d. vertical distance measurement accuracy

9. Doppler flow phantoms are useful for determining:
   a. maximum depth of Doppler signal detection
   b. vertical distance measurement accuracy
   c. acoustic output during color flow imaging
   d. horizontal distance measurement accuracy

10. To produce echo signals that are of a similar magnitude as blood in the body, what two factors in a Doppler phantom must be comparable to human tissues?
    a. phantom material attenuation and mimicking material blood echogenicity
    b. phantom material density and mimicking material blood attenuation
    c. mimicking material blood viscosity and attenuation
    d. mimicking material blood velocity and acceleration

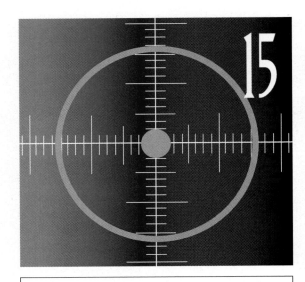

15 Quality Assurance in Nuclear Medicine

● Joanne Metler

Objectives

At the completion of this chapter the reader will be able to do the following:

- Describe the principles of radiation detection and measurement
- Describe the scintillation crystal
- Describe the basic principles of the gamma camera
- Describe the scintillation camera performance characteristics of image linearity, image uniformity, intrinsic spatial resolution, detection efficiency, and counting rate problems
- Describe the design and performance characteristics of commonly used collimators
- Describe planar camera quality control testing methods of calibration, gamma energy spectrum, window determination, daily floods (intrinsic and extrinsic), weekly resolution (intrinsic and extrinsic), counting efficiency and sensitivity, and multiwindow spatial registration
- Describe gamma camera single-photon emission computerized tomography (SPECT) systems
- Describe SPECT quality control, that is, flood uniformity, center of rotation (COR), attenuation correction, and pixel size
- Describe positron emission tomography (PET) and its quality control
- Describe nuclear medicine non-imaging equipment and related quality control procedures, that is, gas-filled detectors such as dose calibrators, survey meters and Geiger-Müeller meters, and scintillation detectors such as the multichannel analyzer and thyroid probe
- Describe quality control procedures in a radiopharmacy and radionuclide generator quality control evaluation of contaminant, such as molybdenum, aluminum, and hydrolyzed reduced technetium

Key Terms

bioassay
center of rotation (COR)
chemical impurity
chi-square
chromatography
collimator
count rate
counts per minute (cpm)
dose calibrator
disintegrations per minute (dpm)
energy resolution
field uniformity
gamma camera
gas-filled detectors
Geiger-Müeller (GM) meter
hydrolyzed reduced technetium
Joint Commission on Accreditation of Hospital Organizations (JCAHO)
multichannel analyzer
molybdenum-99
Nuclear Regulatory Commission (NRC)
Occupational Safety and Health Administration (OSHA)
photomultiplier tube (PMT)
photon
photopeak
pixel size
positron emission tomography (PET)
pulse height analyzer (PHA)
radionuclide impurity
scintillation crystal

Outline

The Scintillation Gamma Camera
Quality Control Procedures for Imaging Equipment
Energy resolution and photopeaking

Nuclear medicine technology is a scientific and clinical discipline involving the diagnostic, therapeutic, and investigative use of radionuclides. The nuclear medicine professional performs a variety of responsibilities in a typical day, including formulating, dispensing, and administering radiopharmaceuticals; performing in vivo and in vitro laboratory procedures; acquiring, processing, and analyzing patient studies on a computer, performing all daily equipment testing; preparing the patient for the studies; operating the imaging and non-imaging equipment, and maintaining a radiation safety program. Because of the variety of responsibilities in the nuclear medicine department the **Joint Commission on Accreditation of Healthcare Organizations (JCAHO)** has recognized the necessity for an established quality assurance program in nuclear medicine. JCAHO states that "There shall be quality control policies and procedures governing nuclear medicine activities that assure diagnostic and therapeutical reliability and safety of the patients and personnel."[1] This chapter discusses the many quality assurance procedures routinely performed in nuclear medicine.

THE SCINTILLATION GAMMA CAMERA

The scintillation **gamma camera** was first developed by Hal Anger in 1958 and has undergone many changes in design and electrical sophistication since its inception. However, the basic components of the gamma camera remain the same (Figure 15-1)[2]. The camera consists of a circular or rectangular detector mounted on a gantry, which allows flexible manipulation around a patient, and electronic processing and display components. In addition, the camera system is interfaced to a computer to control study acquisition, analysis, and display. The detector head contains a thallium-activated sodium iodide crystal, NaI(Tl), photomultiplier tubes (PMTs), preamplifiers, a position energy circuit, a pulse height analyzer, and a display mechanism. Because radiation is a random process, gamma rays are not easy to control. The energy of the ionizing gamma radiation is too high to be deflected like visible light. However, the gamma **photon** can be directed through holes in a **collimator** while blocking tangential or scattered photons. To obtain a resolving image, the collimator must be placed on the face of the detector head, allowing the desirable gamma

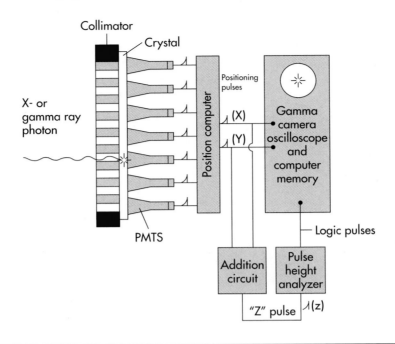

FIGURE 15-1

Basic scintillation camera detector components. (From Thrall JH, Ziessman HA: *Nuclear medicine: the requisites*, St Louis, 1995, Mosby.)

photons to pass through to the NaI(Tl) crystal. A collimator is a lead filtering device that consists of holes through which a gamma photon can pass. These holes are separated by lead septa (Figure 15-2). The photons that are not absorbed or scattered by the lead septa pass straight through to the NaI(Tl) crystal and subsequently create an image of the isotope distribution from the patient. With high-energy photons, thicker lead septa are required to prevent scatter from degrading the image. Collimators are available from several manufacturers. The collimator chosen for a patient study depends on the isotope energy and resolution required for the specific diagnostic procedure. Some examples of the types of collimators commonly used in nuclear medicine include low-, medium-, and high-energy parallel hole; high-resolution parallel hole; high-sensitivity parallel hole; general all purpose parallel hole; pinhole; and converging and diverging.[5] Because collimators are made specifically to operate within a gamma photon's energy range, it is necessary for a nuclear medicine department to procure collimators suitable for several types of applications. The most common type used for diagnostic studies is the parallel-hole collimator. The parallel-hole collimator is preferred because it directs photons from a patient onto the scintillation crystal without varying the image. Once the photon passes through the collimator, it reaches the NaI(Tl) **scintillation crystal** and is converted to light. The number of light photons produced is directly proportional

to the energy of the gamma photon. There are typically 30 photons produced per keV of energy.[15] The NaI(Tl) crystals vary in diameter, shape, and thickness. Changing the parameters of the crystal affects sensitivity or resolution (i.e., if sensitivity is increased by using a thicker crystal, then the resolution will be compromised and vice-versa). The NaI(Tl) crystal is hygroscopic and extremely sensitive to sudden temperature changes. The environment of the gamma camera must remain stable, and precautions must be taken to prevent moisture from entering the NaI(Tl) crystal, as well as preventing sudden temperature shifts.[5] In addition, an accidental impact may cause the crystal to crack.

The scintillation, or light, photon interacts with the **photomultiplier tube (PMT)**. The light generated in the NaI(Tl) crystal is then converted to electrical signals. The electrons produced are amplified and accelerated 1 million-fold in the PMT system. Following conversion to an electrical pulse, a position circuit produces *X* and *Y* position signals, which are directly related to the location of the photon interaction on the NaI(Tl) crystal. Because of the high potential of ionizing radiation to interact with matter, not all the gamma photons detected by the NaI(Tl) crystal are the original primary gamma photons of interest. The interactions with matter from the patient and through the camera system can cause scatter radiation. Too much scatter radiation can cause degradation in the resolution of the

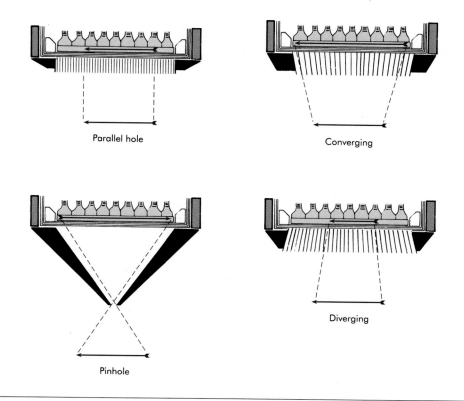

FIGURE 15-2

Four common types of collimators used on gamma cameras. (From Bernier DR, Christian PE, Langan JM: *Nuclear medicine: technology and techniques,* ed 3, St Louis 1994, Mosby.)

final image. It is therefore possible to electronically exclude undesirable photons by only accepting the gamma photons above a certain energy. The discrimination and selection of the gamma photon is performed by a **pulse height analyzer (PHA)**. The pHA can be preset to accept only specific energy signals from the detector. The gamma photon energy required is specified by creating an energy "window" in the PHA. The energy window designates lower and upper limits of the gamma photon energy of interest. Depending on the model and age of equipment, windows can be set by three different methods. A threshold window may be set with a window reading above it, usually expressed in percent of total keV of the gamma energy in question. A midline energy may be set at the energy of the gamma ray or at the maximum count position of the voltage or gain adjustment. The percent window is then applied above and below this midpoint or peak. Lastly, some instruments allow setting window thresholds at any position, including overlapping energies and multiple discrete windows for multiple isotope studies. Multiple windows may also be set up for those radionuclides that emit more than one gamma ray (e.g., thallium-201, indium-111, gallium-67, etc.). The signal is then sent to a display controller to produce a numeric display and an image. The display can occur simultaneously on a cathode ray tube, a scalar, a film, and a computer screen. Many camera systems can display the image in analog, digital, or both. An analog camera allows the image to be displayed directly onto film in a cassette with or without the use of a computer. The analogue camera may also be interfaced to a computer that simultaneously collects the image in the computer and displays it digitally. Finally, a digital camera digitizes the output of each PMT tube to create a digital image.

A variety of gamma camera configurations are available. The gamma camera detector may have a small or large field of imaging capability. The detector also may be circular or rectangular. In addition, the gamma camera system may hold one, two, or three detectors. These configurations are better known as single-, dual-, or triple-head cameras. In addition, some gamma cameras are fixed, whereas others are mobile. The scintillation gamma camera system is a very complex mechanism accompanied by a variety of components that are crucial to producing a reliable and factual clinical image. The quality of the nuclear medicine image is determined by a variety of parameters. These parameters must be perpetually evaluated to guarantee that the image the physician is interpreting is accurate and truly diagnostic of the patient's pathology.

Box 1-1 NEMA Acceptance Tests for Scintillation Cameras (SPECT)

Intrinsic Spatial Resolution
Intrinsic Energy Resolution
Intrinsic Field Uniformity
Intrinsic Count Rate Performance
Intrinsic Spatial Linearity
Multiple Spatial Registration
Sensitivity
Angular Variation of Spatial Position
Angular Variation of Flood Field Uniformity and Sensitivity
Reconstructed System Spatial Resolution
Spatial Resolution with and without Scatter
System Count Rate Performance with Scatter

From National Electrical Manufacturers Association: *NEMA standards for performance measurements of scintillation cameras*, Pub No NUI-1986, Washington DC, 1986, The Association.

Table 15-1   Gamma Camera Quality Control

Quality control procedure	Frequency
Peaking	Daily and before each new radionuclide used
Counting rate limits	Daily
Field uniformity	Daily, after repair
Spatial resolution	Weekly, after repair
Spatial linearity	Weekly, after repair
Sensitivity	Quarterly

According to the National Electrical Manufactures' Association (NEMA) 12 acceptance tests standards are performed at the factory on all gamma cameras.[14,16,17] Box 15-1 lists the type of testing that NEMA performs. The quality control measures taken at the factory ensure the good working condition of the new system. However, once in the nuclear medicine department, it is not practical and sometimes not possible to perform all of the NEMA standard acceptance tests.[22] However, the quality control procedures listed in Table 15-1 are required JCAHO[1] and regulatory agencies and are to be performed routinely.[18] The quality control procedures performed on all imaging equipment ensure that the patient's diagnostic study is safe and accurate.

QUALITY CONTROL PROCEDURES FOR IMAGING EQUIPMENT

Energy Resolution and Photopeaking

Before any quality control or patient procedure, the correct energy setting for the radionuclide being used must be se-

lected and the primary gamma ray energy, or **photopeak**, centered around an energy window. The quality control is performed daily either manually or automatically depending on the manufacturer's specifications. The PHA is centered about the photopeak(s) of the radionuclide of interest, usually using a 5% to 10% window. This is generally referred to as "peaking" the camera. It is accomplished by adjusting the baseline window setting of the PHA around the specific energy of the gamma ray. For example, **technetium-99m** (^{99m}Tc) is used daily in a nuclear medicine department. ^{99m}Tc's primary gamma ray has an energy of 140 keV. The window generally used for imaging is 20% around 140 keV. Therefore resetting a 20% window "tells" the PHA to accept only gamma photons with energies from 126 to 154 keV and to center the photopeak at 140 keV. It is important to note that the camera must be peaked before any radionuclide is used.

Because radioactive decay is random, each step in converting the radiation to an electrical current is subject to random error. The **spectrum** (curve) of the radionuclide of interest is not a straight line representing complete absorption of the gamma ray, but a Gaussian distribution as a result of random error, Compton scatter, and/or material attenuation (Figure 15-3). The light photons emitted by the NaI(Tl) crystal are given off in all directions with random probability. The **energy resolution** can then be expressed as the spread, or width, of the spectrum divided by the center photopeak. The spread of the spectrum or the full width at half maximum (FWHM) is the energy range of the widest width of the spectrum, which is halfway down from the photopeak (Figure 15-4). The energy resolution is calculated as follows:

$$\text{Percent energy resolution} = \frac{\text{FWHM at half maximum}}{\text{Photopeak center}} \times 100$$

The narrower the curve, the better is the energy resolution of the detector. *A good energy resolution is between 8% and 12% and enables the camera system to better discern gamma rays with close energies.* A reliable energy resolution is significant because it represents the system's ability to accurately depict two separate events in space, time, or energy. The ability of a system to detect separate radiation events becomes clinically relevant especially when used for in vitro or in vivo counting, which potentially leads to a patient's clinical diagnosis.

Counting Rate Limits

The sensitivity (counting ability) of a gamma camera generally decreases with increased amounts of activity. If the activity is too high, the detector is "paralyzed" and cannot count. The system's inability to count is referred to as *dead time*. Dead time describes the duration the detector re-

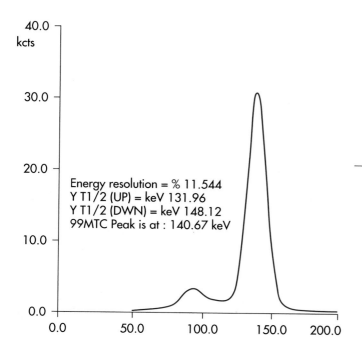

FIGURE 15-3

Energy spectrum of the radionuclide technetium-99m.

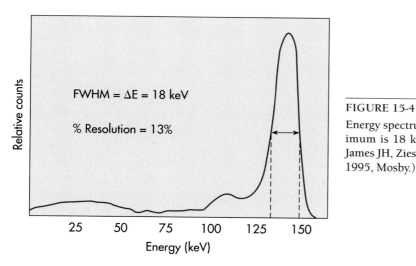

FIGURE 15-4

Energy spectrum of technetium-99m. The full width at half maximum is 18 keV. The energy resolution is 13%. (From Thrall James JH, Ziessman HA: *Nuclear medicine: the requisites*, St Louis, 1995, Mosby.)

quires to process the ionizing events as they occur in the NaI(Tl) crystal. The manufacturer's specification of the **count rate** limit per second states that the observed count rate through a 20% window shall not exceed 20% of the counts lost as a result of dead time.[10a] The electronic circuitry of the majority of contemporary gamma cameras reach counting limits of 120,000 to 150,000 counts per second before experiencing a 20% loss because of dead time.[11] Before performing any quality control procedure, the count rate of the radioactive point or flood source must be determined to ensure that the counts per second do not exceed the manufacturer's specifications. Once the count rate is determined to be within the counting rate limits for that gamma camera, only then can the quality control testing continue. The procedure to determine count rate is quite simple. The radioactive source is placed at the appropriate location necessary for quality control and the time/count scalar continuously displays the counts per second. Count rates that exceed the gamma camera's design limits can result in degradation of the images and loss of counts.[11] If the counts per second rate is too high and it is necessary to decrease the count rate, the radioactive source is repositioned at an increased distance or the amount of radioactivity in the source decreased.

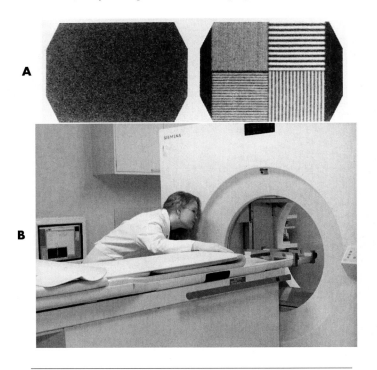

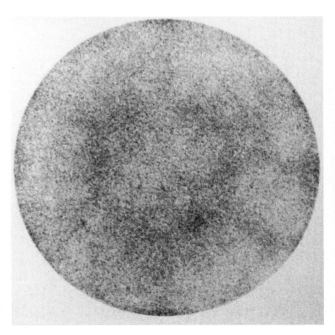

FIGURE 15-5

A, Field uniformity flood and resolution pattern. B, Nuclear medicine technologist preparing to obtain a field flood uniformity on a dual-head camera system. (B, courtesy Northwest Community Hospital, Arlington Heights, Ill.)

FIGURE 15-6

Mispositioned photopeak resulting in a nonuniform flood.

Field Uniformity

Field uniformity refers to the gamma camera's ability to detect a uniform source of radiation and respond exactly the same at any location within the imaging field. The uniform response of the gamma camera results in an image with an even distribution of radioactivity (Figure 15-5). The uniformity of the gamma camera is dependent on the uniform response of the NaI(Tl) crystal and the PMTs. The response of each PMT must match that of all the other PMTs. In addition, the counting window must be centered around the photopeak. Mispositioning the photopeak may alter the field uniformity (Figure 15-6). Nonuniformity may also arise from employing the incorrect photopeak for a specific radionuclide, malfunctioning PMT, cracked NaI(Tl) crystal, total system malfunction, and so on (Figure 15-7). *Because the uniformity of the camera ultimately determines the accuracy of a patient's image and, ultimately, the diagnosis, it is imperative that the field uniformity or flood be performed daily.* This quality control procedure must be performed before any patient studies. The measurement of the daily field uniformity can be performed intrinsically or extrinsically. Intrinsic uniformity is the measurement of the uniformity of the gamma camera detector with no collimator in place. The procedure is generally performed with

a point source of radioactivity placed at a distance equivalent to 4 to 5 diameters of the detector's field of imaging. Take precautions that the counts per second rate does not exceed that particular system's limits. The intrinsic uniformity determines the integrity of the NaI(Tl) crystal, as well as its electronic components. The phenomenon known as *edge packing* can show up as a bright rim of activity around the perimeter of the flood. To prevent edge packing, most manufacturers provide a lead-shielded ring that masks the effect when attached to the edge of the camera head.

Extrinsic uniformity testing is also the measurement of the camera's field uniformity; however, it is performed with the collimator (which is used for imaging) in place. It is performed by placing a uniform flood source of radioactivity directly on the collimated camera (Figure 15-8). There are two commonly used extrinsic radioactive sources: (1) a Plexiglas container filled with water and generally 1 to 10 mCi of ^{99m}Tc and (2) a solid sealed 10 mCi cobalt-57 sheet.[25] The ^{99m}Tc liquid-filled Plexiglas source does have some disadvantages. It must be manually filled with technetium and thoroughly mixed to secure even distribution of the radionuclide. The procedure increases the risk of radioactive contamination to the technologist and equipment, thus increasing the risk of radiation exposure to the

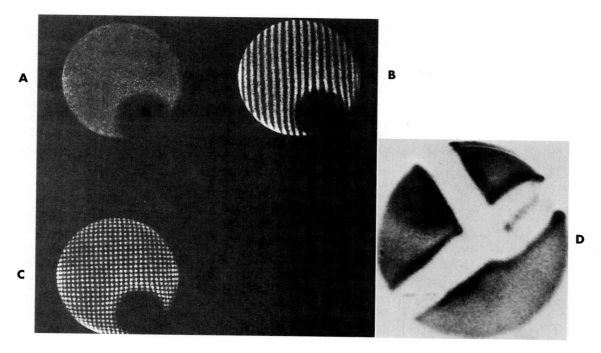

FIGURE 15-7

Example of a nonfunctioning photomultiplier tube seen in the flood field (**A**), the orthogonal hole resolution pattern (**B**), and the PLES phantom (**C**). **D**, Examples of nonuniform flood fields caused by a cracked crystal. (From Early PJ, Sodee BS: *Principles and procedures of nuclear medicine*, ed 2, St Louis, 1995, Mosby.)

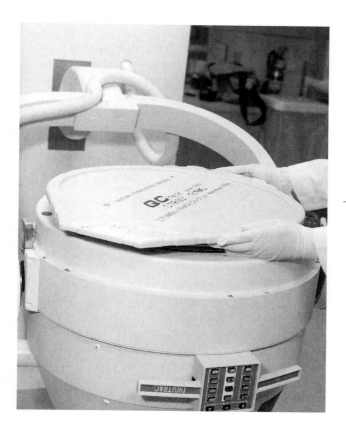

FIGURE 15-8

Extrinsic flood uniformity using a cobalt-57 sheet source.

technologist. The extrinsic uniformity, in addition to evaluating the NaI(Tl) crystal and electrical components, allows visualization of a defect or damage to the collimator. Annual inspection of collimators using extrinsic field uniformity testing is recommended and should become a routine part of any quality assurance program. A defect in a collimator will image as photopenic areas (Figure 15-9).

A flood field image of 1 to 3 million counts is generally acquired whether the intrinsic method or extrinsic method is used. However, it is recommended that the quality control for each gamma camera be carefully evaluated according to the manufacturer's specifications and the department's needs. The quality control test used should remain consistent. The consistency allows visual inspection of any nonuniformity of the camera system to be easily monitored. The uniformity flood must be performed daily on every piece of imaging equipment. Visual inspection of the flood and comparison with that of the previous days will reveal any subtle changes in uniformity that are not always apparent by looking at one image. Any areas of nonuniformity of the detector must be noted and repaired before clinical use. In addition to performing daily floods, the JCAHO quality assurance program recommends that every piece of equipment also have a preventive maintenance program performed biannually.[1]

Gamma cameras of the late 1970s through the present have been developed to correct some of the nonuniformities seen in older images. A microprocessor built into the gamma camera generates a correction factor for each pixel of the matrix, based on variation in counts of different pixels.[23] Figure 15-10 demonstrates the difference between an uncorrected and corrected uniformity flood. Subsequently, when patient images are generated, the correction factors are applied to each pixel, thus reducing nonuniformity.[23]

Spatial Resolution and Spatial Linearity

Spatial resolution is the gamma camera's ability to reproduce small details of a radioactive distribution.[10a] The smaller the details that a camera can reproduce, the better is the spatial resolution of that system. ● *The spatial resolution quality control procedure is required to be performed a minimum of once a week on every imaging system.* The quality control determines the camera's ability to detect and image fine differences of a radioactive distribution that exist in closely spaced areas. In essence, the gamma camera detects the small abnormalities of different radioactive con-

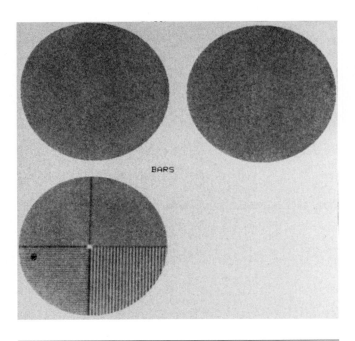

FIGURE 15-9

Note the photopenic area in the flood field and the resolution bar pattern. This is due to collimator damage.

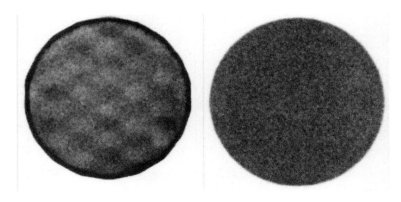

FIGURE 15-10

An uncorrected and a microprocessor corrected uniformity flood.

centrations that may subsequently be seen on patient images. To determine the exact spatial resolution of a gamma camera system, one of the following resolution test pattern transmission sources must be used: 4-quadrant bar phantom with varying size bars; parallel-line equal-spacing (PLES) bar pattern with constant bar and spacing sizes, or an orthogonal hole phantom with varying sizes of holes.[4,5]

The manufacturer of every gamma camera system determines the intrinsic spatial resolution specific for its gamma camera. This is important when choosing the type and size of a transmission resolution pattern. For example, if the manufacturer specifications say that gamma camera 1 has an intrinsic spatial resolution of 3 mm, then the four-quadrant bar phantom used must have bars between 2 and 5 mm. The resolution pattern is placed on the collimator or camera for an intrinsic resolution quality control test and on the collimator for an extrinsic resolution quality control test. The resolution pattern is placed in the center of the field of view (FOV) in such a way that the center of the patterns is directly over the center of the detector. A ^{99m}Tc or ^{57}Co sheet source is then placed on the resolution pattern so that the radioactivity is transmitted through the resolution pattern. It is recommended that when using the four-quadrant bar pattern, four images are obtained at 90 degrees between positions.[4,11] This allows verification of the spatial resolution in the X and Y positions, as well as allowing the bars barely resolved to be evaluated in each quadrant of the FOV (Figure 15-11).

The PLES bar resolution pattern is sometimes preferable to the four-quadrant pattern. A PLES is preferable for testing spatial resolution because it was specifically designed to minimize the number of images that are actually required to evaluate resolution.[11] Only two images are required to evaluate the camera spatial resolution because the size of the bars and the spacing between the bars are constant (Figure 15-12). The orthogonal hole phantom is a hexagonal lead sheet containing holes of equal diameter at right angles to each other. Only one image is required to determine the resolution and uniformity over the entire FOV of the camera detector.

Regardless which resolution test pattern is used routinely for a gamma camera system, it is important to visually inspect each image to detect any fluctuation in resolution. This is done by comparing the weekly resolution image with the previous ones. A change in the resolution can be caused by several factors. If there is a change in resolution, the photopeak, window, source, source distance, gamma photon, energy, and the type of collimator used should all be verified. Any malfunction or misposition of the above factors can detrimentally affect the spatial resolution. If all of the above are properly functioning and in proper position, the crystal must then be evaluated for damage or degradation.

The **spatial linearity** of a gamma camera system is its ability to produce a linear image with straight lines corresponding to the same straight lines of the bar pattern. Most

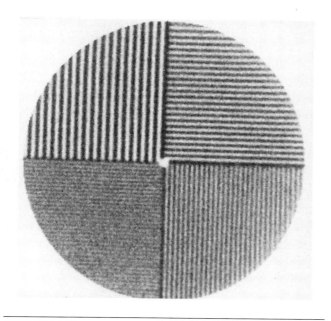

FIGURE 15-11
Spatial resolution using a four-quadrant bar pattern. Four images are obtained 90 degrees apart.

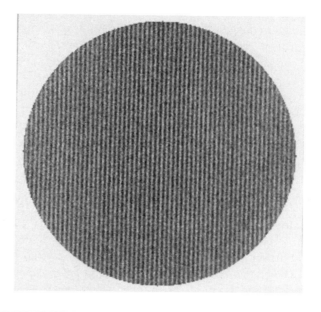

FIGURE 15-12
PLES bar resolution pattern.

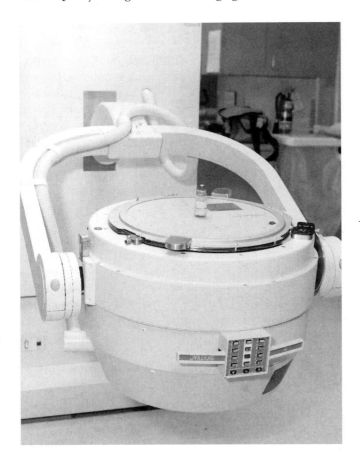

FIGURE 15-13
Sensitivity testing using a known cobalt-57 source.

modern gamma camera systems have circuits that correct for nonlinearity. Linearity is generally assessed and can be seen by visual inspection of any of the spatial resolution test pattern images. This is done by carefully inspecting the linearity of the bars or holes in both the X and Y positions and comparing the results with the acceptance test results and the results from previous weeks. Any nonlinearity can cause extreme image artifacts, especially in reconstructed tomographic images. A nonlinear image indicates that the gamma camera should be serviced and reevaluated before further clinical use. This will ensure the accuracy of the diagnostic images, both planar and tomographic.

Sensitivity

Sensitivity is another quality control procedure performed to determine the gamma camera detector's ability to detect the ionizing events that occur in the NaI(Tl) crystal. The events recorded as **counts per minute (cpm)** are calculated and expressed as counts per minute per microcurie (μCi) of activity present. The sensitivity quality control is performed biannually. It is performed by placing a sealed point source such as Co[57] at different locations (center and at least four peripheral locations) on the camera head and counted for a set time (Figure 15-13).[5,17] The sensitivity is

equal to the net counts per time divided by the actual activity of the sealed source:

$$\text{Sensitivity} = \frac{\text{Net counts/time}}{\text{Activity of the sealed source in μCi (on that day)}}$$

The sensitivity is compared with the previous documented sensitivity tests and the manufacturer's specifications to ensure there is no change in the ability of the gamma camera to detect ionizing events.

Multiple-Window Spatial Registration

Gamma cameras are equipped with multiple pulse height analyzer windows to use with photons of different energies. The multiplicity capability must be evaluated for spatial registration. The position of the X and Y signals must be the same for each energy window. If a study is performed using a radionuclide that has multiple gamma photons of different energies, the photons must be received by their perspective windows and positioned on the cathode ray tube in the same locations. If they are received in different locations, the resolution of that image will be compromised. It is recommended by NEMA that a gallium-67 source be used with a bar pattern phantom and sequential images acquired using the three imaging gamma peaks of

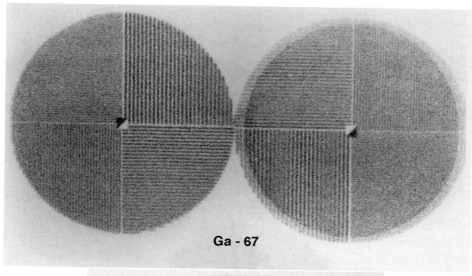

Ga - 67

FIGURE 15-14

Multiwindow spatial resolution testing. (From Henkin RE, Boles MA, Dillehay GL et al: *Nuclear medicine,* vol 1, St Louis, 1996, Mosby.)

[67]Ga (93keV, 184keV, 296keV). The individual images are then acquired using each peak individually, and the final images are made using combinations of two peaks. The images are then evaluated for best time and best resolution. In addition, the three floods are superimposed on each other to evaluate the match (Figure 15-14).[5]

QUALITY ASSURANCE OF SPECT CAMERAS

Tomographic techniques have been developed in nuclear medicine for both **single-photon emission computerized**

tomography, (SPECT) and **positron emission tomography (PET)**.[6-8] The research and development of various tomographic systems have given way to the rotating gamma camera. The rotating system, with the aid of a computer and reconstruction software, has the ability to perform true transaxial tomography. Rotational SPECT, CT, and PET all share the characteristic that only data arising in the particular image plane is used in the reconstruction of the tomographic image, thus allowing higher image contrast.[3,4] SPECT systems are commercially available with single, dual, triple, and quadruple heads. The multiple-head SPECT systems are becoming the preferred model because more information with increased resolution can be ob-

Table 15-2   SPECT Gamma Camera Quality Control*

Quality control procedure	Frequency
Uniformity correction flood	Weekly
Center of rotation	Weekly for every collimator used for tomography
Pixel size	Monthly
Cine to detect patient motion	After each patient acquisition

*Quality control procedure in addition to routine gamma camera quality control procedures.

tained in a given period. The camera head(s) is attached to a mechanical gantry that allows the head to rotate 360 degrees in a circular or an elliptical orbit about the patient. The gantry unit is designed to enable the camera head to come as close to the patient as possible to guarantee the best resolution at the face of the detector head. Some cameras are also designed to follow the patient's body contour in a noncircular orbit (whole body scanner capability). SPECT systems also require a computer to control the gantry, acquire the data, and reconstruct the tomographic images. The quality assurance of a SPECT system requires stricter controls. SPECT quality assurance procedures are not as tolerant as for planar imaging. For example, a ±5% field uniformity is acceptable for planar imaging; however, variations in uniformity for SPECT cannot exceed ±1%.[11,17] In addition, the camera coordinates must be properly aligned with the axis of rotation of the gantry and the computer image matrix. The SPECT system must adhere to the required quality control procedures of the scintillation gamma camera as discussed above, that is, energy calibration, field uniformity, spatial resolution and linearity, sensitivity, and multiple window registration. However, additional procedures must be performed to ensure maximum SPECT camera performance.[9,10] Table 15-2 lists the required and recommended quality control procedures of a SPECT system.[9]

Uniformity Correction Flood

Field uniformity corrections are much more critical in SPECT imaging than in other forms of imaging. Small changes in extrinsic uniformity may alter the reconstructed images. Acquiring the 1 to 3 million counts needed in a planar system is just not adequate for the SPECT. Acquiring less than 30 million counts for a **uniformity correction flood** may result in a ring artifact (Figure 15-15). The 30 million count figure used for uniformity correction is acquired so that there are about 10,000 counts per pixel in a

64 × 64 matrix. *The system's manufacturer requires that a camera with a collimator in place must have uniformity with variations of less than 1%.* In addition, there are some internal software programs used to verify a 1% standard deviation. Acquiring 10,000 counts per pixel is necessary to obtain the recommended percent relative standard deviation (SD) of 1%.

$$\text{Percent SD} = \frac{100}{10,000} = 1\%$$

A uniform ^{99m}Tc or ^{57}Co source is placed on the collimator. The uniformity correction flood of 30 to 60 million counts using a 64 × 64 matrix is acquired weekly for each collimator used. The image is stored in the computer and later employed to correct raw data used in reconstruction of the tomographic images.

Center of Rotation

It is very important that there is no misalignment between the physical or mechanical **center of rotation** (COR) of the SPECT system and the center of rotation in the reconstruction computer matrix. The pixel matrix that forms the projection images of the SPECT acquisition is a function of the computer, not the camera. The alignment of the computer matrix may not be perfectly aligned with the camera head or gantry or both. The basic mechanical parts of the SPECT system, such as the gears and bearings, as well as patient diversity, prevent a consistent symmetry. In addition, daily use and wear and tear of the system could cause rotational discrepancies.[7,10a] The center of rotation is important to all SPECT systems, from single- to quadruple-head systems. However, multiple-head systems also require software to guarantee synchronization between the heads.

To determine if the center of rotation is properly calibrated, a point source placed in the center of the detector head orbit should project to the center of the 64 × 64 computer matrix, or pixel 32. The center of rotation discrepancies of most SPECT systems are less than 2 mm from the center of the matrix, but the goal is to be no more than 1 mm from pixel 32.[7,10a] A point source of ^{57}Co or ^{99m}Tc is used to calculate the center of rotation and the pixel size. A SPECT study is performed on the point source, and the images are reconstructed. A misaligned center of rotation will show the point source to appear larger, blurred, or containing a ring artifact. A center of rotation shift of 3 mm or more can affect the quality of the reconstructed images. *The center-of-rotation quality control must be performed weekly on all SPECT systems.* Many SPECT systems now use computer processing to construct a linear representation to ensure stability. If there is a deviation or a mis-

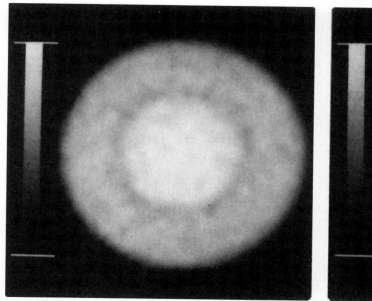
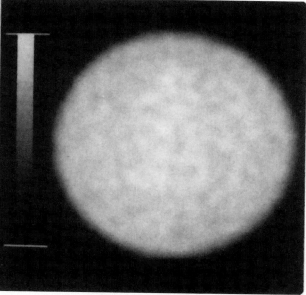

FIGURE 15-15

Ring artifact. (From Greer et al: *J Nucl Med Technol* 13:76, 1985.)

alignment, the computer will generate a straight line with areas appearing outside the line.

Pixel Size

Pixel size of the matrix must be calibrated properly because pixels take on the three-dimensional characteristic of depth in SPECT. Any change in the pixel size will change depth or distance and subsequently alter attenuation correction factors used in the tomographic reconstructed images. The sizes of the pixels should be monitored monthly for any fluctuations. The pixel size can be adjusted by setting of the analog-to-digital converters and should be checked in both the X and Y directions.[28] The pixel width should be the same in both directions. Any difference in the pixel dimensions will cause problems in reformatting of the image data. In addition, a shift in the analog-to-digital converter can also move the center of rotation matrix.

SPECT Quality Control During and After Patient Procedures

SPECT quality control of the camera and computer systems is important to ensure accurate and optimal image quality for the patient. However, in addition to the quality control of the mechanics of the SPECT system, quality assurance must be practiced during a patient study. It is important to remove any materials from the patient's body that might attenuate the radioisotope being imaged or interfere with image acquisition and reconstruction. This is especially crucial when imaging myocardial perfusion. Examples of external attenuators on a patient are metal coins left in a shirt pocket, a necklace with a hanging metal, an ECG lead left on, or a prosthesis. Breast tissue may also attenuate data and should be noted. Many software programs are able to correct for this. The patient must also be closely monitored for motion. Any vertical or horizontal motion can create artifacts in the reconstruction. In addition, the camera head must be level when the acquisition begins and remain level throughout the study. Once the study acquisition is completed, patient motion can be detected on the computer. The computer programs used today allow inspection for patient motion by either summed projection, sinograms, or cine displays. In a summed projection, patient motion appears as a change in the height of the organ imaged. A sinogram is a plot of each projection. If the patient did not move during the acquisition, the plot will appear as a bright line. A break in the line indicates patient motion from left to right. A cine display, a raw motion picture of the acquired projections, is a simple way to detect patient motion. If the motion is significant, the study is invalid and must be repeated (Figure 15-16).

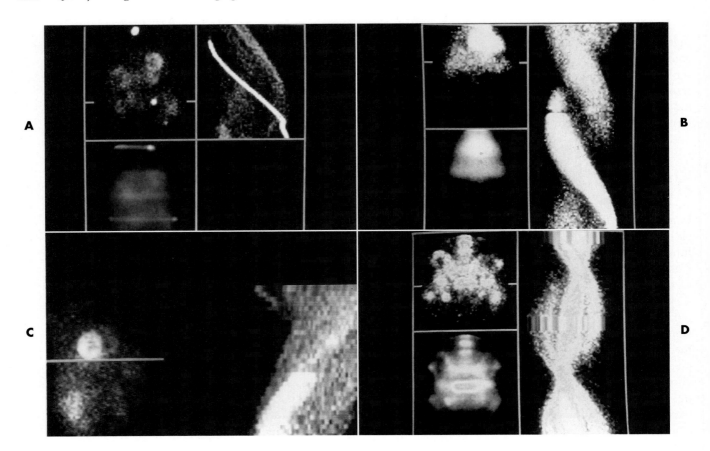

FIGURE 15-16
Problems identified with the patient motion quality control displays. **A,** SPECT catches patient's bed during rotation. **B,** Patient sits up during acquisition. **C,** Patient's bed translates axial during acquisition. **D,** Gantry stops befor completion of study. (From Henkin RE, Boles MA, Dillehay GL et al: *Nuclear medicine,* vol 1, St Louis, 1996, Mosby.)

POSITRON EMISSION TOMOGRPAHY

Positron emission tomography (PET) is a fast-growing imaging modality of nuclear medicine that produces tomographic images of the distribution of positron-emitting radiopharmaceuticals. The excitement surrounding PET technology is that the images depict both physiologic and biochemical processes of the human body. The study of nuclear physics follows that positrons are emitted from proton-rich nuclei that only travel a short distance before encountering an electron, resulting in annihilation of both particles. Upon annihilation, two gamma rays of 511 keV are produced and travel 180 degrees apart in opposite directions. A great quantity of energy is required for positron emission to occur. The radionuclides that emit positrons must be artificially produced in a linear or cyclotron accelerator. An example of the more common radioisotopes used for PET are carbon-11, oxygen-15, nitrogen-13, and fluorine-18. In addition, generator-produced positron-emitting radioisotopes, rubidium-82, copper-62, and gallium-68, are also used. The chemical characteristics of the radioisotopes used for PET enable the synthesis of molecules that are used in tissue metabolism. The metabolic radiopharmaceuticals presently being studied and researched entail diagnostic applications in tumor biology, neurology, psychiatry, and cardiology.

The PET camera is a system that has many crystal detectors, the most common of which is bismuth germanate (BGO), placed in a circular configuration about the patient. The system hardware configuration looks similar to the CT; however, the operation has no similarity. A positron-emitting radiopharmaceutical is administered to the patient. The crystal detectors are paired off 180 degrees apart to count simultaneously, detecting the 511 keV photons.[8] The PET system then establishes where the event occurred simultaneously and acquires the data.[8] The computer software then manipulates the data and reconstructs tomographic slices of the original images.

The PET system is a very complicated detection device that can have literally thousands of crystals. The quality control tests required at installation and thereafter and described and outlined in depth by Karp et al[12,16] are radial resolution, tangential resolution, axial resolution, sensitivity, linearity, uniformity, attenuation accuracy, scatter determination, and dead time corrections.[11]

QUALITY CONTROL OF NON-IMAGING EQUIPMENT

In addition to the variety of imaging systems used in nuclear medicine, non-imaging equipment is essential for the function and safety of all nuclear medicine departments. Non-imaging devices are used daily in radiation protection, in vitro studies, and all radiopharmacy procedures. A radiation protection quality assurance program is essential and required by JCAHO[1] and the **Nuclear Regulatory Commission (NRC)**.[29] A radiation protection program ensures that the work place, employees, and patients are safe and not exposed to any ionizing radiation needlessly. A quality assurance program is also crucial in the radiopharmacy of any nuclear medicine department. Radionuclides must be produced and radiopharmaceuticals prepared and subsequently dispensed and administered to the correct patients. In addition, the procedure of Universal Precautions, enacted into law and enforced by the **Occupational Safety and Health Administration (OSHA)**,[26] must be an integral component of any nuclear medicine quality assurance program to secure a safe environment for both the patient and the healthcare worker. This is especially important to all individuals that may come in contact with needles and blood products. To guarantee safe and accurate diagnostic and therapeutic studies, it is imperative that there are quality control procedures in place from the moment a radionuclide is produced or received until the patient study is completed.

Gas-Filled Detectors

Many radiation detection devices not only detect radiation but also quantitate the amount of ionizing radiation present. The **gas-filled detector** is one type of radiation detection device. The gas-filled detector is a mechanism that consists of a chamber filled with a gas, an anode, a cathode, an external voltage source, and a display meter. The operation of gas-filled detectors is based on the principle that that the ionization-induced electrical currents are produced within the gas chambers of these detectors. As radiation passes through the gas chamber, ions are produced, and the positive ions migrate to the cathode, while the electrons migrate to the anode. The amount of ion pairs collected is a function of the voltage applied and is directly proportional to the energy and quantity of gamma rays entering the chamber. The detector then responds to the presence of radiation by detecting the ionization-induced electrical currents and displaying the current to read in radiation units. Ionization chambers and Geiger-Müller meters are the most common gas-filled detectors used in nuclear medicine. ● *NRC regulation 10 CFR 35.50[29] requires that nuclear medicine departments must assay all radionuclides administered to patients in a dose calibrator, a specialized ionization chamber.*

Ion-Detecting Radiation Detectors

Three types of ion-detecting radiation detectors are commonly used in nuclear medicine. The *ionization survey meter,* which includes the cutie-pie* type, measures radiation exposure rates, (roentgens/hour [R/hr]); the *dose calibrator* measures the quantity of the radiation dosage in microcuries (µCi) to curies (Ci); and the *Geiger-Müller survey meter* and *room monitor* measures qualitative exposure rates. ● *The NRC requires that nuclear medicine departments possess all three types of radiation detectors.[11]*

The ionization survey meter is generally battery operated and portable. The ionization survey meter is commonly used in the nuclear medicine department to secure radiation safety of the personnel and the work environment. ● *The NRC states in section 35 of the Code of Federal Regulation,[32] that any licensee using radioactive materials or radiopharmaceuticals is required to possess a portable radiation survey meter.[11] In addition, the NRC regulations state that a daily area survey must be performed in any area where radioactive materials are used and stored. Unrestricted areas must not exceed 2 mrem in any 1 hour.[30] The NRC requires that the survey meter be capable of detection of dose rate from 0.1 to 100 mR/hr.[11,30]*

To ensure that all monitoring and daily survey radiation exposure readings are true values and conform to the NRC regulations, it is very important that the radiation monitoring equipment is functioning accurately and properly. ● *The NRC requires that all survey meters undergo an annual calibration and a daily reference check before use.* The survey meter must be calibrated; otherwise, the values it produces when exposed to radiation will have no meaning. The survey meter must be calibrated against a point source that is traceable to a standard certified within 5% accuracy by the U.S. National Institute of Standards and Technology (NIST).[28] The survey meter is adjusted if necessary to read the calculated value of the standard, that is, cesium-137. ● *The survey meter should be calibrated on three to five scales (0.1, 10, 100). The procedure and requirements of the NRC can be found in 10 CFR 35.51.[32]*

---

*The cutie-pie is considered more accurate and linear over all of its ranges compared with the Geiger-Müeller tubes.

The reference check is a simple procedure that requires that the instrument measures a standard long-lived radioactive source at the same geometry. The readings obtained in the reference check must be within 20% of the exposure rate checked at calibration, which must always be posted on the side of the instrument.[32] The reference check of the survey meter ensures that the instrument is maintaining calibration. In addition, because the survey meter is battery operated, it is good practice to perform a battery check on the instrument before each use.

Geiger-Müeller Meters

The **Geiger-Müeller (GM) meter** is a survey meter used mainly for radiation protection purposes as a survey instrument and an area monitor. One of its uses is as a room monitor. The audible mechanism allows a quick and inexpensive way to determine the presence of ionizing radiation and is a reminder to work quickly. The intensity of the sound increases with the intensity of the ionizing radiation field. However, the GM meter is not capable of accurately measuring and quantitating radiation exposure caused by diverse energy photons commonly found in a nuclear medicine department. It is important to note that the GM meter cannot accurately measure radiation exposure or dose rate, although calibrated in mR/hr or cpm. It can only indicate the presence of ionizing radiation. ● *The NRC requires that all GM meters undergo the same quality control as the ionization survey meters. The GM meter must be calibrated annually and the reference and battery checked before use.*[32]

Dose Calibrator

A **dose calibrator** is an ionization chamber that is used to verify radioactivity measurements of all radionuclides, radiochemicals, and radiopharmaceutical doses subsequent to administration to the patient. To avoid confusion in the terminology used in the radiopharmacy, the definitions of the "radio" terms follow:

- *Radionuclide:* any radioactive atom
- *Radiochemical:* a radionuclide that has combined with a nonradioactive chemical molecule
- *Radiopharmaceutical:* a radionuclide combined with a biologically active molecule

Radioactive material may require the addition of stabilizers, reagents, or buffering agents. In addition, a radiopharmaceutical requires approval by the Food and Drug Administration (FDA) before clinical use.[28] ● *The four NRC-required quality control tests performed on a dose calibrator are accuracy, constancy, geometry, and linearity.*

The accuracy test evaluates the ability of the radionuclide dose calibrator to accurately measure the activity of standard sources such as ^{57}Co, ^{55}Cs, and ^{133}Ba. These reference sources must be traceable to the National Institute of Standards and Technology. The accuracy test, performed annually, compares the actual activity of the standard sources to the observed readings of the dose calibrator. ● *If the dose calibrator readings vary from the reference sources by greater than 10%, then the instrument must be recalibrated, repaired or replaced (Figure 15-17).* *

The constancy test assesses and verifies the precision of the dose calibrator. A long-lived sealed reference source, such as ^{57}Co, ^{137}Cs, or radium-226, is assayed daily on all commonly used radionuclide settings, and the readings are compared with the standard reference source. ● *The dose calibrator readings must not vary from the reference source activity by more than 10%.* *

---

*Please note that the 10% variance refers to the Nuclear Regulatory Commission regulations. The accepted variance is 5% in most agreement states. Please check with your individual state's regulations for the correct value.

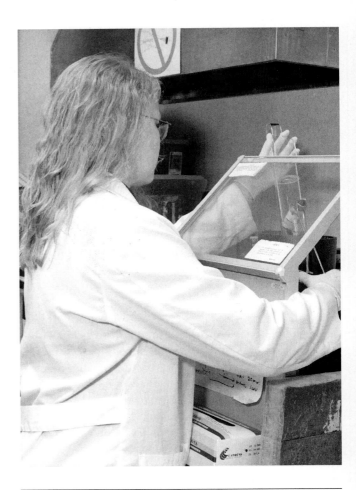

FIGURE 15-17

Nuclear medicine technologist performing the quality control tests on a dose calibrator.

There may be significant variation in measured values versus actual radioactivity present as a result of a variation of sample volume. For example, 10 mCi (370 MBq) contained in the volume of a 1-mL syringe or a 20-mL syringe or vial might vary significantly. ● *If the geometric variations cause the actual measurements to vary by greater than 10% from the true value, correction factors are calculated and used for that specific volume.** The geometric variation test is required upon installation of the dose calibrator and after any repair.

Radionuclide dose calibrators should display the actual radioactivity of a sample. A linearity test determines the accuracy of the dose calibrator's response to measure a wide range of activities. The dose calibrator should be able to measure a full range of activities from microcuries to millicuries. ● *Two methods are readily used and accepted by the NRC.* The first linearity test requires assaying a decaying source of ^{99m}Tc sequentially over 3 to 5 days. The readings are compared with the actual decay of ^{99m}Tc at the same time intervals. The second method involves using precalibrated lead sleeves that are placed sequentially over the same source. The advantage of using the lead sleeves is that the procedure only takes about 5 minutes, resulting in a much lower level of radiation exposure to the technologist. The linearity test is performed at installation, quarterly, and after any repair. ● *The observed values in either method must be within 10% of the actual calculated activities.**

Non-imaging Scintillation Detectors

Along with the scintillation gamma camera systems mentioned previously, there are also non-imaging systems found in nuclear medicine that use the NaI(Tl) crystal and detect radiation with the same basic principle of scintillation. The **scintillation detectors** used in nuclear medicine have many functions. The single- or **multichannel analyzers** (well counters) are scintillation detectors that are used to count blood and urine samples obtained from in vitro procedures such as red cell mass and plasma volume determinations and Schilling tests. In addition to in vitro patient studies, well counters are used to count the quality control **chromatography** strips required to evaluate radionuclides and radiopharmaceuticals.[37] The advantage of the multichannel over the single channel analyzer is that samples that have multiple radioisotopes presenting low to high energy can be analyzed simultaneously. In addition, because the spectrum display is directly proportional to the radionuclide energy, it is possible to determine the un-

known radiation that might be present in some contamination. It is also possible to see at a glance the whole spectrum and proper peaking over the energy of interest. This is important when performing NRC-required daily area wipe surveys to locate, identify, and quantitate any contamination. The quality control procedures required for a scintillation detector are listed in Table 15-3.

Calibration is performed to determine and preset the correct operating voltage that is necessary for the detector to place the gamma energy peak in the center of the spectrum window. This results in achieving the highest and most accurate count rate. Generally, a long-lived radionuclide such as ^{137}Cs, with a gamma photon energy of 662 keV, is used. The voltage is adjusted so that the pulse height of 662 keV is at the center of the spectrum, and the window is spaced equally above and below 662 keV.

Because the scintillation detectors count a variety of radionuclides (^{99m}Tc, iodine-123, ^{125}I, ^{131}I, ^{57}Co, etc.), the detector must be photopeaked before each new radionuclide is counted. Once this is accomplished, the detector's high voltage is adjusted properly for that specific radionuclide. When counting environmental samples for contamination, windows are set wide to capture the gamma rays of all radionuclides that may be potentially released as contaminants. Matching the photopeaks on the spectrum to specific energies allows identification of the radionuclide in the sample.

A background measurement with no radionuclide present is taken to ensure that there is no contaminating radioactivity present that can affect the true counts. The background is taken for the same period that the sample will be counted. The background counts must be subtracted from each sample's gross counts to obtain the true, or net counts, that is, *net counts = gross counts − background counts*. A new background count must be taken for each radionuclide and for each separate procedure to obtain accurate clinical data.

Table 15-3 Scintillation Detector Quality Control

Quality control procedure	Frequency
Energy calibration	Daily
Peaking	Daily and before each new radionuclide used
Background	Daily and for each new radionuclide used
Constancy	Daily
Instrument calibration	Annually, after repair
Energy resolution	Annually, after repair
Efficiency	Annually, after repair
Chi-square test (reproducibility)	Quarterly, weekly recommended

---

*Please note that the 10% variance refers to the Nuclear Regulatory Commission regulations. The accepted variance is 5% in most agreement states. Please check with your individual state's regulations for the correct value.

A constancy test is performed daily to verify the stability of the detector. A long-lived source such as ^{137}Cs is counted and the counts/min (cpm)/microcurie (µCi) is determined and compared with the cpm/µCi at the time of calibration. A change of greater than 10% indicates repair is necessary.[9]

An annual calibration is performed to regulate the gain and high-voltage settings in such a way that dial settings of the channels read directly to the energy keV of the radionuclide. A ^{137}Cs source is used in the detector, and the energy peak is set on 662 keV with a 5% window. The voltage and gain are adjusted until the center, or photopeak, is exactly centered on 662 keV.

The energy resolution can be thought of as the ability of the scintillation detector to accurately discern two different energies as separate. Energy resolution quality control is discussed in the section on quality control of imaging equipment. To review, the energy resolution can then be expressed as the spread or width of the spectrum divided by the center photopeak. The spread of the spectrum or the full width at half maximum (FWHM) is the energy range of the widest width of the spectrum, which is halfway down from the photopeak. The energy resolution is calculated as follows:

$$\text{Percent energy resolution} = \frac{\text{FWHM at half maximum}}{\text{Photopeak center}} \times 100$$

The energy resolution of most scintillation systems using ^{137}Cs is between 8% and 12%.[3,4]

The efficiency of a counting detector is measuring the sensitivity of the detector. It is expressed as the observed count rate divided by the disintegration rate of a radioactive sample.[24]

$$\text{Percent efficiency} = \frac{\text{Counts per minute}}{\text{Disintegrations per minute}}$$

This concept is important because counts per minute (cpm) must be converted into **disintegrations per minute (dpm)** for the technologist to know that whether regulatory requirements are being met for keeping environmental contamination within specific contamination limits for both fixed and removable contamination. For the same sample activity and geometry, every instrument will register a different cpm based on several detector design factors. Therefore an efficiency factor must be determined for each instrument used to count in cpm and convert to dpm.

Radioactive decay of an atom is a random process. So when a radioactive source is said to undergo a number of disintegrations per second, the value represents only the average. Because the number of disintegrations per unit time varies, it can be expected that the counts obtained will also vary. The variation to be expected when counting the same sample is due to random error. A statistical test called **chi-square** test is used to evaluate the reliability of the detector. The results of the chi-square test indicate whether the error that exists in counting is due to randomness. If the error is due to some other problem, such as technical or mechanical error, the detector must be serviced before clinical use. The chi-square quality control test is easy to perform. A radioactive sample is counted 10 times for 1 minute each time. The sample must be placed at a distance from the detector that will result in a minimum of 10,000 counts. The 10,000 counts are necessary to obtain good statistical data within 1% standard deviation. The data is then used to determine the chi-square value:

$$\text{Chi-square} = \frac{\text{Sum }(x_i - \text{mean})^2}{\text{Mean}}$$

where x_i = individual count rates.

The result is then located on the table of chi-square values to determine the probability that the discrepancy between the observed and expected frequency is due to random error. Most scintillation detectors are computer driven and maintain the statistical programs that automatically calculate the chi-square values.

Another NaI(Tl) scintillation detector used in nuclear medicine is the thyroid uptake probe. The thyroid probe is used clinically to determine the function of the patient's thyroid. A percent uptake of an ingested radioisotope of iodine is calculated. The thyroid uptake probe is a multichannel analyzer with a flat face crystal and photomultiplier tube encased in an open-field collimator that faces the patient's thyroid during the procedure. The collimator is generally 20 to 30 cm long, which is the length required to obtain the proper counting geometry of the patient's thyroid. All of the quality control procedures required for a scintillation detector are performed on the thyroid probe. However, because distance and geometry are crucial in measuring a patient's iodine uptake, a thyroid phantom is used in all daily quality control procedures (Figure 15-18).

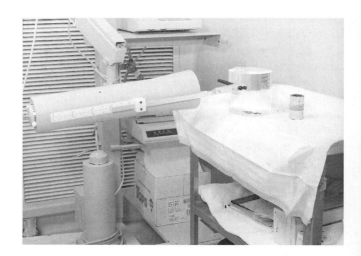

FIGURE 15-18

Thyroid probe quality control using a neck phantom.

The thyroid phantom has been designed to mimic the location of a thyroid in a patient. The phantom ensures that the quality control procedures are accurate and can be related to the patient study.

QUALITY ASSURANCE IN THE RADIOPHARMACY

Sealed Radioactive Source

The sealed sources used in the above calibrations and for calibration of other non-imaging and imaging equipment must be tested for any leakage of radioactive material. ● *The NRC requires that all photon-emitting sealed sources containing 100 µCi or more be tested for leakage biannually.*[30] *Any sealed sources found to have more than 0.005 µCi of removable activity per test must immediately be removed, properly stored, and reported to the NRC.*[31] *In addition, the NRC requires that all sealed sources be inventoried and surveyed for radiation exposure quarterly.*

Molybdenum-99/Technetium-99 Radionuclide Generator

The radionuclide generator system, a long-lived parent yielding to a shorter-lived daughter, allows the production of useful radionuclides for clinical use. The combination of half-lives of the radionuclides in the generator system makes the shipping of radionuclides from a commercial pharmacy to a hospital more cost-effective, requiring deliveries once a week rather than daily. Most of the radiopharmaceuticals prepared by the nuclear medicine technologist are labeled with ^{99m}Tc. The most commonly used generator system in hospitals and clinics is the **molybdenum-99**/technetium-99m (^{99}Mo/^{99m}Tc) system. The ^{99}Mo/^{99m}Tc generator is an alumina ion-exchange column onto which ^{99}Mo, the parent, has a high affinity. Subsequently, ^{99m}Tc has a lower affinity to the column, therefore making the separation of ^{99m}Tc from the parent, ^{99}Mo, simple. When saline is pulled through the alumina column via an evacuated collection vial, the daughter, Tc^{99m}, is removed, or eluted, from the column. The technetium eluted is in the radiochemical form ^{99m}TcO$_4$, **technetium pertechnetate**, and the ^{99m}Tc is in the valence state of +7. Quality control procedures are essential on the technetium eluant each time the generator is eluted, to ensure that the eluant does not contain any contaminants or impurities including: **radionuclide impurity** of ^{99}Mo, molybdate, **chemical impurity** of Al^{+3}, alumina, or radiochemical impurity of **hydrolyzed reduced technetium** (HR-Tc).

A common contaminant found in the generator eluant is the parent, ^{99}Mo. The appearance of ^{99}Mo in the eluant is called *moly breakthrough*. If any ^{99}Mo is injected to a patient, the ^{99}Mo is taken up by the liver and delivers an unnecessary radiation to the liver.

Testing for moly breakthrough is simple to perform. A lead container is used, which absorbs the ^{99m}Tc 140 keV energy but allows the passage of the higher-energy 740 and 780 keV ^{99}Mo photons. The generator eluant vial is placed in the moly lead shield and assayed in the dose calibrator. The amount of ^{99}Mo contamination is calculated by dividing the total amount of ^{99}Mo assayed by the total amount of ^{99m}Tc. ● *The NRC allowable limit is 0.15 µCi of ^{99}Mo activity per 1 mCi of ^{99m}Tc activity at time of injection of the administered dose.*[31] This is critical because the concentration of ^{99}Mo/^{99m}Tc may creep up, exceeding limits several hours after elution.

The chemical impurity that can be present in the generator eluant is alumina, Al^{+3}, which comes from the ion-exchange column. ● *The United States Pharmacopoeia (USP) has established that the Al^{+3} concentration limits not exceed 10 µg Al^{+3}/mL eluant.* Aurin tricarboxylic acid is used for colorimetric spot testing.[28] The color reaction for a standard alumina sample is compared with the generator eluate. The comparison is qualitative and made by visual inspection. Excessive levels of aluminum can interfere with normal distribution of some radiopharmaceuticals.

In addition, the radiochemical impurity that may exist in the eluant solution is hydrolyzed reduced ^{99m}Tc (HR-Tc). Technetium that is eluted is expected to have a valence state of +7, which is the desired chemical form for most kit preparations. If the ^{99m}Tc is present in other forms, then the distribution of the final radiopharmaceutical product in a patient is altered. Unbound, or free, technetium pertechnetate accumulates in the stomach, thyroid, and salivary glands. ^{99m}Tc-colloidal uptake occurs in the reticuloendothelial system, especially the liver. ● *The USP standard for the generator eluant is that 95% or greater of the Tc activity be in the +7 valence state.*[13]

Radiopharmaceuticals

Because radiopharmaceuticals are intended for diagnostic and therapeutic patient procedures, quality control procedures are crucial in ensuring the safety and effectiveness of these preparations.[37] When a nuclear medicine department uses unit doses provided by a commercial nuclear pharmacy, the preparations undergo extensive quality control procedures by the manufacturer and/or the commercial nuclear pharmacy. However, many radiopharmaceutical preparations are prepared using lyophilized radiopharmaceutical preparation kits and short-lived radionuclides, such as ^{99m}Tc. As a result, the absolute responsibility for the quality assurance of the radiopharmaceuticals lies with the radiopharmacist or the nuclear medicine technologist preparing the kits.

Whether the radiopharmaceuticals are prepared commercially or at the hospital nuclear pharmacy, they must be subjected to physiochemical and biologic testing, including physical state examination, osmolality, pH, chemical, radionuclidic and radiochemical purity, sterility, and pyrogenicity testing.[37]

Sterility represents the absence of metabolic products such as endotoxins in the final product. The sterility testing uses *USP* standard media such as thioglycollate and soybean casein digest media to determine the presence of bacteria and fungi in the radiopharmaceutical solution.[28] Because many radiopharmaceuticals are prepared just before patient administration, the sterility test must be performed retrospectively. Pyrogens or microorganism metabolites that may exist in the radiopharmaceutical solution can cause a fever if injected into a patient. The pyrogen test uses the *USP* limulus amebocyte lysate test (LAL) to detect the presence of pyrogens.

The radiochemical and radionuclidic purity of a radiopharmaceutical may be assessed by many different methods, including paper chromatography, thin layer chromatography, high-performance liquid chromatography, and gel electrophoresis.[21,35-37] Because of the characteristics of the short-lived radionuclides used in the preparation of radiopharmaceuticals, time is critical. Miniaturized chromatography procedures are used to evaluate the radiochemical purity of radiopharmaceuticals because they are rapid and easy to use.[34,36] The miniaturized chromatography system developed by Zimmer[36] uses a support medium such as thin layer chromatography and a developing solvent to routinely evaluate radiopharmaceutical preparations subsequent to patient administration.[27]

The chromatography procedures involve spotting the radiopharmaceutical being tested on the origin line of the respective paper strips and eluting the strips in the designated solvent system (Figure 15-19). Following solvent migration to the solvent front line, the strips are removed, cut at the cut line, and counted for activity using appropriate counting systems, such as the dose calibrator or the well counter (Figure 15-20). The labeling efficiency or the fraction of total radioactivity incorporated into the radiolabeled material is calculated by subtracting the sum of the fraction of the impurities of free technetium and HR-Tc from 100%.

Percent labeling efficiency = 100 − (Sum of all impurities)

● *The percent labeling efficacy for most radiopharmaceuticals should be greater than 98%.*[1]

Radiation Protection of Nuclear Medicine Personnel

The cooperation of the regulatory agencies regulates the radiation exposure of radiation workers in the United States. The Department of Transportation (DOT), Environmental Protection Agency (EPA), Occupational Safety and Health Administration (OSHA), individual state nuclear safety agencies, and United States Nuclear Regulatory Commission Council on Radiation Protection and Measurements (NCRP) determined and provided the radiation dose exposure recommendations used for establishing the regulations and statutes of the NRC.[4] Table 15-4 lists the current acceptable radiation dose limits for occupational radiation workers.[33]

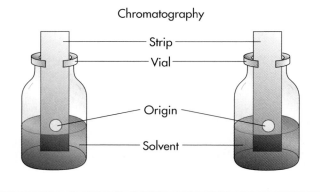

FIGURE 15-19
Eluting chromatography strips.

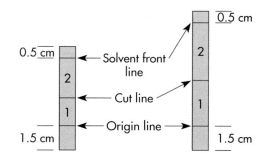

FIGURE 15-20
Typical chromatography strips.

Table 15-4   Nuclear Regulatory Commission Dose Equivalent Limits per Year

Anatomic category	Dose equivalent limit/year*
Whole body, head and trunk blood-forming organs, gonads, and lens of the eyes	5 rem (50 milliSieverts)
Hands, forearms, feet, and ankles	50 rem (500 milliSieverts)
Skin of whole body	30 rem (300 milliSieverts)
Fetus of radiation worker	0.5 rem (5 milliSieverts)* for entire gestation period

To ensure that the occupational radiation worker maintains an exposure far below the federal limits, the radiology communities adhere to the philosophy that the radiation dose exposure be "As Low As Reasonably Achievable," or ALARA.[4] ● *The NRC states that the ALARA concept should maintain radiation doses to personnel working in radiation areas of a medical institution to less than 10% of the federal limits of occupational exposure.*[3,4]

Personnel Monitoring

All radiation workers in the medical institution that may run the risk of exposure to ionizing radiation during routine duties must be provided with and wear a photographic film or **thermoluminescent (TLD)** personal radiation detector.[19] The detector must be worn on the body part likely to receive the highest radiation exposure. It is recommended that the detector be worn between the shoulders and the waist. Nuclear medicine technologists or others who handle radionuclides or radiopharmaceuticals must also wear a ring or wrist radiation monitor so radiation exposure of fingers and extremities can be estimated. The average period that a radiation worker routinely wears the radiation detectors is recommended not to exceed 1 month.[30] In addition, it is the responsibility of the radiation safety officer to review at least quarterly the results of personnel radiation monitoring and investigate and document any radiation dose exposure exceeding action Level II (30% of the federal limit).[19]

In addition to personnel monitoring, any individual handling certain amounts of radioiodine[32] must have a **bioassay** performed. The bioassay is performed to determine if any iodine activity in the thyroid is due to ingestion or inhalation. The assay is performed using the thyroid uptake probe. The bioassay must be performed between 6 and 72 hours after handling for any individual dispensing, preparing, or administering a therapeutic dose of sodium iodide-131. Individuals that handle less than 30 mCi of iodine are required to have a bioassay each calendar quarter. ● *The NRC recommends corrective action be taken if the* [131]*I thyroid activity of the radiation worker exceeds 40 nanocuries (nCi).*

Area Monitors

In addition to monitoring radiation exposure using personal dosimeters, individuals working in areas with radioactive materials must also monitor themselves before meals and before going home. The individuals can use a portable survey instrument, such as a survey meter, to determine any contamination to the body or clothing. In addition, every radiation work area must be surveyed daily to ensure that only background levels of radiation are present. If an area exceeds background radiation, then that area must be decontaminated. ● *Because the survey meter is*

best to detect radiation but not quantitate or identify radionuclide contaminant, a daily wipe test is also required in any radiation areas. The wipe test is a survey designed to detect any removable radiation contamination by wiping the area to be evaluated with a cotton swab or some other absorbent paper, such as filter paper. The wipe sample is analyzed in a scintillation detector, such as a well counter or multichannel analyzer, to determine the extent of the radionuclidic contamination. ● *Although the NRC only requires a detector sensitive enough to detect any contamination of 2000 disintegrations per minute (dpm), it recommends that if the wipe sample results are greater than or equal to 200 dpm/100cm^2, the specific area must be decontaminated and checked again.*[30]

● *Areas where radioactive gaseous materials are used, such as the nuclear pharmacy and rooms where xenon-133 lung ventilation studies are performed, are mandated by the NRC to have negative airflow pressure with respect to surrounding areas.*[30] *This allows airborne activity that might be generated within the room to be removed by the exhaust system. The negative airflow pressure will not permit Xe^{133} to passively diffuse into any surrounding areas. The exhaust must be a dedicated system and provide enough ventilation to dilute and remove radioactive concentrations that may be released into the room.*[30] *The exhaust must also release at a distance away from the public, such as the roof top, and meet EPA regulations for effluents released.* Quality control procedures must be performed to demonstrate that the airflow at the perimeters of these rooms is toward the room.[20] ● *The airflow must be checked a minimum of every 6 months to demonstrate proper and unchanged ventilation.*

Radioactivity Sign Posting

● *Specific signs are required by the NRC.*[3,4,30] They must be posted near the entrance to any room where radioactive material may be used or stored. This is done to inform anyone entering the area of the potential hazard of radiation exposure. Each of the signs must bear the three-bladed international warning symbol for ionizing radiation (Figure 15-21). The three-bladed symbol is magenta on a yellow background. Four different signs are used depending on the amount of potential exposure, as listed in Table 15-5.

Package Shipment, Receipt, and Opening

● *NRC Regulation Part 20 recommends that all radioactive materials be monitored upon receipt or within 3 hours if received during normal working hours or within 18 hours if received after normal working hours.*[31] A good quality assurance program recommends that any radioactive package be handled with disposable gloves, visually inspected, verified for contents, and checked for breakage or leaks. The radiation safety officer is to be notified of any irregularities. The package then must be monitored with a survey

FIGURE 15-21

The three-bladed international warning symbol for ionizing radiation.

Table 15-5   Radiation Signs

Type of sign	Radiation exposure potential
CAUTION, RADIOACTIVE MATERIALS	Areas in which radioactive material is stored or used in amounts not exceeding 5 mrem in 1 hour.
CAUTION, RADIATION AREA	Areas in which an exposure could be more than 5 mrem in 1 hour or more than 100 mrem in 5 consecutive days.
CAUTION, HIGH RADIATION AREA	Areas in which an exposure could result in excess of 100 mrem in any 1 hour.
CAUTION, AIRBORNE RADIOACTIVITY AREA	Areas in which the airborne radioactivity level may exceed the restricted limit or may exceed 25% of the restricted area limit when averaged over 1 week.

meter at the surface of the package and at 3 feet from the package. In addition, a wipe survey of the exterior surface is performed to determine any removable contamination present. ● *Any value in excess of 0.01 μCi/100 cm² of surface area tested is a reportable level and must be decontaminated. In addition, exposure levels exceeding 200 mR/hr on the surface or 100 mR/hr at 3 feet from the package require notification of the radiation safety officer.*[31] This must be documented daily on receiving forms.

Infection and Radiation Exposure Control

Protective shielding in a variety of forms must be used when working with radioactive material. To minimize radiation contamination and exposure, several protective mea-

sures must be followed. Some examples of shielding protection materials are lead bricks, disposable gloves, leaded glass, shielded bench tops, syringe shields, vial lead containers, lead container "pigs" to transport the dose, lead-shielded containers to transport radioactive materials outside of the nuclear medicine department, and shielded waste receptacles. The use of the above gloves and shielding are considered mandatory for the nuclear medicine worker.

In addition, OSHA requires that any personnel who work with needles and blood products must minimize their chance of exposure to human immunodeficiency virus (HIV) and the hepatitis virus by practicing Universal Precautions.[26] It is now mandatory to wear disposable gloves when working with patient procedures using needles and patient blood products. The Universal Precaution guidelines assert the prevention of recapping of needles at all costs. The used syringe must be placed in an approved infectious control needle and syringe receptacle, or sharps container (Figure 15-22). Because nuclear medicine deals with radioactive needles and syringes, the sharps container must also be properly shielded, decayed, and stored a minimum of 10 half-lives before disposal to the biohazard department.

Radiopharmaceutical Administration

Following preparation and quality control testing, the radiopharmaceutical is ready to be dispensed and administered to a patient. Quality assurance does not stop here. The individual that will be dispensing and injecting the radiopharmaceutical should again verify the requisition, the identity of the radiopharmaceutical, the activity, and the patient. The following information must be visually inspected and verified on every request before initiating the nuclear medicine procedure:

- Patient's name
- Hospital identification number and room number
- Requesting physician's name
- Patient history, condition, and preliminary diagnosis
- Examination agreement with the physician's orders and possible diagnosis of the patient
- Correct radiopharmaceutical for the examination
- Contraindications that can interfere with the radiopharmaceutical biodistribution
- Patient's physical limitations
- Allergies or potential drug interactions
- Potential nuclear medicine radiopharmaceutical interference with other diagnostic or therapeutic procedures
- Patient concerns

After the above checks have been accomplished and it is determined that the examination is correct, the person who

FIGURE 15-22
Following Universal Precautions.

will be administering the radiopharmaceutical must continue to practice good quality assurance. The radiopharmaceutical, the activity, and the volume to be administered must be verified. Before administration, the patient's name and hospital identification number must be verified on the patient's wristband. And, finally, if the patient is an outpatient, the patient must be identified by name, birth date, and social security number. If a misadministration occurs, the radiation safety officer must be notified immediately. ● *The radiation safety officer determines what NRC classification of misadministration has occurred and immediately takes appropriate action,[33] including notification of ordering physician, medical director, patient, and NRC or agreement state. An investigation must be conducted to determine all factors contributing to the misadministration and a plan made of corrective action, including training, to prevent future occurrences.*

References

1. *Accreditation Manual for Hospitals,* vol 1, *Standards,* Oakbrook Terrace, Ill, 1993, Joint Commission on Accreditation of Healthcare Organizations.
2. Anger HO: Scintillation camera, *Rev Scient Inst* 29:27, 1958.
3. Bernier DB, Christian PE, Langan JM et al, editors: *Nuclear medicine: technology and techniques,* ed 4, St Louis, 1997, Mosby.
4. Bernier DB, Christian PE, Langan JM et al, editors: *Nuclear medicine: technology and techniques,* ed 4, St Louis, 1997, Mosby.
5. Early PJ, Sodee BD: *Principles and practices of nuclear medicine,* ed 2, St Louis, 1995, Mosby.
6. Eisner R: Principles of instrumentation in SPECT, *J Nucl Med Technol* 13:23, 1985.
7. English RJ: *SPECT single-photon emission computerized tomography: a primer,* ed 3, Reston, Va, 1995, The Society of Nuclear Medicine.
8. Esser PD, Sorenson JA, Westerman BR, editors: *Emission computed tomography,* New York, 1983, The Society of Nuclear Medicine.
9. Graham SL, Kirchner PT, Siegel BA, editors: *Nuclear medicine: self study program II: instrumentation,* Reston, Va, 1996, The Society of Nuclear Medicine.
10a. Greer K, Jaszczak R, Harris C et al: Quality control in SPECT, *J Nucl Med Technol* 13:76, 1985.
12. Halama JR, Henkin RE: Quality assurance in SPECT imaging, *Appl Radiol,* May 1987.
11. Henkin RE, Boles MA, Dillehay GL et al: *Nuclear medicine,* vol 1, St Louis, 1996, Mosby.
12. Karp JS, Dauber-Witherspoon ME, Hoffman EJ et al: Performance standards in positron emmission tomography, *J Nucl Med* 32:2342, 1991.
13. Klingensmith III WC, Eshima D, Goddard J: *Nuclear medicine procedure manual: 1995-1996,* Englewood, Colo, 1995, Wick.
14. Murphy PH: Acceptance testing and quality control of gamma cameras including SPECT, *J Nucl Med* 28:1221, 1987.
15. Murray IPC, Ell PJ, editors: *Nuclear medicine in clinical diagnosis and treatment,* vol 1, Edinburgh, 1994, Churchill Livingstone.
16. National Electrical Manufactures Association: *NEMA standards for performance measurements of scintillation cameras,* Pub No NUI-1986, Washington DC, 1986, The Association.
17. National Electrical Manufactures Association: *Performance measurements of scintillation camera,* Washington DC, 1980, The Association.
18. Rao DV, Early PJ, Chu RY et al: *Radiation control and quality assurance surveys: nuclear medicine-a suggested protocol,* Rep No 3, 1986, American College of Medical Physicists.
19. Regulatory Guide 8.7: *Instructions for recording and reporting occupational radiation exposure data,* Washington, DC, 1992, U.S. Nuclear Regulatory Commission.
20. Regulatory Guide 8.25: *Air sampling in the workplace,* Washington, DC, 1992, U.S. Nuclear Regulatory Commission.
21. Robbins PJ: *Chromatography of technetium-99m radiopharmaceuticals: a practical guide,* New York, 1984, The Society of Nuclear Medicine.
22. *Scintillation camera acceptance testing and performance evaluation,* Rep 6, Chicago, 1980, American Association of Physicists in Medicine.
23. Saha, GP: *Physics and radiobiology of nuclear medicine,* New York, 1993, Springer-Verlag.
24. Sorenson JA, Phelps ME: *Physics in nuclear medicine,* ed 2, Philadelphia, 1987, WB Saunders.
25. Steves, AM: *Review of nuclear medicine technology,* New York, 1992, The Society of Nuclear Medicine.
26. Strasinger SK, Di Lorenzo MA: *Phlebotomy workbook for the multiskilled healthcare professional,* Philadelphia, 1996, FA Davis.
27. Taukulis RA, Zimmer AM, Pavel DG et al: Technical parameters associated with miniaturized chromatography systems, *J Nucl Med Technol* 7:19, 1979.
28. Thrall JH, Ziessman HA: *Nuclear medicine: the requisites,* St Louis, 1995, Mosby.

29. USNRC Title 10, Code of Federal Regulation, Part 20: *Standards for protection against radiation,* Washington, DC, 1987, US Nuclear Regulatory Commission.

30. Regulatory Guide 8.18: *Information relevant to insuring that occupational radiation exposures at medical institutions will be as low as reasonably achievable,* Washington, DC, 1977, US Nuclear Regulatory Commission.

31. USNRC Title 10, Code of Federal Regulations, Part 20: Standards for protection against radiation, *Fed Reg* 56(89):23390, 1987.

32. USNRC Title 10, Code of Federal Regulations, Part 35: *Human uses of byproduct material,* Washington, DC, 1987, US Nuclear Regulatory Commission.

33. USNRC Title 10, code of Federal Regulations, Part 20: Standards for protection against radiation, *Fed Reg* 56(98):23390, 1991.

34. Webber DI, Zimmer AM, Spies SM: Common errors associated with miniaturized chromatography, *J Nucl Med Technol* 11:66, 1983.

35. Zimmer AM, Spies SM: Quality control procedure for newer radiopharmaceuticals, *J Nucl Med Technol* 19:210, 1991.

36. Zimmer AM, Pavel DG: Rapid miniaturized chromatographic quality control procedures for Tc-99m radiopharmaceuticals, *J Nucl Med* 18:1230, 1977.

37. Zimmer AM: *Miniaturized chromatography procedures for radiopharmaceuticals,* Chicago, 1991, Northwestern University Medical Center.

Review Questions

1. The scintillation detector is based on the principle that certain crystals _____ after deposition of energy by some ionizing radiation.
   a. vibrate
   b. refract
   c. emit
   d. trap

2. The crystal that is used in most planar and SPECT gamma cameras is the _____ crystal.
   a. CsI(T1)
   b. CsF
   c. LiI(Eu)
   d. NaI(T1)

3. _____ testing involves performing a quality control performance evaluation of the camera system without the collimator.
   a. extrinsic
   b. intrinsic
   c. phantom
   d. dead time

4. The two most important quality control procedures that must be performed on a scintillation gamma camera are:
   a. intensity; persistence
   b. counting efficiency; sensitivity
   c. flood field uniformity; spatial resolution
   d. linearity; geometry

5. A dose calibrator is an example of an ionization chamber. The following quality control procedures are mandated by the NRC *except* for:
   a. geometry
   b. chi-square
   c. linearity
   d. accuracy
   e. constancy

6. The allowable (NRC) limit of molybdenum in the generator eluant of ^{99m}Tc pertechnetate is:
   a. 0.0015 microcuries/millicurie
   b. 0.015 microcuries/millicurie
   c. 0.15 microcuries/millicurie
   d. 1.5 microcuries/millicurie
   e. 1.5 millicuries/microcurie

7. _____ is the gamma camera's ability to see detail in any image.
   a. spatial linearity
   b. spatial resolution
   c. relative position
   d. energy resolution

8. In addition to the routine quality assurance procedures required for planar gamma cameras, the SPECT systems require evaluation of its tomographic performances, as well as reconstruction algorithms. Uncorrected center-of-rotation errors greater than ½ pixel can produce significant loss of spatial resolution. The quality control procedure COR (center of rotation) aligns the center of rotation projected onto the computer matrix with the center of the _____ used for reconstruction.
   a. camera
   b. patient
   c. computer matrix
   d. camera gantry

9. It is important to not only evaluate the equipment used in a SPECT system but also to evaluate each patient study for artifacts or errors. The sinogram of a selected tomographic slice is a summed image of all the projection data. It is useful in detecting _____, which can degrade the quality of the SPECT study.
   a. patient motion
   b. dead time
   c. correct acquisition time
   d. incorrect radionuclide energy

10. Impurities found in radiopharmaceutical preparations are placed in all of the following categories except:
    a. chemical impurities
    b. nuclidic impurities
    c. radionuclide impurities
    d. radiochemical impurities

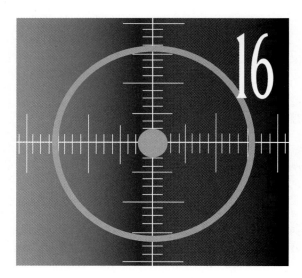

16 Sample Quality Management Examination

This chapter contains a sample Quality Management Examination that is similar in format to the Quality Management Advanced Examination offered by the American Registry of Radiologic Technologists. The examination consists of 140 questions divided into the following content categories:

A. Radiographic and Mammographic
   Quality Control   77
B. Quality Improvement   42
C. Program Standards and Guidelines   21

1. As the x-ray tube filament ages, it becomes progressively thinner as a result of evaporation. The vaporized tungsten frequently is deposited on the window of the glass envelope. This may:
   1. act as an additional filter
   2. reduce the amount of x-rays emitted from the tube
   3. result in arcing and tube puncture
   a. 1 only
   b. 1 and 2 only
   c. 2 and 3 only
   d. 1, 2, and 3

2. Viewbox illuminators must be periodically evaluated for which of the following?
   1. color of emitted light
   2. cleanliness of the viewbox surface
   3. intensity of the light from the viewbox
   a. 1 and 2 only
   b. 2 and 3 only
   c. 1 and 3 only
   d. 1, 2, and 3

3. Which of the following are essential elements of a quality control program?
   1. performance evaluation
   2. image interpretation
   3. error correction
   a. 1 and 2 only
   b. 1 and 3 only
   c. 2 and 3 only
   d. 1, 2, and 3

4. Which of the following is represented by the illustration in Figure 16-1?
   a. tomographic evaluation phantom
   b. mammographic accreditation phantom
   c. film-screen spatial resolution phantom
   d. anthropomorphic phantom

(FIGURE 16-1)

5. A wire mesh test is performed to diagnose film-screen:
   a. lag
   b. spatial resolution
   c. receptor system speed
   d. contact

6. Collimation devices for radiographic equipment should be accurate to within ____% of the SID.
   a. 2
   b. 5
   c. 10
   d. 15

7. Mammographic quality assurance phantoms should represent an average breast compressed to ____ centimeters.
   a. 2.5
   b. 3.0
   c. 4.5
   d. 6.0

8. Radiographic kVp variance should be evaluated:
   a. weekly
   b. monthly
   c. semiannually
   d. annually

9. Which of the following target materials is most likely to create characteristic x-ray photons with the greatest energy?
   a. rhodium (Z = 45)
   b. tungsten (Z = 74)
   c. molybdenum (Z = 42)
   d. beryllium (Z = 4)

10. Reproducibility variance of radiographic equipment must be within ____%.
    a. 1
    b. 3
    c. 5
    d. 10

11. When the focal spot in an x-ray tube undergoes a change in size with age or high mA, the effect is known as:
    a. saturation
    b. field emission
    c. blooming
    d. vignetting

12. A synchronous spinning top rotating at 1 rps is used to assess the timer of a three-phase x-ray generator. If the exposure time is 10 ms, the proper arc size should be ____ degrees.
    a. 0.9
    b. 1.8
    c. 3.6
    d. 7.2

13. The most practical form of silver reclamation for most diagnostic application is:
    a. metallic replacement
    b. electrolytic
    c. chemical
    d. all are equally practical

14. The classification of artifacts includes all except _____ artifacts.
    a. exposure
    b. processing
    c. storage
    d. location

15. Which type of test can use a Wisconsin test cassette?
    a. focal spot evaluation
    b. kVp measurement
    c. mR/mAs measurement
    d. film-screen contact

16. A hospital radiology department performs 1356 views during a 1-month period. Of these, 187 have to be repeated. What is the repeat rate for this department?
    a. 1.4%
    b. 14%
    c. 18%
    d. 33%

17. The most serious outcome following an FDA/MQSA inspection is:
    a. Level 1
    b. Level 2
    c. Level 3
    d. no finding

18. The eight penny test can be used to evaluate:
    a. focal spot size
    b. collimation
    c. film-screen contact
    d. image receptor system spatial resolution

19. During a filtration check, the first HVL is determined to be 1.3 mm and the second HVL is calculated to be 2.5 mm. What is the homogeneity coefficient?
    a. 0.52
    b. 1.3
    c. 1.9
    d. 2.5

20. The radiographic collimation system should be evaluated at least:
    a. weekly
    b. monthly
    c. semiannually
    d. annually

21. According to NEMA standards, a 0.5-mm focal spot cannot vary by more than ____% of the manufacturer's stated size.
    a. 50
    b. 40
    c. 30
    d. 10

22. Wire mesh tests on intensifying screens should be performed at least:
    a. weekly
    b. monthly
    c. semiannually
    d. annually

23. A department performs a total of 1720 views per month; 146 views must be repeated. What is the repeat rate of this department?
    a. 1.5%
    b. 4.2%
    c. 5.7%
    d. 8.5%

24. What are the primary advantages of extended processing for mammographic images?
    a. decreased contrast and patient dose
    b. increased contrast and decreased patient dose
    c. decreased contrast and increased patient dose
    d. increased contrast and patient dose

25. The minimum brightness of a collimator illuminator bulb is ____ ft-cd at 100 cm.
    a. 10
    b. 15
    c. 30
    d. 500

26. Which of the following are methods of silver recovery commonly used in diagnostic imaging departments?
    1. electrolytic
    2. metallic replacement
    3. resin
    a. 1 only
    b. 1 and 2 only
    c. 2 and 3 only
    d. 1, 2, and 3

27. Viewboxes for mammographic images are:
    a. less bright than conventional viewboxes
    b. the same as conventional viewboxes
    c. brighter than conventional viewboxes
    d. none of the above

28. A processor control chart shows the B + F, speed indicator, and contrast indicator all increasing on successive days. Which of the following could be the cause?
    1. developer temperature too high
    2. contamination of developer with fixer
    3. insufficient developer replenishment
    a. 1 only
    b. 1 and 2 only
    c. 2 and 3 only
    d. 1, 2, and 3

29. The relationship between the intensity of radiation absorbed by the film to the optical density produced defines:
    a. densitometry
    b. film or inherent contrast
    c. sensitometry
    d. speed or sensitivity

30. Film is more sensitive to safelight fog:
    a. before exposure
    b. after exposure
    c. equally before or after exposure
    d. none of the above

31. The action of two agents working together is greater than the sum of the action of two agents working independently. This is known as:
    a. oxidation
    b. reduction
    c. synergism
    d. contamination

32. The margin of error for the specific gravity of processing solutions is _____.
    a. 0.002
    b. 0.004
    c. 0.006
    d. 0.100

33. What is the best way to avoid bromide drag on a sensitometer film?
    a. feed the film in the same side of the feed tray
    b. process early in the morning after the processor has warmed-up
    c. feed the least dense end of the sensitometry strip into the processor first
    d. use a 21-step sensitometer to expose the film

34. What is the maximum variation in B + F value for daily sensitometry films?
    a. ±0.01
    b. ±0.05
    c. ±0.10
    d. ±0.20

35. What is the maximum variation in the speed indicator for daily sensitometry films?
    a. ±0.01
    b. ±0.05
    c. ±0.10
    d. ±0.20

36. Which processing chemical is responsible for creating the D_{max} and contrast indicator values on sensitometry films?
    a. phenidone
    b. hydroquinone
    c. Elon
    d. Metol

37. What is the maximum value in the contrast indicator for daily sensitometer films?
    a. ±0.01
    b. ±0.05
    c. ±0.10
    d. ±0.20

38. A device designed to give precise, reproducible, and graded light exposures to a film is called a:
    a. densitometer
    b. photometer
    c. sensitometer
    d. penetrometer

39. Optical density is measured by an instrument called a:
    a. densitometer
    b. photometer
    c. sensitometer
    d. penetrometer

40. Chemical fog influences the final image such that:
    a. B + F increases, contrast increases, speed decreases
    b. B + F decreases, contrast decreases, speed increases
    c. B + F increases, contrast decreases, speed increases
    d. B + F decreases, contrast increases, speed decreases

41. The best time to process sensitometric strips is in the:
    a. morning, after the processor is warmed-up
    b. late morning or midday after peak demand period
    c. late afternoon during low demand period
    d. evening during the lowest demand period

42. If the developer temperature is set on 96° F, the wash water temperature should be _____° F.
    a. 86
    b. 91
    c. 96
    d. 101

43. Sensitometrically, the contrast indicator is defined as the difference between ___ above B + F and ___ above B + F.
    a. 1.0; 0.25
    b. 1.0; 0.5
    c. 2.0; 0.25
    d. 2.0; 0.5

44. After routine processing of a sensitometric strip, the speed and contrast indicators have risen sharply and suddenly. What is the most likely source of this problem?
    a. safelight fog
    b. decreased patient load
    c. increased developer temperature
    d. decreased replenishment

45. In reviewing the processor control chart, you notice that the speed and contrast indicators have gradually decreased over the past 5 days. What is the most likely source of this problem?
    a. decreased replenishment of the developer
    b. increased developer temperature
    c. increased developer replenishment
    d. contamination of developer with fixer

46. Radiographs begin coming out too dark from one particular processor in the department. This could be a result of:
    a. overreplenishment
    b. increased developer temperature
    c. increased developer time
    d. all of the above

47. Images of radiographic grids taken with a homogenous phantom are used for evaluation of grid:
    a. frequency
    b. latitude
    c. uniformity
    d. ratio

48. Which of the following would cause a change in the emission spectra in Figure 16-2 from curve *A* to curve *B*?
    a. changing the mA
    b. changing the atomic number of the target material employed
    c. changing the voltage waveform of the x-ray generator
    d. changing the kVp

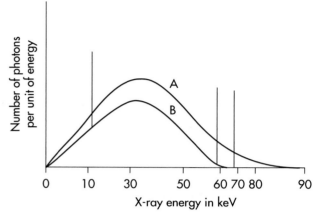

(FIGURE 16-2)

49. If a 400-speed imaging system were replaced by a 200-speed system, which of the following would be likely to occur?
    1. image resolution will increase
    2. lower mAs will be required to maintain optical density
    3. patient dosage will decrease
    a. 1 only
    b. 2 only
    c. 3 only
    d. 1, 2, and 3

50. A photometer using a photometric filter and a cosine diffuser are used for measurement of:
    a. fluorescence
    b. luminescence
    c. illuminescence
    d. phosphorescence

51. Which of the following test objects are used to mimic anatomic structures of a given region?
    a. homogenous phantom
    b. accreditation phantom
    c. anthropomorphic phantom
    d. wire mesh phantom

52. A radiograph emerges from a processor with numerous dark, treelike or branching artifacts. The most likely cause is:
    a. water on the feed tray
    b. hyporetention
    c. static electricity
    d. bending the film before processing

53. A 40-wire-per-inch mesh tool is used in a quality control program to evaluate:
    a. spectral matching of the film and screen
    b. grid uniformity
    c. film-screen contact
    d. focal spot size

54. A speed indicator value below the 0.10 lower control limit can be caused by:
    a. insufficient developer temperature
    b. overreplenishment
    c. hyporetention
    d. excessive developer immersion time

55. A fixer retention test to monitor archival quality should be performed at least:
    a. daily
    b. weekly
    c. monthly
    d. semiannually

56. A sensitometric strip is used in a quality control program to evaluate:
    a. focal spot size
    b. voltage waveform
    c. processor function
    d. image receptor system resolution

57. The mR/mAs value can be used to measure the:
    a. mA accuracy
    b. kVp accuracy
    c. output of the x-ray generator
    d. timer accuracy

58. In a radiographic unit with positive beam limitation, the sum of the misalignment between the x-ray field and image receptor should not vary by more than ____% of the SID.
    a. 2
    b. 4
    c. 10
    d. 15

59. Beam quality is best defined as the ____ energy of the photons in the x-ray beam.
    a. minimum
    b. maximum
    c. average
    d. none of the above

60. The voltage ripple of a three-phase, six-pulse x-ray generator is about ____%.
    a. 1
    b. 3.5
    c. 13
    d. 100

61. The standard unit used for measuring illumination is the:
    a. lumen
    b. lux
    c. nit
    d. candela

62. The coulomb/kg of air is an SI unit for measuring radiation intensity. The older special unit for radiation intensity is the:
    a. rem
    b. rad
    c. roentgen
    d. curie

63. The ability of an x-ray machine to produce constant radiation output at various conditions of mA and exposure time producing the same mAs is called:
    a. reproducibility
    b. linearity
    c. reciprocity
    d. accuracy

64. A test image made with an anthropomorphic phantom can be used to determine:
    a. the presence of screen artifacts
    b. film-screen contact
    c. low-contrast resolution
    d. if the image receptor demonstrates adequate contrast and recorded detail

65. To ensure the integrity of lead aprons and gloves in reducing exposure of radiation to the wearer, they should undergo a (an):
    a. visual inspection
    b. electrical inspection
    c. radiographic or fluoroscopic inspection
    d. ultrasonic inspection

66. The diagram in Figure 16-3 is known as a:
    a. fishbone diagram
    b. scatter diagram
    c. Pareto chart
    d. control chart

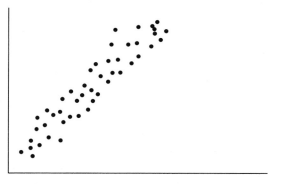

(FIGURE 16-3)

67. The chart in Figure 16-3 demonstrates a _____ correlation between the measured variables.
    a. positive
    b. negative
    c. zero
    d. cannot determine

68. Which of the following are most likely to cause a sentinental event indicator?
    a. tomographic examinations
    b. angiographic examinations
    c. routine diagnostic radiographs
    d. routine fluoroscopic procedures

69. The distribution of continuous data can be best demonstrated by the use of:
    a. histograms
    b. control charts
    c. scatter diagrams
    d. Pareto charts

70. An individual event or phenomenon that is significant enough to trigger further review each time it occurs is known as a (an):
    a. threshold event
    b. sentinental event
    c. aggregate data indicator
    d. routine event

71. The appropriateness of care is most closely related to the:
    a. physicians and their role
    b. administration and their role
    c. nurses and their role
    d. healthcare team's role

72. An ordered series of steps that aid in the achievement of a desired outcome is called a (an):
    a. process
    b. program
    c. indicator
    d. efficacy

73. An individual, department, or organization that provides input toward achieving a desired outcome is called a (an):
    a. customer
    b. supplier
    c. provider
    d. indicator

74. The degree to which an indicator specifically identifies a sentinental event is called the indicator:
    a. validity
    b. reproducibility
    c. reliability
    d. none of the above

75. Of the following, who could be considered external customers?
    1. patient family members
    2. the community
    3. third party payers
    a. 1 only
    b. 2 only
    c. 3 only
    d. 1, 2, and 3

76. A flowchart is best defined as a:
    a. pictorial relationship between quantities
    b. causal analysis tool, also called a fishbone chart
    c. a data display tool in the form of a bar graph
    d. pictorial representation of the individual steps in a process

77. Any data collected during the time in which healthcare is provided is known as _____ data.
    a. concurrent
    b. internal
    c. external
    d. aggregate

78. The standard deviation for a sample size of 81 items is approximately:
    a. 3.14
    b. 9
    c. 12
    d. 36

79. The primary focus of an effective quality improvement program is the:
    a. internal customer
    b. external customer
    c. supplier
    d. provider

80. Benchmarking is a process in which an:
    a. individual can reduce performance variations
    b. organization can compare performance with another
    c. organization can process data
    d. organization can achieve accreditation

81. The FOCUS-PDCA is a process for:
    a. quality control
    b. brainstorming
    c. quality improvement
    d. healthcare reform

82. The frequency of data collection is determined by the event:
    1. severity
    2. frequency
    3. expense
    a. 1 and 2 only
    b. 1 and 3 only
    c. 2 and 3 only
    d. 1, 2, and 3

83. The level of benefit expected when healthcare services are applied under ideal conditions is known as the _____ of care.
    a. continuity
    b. reliability
    c. appropriateness
    d. efficacy

84. A threshold can best be defined as:
    a. a process indicator
    b. the minimum cost of goods or services
    c. a preestablished level of performance for a given indicator
    d. a process for quality improvement

85. A quality management program should encourage:
    1. staff innovation and participation
    2. staff diversity
    3. reduction of abusive management behavior
    a. 1 only
    b. 2 only
    c. 3 only
    d. 1, 2, and 3

86. Which of the following is not a tool for data presentation?
    a. control charts
    b. brainstorming
    c. Pareto charts
    d. cause and effect diagrams

87. A group process used to develop a large sample of ideas without judgment as to merit or validity is known as:
    a. storyboarding
    b. brainstorming
    c. benchmarking
    d. focus group

88. The labels found on the bottles of processing solutions are required to contain all of the following except:
    a. product chemical name
    b. manufacturer name and address
    c. basic product warnings
    d. specific health hazards

89. According to OSHA regulations, a policy must be in place for workplace environments where workers may come in contact with:
    1. nonsterilized instruments
    2. body and blood products
    3. infectious materials
    a. 1 and 2 only
    b. 1 and 3 only
    c. 2 and 3 only
    d. 1, 2, and 3

90. Which of the following would not require a medical device report?
    a. a malfunctioning bed that injures the patient
    b. an allergic reaction to contrast media during angiography
    c. a nonworking defibrillator resulting in patient death
    d. a defective cardiac pacemaker resulting in patient death

91. The reliability of mammographic diagnosis can be affected by:
    1. viewbox intensity
    2. ambient light intensity
    3. ambient temperature of the viewing room
    a. 1 and 2 only
    b. 1 and 3 only
    c. 2 and 3 only
    d. 1, 2, and 3

92. Which of the following is not considered personal protective equipment?
    a. pocket mask
    b. laboratory coat
    c. protective eyewear
    d. hospital uniform

93. The variation in optical density allowed when evaluating different screens for screen uniformity is _____.
    a. 0.05
    b. 0.25
    c. 0.75
    d. 1.00

94. The FDA requires medical facilities to report medical devices that have:
    1. caused serious injury to a patient
    2. caused death to a patient
    3. failed to perform to manufacturer's specifications
    a. 1 and 2 only
    b. 1 and 3 only
    c. 2 and 3 only
    d. 1, 2, and 3

95. Which of the following results in the lowest possible occupational exposure?
    a. distance from the source as short as possible
    b. time of exposure as long as possible
    c. time of exposure as short as possible
    d. shielding material as thin as possible

96. Radiation protection protocols for medical facilities include:
    a. monitoring all hospital personnel
    b. providing technologist continuing education
    c. having an orientation program on radiation safety for new technologists
    d. monitoring all patient radiation exposure

97. The special unit for measuring dose equivalent is the:
    a. curie
    b. rem
    c. rad
    d. roentgen

98. The kVp accuracy for mammographic units should be evaluated at least once each:
    a. day
    b. week
    c. month
    d. 6-month period

99. The one value in a data sample that occurs with the greatest frequency is called the:
    a. mean
    b. median
    c. mode
    d. standard deviation

100. Variables that have an infinite range of mathematical values are known as:
    a. continuous variables
    b. dichotomous variables
    c. central tendency variables
    d. processes

101. Which of the following processor artifacts run in the same direction as film travel?
    a. hesitation marks
    b. pi lines
    c. guide shoe marks
    d. all of the above

102. Which processing artifact occurs as a result of drastic differences in solution temperatures?
    a. dichroic stains
    b. streaking
    c. curtain effect
    d. reticulation marks

103. An exposure artifact that appears as a result of very low mAs exposure factors is:
    a. motion
    b. patient artifact
    c. quantum mottle
    d. poor film/screen contact

104. The average set of observations in a data set is termed:
    a. mean
    b. median
    c. mode
    d. standard deviation

105. The number of times a particular value of a variable occurs is termed:
    a. sample
    b. frequency
    c. central tendency
    d. standard deviation

106. What is the median for the following set of numbers: 3, 5, 7, 9, 11?
    a. 3
    b. 5
    c. 7
    d. 11

107. What is the mean for the following set of numbers: 3, 5, 7, 9, 11?
    a. 3
    b. 5
    c. 7
    d. 11

108. The square of the standard deviation is termed the:
    a. range
    b. mode
    c. variance
    d. frequency

109. Which of the following involves comparing one organization's performance with that of another but focuses on the other organization's key processes that achieve performance rather than numbers and statistical data?
    a. aggregate external reference database
    b. historical patterns of performance
    c. desired performance limits
    d. benchmarking

110. Translating data collected during measurement into information that can be used to change processes is termed:
    a. design
    b. measure
    c. assess
    d. improve

111. The level of benefit expected when healthcare services are applied under ideal conditions is termed the ____ of care.
    a. appropriateness
    b. effectiveness
    c. efficacy
    d. efficiency

112. Which of the following are valid data collection methods?
    1. patient surveys and questionnaires
    2. patient care logs
    3. focus groups
    a. 1 only
    b. 1 and 2 only
    c. 2 and 3 only
    d. 1, 2, and 3

113. Sources of natural background radiation exposure include:
    1. building materials
    2. transcontinental flights
    3. diagnostic x-rays
    a. 1 only
    b. 1 and 2 only
    c. 2 and 3 only
    d. 1, 2, and 3

114. The unit of measure used to express occupational exposure is the:
    a. roentgen
    b. rad
    c. rem
    d. RBE

115. The effective dose equivalent for occupationally exposed individuals is valid for:
    a. alpha, beta, and gamma radiation only
    b. beta, x, and gamma radiation only
    c. x and gamma only
    d. all ionizing radiation

116. Which of the following would be considered personal monitoring devices?
    1. film badge
    2. TLD
    3. cutie pie ionization chamber
    a. 1 only
    b. 1 and 2 only
    c. 2 and 3 only
    d. 1, 2, and 3

117. What is the annual whole body effective dose equivalent for occupational workers?
    a. 0.1 rem
    b. 0.5 rem
    c. 5.0 rem
    d. 10.0 rem

118. Which of the following procedures involves the highest occupational exposure?
    a. lumbar spine
    b. interventional procedures
    c. skull series
    d. scoliosis survey

119. All of the following affect patient dose except:
    a. inherent filtration
    b. added filtration
    c. focal spot size
    d. SID

120. Methods of reducing radiation exposure to patients and/or personnel include:
    1. collimation
    2. shielding
    3. high kVp, low mAs exposure factors
    a. 1 only
    b. 1 and 2 only
    c. 2 and 3 only
    d. 1, 2, and 3

121. How many HVLs are required to reduce the intensity of an x-ray beam to less than 10% of its original value?
    a. 2
    b. 3
    c. 4
    d. 5

122. Which federal law set the standards for the manufacture and operation of diagnostic x-ray equipment?
    a. Radiation Control for Health and Safety Act
    b. Consumer-Patient Radiation Health and Safety Act
    c. Safe Medical Devices Act of 1991
    d. Mammography Quality Standards Act

123. How does filtration affect the primary beam of x-rays?
    a. it increases the average energy
    b. it decreases the average energy
    c. it makes it more penetrating
    d. it increases the intensity

124. Given the following data, what is the HVL of an x-ray beam whose initial value is 150 R/min?
    a. 0.3 mm Al; 126 R/min
    b. 0.75 mm Al; 99 R/min
    c. 1.5 mm Al; 75 R/min
    d. 3.0 mm Al; 55 R/min

125. The likelihood of a patient obtaining a negative diagnosis when no disease is present is known as:
    a. sensitivity
    b. specificity
    c. accuracy
    d. efficacy

126. The human eye possesses maximum sensitivity to light in the _____ region of the color spectrum.
    a. green
    b. yellow
    c. red
    d. blue-violet

127. What is the minimum suggested level of luminance for a viewbox used for mammographic images?
    a. 1000 nit
    b. 1500 nit
    c. 2500 nit
    c. 3500 nit

128. The most important acceptance test to perform on radiographic grids is the evaluation of grid:
    a. focusing distance
    b. purchase price
    c. uniformity
    d. size

129. Which of the following is required during evaluation of AEC systems?
    1. response to changes in mA
    2. response to changes in ambient temperature
    3. density selector switch function
    a. 1 and 2 only
    b. 2 and 3 only
    c. 1 and 3 only
    d. 1, 2, and 3

130. The energy peaks on an x-ray emission spectrum graph is the result of:
    a. Compton x-rays
    b. bremsstrahlung x-rays
    c. characteristic x-rays
    d. naturally occurring background radiation

131. Exposure linearity of x-ray generators must be maintained to within a limit of _____%.
    a. 2
    b. 5
    c. 10
    d. 15

132. As the anode angle of an x-ray tube decreases, the:
    a. focal spot size increases
    b. field size decreases
    c. anode heel effect decreases
    d. anode rotation speed decreases

133. The spectrum of light emitted by a viewbox is measured by a property called the:
    a. luminance
    b. illuminance
    c. spectral response
    d. color temperature

134. What is the suggested frequency of light bulb replacement for mammographic viewboxes?
    a. twice a year
    b. yearly
    c. every 2 years
    d. every 3 years

135. Which device is used to evaluate the relationship between the central ray and the field of exposure?
    a. resolution chart
    b. pinhole camera
    c. wire mesh tool
    d. beam alignment tool

136. Compression of the breast during mammographic imaging improves the technical quality of the image because:
    1. geometric unsharpness is decreased
    2. less scattered radiation is produced
    3. patient motion is reduced
    a. 1 only
    b. 3 only
    c. 2 and 3 only
    d. 1, 2, and 3

137. The repeat rate for mammographic departments should not be greater than _____%.
    a. 2
    b. 5
    c. 10
    d. 12

138. Off-focus radiation may be minimized by:
    a. avoiding the use of high kVp
    b. restricting the x-ray beam close to the source
    c. using compression devices to reduce tissue thickness
    d. avoiding extreme collimation

139. Which of the following tests is performed to evaluate effective focal spot size?
    a. spinning top test
    b. wire mesh test
    c. Wisconsin test cassette
    d. pinhole camera

140. Using the H & D curve found in Figure 16-4, which film demonstrates the effect of excessive developer temperature?
    a. film I
    b. film II
    c. film III
    d. unable to determine

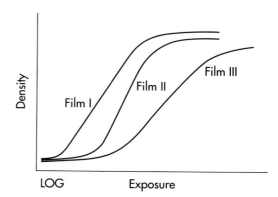

(FIGURE 16-4)

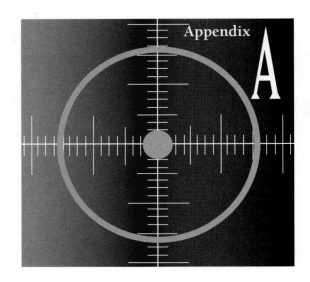

Review of Radiographic Quality

Outline

R adiographic imaging is a multistep process in which the x-ray intensity following attenuation inside of the patient is transferred to different types of information carriers (e.g., as intensifying screens, film, etc.) along the imaging chain. Once the image is created, the radiographic quality must be sufficient to demonstrate the anatomy of the patient.

Radiographic quality is defined as the fidelity with which an anatomic structure is represented in a radiographic image and is determined by four factors: optical density, contrast, recorded detail, and distortion.

- *Optical density:* The amount of black metallic silver remaining on a portion of film after processing is complete.
- *Contrast:* the differences between optical densities on the processed radiograph.
- *Recorded detail:* The sharpness of structure lines or minute details in a radiographic image.
- *Distortion:* Any misrepresentation of the true size, shape, or spatial relationship of the part in the radiographic image.

OPTICAL DENSITY

The function of optical density is to provide information in the radiographic image. Without black silver present on the polyester plastic film base, no information concerning the patient's anatomy would be present. Optical density is measured by a device called a *densitometer,* which measures the amount of light transmission through a portion of film and assigns a numeric value ranging from 0 to 4 using the following equation:

$$\text{Optical density} = \frac{\text{Log}_{10} \text{ incident light}}{\text{Transmitted light}}$$

Factors That Influence Optical Density

Factors that influence optical density include the following:

- *kVp:* An increase in kVp increases the optical density because the x-ray beam is more penetrating (so more of it reaches the image receptor) and because a higher percentage of scatter versus absorption occurs. The kVp and the optical density have an exponential, or logarithmic, mathematical relationship.
- *mAs:* An increase in mAs increases optical density because a greater quantity of x-rays are being emitted from the x-ray tube. A direct, or linear, mathematical relationship exists between mAs and optical density, making it the major control of optical density.
- *Source-Image-Distance (SID):* An increase in SID causes a decrease in optical density as a result of the divergent

effect of the x-ray beam, reducing the number of x-ray photons per unit area. An inverse square mathematical relationship exists between the SID and optical density.
- *Part thickness and tissue density:* An increase in either or both factors decreases optical density if no other factors are altered. This is because of the extra absorption of primary beam x-rays.
- *Development:* An increase in developer time, temperature, pH, concentration, or replenishment rate increases the optical density of a radiographic image and vice versa.
- *Field size:* A significant reduction in field size causes a decrease in image optical density as a result of less scattered radiation being produced in the patient.
- *Grid ratio:* A higher grid ratio decreases image optical density because of a greater absorption of primary x-rays.
- *Intensifying screen speed:* A faster speed screen increases the emission of light and therefore increases the optical density of the resulting image.
- *Film speed:* Faster speed film emulsions increase optical density.
- *Object-Image-Distance (OID):* A significant increase in OID decreases optical density as a result of the reduction of scattered radiation reaching the film (air gap technique).
- *Fogging:* Fog is defined as noninformational optical density and increases the overall optical density of the resulting image if present.
- *Pathology:* Certain pathologic conditions alter the normal tissue density of an anatomic region and therefore alter the optical density of the resulting image. Disease processes that decrease the normal tissue density tend to increase image optical density if no other exposure factors are changed and vice versa.
- *Voltage waveform:* High-frequency and three-phase x-ray generators emit more x-rays in a given period than single-phase x-ray generators, thereby increasing the image optical density.
- *Filtration:* An increase in filtration decreases the image optical density as a result of the absorption of primary beam x-rays.

Inherent Densities

There are two types of optical densities inherent in film without prior exposure to radiation.

- *Base density:* Caused by the blue tint added to the film base and having a value of 0.05.
- *Fog density:* The development of silver grains that contain no useful information, caused by age fog, improper storage conditions, and improper safelight conditions. This value can vary between 0.05 and 0.15.

The base and fog density values are usually combined into the base-plus-fog (B + F) density that is used in sensitometric testing.

CONTRAST

Contrast is the differences between optical densities on a processed radiograph and functions to make details visible. There are three types of contrast to consider: radiographic, subject, and film or inherent.

Radiographic Contrast

Radiographic contrast is the contrast as it appears on the finished image and is normally classified as either long scale or short scale.

- *Long scale, or low, radiographic contrast:* A small, gradual change between the different optical densities, yielding a relatively large number of gray shades.
- *Short scale, or high, radiographic contrast:* Large or abrupt differences between optical densities, yielding an image with a relatively small number of gray shades (image appears more black and white).

Subject Contrast

Subject contrast is the difference in the quantity of radiation transmitted by a particular part as a result of the different absorption characteristics of the tissues and structures within the part. The subject contrast helps determine the radiographic contrast. Several factors that affect subject contrast are radiation quality, radiographic part, contrast media, scattered radiation, and fogging.

- *Radiation quality:* As the quality (energy) of radiation increases, the subject (and therefore radiographic) contrast decreases because of greater penetration of the structures within the part. Radiation quality is influenced by the kVp selected, voltage waveform of the x-ray generator, and amount of filtration in the beam.
- *Radiographic part:* The distribution of tissue densities within the anatomic part significantly effect the subject contrast. If similar tissue densities exist within a particular part (i.e., breast), low subject contrast will occur. Widely different tissue densities (i.e., chest) demonstrate a high subject contrast.
- *Contrast media:* The use of contrast media increases the subject contrast of a particular region by changing the tissue density of the structure in which it is located.
- *Scattered radiation:* Scattered radiation always reduces subject contrast. Therefore any device or procedure that reduces the amount of scattered radiation reaching an image receptor always increases subject (and therefore radiographic) contrast.
- *Fogging:* Any amount of fogging reduces subject contrast.

Film or Inherent Contrast

The contrast that is built into the film emulsion by the manufacturer helps determine the radiographic contrast and subject contrast. This relationship can be demonstrated mathematically by the following equation:

Radiographic contrast = Subject contrast × Film contrast

Factors that affect film contrast are film emulsion, development, and image receptor system speed.

- *Film emulsion:* Faster speed emulsions generally yield higher-contrast images.
- *Development:* Any increase in development time, temperature, pH, concentration, or replenishment from the normal values decreases contrast.
- *Image receptor system speed:* Faster speed systems tend to create higher contrast images.

Sensitometric Curve

The relationship between the above factors and film contrast can be demonstrated graphically by using a sensitometric curve (also known as a *characteristic curve, Hurter and Driffield curve [H & D curve]*, or a *D log E curve*). This curve plots the optical density on the Y axis and the log of exposure to the film on the X axis. The curve is divided into three main portions (Figure A-1), the toe, straight line portion, and shoulder.

- *Toe:* Indicates the B + F optical density values
- *Straight line portion:* Contains the diagnostically useful optical densities.
- *Shoulder:* Indicates the maximum optical density value obtained.

The steeper the straight line portion of the curve, the greater is the film contrast (Figure A-2).

Other quantities that can be demonstrated with a characteristic curve include film speed or sensitivity, exposure latitude, and solarization or image reversal.

- *Film speed or sensitivity:* The relative exposure needed to produce an optical density of 1 above the B + F. The closer this point is to the Y axis, the faster is the speed of the film (Figure A-2).
- *Exposure latitude:* The range of exposures over which the film will respond with optical densities in the diagnostically useful range of 0.5 to 2.5. Exposure latitude and contrast are inversely proportional. Therefore high-contrast

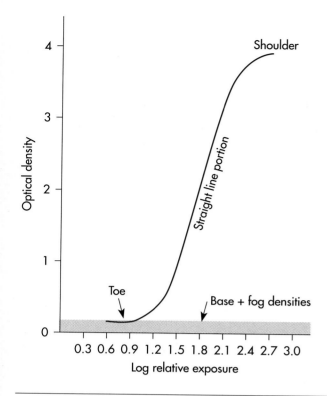

FIGURE A-1

The three main portions of the sensitometric curve.

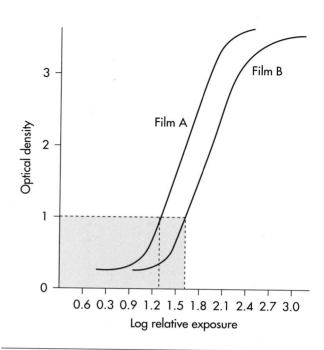

FIGURE A-2

Film **A** demonstrates a higher contrast and faster speed than film **B**.

film has narrow exposure latitude, and low-contrast film has wide exposure latitude (Figure A-3).

• *Solarization or image reversal:* A decrease in optical density occurs as the amount of exposure increases beyond the maximum optical density. This is believed to be caused by a chemical reaction in the film emulsion, known as *rebromination*. This principle is used in duplicating film that has been exposed to the maximum density before purchase (Figure A-4).

RECORDED DETAIL

Recorded detail is the sharpness of structure lines or minute details in a radiographic image and is often referred to as *definition* or *sharpness*. Four sets of factors affect recorded detail: geometric, motion, image receptor, and absorption.

Geometric Factors

Geometric factors deal with the geometry of the x-ray beam and include the following:

• *Effective focal spot size:* The smaller the effective focal spot size, the greater is the recorded detail.
• *Source-Image-Distance (SID):* The greater the SID, the

greater is the recorded detail.
• *Object-Image-Distance (OID):* The greater the OID, the poorer is the recorded detail.
• *Heel effect:* The amount of geometric unsharpness is poorer at the cathode end of the x-ray field.

Motion Factors

Any motion of the patient, x-ray source, or image receptor always reduces the recorded detail within the image.

Image Receptor Factors

The type of image receptor system effects the level of recorded detail in the resulting image.

• *Single screen versus double screen:* Single screen imaging systems demonstrate greater recorded detail than double screen systems because of the cross-over effect.
• *Screen active layer thickness and crystal size:* An increase in either of these variables decreases the level of recorded detail.
• *Film speed:* In general, fast-speed film emulsions demonstrate poorer recorded detail than slow-speed emulsions because of the graininess that occurs as a result of larger crystal size.

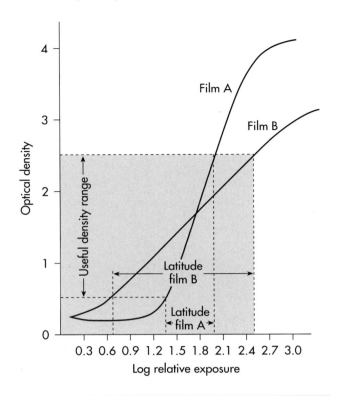

FIGURE A-3

Film **A** demonstrates a narrower exposure latitude than film **B**.

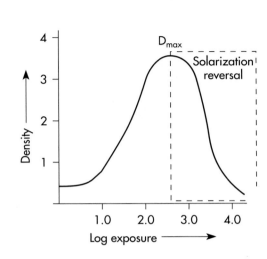

FIGURE A-4

Sensitometric curve demonstrating the effect of solarization. A decrease in optical densities occurs after the maximum density has been achieved.

Absorption Factors

The size or shape of the part being radiographed can decrease the level of recorded detail. In general, larger objects have less recorded detail than smaller objects because structures are further away from the image receptor.

DISTORTION

Distortion is a misrepresentation of the true size, shape, or spatial relationship of an object in a radiographic image. The three types of distortion are size, shape, and spatial.

Size Distortion

Also known as *magnification,* size distortion is the result of the divergence of the x-ray beam from its source. The degree of size distortion is chiefly dependent upon the SID and OID.

- *SID:* An increase in SID decreases the amount of size distortion.
- *OID:* An increase in OID increases the amount of size distortion.

Shape Distortion

Shape distortion is caused by improper alignment of the part with respect to the x-ray source and image receptor. The two main types of shape distortion are elongation and foreshortening.

- *Elongation:* The object appears longer in the image, usually because of the central ray not being perpendicular to the image receptor.
- *Foreshortening:* The object appears shorter in the image as a result of the object superimposing upon itself. The most common cause of this type of shape distortion is the position of the part (e.g., in the oblique position).

Spatial Distortion

Spatial distortion is a misrepresentation of the true spatial relationship between the various parts of the patient in the radiographic image. To overcome spatial distortion, two views of the patient are normally taken at 90 degrees during most radiographic procedures.

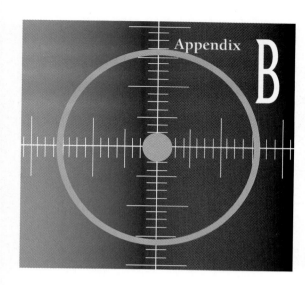

Sample Documentation Forms

Outline

Darkroom Safelight Test Form

ITEM	PASS	FAIL	COMMENTS
Safelight distance			
Safelight wattage			
Safelight color			
Filter condition or shutter opening			
Safelight test film			
Overall safelight evaluation			

Safelight Test Film

Optical density of each step

1 _____

2 _____

3 _____

4 _____

5 _____

6 _____

7 _____

8 _____

9 _____

10 _____

Viewbox Quality Control Test

ITEM	PASS	FAIL	COMMENTS
Conditions of Plexiglas front			
Condition of fluorescent bulb			
Intensity of viewbox light			
Uniformity of viewbox light (±10%)			
Overall viewbox evaluation			

Light Intensity Measurement

_____ **Light meter**   _____ **35-mm camera**

Center of viewbox   _____

Right upper quadrant   _____

Right lower quadrant   _____

Left upper quadrant   _____

Left lower quadrant   _____

Processor Quality Control Form

DAILY SENSITOMETRIC TEST
Chemical Activity

Developer temperature   _____   Fixer temperature   _____

Developer specific gravity   _____   Fixer specific gravity   _____

Developer pH   _____   Fixer pH   _____

      Water temperature   _____

Sensitometric Test

Step number	Optical density
1	_____
2	_____
3	_____
4	_____
5	_____
6	_____
7	_____
8	_____
9	_____
10	_____
11	_____
12	_____
13	_____
14	_____
15	_____
16	_____
17	_____
18	_____
19	_____
20	_____
21	_____

Base + Fog   _____

Speed indicator   _____

D_{max} _____

D_{min} _____

Contrast indicator   _____

Plot the B + F, speed indicator, and contrast indicator values daily on the control chart.

Automatic Film Processor Checklist

Transport System

	Rollers	Guide Shoes	Gears	Chains
Entrance rack				
Developer rack				
D-F crossover				
Fixer rack				
F-W crossover				
Wash rack				
Squeegee rack				
Dryer rollers				
Main drive motor				
Worm gear				
Feed tray cleanliness				

Circulation System

Pump	
Tubing	
Filter	
Circulation rate	

Replenishment System

Microswitch function	
Audible signal	
Replenishment rate	

Dryer System

Drive belt	
Heater	
Thermostat	
Air tubes	

Place a P in the column if the component passes the visual inspection and an F if it fails. Mark NA for items that are nonapplicable.

Radiographic System Visual Inspection

Control Booth	Date				
Panel switches/meters/lights					
Overload protection					
Heat sensors					
Exposure switch placement					
Window					
Technique chart					

Overhead Tube Crane					
High-voltage cables					
System stability/movement					
SID indicator					
Angulation indicator					
Lock function					
Bucky center light					
Collimator light brightness					
Interlock function					

Radiographic Table	Date				
Cleanliness/surface condition					
Bucky tray lock					
Cassette lock					
Table angulation indicator					
Stability					

Miscellaneous					
Lead aprons					
Lead gloves					
Gonadal shields					
Positioning aids					

Place a P in the column if the item has passed the visual inspection and an F if it fails. Mark NA if the item is nonapplicable.

Radiographic Survey

kVp ACCURACY

Digital meter	Test cassette	Generator kVp	Measured kVp	Percent variance	Acceptable yes/no

REPRODUCIBILITY OF EXPOSURE

	mR	mR/mAs
1.		
2.		
3.		
4.		
5.		

PERCENT VARIANCE _____

TIMER ACCURACY

Generator set time	Angle measured time	Percent variance	Acceptable yes/no

mA LINEARITY

	mA	mAs	mR	Variance	Acceptable yes/no
1.				XXXXXXX	XXXXXXX
2.				XXXXXXX	XXXXXXX
3.				XXXXXXX	XXXXXX
4.				XXXXXXX	XXXXXXX
5.					

Radiographic Survey—cont'd

RECIPROCITY

mAs	mA	Time	mR	Variance	Acceptable yes/no
20 mAs				X X X X	X X X X
20 mAs				X X X X	X X X X
20 mAs				X X X X	X X X X
20 mAs				X X X X	X X X X
20 mAs					

FOCAL SPOT SIZE

Large

Stated size	Measured size	Percent variance	Acceptable yes/no

Small

Stated size	Measured size	Percent variance	Acceptable yes/no

COLLIMATION

Stated field size X Y	Measured field size X Y	Percent variance	Acceptable yes/no

BEAM ALIGNMENT

SID	Screw shadow within washer yes/no	Acceptable yes/no

HVL Evaluation Form

Room: _____   Tube number: _____   Date: _____

kVp: _____   mA: _____   Time: _____   SID: _____

mm of Aluminum	Dosimeter Reading (mR)

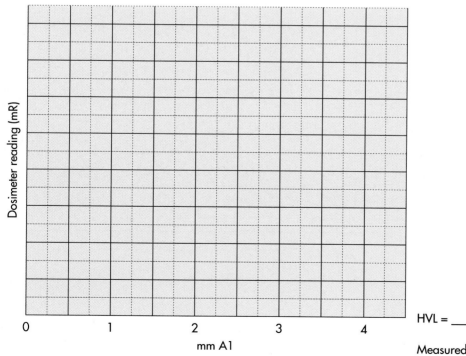

HVL = _____ mm A1

Measured by: _____

Place a P in the column if the item has passed the visual inspection and an F if it fails. Mark NA if the item is nonapplicable.

Grid Alignment Quality Control Form

Room: _____   Unit: _____   Grid tested: _____

Grid ratio: _____   Line no.: _____   Focal distance: _____

SID: _____   kVp: _____   mA: _____   Time: _____

Date	Measured Optical Density					Comments	Checker's initials
	Reference Location (Three small marking holes toward the front of the table)						
	2	1	0 Center	1	2		

Tomographic Quality Assurance Survey Form

Dept: _____   Room no.: _____   Generator: _____

Surveyor: _____   Type of motion: _____   kVp: _____   mAs: _____

DEPTH (PLANE) AND THICKNESS OF CUT

Date	Set depth	Clear numbers	Angle	Measured thickness	Measured depth	Acceptable Yes	Acceptable No

RESOLUTION

Date	Angle	Smallest mesh resolved	Acceptable Yes No	Comments

EXPOSURE UNIFORMITY AND BEAM PATH

Date	Angle	Beam path	Acceptable Yes No	Optical density uniformity	Acceptable Yes No	Comments

Fluoroscopic System Visual Inspection

Date: _____

ITEM				
Fluoroscopic tower				
Table locks				
Power assist				
Protective curtain				
Bucky slot cover				
Exposure switch				
Fluoroscopic timer				
Lights/meter function				
Compression device/ spoon observation				
Park position interrupt				
Primary protective barrier				
Collimation shutters				
Monitor brightness/ contrast				
Table angulation and motion				
Lead aprons/gloves				

Place a P in the column if the item passes the visual inspection and an F if it fails. Place NA in the column if the item is nonapplicable.

Fluoroscopic Quality Assurance Survey

Room: _____ Tube: _____ II Tube: _____ Date: _____ Surveyor: _____

kVp	Generator kVp set	mA/Time	Match step	Measured kVp	kVp variance	Percent variance	Acceptable Yes	No
Spot film A								
Mode B								
C								
D								
Fluoro A								
Mode B								
C								
D								

HVL	Set 60 kVp	mAs 1 Ø / 3 Ø _____	Match step	Estimated HVL mm A1	Acceptable Yes	No

Maximum output	Dosimeter between tube and phantom	kVp _____ mA	Exposure Time _____	R/min _____	Acceptable Yes	No

Focal spot	Specified spot size	SID (24")	Technique used	Smallest group resolve	Measured focal spot size	Percent variance	Acceptable Yes	No
Large								
Small								

Automatic brightness control	kVp (80 if constant)	mA	Image brightness Change	No change	Acceptable Yes	No
Phantom Thickness 1/32"						
3/4"						
1½"						
1½" and lead						

High-contrast resolution	kVp	mA	Smallest mesh resolved — Direct view Center	Edge	Television Center	Edge	Acceptable Yes	No
6"								
9"								
mag.								

Low-contrast resolution	kVp	mA	4% Contrast — Number of holes resolved — Direct view	Television	2% Contrast — Number of holes resolved — Direct view	Television	Acceptable Yes	No
6"								
9"								
mag.								

AEC	kVp (Constant)	mA	Phantom thickness	Spot film density No change	Change ΔD	Acceptable Yes	No
1							
2							
3							

Plot the B + F, speed indicator, and contrast indicator values daily on the control chart.

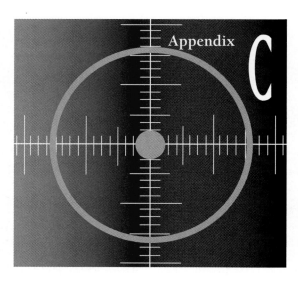

Agencies, Organizations, and Committees in Quality Assurance

American Association of Physicists in Medicine
335 East 45th Street
New York, New York 10017

American College of Medical Physics
1891 Preston White Drive
Reston, Virginia 22091

American College of Radiology
1891 Preston White Drive
Reston, Virginia 22091
www.acr.org

American Society of Radiologic Technologists
15000 Central Avenue S.E.
Albuquerque, New Mexico 87123
www.asrt.org

Conference of Radiation Control Program Directors
205 Capital Avenue
Frankfort, Kentucky 40601
http://www.webpub.com/crcpd/

FDA/CDRH
5600 Fishers Lane
Rockville, Maryland 20857
http://www.FDA.gov

FDA/CDRH/MQSA
1350 Piccard Drive
Rockville, Maryland 20850
http://www.FDA.gov

Gammex-RMI
2500 W. Beltline Highway
Middleton, Wisconsin 53562-0327
www.gammex.com

Joint Commission on the Accreditation of Healthcare Organizations
1 Renaissance Boulevard
Oak Brook Terrace, Illinois 60181

National Council on Radiation Protection and Measurements
7910 Woodmont Avenue
Suite 1016
Bethesda, Maryland 20814

Radiological Society of North America, Inc.
1415 West 22nd Street, Tower B
Oak Brook, Illinois 60521

Victoreen, Inc.
6000 Cochran Road
Cleveland, Ohio 44139-3395
www.victoreen.com

Bibliography

Adams H, Arora S: *Total quality in radiology,* Delray Beach, Fla, 1994, GR/St Lucie Press.

American Association of Physicists in Medicine: *Basic quality assurance in diagnostic radiology,* Rep No 4, Chicago, 1978, The Association.

American College of Radiology Committee on Quality Assurance in Mammography: *Mammography quality control: radiologic technologists manual,* Reston, Va, 1990, American College of Radiology.

Anderson R: Darkroom disease: a matter of debate, *ASTR Scanner* 28(10):1, 1996.

Ball J, Price T: *Chesneys' radiologic imaging,* ed 5, Boston, 1989, Blackwell Scientific.

Balter S: Fundamental properties of digital images, *Radiographics* 13:129, 1993.

Bushberg J, Seibert J, Boone J et al: *The essential physics of medical imaging,* Baltimore, 1994, Williams & Wilkins.

Bushong S: *Radiologic science for technologists: physics, biology, and protection,* ed 6, St Louis, 1997, Mosby.

Carlton R, Adler A: *Principles of radiologic imaging,* ed 2, Albany, 1996, Delmar.

Carroll Q: *Fuchs' principles of radiologic exposure,* ed 4, Springfield, Ill, 1990, Charles C Thomas.

Curry T, Dowdey J, Murry R et al: *Christensen's physics of diagnostic radiology,* ed 4, Philadelphia, 1990, Lea & Febiger.

Deming WE: *Out of the crisis,* Cambridge, Mass, 1986, MIT Press.

Forster E: *Equipment for diagnostic radiography,* Boston, 1985, MPT Press.

Gaucher E, Coffey R: *Total quality in health care,* San Francisco, 1993, Jossey-Bass, Inc.

Graham N: *Quality in health care,* Gaithersberg, Md, 1995, Aspen.

Gray J, Winkler N, Stears J et al: *Quality control in diagnostic imaging,* Baltimore, 1983, University Park Press.

Hendee WR, Ritenour ER: *Medical imaging physics,* ed 3, St Louis, 1992, Mosby.

Hendrick RE et al: *Mammography quality control,* Reston, Va, 1994, American College of Radiology.

Joint Commission on Accreditation of Healthcare Organizations: *Forms, charts & other tools for performance improvement,* Oak Brook Terrace, Ill, 1994, The Commission.

Lam R: *Continuous quality improvement for hospital diagnostic radiology services.* I, II. Albuquerque, 1994, American Society of Radiologic Technologists.

Lam R: *Processor quality control of radiographers,* Albuquerque, 1994, American Society of Radiologic Technologists.

Lederer W: *Regulatory chemicals of health and environmental concern,* New York, 1985, Van Nostrand Reinhold Co.

Lohr KN: Outcomes measurement: concept and questions, *Inquiry* 25:37, 1988.

Mammography quality standards, 21 CFR part *900, Fed Reg* 21:471, 1994.

McKinney W: *Radiographic processing & quality control,* Philadelphia, 1988, JP Lippincott.

McLemore J: *Quality assurance in diagnostic radiology,* St Louis, 1981, Mosby.

Meisenheimer C: *Improving quality,* ed 2, Gaithersberg, Md, 1997, Aspen.

National Council on Radiation Protection, Rep No 85, Bethesda, Md, 1986, The Council.

National Council on Radiation Protection, Rep No 99, Bethesda, Md, 1986, The Council.

National Council on Radiation Protection, Rep No 103, Bethesda, Md, 1989, The Council.

National Council on Radiation Protection, Rep No 105, Bethesda, Md, 1988, The Council.

National Council on Radiation Protection, Rep No 116, Bethesda, Md, 1993, The Council.

Parelli R: *Principles of fluoroscopic image intensification and television systems,* Delray Beach, Fla, 1997, GR/St Lucie Press.

Thompson M, Hattaway M, Hall J et al: *Principles of imaging science and protection,* Philadelphia, 1994, WB Saunders.

Tortorici M: *Medical radiographic imaging,* Philadelphia, 1992, WB Saunders.

Vyborny C, Schmidt R: Mammography as a radiographic examination: an overview, *Radiographics* 9:723, 1989.

Wentz G: *Mammography for radiologic technologists,* New York, 1992, McGraw-Hill.

Wolbarst A: *Physics of radiology,* Norwalk, Conn, 1993, Appleton & Lange.

Zandlerk et al: *Managing outcomes through collaborative care,* 1995, American Hospital Publishing.

Glossary

acceptance testing Quality control testing performed on new equipment upon delivery and installation.

accuracy The extent to which a measurement is close to the true value.

action The activity to achieve the desired outcome.

actual focal spot The actual area of the x-ray tube target from which x-rays are emitted.

aggregate data indicator Quantifies a process or outcome related to many cases.

agitation Stirring, swirling, or shaking of processing solutions.

ALARA As Low As Reasonably Achievable. Philosophy of keeping radiation exposure to a minimum.

appropriateness of care Whether the type of care is necessary.

archival film Film images made before 1974 and containing 20% more silver than film made afterward.

archival quality How well an image can be stored over time.

AEC Automatic Exposure Control. Electronic system that terminates the x-ray exposure once an adequate amount of radiation has been emitted.

automatic brightness stabilization Electronic method of regulating fluoroscopic image brightness.

automatic gain control Electronic method of regulating image brightness.

avoirduprois ounce Unit of weight in the English system more commonly known as the *standard ounce.*

axial resolution Minimum reflector spacing along the axis of an ultrasound beam that results in separate, distinguishable echoes on the display.

base + fog Inherent optical densities in film resulting from the tint added to the base of the film and silver grains not exposed to radiation.

benchmarking Involves comparing one organization's performance with that of another.

beryllium window A portion of the mammographic x-ray tube where the useful beam exits.

bioassay The laboratory determination of the concentration of a drug or other substance in a specimen.

brainstorming A group process used to develop a large collection of ideas without regard to their merit or validity.

brightness gain The degree of image brightness increase obtained with an image intensifier.

bromide drag Decrease in optical density caused by halides being deposited on trailing areas of the film during automatic processing.

cause-effect diagram A causal analysis tool. Also known as a *fishbone chart* or *Ishikawa diagram.*

center of rotation (COR) The fulcrum, or pivot point, of tomographic equipment motion.

central tendency The central position of a sample frequency.

channeling A potential problem in certain metallic replacement silver recovery units whereby the fixer forms a straight channel that reduces efficiency.

charge-coupled device (CCD) A solid-state television camera.

chemical activity How well the processing solutions perform their desired function.

chemical impurity The presence of a chemical or other substance that normally should not be present.

chi-square A statistic test for an association between observed data and expected data represented by frequencies.

chromatography Any one of several processes for separating and analyzing various gaseous or dissolved chemical materials.

cinefluorography The recording of a fluoroscopic image onto motion picture film.

collimator (1) A device that regulates the area of x-ray beam exposure. (2) A device for improving image resolution in nuclear medicine procedures.

comparator A portion of an automatic exposure control system that compares the amount of radiation detected with a preset value.

compression Applying pressure to a body area to reduce part thickness.

concurrent data Data collected during the time of care.

continuity of care The degree to which the care is coordinated among practitioners and/or organizations.

continuous variables Variables that have an infinite range of mathematic values.

contrast indicator Value obtained during sensitometric testing, which indicates film contrast.

contrast resolution The ability of an imaging system to distinguish structures with similar transmission as separate entities.

control chart A modification of the trend chart in which statistically determined upper and lower control limits are placed.

coulomb/kg SI unit of radiation intensity equivalent to 3876 roentgen.

count rate Measurement of the activity of a radioactive substance.

counts/minute A measure of the decay rate of ionizing emissions by radioactive substances.

critical path Documents the basic treatment or action sequence in an effort to eliminate unnecessary variation.

customer A person, department, or organization that needs or wants the desired outcome.

darkroom Area protected from white light where films are processed.

daylight system A system for loading and unloading film from image receptors outside of a darkroom.

densitometer Electronic device for measuring the optical density of a film.

depth of visualization Depth into a patient or phantom at which signals from scattered echoes can create an image.

developer A processing solution responsible for conversion of the latent image to a manifest image in film.

dichotomous variables Variables that have only two values or choices.

digital fluoroscopy Computerized enhancement of fluoroscopic images.

digital radiography A method of obtaining a radiographic image using computer hardware and software instead of a film/screen combination.

digital subtraction angiography An electronic method of enhancing visibility of vascular structures involving digital fluoroscopy.

dose calibrator A component in nuclear medicine equipment for determining the amount of radionuclide.

DPM Disintegrations Per Minute. A measure of the rate of ionizing emissions by radioactive substances.

dwell time The amount of time that the fixer solution is in contact with the active portion of the silver recovery device.

edge spread function A graphic indication of image resolution.

effective focal spot The area of the x-ray tube target that emits x-rays when viewed from the perspective of the image receptor.

effectiveness of care The level of benefit when services are rendered under ordinary circumstances by average practitioners for typical patients.

efficacy of care The level of benefit expected when health-care services are applied under ideal conditions.

efficiency of care The highest quality of care delivered in the shortest amount of time with the least amount of expense and a positive outcome.

electrolysis A process in which an electric charge causes a chemical change in a solution or molten substance.

emission spectrum Graphic demonstration of the component energies of emitted electromagnetic radiation.

energy resolution The amount of variation in pulse size or spreading of the spectrum produced by a detector.

extended processing A method of film processing that extends the normal developer time to increase image contrast.

field uniformity Refers to the even distribution of magnetic field strength in the region of interest.

fixer Processing solution responsible for removal of undeveloped silver halide and hardening of the film emulsion.

flood replenishment A timed method of replenishing processing solutions with an automatic processor.

flowchart A pictorial representation of the individual steps required in a process.

flow meter A device for measuring the volume of liquid flowing through it.

flux gain The gain in image brightness occurring with an image intensifier during fluoroscopy resulting from the high voltage across the tube.

focal spot blooming An increase in stated focal spot size, usually as a result of an increase in mA.

focus group Group dynamic tool for problem identification and analysis.

FOCUS-PDCA A quality management method developed by the Hospital Corporation of America.

frequency The number of repetitions of any phenomenon within a fixed period.

gamma camera A device used for image acquisition in many nuclear medicine procedures.

gas-filled detector A category of radiation detector consisting of a gas-filled chamber.

Geiger-Müeller tube A type of gas-filled radiation detector.

green film Film that has not been processed.

grid latitude The margin of error in centering the central ray of the x-ray beam to the center of the grid.

half-value layer The amount of filtering material that reduces the intensity of radiation to one half of its previous value.

high-contrast spatial resolution The minimum distance between two objects that allows them to be seen as separate and distinct.

high-frequency generator A type of x-ray generator that dramatically increases the frequency of alternating current sent to the x-ray tube.

histogram A data display tool in the form of a bar graph that plots the most frequent occurrence of a quantity in the center.

homogenous phantom A device used in quality control testing that is uniform in thickness and density.

horizontal distance measurement A quality control test for ultrasound equipment requiring measurements taken perpendicular to the sound beam axis.

humidity A measurement of the relative level of moisture in the air.

hydrolyzed reduced technetium A type of technetium-99m used in radionuclide imaging.

hydrometer A device for measuring specific gravity.

hyporetention A residue of fixer components remaining on a film after processing.

IMACS Image Management And Communication System. A computerized system for storing patient images and medical records.

image enhancement The use of a computer to improve or enhance an image.

image intensifier An electronic device that brightens a fluoroscopic image.

image lag An image persisting on a cathode ray tube even after termination of radiation.

image restoration A process in digital imaging whereby the final image is displayed.

image uniformity A uniform brightness level throughout the image when visualizing a homogenous phantom.

incident light The emitted light from its source before striking the film.

indicator A valid and reliable quantitative process or outcome measure related to one or more dimensions of performance.

input Information or knowledge necessary to achieve the desired outcome.

intensification factor A measurement of intensifying screen speed.

ion chamber A type of gas-filled radiation detector.

JCAHO Joint Commission on the Accreditation of Healthcare Organizations. A private agency responsible for accreditation of healthcare systems.

kilowatt rating A rating of power output for x-ray generators.

latent image An invisible image present after exposure but before processing.

lateral resolution A measure of how close two reflectors can be to one another perpendicular to the beam axis and still be distinguished as separate.

Law of Reciprocity Law stating that the amount of x-ray intensity should remain constant at a specific mAs value despite the mA and time combination.

line focus principle A principle stating that the effective focal spot always appears smaller than the actual focal spot because of the anode angle.

line spread function A graphic indication of image resolution.

linear tomography A type of conventional tomography whereby the x-ray source and image receptor undergo reciprocal motion in a straight line.

linearity Sequential increases in mAs should produce the same sequential increase in exposure rate.

locational effect A variation in film quality caused by the sensitometric test film being inserted in different portions of the feed tray.

low-contrast resolution Performance variable measuring the ability to image structures of similar density.

manifest image The final visible image.

mean The average set of observations.

mean CT number Average pixel value calculated by dividing the total CT value by the total number of pixels in a sample.

median A point on a scale of measurement above which are exactly one half of the values and below which are the other half.

metallic replacement A method of silver recovery from used fixer solution.

minification gain An increase in brightness with image intensifier tubes as a result of the difference in size between the input and output phosphors.

mobile generator A smaller-size x-ray generator mounted on wheels, which can be transported to various locations.

mode The one value that occurs with the most frequency.

modulation transfer function A graphic or numeric indication of image resolution.

molybdenum-99 The parent element of technetium-99m.

MQSA Mammography Quality Standards Act. Federal legislation mandating quality standards for all mammographic procedures.

multichannel analyzer A specialized scintillation detector that can select specific energy levels for detection.

multifield image intensifier A specialized image intensifier that allows for magnified fluoroscopic images.

noise Random signals or disturbances that interfere with proper image formation or demonstration.

NRC Nuclear Regulatory Commission. Federal agency that enforces radiation safety guidelines.

objective plane The region remaining relatively sharp in detail during tomographic procedures.

orthicon A type of television camera tube.

orthochromatic A type of film that is sensitive mainly to light in the green portion of the visible light spectrum.

OSHA Occupational Safety and Health Administration. Federal agency that oversees the workplace environment.

oxidation/reduction reaction A chemical change in which electrons are removed (oxidation) from an atom, ion, or molecule, accompanied by a simultaneous transfer of electrons to another atom, ion, or molecule (reduction). Also known as *redux*.

PACS Picture Archiving and Communication System. A computerized system that stores patient images.

panchromatic A type of film that is sensitive to all wavelengths of the visible light spectrum.

Pareto chart A causal analysis tool that is a variation of a histogram.

PET Positron Emission Tomography. An imaging technique whereby a positron-emitting radionuclide is administered to a patient, resulting in the release of photons by an annihilation reaction.

PHA Pulse Height Analyzer. A device that accepts or rejects electronic pulses according to their amplitude or energy.

phantom A quality control test tool used to simulate human tissue or body parts or demonstrate certain image characteristics.

photodetector An electronic device used for detecting photons of light, x-rays, or gamma rays.

photoemission The emission of electrons from a material following exposure to light or other ionizing radiation.

photofluorospot A method of recording static images during fluoroscopy.

photon The smallest quantity of electromagnetic energy.

photopeak The peak amplitude on an oscilloscope display.

pincushion distortion A type of distortion in image-intensified images caused by the projection of a curved image onto a flat surface.

pixel Abbreviation for *picture elements*. Small cells of information that make up the digital image on a computer monitor screen.

plumbicon A type of television camera tube.

pluridirectional tomography A specialized type of tomographic unit that allows for multiple-direction motion of the x-ray source and image receptor.

PMT Photomultiplier Tube. A device used in many radiation detection applications that converts low levels of light into electronic pulses.

point spread function A graphic demonstration of image resolution.

population Any group measured for some variable characteristic from which samples may be taken for statistical purposes.

portable generator A type of x-ray generator that is small enough to be carried from place to place by one person.

precipitation A process whereby silver particles are made to settle out of a used fixer solution.

process An ordered series of steps that help achieve a desired outcome.

psychrometer An instrument for measuring the degree of humidity in the atmosphere.

quality assurance An all-encompassing management program used to ensure excellence.

quality control The part of the quality assurance program that deals with techniques used in monitoring and maintenance of technical systems.

quantum mottle Image noise caused by statistical fluctuations in the number of photons creating the image.

radionuclide impurity The presence of other substance(s) in the radiopharmaceutical for nuclear medicine procedures.

reciprocity The amount of x-ray intensity should remain constant at a specific mAs value despite the mA and time combination.

recirculating electrolytic A type of electrolytic silver recovery device that recirculates fixer back into the processor after silver reclamation.

region of interest (ROI) A specified region of the image that is selected for display or analysis.

relative conversion factor Measures the amount of light produced by the output phosphor per unit of x-radiation incident upon the input phosphor.

relative speed A relative number indicating the speed of an intensifying screen imaging system.

repeat analysis A data collection of repeat images to determine the cause of the repeats so they may be prevented in the future.

reproducibility The same technique setting should always create the same exposure rate at any time.

resonance frequency (1) The frequency for which the response of a transducer to an ultrasound beam is a maximum. (2) In MRI, the frequency at which a nucleus absorbs radio energy when placed in a magnetic field.

roentgen The special unit of radiation exposure or intensity.

S distortion An artifact that can occur in image intensifier tubes consisting of a warping of the image along an S-shaped axis.

safelight A light source that will not fog film.

sample The number of items that are actually measured from a population.

scan image uniformity The uniformity in brightness of an image created with a homogenous phantom.

scatter plot A graph that demonstrates a possible correlation between two variables.

scintillation crystal A sodium iodide crystal used in scintillation detectors.

scintillation detector A radiation detector consisting of a sodium iodide crystal coupled to a photomultiplier tube.

scrap exposed film Exposed and processed film that is not of diagnostic use and is disposed of for silver recovery.

screen speed The amount of light that is emitted from an intensifying screen for a given amount of x-ray exposure.

sensitivity Indicates the likelihood of obtaining a positive diagnosis in a patient with the disease.

sensitometer An electrical device that exposes the film to a premeasured light source for quality control purposes.

sensitometry The study of the relationship between the amount of radiation exposing a film and the optical density that is produced.

sensor The radiation detector assembly in an automatic exposure control system.

sentinental event indicator An individual event or phenomenon that is significant enough to trigger further review each time it occurs.

signal-to-noise ratio (SNR) Used to describe the relative contributions to a detected signal of the true signal and random superimposed signals or noise.

single-phase A type of x-ray generator using a single source of alternating current.

slice position The relative position of the image section and the patient.

slice thickness The thickness of the image section.

SMDA Safe Medical Devices Act. Federal legislation governing the safe use of medical devices and appliances.

solarization A decrease in optical density with an increase in exposure. Also known as *image reversal*.

solid-state detector A radiation detector using silicon or germanium crystals.

spatial resolution The ability of an imaging process to distinguish small adjacent high-contrast structures in the object.

specificity Indicates the likelihood of a patient obtaining a negative diagnosis when no disease is present.

SPECT Single-Photon Emission Computerized Tomography. A nuclear medicine procedure that creates cross-sectional images.

spectral matching The matching of film sensitivity with the color of light emitted by the intensifying screen.

spectrum A display of electromagnetic energy on the basis of wavelength and frequency.

speed indicator The step closest to 1 above the base + fog on a sensitometric test film.

standard deviation The amount of variance in a sample.

static electricity Electrical charges created by friction, which can cause artifacts on unprocessed film.

string test A quality control test for Doppler ultrasound equipment.

sulfurization A build-up of sulfur on the electrodes in an electrolytic silver recovery unit as a result of incorrect amperage setting.

supplier One who provides goods or services.

synergism The action of two agents working together is greater than the sum of the action of the agents working independently.

target composition Refers to the elemental composition of the x-ray tube anode.

technetium pertechnetate A radionuclide used in nuclear medicine procedures, which consists of technetium-99m.

temperature A measure of the average kinetic energy in atoms and molecules of matter.

terminal electrolytic An electrolytic silver recovery device in which the used fixer is removed for disposal.

three-phase An alternating-current power source made up of three single-phase currents that are staggered by 120 degrees.

threshold A preestablished level of performance applied to a specific indicator.

time of day variability A possible variable in sensitometric testing in which test films are processed at different times during the day, varying in optical density.

TLD Thermoluminescent Dosimeter. A type of radiation detector using crystals such as lithium fluoride that release light when heated that is proportional to the amount of incident radiation.

tomography A radiographic process whereby specific slices of the body are imaged.

transmitted light The amount of viewbox light that is transmitted through a film image.

trend chart A graph that pictorially demonstrates whether key indicators are moving up or down over a given period. Also called a *run chart*.

troy ounce A unit of weight used for precious metals such as silver. 14.58 troy ounces = 16 standard ounces.

ultraviolet radiation A type of electromagnetic radiation in between visible light and x-rays.

uniformity correction flood A quality control procedure for nuclear medicine equipment.

variance A numeric representation of the dispersion of data around the mean in a given sample.

veiling glare Glare caused by light being reflected from the window of the output phosphor in an image intensifier. Also known as *flare*.

ventilation The process by which air is changed into and out of a specific area.

vertical distance measurement A quality control test variable for ultrasound equipment measuring along the sound beam axis. Also known as *depth calibration accuracy*.

vidicon A type of television camera tube.

viewbox illuminator An electronic device for viewing transparency images such as radiographs.

vignetting A decrease in brightness toward the periphery of a fluoroscopic image when using an image intensifier tube.

voltage ripple The variation from the peak voltage through the x-ray tube in an x-ray generator.

volume replenishment A type of system in an automatic processor that replenishes a volume of solution for each film introduced.

window level A value in digital imaging that selects the level of the displayed band of values within the complete range.

window width A value in digital imaging that selects the width of the band of values in the digital signal that can be represented as gray tones in the image.

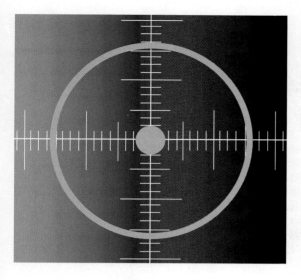

Answers to Review Questions

CHAPTER 1	CHAPTER 4	CHAPTER 7	CHAPTER 10
1. a	1. b	1. d	1. a
2. c	2. c	2. b	2. a
3. b	3. b	3. c	3. b
4. d	4. a	4. c	4. d
5. c	5. c	5. d	5. c
6. d	6. c	6. b	6. d
7. d	7. b	7. a	7. b
8. c	8. d	8. b	8. c
9. b	9. b	9. c	9. d
10. d	10. c	10. b	10. a

CHAPTER 2	CHAPTER 5	CHAPTER 8	CHAPTER 11
1. b	1. c	1. a	1. b
2. b	2. a	2. b	2. a
3. d	3. b	3. c	3. d
4. c	4. b	4. d	4. c
5. b	5. a	5. c	5. c
6. d	6. d	6. b	6. d
7. a	7. b	7. d	7. a
8. c	8. c	8. b	8. b
9. b	9. d	9. c	9. d
10. c	10. c	10. c	10. c

CHAPTER 3	CHAPTER 6	CHAPTER 9	CHAPTER 12
1. d	1. d	1. c	1. c
2. b	2. c	2. d	2. c
3. a	3. b	3. c	3. b
4. a	4. a	4. b	4. b
5. b	5. d	5. c	5. a
6. b	6. c	6. d	6. b
7. d	7. b	7. b	7. a
8. c	8. b	8. d	8. b
9. d	9. d	9. a	9. b
10. b	10. c	10. d	10. c

CHAPTER 13

1. d
2. b
3. a
4. c
5. d
6. a
7. a
8. b
9. a
10. d

CHAPTER 14

1. c
2. c
3. d
4. b
5. b
6. c
7. a
8. b
9. a
10. a

CHAPTER 15

1. c
2. d
3. b
4. c
5. b
6. c
7. b
8. c
9. a
10. b

CHAPTER 16: ANSWERS TO MOCK EXAMINATION*

1. d (6)
2. d (2)
3. b (1)
4. b (11)
5. d (7)
6. a (6)
7. c (11)
8. d (6)
9. b (7)
10. c (6)
11. c (6)
12. c (6)
13. a (5)
14. d (10)
15. b (7)
16. b (10)
17. a (11)
18. b (6)
19. a (6)
20. c (6)
21. a (6)
22. d (7)
23. d (10)
24. b (11)
25. b (6)
26. b (5)
27. c (11)
28. a (4)
29. c (4)
30. b (2)
31. c (3)
32. b (3)
33. c (4)
34. b (4)
35. c (4)
36. b (4)
37. c (4)
38. c (4)
39. a (4)
40. c (3)
41. a (4)
42. b (3)
43. c (4)
44. c (4)
45. a (4)
46. d (3)
47. c (7)
48. d (11)
49. a (7)
50. c (2)
51. c (11)
52. c (10)
53. c (7)
54. a (4)
55. d (3)
56. c (4)
57. c (6)
58. b (6)
59. c (6)
60. c (6)
61. b (2)
62. c (6)
63. c (6)
64. d (11)
65. c (6)
66. b (1)
67. a (1)
68. b (1)
69. a (1)
70. b (1)
71. a (1)
72. a (1)
73. b (1)
74. c (1)
75. d (1)
76. d (1)
77. a (1)
78. b (10)
79. a (1)
80. b (1)
81. c (1)
82. a (1)
83. d (1)
84. c (1)
85. d (1)
86. b (1)
87. b (1)
88. d (2)
89. c (2)
90. b (1)
91. a (11)
92. d (1)
93. a (7)
94. a (1)
95. c (10)
96. c (10)
97. b (6)
98. d (11)
99. c (10)
100. a (10)
101. c (10)
102. d (10)
103. c (10)
104. a (10)
105. b (10)
106. c (10)
107. c (10)
108. c (10)
109. d (1)
110. c (1)
111. c (1)
112. d (1)
113. b (10)
114. c (10)
115. d (10)
116. b (10)
117. c (10)
118. b (10)
119. c (10)
120. d (10)
121. c (6)
122. a (1)
123. a (6)
124. c (6)
125. b (10)
126. a (7)
127. d (11)
128. c (7)
129. c (7)
130. c (11)
131. c (6)
132. b (6)
133. d (2)
134. c (11)
135. d (6)
136. d (11)
137. a (11)
138. b (6)
139. d (6)
140. a (6)

*Number in parentheses is chapter in text where material is covered.

Index

Italics indicates illustration; *t* indicates table.